PENGUIN BOOKS

MARY TUDOR

Anna Whitelock is a historian of early modern Britain and the author of *The Queen's Bed: An Intimate History of Elizabeth's Court*, winner of the PEN/Jacqueline Bograd Weld Award for Biography. She teaches at Royal Holloway College, University of London, and is the director of the London Centre for Public History. A frequent television presenter and media commentator on the Tudors, the monarchy, and royal succession, she has written for the *Guardian*, the *Times Literary Supplement*, and *BBC History*.

Mary Tudor

ENGLAND'S FIRST QUEEN

Anna Whitelock

PENGUIN BOOKS

PENGUIN BOOKS
An imprint of Penguin Random House LLC
375 Hudson Street
New York, New York 10014
penguin.com

First published in Great Britain by Bloomsbury Publishing Plc 2009
First published in the United States of America by Random House,
an imprint of The Random House Publishing Group,
a division of Random House, Inc., 2010
Published in Penguin Books 2016

Published by arrangement with Random House,
a division of Penguin Random House LLC.

Pages 401–402 constitute an extension of this copyright page.

LIBRARY OF CONGRESS CATALOGING-IN-PUBLICATION DATA

Names: Whitelock, Anna, author.
Title: Mary Tudor / Anna Whitelock.
Description: New York, New York : Penguin Books, 2016. | Includes
bibliographical references and index.
Identifiers: LCCN 2015040862 | ISBN 9780143128656
Subjects: LCSH: Mary I, Queen of England, 1516–1558. | Queens—Great
Britain—Biography. | Great Britain—History—Mary I, 1553–1558. | Great
Britain—Kings and rulers—Biography.
Classification: LCC DA347 .W48 2016 | DDC 942.05/4092—dc23

Set in Fournier MT Std

146122990

For Sam, Lily, and Baillie

SHE WAS A KING'S DAUGHTER,

SHE WAS A KING'S SISTER,

SHE WAS A KING'S WIFE.

SHE WAS A QUEEN,

AND BY THE SAME TITLE A KING ALSO.

—*John White, bishop of Winchester,*
in his sermon at Mary's funeral

CONTENTS

PART TWO · A KING'S SISTER

PART THREE · A QUEEN

PART FOUR · A KING'S WIFE

MARY TUDOR'S FAMILY TREE

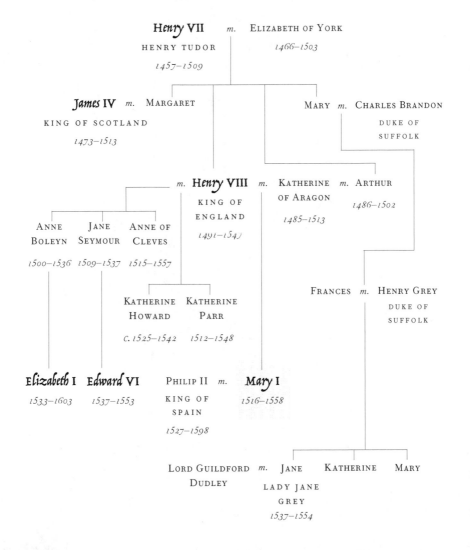

Henry VII *m.* ELIZABETH OF YORK
HENRY TUDOR   1466–1503
1457–1509

James IV *m.* MARGARET   MARY *m.* CHARLES BRANDON
KING OF SCOTLAND   DUKE OF
1473–1513   SUFFOLK

                      m. **Henry VIII** *m.* KATHERINE *m.* ARTHUR
                          KING OF   OF ARAGON
                          ENGLAND   1485–1513   1486–1502
ANNE   JANE   ANNE OF   1491–1547
BOLEYN   SEYMOUR CLEVES

1500–1536 1509–1537 1515–1557

                  KATHERINE KATHERINE   FRANCES *m.* HENRY GREY
                  HOWARD   PARR   DUKE OF
                                                                    SUFFOLK
                  C. 1525–1542 1512–1548

Elizabeth I **Edward VI** PHILIP II *m.* **Mary I**
1533–1603   1537–1553   KING OF   1516–1558
                                SPAIN
                                1527–1598

                  LORD GUILDFORD *m.* JANE   KATHERINE   MARY
                  DUDLEY   LADY JANE
                                    GREY
                                    1537–1554

AUTHOR'S NOTE

M̲ARY'S REIGN HAS LONG BEEN CONSIDERED A TERRIBLE FOOTNOTE in English history, her reputation dominated by the great Elizabethan work of propaganda, John Foxe's *Actes and Monuments*, which so graphically depicted "the horrible and bloudy time of Queene Mary." It is striking that nearly 450 years later Foxe's work continues to have a tenacious hold on the popular imagination. Recently this view found dramatic expression in Shekhar Kapur's 1998 film *Elizabeth*, which portrays the dark, brutal, and barren world of Mary in contrast to the light, liberating accession of Elizabeth. Mary is maligned as a cruel, obstinate Catholic bigot who burned heretics and married an unpopular Spanish prince. As one early biographer concluded, she had "a fatal lack of that subtle appeal that awakens popular sympathies."[1]

This book seeks to challenge such popular prejudice and acceptance of Mary as one of the most reviled women in English history; to "rebrand" her less as the "grotesque charicature" that is "Bloody Mary" and more as the groundbreaking first crowned queen of England. In the last ten years or so the gap between academic writing and popular understanding has grown ever wider, and this has spurred my desire to write. Recent scholarship has questioned twentieth-century verdicts of Mary's reign as one of "sterility" and lack of achievements and of Mary as a "profoundly conventional woman."[2] A number of important revisions can now be made to the pervasive popular view.

Mary's relationship with her mother is key, and Katherine must be understood not as a weak, rejected wife but as a strong, highly accomplished, and defiant woman who withstood the attempts of her husband, Henry VIII, to browbeat her into submission and was determined to defend the legitimacy of her marriage and of her daughter's birth. As one of the most prolific Tudor historians of the twentieth century argued, Mary "had ever been her mother's daughter rather than her father's, devoid of political skill, unable to compromise, set only on the wholesale reversal of a generation's history."[3] Yet Katherine of Aragon can be understood as a figure of immense courage from whom Mary could learn much. Katherine oversaw Mary's early education and highly formative upbringing, which was not a prelude to inevitable failure but an apprenticeship for rule. Mary's Spanish heritage informed her queenship but in a far more positive way than is popularly acknowledged.

Mary's very accession was against the odds and is a too commonly overlooked achievement the scale of which is rarely acknowledged. It was, as one contemporary chronicler described, an act of "Herculean daring" that rarely finds its way into the popular annals. Upon becoming queen, Mary entered a man's world and had to change the nature of politics—her decisions as to how she would rule would become precedents for the future. She gained the throne, maintained her rule, preserved the line of Tudor succession, and set many important precedents for her sister, Elizabeth. Less a victim of the men around her but politically accomplished and at the center of politics, Mary was a woman who in many ways was able to overcome the handicap of her sex. For good or ill, Mary proved to be very much her own woman and a not entirely unsuccessful one at that.

So the Mary of this book is an unfamiliar queen, and hers is an incredibly thrilling and inspirational story. She broke tradition, she challenged precedent; she was a political pioneer who redefined the English monarchy.

RESURRECTION

∴

IN WESTMINSTER ABBEY, AMID THE CHAOTIC GRANDEUR OF ROYAL tombs, lies the marble effigy of a resplendent Tudor queen. It is a striking, iconic image of Elizabeth I, her successes inscribed for "eternal memory" in panegyric Latin verses. Each week hundreds of people file through the north aisle of the Chapel of Henry VII, past this monument dedicated to the great "Gloriana." Many perhaps fail to notice the Latin inscription on the base of this towering edifice:

> *Regno consortes et urna, hic obdormimus Elizabetha et Maria sorores, in spe resurrectionis.* [Partners both in throne and grave, here rest we two sisters, Elizabeth and Mary, in the hope of one resurrection.]

Elizabeth does not lie alone; she inhabits her elder sister's tomb.

Queen Mary I was buried there on December 14, 1558, with only stones from demolished altars marking the spot where she was laid to rest. When Elizabeth died in 1603, her body was placed in the central vault of the chapel alongside the remains of her grandparents Henry VII and Elizabeth of York. But in 1606, James I ordered that the dead queen be moved. Forty-eight years after Mary's death, the stones were cleared from her grave, the vault was reopened, and Elizabeth's coffin was placed within. Seeking to legitimize a new dynasty and preserve his status in posterity, James wanted Elizabeth's place in Henry VII's vault for himself.[1] Having moved her body, he then commissioned a monument, celebrating the life of England's Virgin Queen, to lie upon the tomb of the two dead queens. In doing so James shaped how those queens would be remembered: Elizabeth magnificent, Mary, her body, as her memory, buried beneath. This book seeks to resurrect the remarkable story of Mary, the first queen of England.

MARY'S ACCESSION WAS against the odds. It was, in many ways, emblematic of a life of both fortune and adversity, of both royal favor and profound neglect. Mary was a truly European princess. The heir of the Tudor dynasty in England and a daughter of Spain, she grew up adored at home and feted by courts across Europe. Yet this was a prelude to great personal tragedy. When her parents, Henry VIII and Katherine of Aragon, divorced, Mary, then just seventeen years old, was reduced from a royal princess to a royal bastard. She became the "Lady Mary," spurned by her father and superseded in his affections by the infant Elizabeth. For the next three years she defended her mother's honor, refusing to acknowledge her stepmother, Anne Boleyn, as queen or the illegitimacy of her own birth. Mother and daughter were prevented from seeing each other even when Katherine was dying. Mary was threatened with death as a traitor and forced to submit to her father's authority as supreme head of the English Church. Her submission defined her. From then on she lived according to the dictates of her Catholic conscience, ready to defend her faith at all costs.

Her defiance cast her in opposition to the brother she loved when he became king. Edward VI was determined to enforce a new religious service and outlaw the Mass that Mary held so dear. In repeated confrontations, Edward challenged Mary to submit to his authority, but she proved defiant, even considering flight to the imperial court in Brussels to retain her independence. As Mary refused to capitulate and accept the new Protestant settlement, Edward overturned his father's will to prevent his sister from inheriting the throne. When Edward died, the Protestant Lady Jane Grey was proclaimed queen—though she would never be crowned and anointed—and orders were issued for Mary's arrest. Yet Mary fled and eluded capture. Ready to fight for her throne, she mobilized support across East Anglia. In a dramatic coup in the summer of 1553, she mustered her forces at Framlingham Castle in Suffolk and won her rightful throne.

England had never before had a crowned queen regnant. The accession of Matilda, the daughter of Henry I, in the twelfth century had been challenged by her cousin Stephen and failed. Matilda was never crowned queen of England and granted only the title "Lady of the English."² It was not until Edward VI's death four hundred years later, in 1553, that England once again faced the prospect of female succession. Though there was no Salic law barring a woman from the throne, in practice the idea of female sovereignty was anathema to contemporary notions of royal majesty. The monarch was understood to be God's representative on Earth and a figure of defense and justice. Women were considered to be too weak to rule and overly led by their emotions.

Yet Mary reigned with the full measure of royal majesty; she preserved her throne against rebellion and reestablished England as a Catholic nation.

MARY'S LIFETIME SPANNED years of great European crisis, fueled by a rivalry between Spain and France. Spain had been unified in 1479 as a result of the marriage of Mary's grandparents Ferdinand of Aragon and Isabella of Castile. France had grown in strength since defeating England in the Hundred Years' War (1377–1453) and expelling the English from all its territories except Calais. In 1494, Charles VIII, the king of France, invaded Italy looking to make good his right to the Kingdom of Naples. The rival claims of France and Spain to territories in Italy ignited a conflict that would continue throughout the first half of the sixteenth century. England was now dwarfed as a European power but sought as an ally by each to prevent the ascendancy of the other. The accession of Charles of Habsburg, duke of Burgundy, as king of Spain in 1516 and as Holy Roman Emperor three years later increased the enmity with France. Mary's cousin Charles became ruler of much of central and western Europe; France was virtually encircled by Habsburg lands and challenged the emperor's claims to the disputed territories in Italy and to lands along the Pyrenees. From the eve of Mary's birth to shortly after her death, the Habsburg and Valois kings would be engaged in bitter conflict. For much of her life Mary would represent the prize of an English alliance.

Mary was born on the eve of another great struggle that divided Europe, the Reformation. In October 1517, Martin Luther ignited a battle of faith that shattered the unity of Christendom. His attack on the abuses of the Church, expressed initially in his Ninety-Five Theses, became an onslaught against many of its most fundamental teachings. Luther maintained that a sinner was justified by faith alone and salvation might not be secured by the purchase of indulgences or by other "good works." He denied the authority of the pope in Rome and called on the German princes to take over and reform the Church. With the development of printing, Luther's ideas spread, as people looked to throw off the yoke of Roman Catholicism and embrace the new teaching.

The vast empire of Charles V, Mary's cousin, became riven by rebellion and dissent. As the emperor sought to stanch the flow of Protestantism, he faced the great threat of the Ottoman Turks in the East. Under the leadership of Suleiman the Magnificent, the Turks threatened Spain's trade in the Mediterranean and Habsburg family lands in Austria. Following the fall of Constantinople in 1453, the Turkish advance had been unrelenting; Belgrade was captured and the Kingdom of Hungary conquered. From North African bases the Barbary pirates preyed on shipping and raided the coasts of Spain and Italy. During the sixteenth century, "the threat of Islam" cast a long shadow over Christian Europe, rousing successive popes to make calls for a European crusade and commanding much of the emperor's attention and resources. Throughout her life, Mary would petition Charles to come to her aid and protect her claim to the throne and later her right to practice her religion; but always she would be secondary to his own strategic interests.

England too became the theater of European conflict. Henry VIII's repudiation of Katherine of Aragon and search for a divorce challenged the power of the papacy and of Katherine's nephew Emperor Charles V. Charles was determined to protect the position of his aunt, and for a time Henry's rejection of Katherine and their daughter, Mary, brought the threat of war with Spain and the papacy. Mary would always look to her Habsburg cousin for protection. Her kinship with him gave the struggles of her life a European dimension. Remaining loyal to her Spanish ancestry and looking to preserve England's position in Europe, she chose to marry Philip, the son of the emperor and the future king of Spain. It was a match that revived the Anglo-Spanish alliance founded with her parents' marriage forty-five years before. While protecting her sovereignty as queen and limiting his power, Mary would submit to Philip as a dutiful wife and mourn his long absences abroad.

It is the contrast between Mary as queen and the personal tragedy of Mary as a woman that is the key to understanding her life and reign. Her private traumas of phantom pregnancies, debilitating illnesses, and rejection—first by her father and then by her husband—were played out in the public glare of the fickle Tudor court. The woman who emerges is a complex figure of immense courage and resolve, her dramatic life unfolding in the shadow of the great sixteenth-century struggle for power in Europe.

MARY TUDOR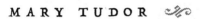

PART ONE

A King's Daughter

CHAPTER I

PRINCESS OF ENGLAND

∴

MARY, THE DAUGHTER OF KING HENRY VIII AND KATHERINE OF Aragon, was born at four in the morning of Monday, February 18, 1516, at Placentia, the royal palace at Greenwich, on the banks of the Thames River in London. Three days later, the nobility of England gathered at the royal apartments to form a guard of honor as the baby emerged from the queen's chamber in the arms of Katherine's devoted friend and lady-in-waiting, Elizabeth Howard, countess of Surrey. Beneath a gold canopy held aloft by four knights of the realm, the infant was carried to the nearby Church of the Observant Friars.[1] It was the day of Mary's baptism, her first rite of passage as a royal princess.

The procession of gentlemen, ladies, earls, and bishops paused at the door of the church, where, in a small arras-covered wooden archway, Mary was greeted by her godparents, blessed, and named after her aunt, Henry's favorite sister. The parade then filed two by two into the church, which had been specially adorned for the occasion. Jewel-encrusted needlework hung from the walls; a font, brought from the priory of Christchurch Canterbury and used only for royal christenings, had been set on a raised and carpeted octagonal stage, with the accoutrements for the christening—basin, tapers, salt, and chrism— laid out on the high altar.[2] After prayers were said and promises made, Mary was plunged three times into the font water, anointed with the holy oil, dried, and swaddled in her baptismal robe. As Te Deums were sung, she was taken up to the high altar and confirmed under the sponsorship of Margaret Pole, countess of Salisbury.[3] Finally, with the rites concluded, her title was proclaimed to the sound of the heralds' trumpets:

> God send and give long life and long unto the right high, right noble and excellent Princess Mary, Princess of England and daughter of our most dread sovereign lord the King's Highness.[4]

Despite the magnificent ceremony, the celebrations were muted. This was not the longed-for male heir, but a girl.

SIX YEARS EARLIER, in the Church of the Observant Friars, Henry had married his Spanish bride, Katherine of Aragon. Within weeks of the wedding, Katherine was pregnant and Henry wrote joyfully to his father-in-law, Ferdinand of Aragon, proclaiming the news: "Your daughter, her Serene Highness the Queen, our dearest consort, has conceived in her womb a living child and is right heavy therewith."[5] Three months later, as England awaited the birth of its heir, Katherine miscarried. Yet the news was not made public, and with her belly still swollen, most likely with an infection, she was persuaded by her physician that she "remained pregnant of another child."[6] A warrant was issued for the refurbishment of the royal nursery, and in March 1511 she withdrew to her apartments in advance of the birth.[7]

For weeks the court waited for news of the delivery, but labor did not come. As Katherine's confessor, Fray Diego, reported, "it has pleased our Lord to be her physician in such a way that the swelling decreased."[8] There was no baby. Luiz Caroz, the new Spanish ambassador, angrily condemned those who had maintained "that a menstruating woman was pregnant" and had made her "withdraw publicly for her delivery."[9] Many councillors now feared that the queen was "incapable of conceiving."[10] Fearing her father's displeasure, Katherine wrote to Ferdinand in late May, four months after the event, claiming that only "some days before" she had miscarried a daughter and failing to mention the subsequent false pregnancy. Do "not be angry," she begged him, "for it has been the will of God."[11]

Hope soon revived, and while writing letters of deceit to her father, Katherine discovered she was pregnant once more.[12] Seven months later, on the morning of New Year's Day, bells rang out the news of the safe delivery of a royal baby. It was a living child and a son; England had its male heir. Celebrations engulfed the court and country, and five days later the child was christened and proclaimed "Prince Henry, first son of our sovereign lord, King Henry VIII." The king rode to the Shrine of Our Lady at Walsingham in Norfolk to give thanks and hold a splendid joust in his son's honor. But the celebrations were short-lived. Three weeks later Prince Henry died. It did not augur well. Over the next seven years, failed pregnancy followed failed pregnancy, each ending in miscarriage, stillbirth, or infant death.

So when in the spring of 1515 the thirty-one-year-old queen fell pregnant for the seventh time, there was a somewhat subdued response. This pregnancy, however, followed its natural course, and in the early weeks of the New Year the royal couple moved to the royal palace at Greenwich, where Henry had been born twenty-four years before and where preparations were now under way for the queen's confinement.

The Royal Book, the fifteenth-century book of court etiquette for all such royal events drawn up by Margaret Beaufort, Henry VIII's grandmother, outlined the necessary arrangements. The queen's chamber was to be turned into a tapestried cocoon, the floor covered with thickly laid carpet; the walls, ceiling, and windows hung with rich arras and one window left loosely covered to allow in air and light. The wall tapestries, the queen's canopied bed, and the bed hangings were to be of simple design, with figurative images avoided for fear of provoking dreams that might disturb mother and child. There was to be a cupboard stacked with gold and silver plate to signify the queen's status, and crucifixes, candlesticks, images, and relics placed on an altar before which she could pray. At the foot of her canopied bed was placed a daybed, covered with a quilt of crimson satin and embroidered with the king and queen's arms, where the birth would take place.[13]

In late January, with all made ready, Katherine began the ceremony of "taking her chamber." First she went to the Chapel Royal to hear Mass; then, returning to the Presence Chamber, she sat beneath her cloth of estate—the mark of her rank—and took wines and spices with members of the court. Lord Mountjoy, her chamberlain, called on everyone to pray that "God would give her the good hour"—safe delivery—and the queen was accompanied to the door of her bedchamber in solemn procession. There the men departed, and Katherine entered the exclusively female world of childbirth. As *The Royal Book* stipulated, "All the ladies and gentlewomen to go in with her, and no man after to come in to the chamber save women, and women to be inside."[14] She would not be in male company again until her "churching," the purification after labor, thirty days after the birth. Officers, butlers, and other servants would bring all manner of things to the chamber door, but there the women would receive them.

After days of seclusion and hushed expectancy, the February dawn was broken with bells ringing in the news: the queen had delivered a healthy baby, but a girl. Writing two days later, Sebastian Giustiniani, the Venetian ambassador, assured the doge and Senate that he would offer their congratulations but added that, had the baby been a son, "[he] should have already done so, as in that case, it would not have been fit to delay the compliment."[15] Eventually, the ambassador sought an audience with King Henry and congratulated him "on the birth of his daughter, and on the wellbeing of her most serene mother Queen." The state would have been "yet more pleased," he added, "had the child been a son." Henry remained optimistic. "We are both young," he insisted; "if it was a daughter this time, by the grace of God, sons will follow."[16]

CHAPTER 2

A TRUE FRIENDSHIP AND ALLIANCE

∴

*We have this moment received news of the death of the most
serene Ferdinand, King of Aragon; and it is supposed this was
known some days ago to his Majesty, but kept secret, because of the
most serene Queen's being on the eve of her delivery.*[1]

—GIUSTINIANI TO THE DOGE
AND SENATE, FEBRUARY 20, 1516

MARY CAME INTO THE WORLD DURING A SEASON OF MOURN-
ing. Just days before her birth, news reached the English court of the
death of Katherine's father. Solemn requiems were sung at St. Paul's,
but the queen was not informed of her loss until after she had safely
given birth.[2] Ferdinand's death marked the passing of the last of Mary's
grandparents, and though she never knew any of them, with her steely
determination, Catholic devotion, and strong sense of her right to rule,
she would prove to be every inch their heir. She was, unmistakably,
both a Spaniard and a Tudor.

Her mother, Katherine, was the daughter of Ferdinand of Aragon
and Isabella of Castile, her father the son of Henry Tudor (Henry VII)
and Elizabeth of York. Both sets of grandparents had brought unity to
their war-torn kingdoms after years of disputed successions. Henry
Tudor's defeat of Richard III at the Battle of Bosworth in 1485 had
ended thirty-three years of incipient civil war between the Houses of
York and Lancaster, two rival branches of the Plantagenet family that
had ruled England since the twelfth century. Henry, a Lancastrian,
claimed the throne through his mother, Margaret Beaufort, and her
descent from John of Gaunt, duke of Lancaster, the son of Edward III.

Following the accession of the Yorkist king, Edward IV, in 1471, Henry had fled to Brittany for fear that Edward would act against him as the remaining Lancastrian claimant. Twelve years later, after Edward had died, his brother Richard, duke of Gloucester, usurped the throne. He imprisoned, and most likely murdered, his nephew Edward V, and was crowned King Richard III on July 6, 1483. Realizing Richard's unpopularity, Henry saw an opportunity to win the throne. He set sail from Brittany with French men and ships and landed at Milford Haven in August 1485. On the twenty-second he overwhelmed the king's forces at Bosworth, near Leicester, and killed Richard III in the midst of the battle. Five months after his accession, Henry married Elizabeth of York, the eldest daughter and surviving heir of the Yorkist king, Edward IV, thereby uniting the warring Plantagenet family. The establishment of the Tudor dynasty was made secure by the birth of their first son and heir, Arthur, on September 19, 1486, a daughter Margaret, and a second son, Prince Henry, five years later, to be followed by another daughter, Mary.

Mary's grandmother Isabella of Castile had also fought to win her throne, after her father disinherited her. Alongside her husband Ferdinand, king of Aragon, she campaigned for five years in a bitter civil war before emerging triumphant and claiming the crown of Castile. The only queen regnant in fifteenth-century Europe, she doggedly reasserted her position in the face of her husband's attempts to share her power. It would be a marriage of equals, with both sovereigns ruling in their own right. Ferdinand and Isabella became the foremost monarchs in Europe, with a crusading zeal that characterized the Spanish monarchy. Their shared aim became the Reconquista of Granada, the last Muslim kingdom in Spain. The Reconquista was to be the climax of the Crusade, the medieval Christian enterprise against the Muslims that had begun in the twelfth century. Isabella, determined, single-minded, and fervently Catholic, saw the campaign as her divine purpose and rode with her knights, rallying her troops. The war lasted for ten years before finally, on January 2, 1492, the last Muslim leader, Muhammad II, surrendered complete control of Granada. It was the culmination of several centuries of reconquest and a great Christian triumph. In the years that followed, the Spanish Inquisition, established first in Castile and then in Aragon, secured the expulsion of all remaining

Jews and Muslims. "The Catholic Kings," as they were entitled by Pope Alexander IV, had created a unified Spain and an entirely Catholic kingdom.

Katherine, the youngest of Ferdinand and Isabella's five children, was born on December 16, 1485, in the midst of the Reconquista at the archbishop of Toledo's palace northeast of Madrid. She was named after her mother's English grandmother, a daughter of John of Gaunt, duke of Lancaster, who had married Enrique III of Castile. Following the defeat of the Moors, the Alhambra—the former residence of the Muslim kings—became Katherine's home, and from there she witnessed the expulsion of the Jews and the activities of the Inquisition.

Isabella was determined that her four daughters be educated properly and have what she had been denied. She had received only a meager schooling as a child and had later taught herself to read Latin while campaigning. Along with learning the "female arts" of dancing, music, needlework, and embroidery, Katherine learned the works of the Latin Fathers of the Church—Ambrose, Augustine, Gregory, and Jerome—and those of the Latin Christian poets. But whereas her brother, Juan, was educated to rule, Katherine and her sisters were expected to cement foreign policy alliances as the wives of European princes. First Isabella, Katherine's eldest sister, was married to Prince Alfonso of Portugal, then Juana to the Archduke Philip of Burgundy, and later Maria to Prince Manoel of Portugal. When it was Katherine's turn, her parents looked to England.

Ferdinand and Isabella wanted an Anglo-Spanish alliance as a counterpoise to French aggression in Italy. For Henry VII a union with Spain was a great diplomatic coup, a means to bolster the fledgling Tudor dynasty and England's place in Europe. Founded on their common interest of restraining the growing power of France, the Treaty of Medina del Campo of March 28, 1489, provided for mutual cooperation. It would form the basis of an Anglo-Spanish bond that would endure for the first half of the sixteenth century.

A true friendship and alliance shall be observed henceforth between Ferdinand and Isabella, their heirs and subjects, on the one part, and Henry, his heirs and subjects, on the other part. They promise to assist one another in defending their present and future dominions against any enemy whatsoever. . . . As often as and whenever Ferdinand and Isabella make war with France, Henry shall do the same, and conversely. . . . In order to strengthen this alliance the Princess Katherine is to marry Prince Arthur. The marriage is to be contracted *per verba de futuro* as soon as Katherine and Arthur attain the necessary age.[3]

Isabella "made very particular honour [of the English ambassadors], for she prized her Lancastrian kinship with Henry, and saw a connection with England, as with Burgundy, important to pre-eminence in Europe."[4] And so, from the age of three, Katherine knew her future would be as an English queen. Her mother was reluctant for her to go: she was the youngest of her children and the last to marry; but finally, aged sixteen, Katherine set sail for England to marry Henry VII's son Arthur.[5] Upon the Spanish princess's arrival at Plymouth, the licentiate Alcares wrote to tell Isabella that "she could not have been received with greater rejoicings if she had been the Saviour of the World."[6]

Katherine and Arthur were married on November 14, 1501, at St. Paul's Cathedral. It was a magnificent ceremony and one that heralded the Anglo-Spanish alliance—the defining moment of the Tudor dynasty.[7] After a week of splendid banquets and tournaments, the royal couple journeyed to Ludlow in Shropshire to govern the Principality of Wales, as was the ancient custom for the heir to the throne. But though long in the making, the marriage was to last less than six months. On April 2, Arthur, then sixteen, died suddenly; most accounts suggest it was tuberculosis, or "consumption." The foundations on which the Anglo-Spanish entente had been constructed had crumbled.

Yet it was an alliance too important for either party to lose. As soon as news reached Spain of Arthur's death, Ferdinand and Isabella mooted the possibility of Katherine marrying the new heir to the throne, ten-year-old Prince Henry. Because of their consanguinity, a dispensation had to be sought from Pope Julius II, although Katherine insisted that her marriage to Arthur had never been consummated. On June 23, 1503, a new treaty was signed and agreement reached for Prince Henry and Katherine to be married in five years' time. But when Queen Isabella died in November 1504, the personal union of Castile and Aragon, founded on her marriage with Ferdinand, was shattered. Isabella had bequeathed Castile to her daughter Juana, who was married to Philip of Burgundy. He claimed the throne in her name, while Ferdinand of Aragon took power as regent. Katherine's worth as a bride fell dramatically. She was no longer princess of the Iberian Peninsula, and an alliance with Aragon alone was of limited value. Henry VII now abandoned marriage negotiations with Ferdinand.

Katherine, meanwhile, was stranded. She remained in England, mourning the loss of her mother, with little money and no clear status. She petitioned her father to come to her aid, describing how she was in debt and how greatly she needed money "not for extravagant things" but "only for food"; she was "in the greatest trouble and anguish in the world."[8]

ON APRIL 21, 1509, amid scenes of great celebration, seventeen-year-old Prince Henry was proclaimed king of England. "Heaven and earth rejoices," wrote Lord Mountjoy to the Dutch humanist Desiderius Erasmus; "everything is full of milk and honey and nectar. Avarice has fled the country. Our King is not after gold, or gems, or precious metals, but virtue, glory, immortality."[9] Soon after his accession, Henry sought to establish his European status by reasserting England's claim to the French Crown. He needed allies and looked to renew the alliance with Ferdinand of Aragon and marry his brother's widow, Katherine. On June 11 they exchanged vows at the Franciscan church at Greenwich.

"Most illustrious Prince," Henry was asked, "is it your will to fulfil the treaty of marriage concluded by your father, the late King of England and the parents of the Princess of Wales, the King and Queen of Spain; and, as the Pope has dispensed with this marriage, to take the Princess who is here present for your lawful wife?" Both parties answered, "I will."[10]

Two weeks later, Henry and Katherine were crowned together at Westminster Abbey. He was eighteen, handsome, and athletic; she was twenty-three and described as "the most beautiful creature in the world." Well educated and accomplished, she loved music, dancing, and hawking almost as much as Henry did. She was, in many ways, the ideal royal bride. Both were equally learned and pious and were keen readers of theological works. Katherine spent hours at her devotions, rising at midnight to say Matins and at dawn to hear Mass, and, very much her mother's daughter, she proved to be politically able and determined. As Henry prepared for war with France in 1512, Katherine was closely involved. "The King is for war, the Council against and the Queen for it," one Venetian diplomat reported.[11]

While Henry embarked on his campaign, capturing the towns of Thérouanne and Tournai in northern France, Katherine remained in England as "Regent and Governess of England, Wales and Ireland," with authority to raise troops and supervise preparations for war against the Scots. Ten years earlier, when James IV of Scotland had married Henry's elder sister, Margaret, he had sworn "perpetual peace" with England. He had now been persuaded by the French to renew their "auld alliance" against England. War was declared in August, and James launched an invasion across the border. As Peter Martyr, the contemporary Italian historian, reported:

> Queen Katherine, in imitation of her mother Isabella . . . made splendid oration to the English captains, told them to be ready to defend their territory . . . and they should remember that English courage excelled that of all other nations. Fired by these words, the nobles marched against the Scots . . . and defeated them.[12]

The Scottish king was killed at Flodden Field. It was one of England's most resounding victories over the Scots and Katherine's finest hour. She wrote triumphantly to Henry, "In this your grace shall see how I can keep my promise, sending you for your banners a King's coat. I thought to send himself unto you, but our Englishmen's hearts would not suffer it."[13] Following in the footsteps of her mother, Isabella, she had proved to be a great warrior queen, mustering troops and delivering rousing orations. Ironically, it would be the womanly "duties" of pregnancy and childbirth—her inability to provide a male heir—that would be her undoing.

CHAPTER 3

ARE YOU THE DAUPHIN
OF FRANCE?

⋮

ONCE MARY HAD BEEN CHRISTENED, KATHERINE ENTRUSTED HER care to the staff of the royal nursery. Katherine carefully selected each of them: a lady mistress, Lady Margaret Bryan, formerly one of Katherine's ladies-in-waiting, headed the small establishment; a wet nurse, Katherine Pole, suckled the young princess; three "rockers" took it in turn to soothe her; and a laundress performed the endless task of washing the infant's clothes. In the inner room of her nursery suite, Mary slept in an "everyday" cradle. In the outer chamber, she received visitors in a specially constructed "cradle of estate," draped in a quilt of ermine and framed by a canopy embossed with the royal arms.¹ Courted by princes from around the world, she was at once dependent infant and esteemed European princess.

Her father doted on her. According to Sebastian Giustiniani, one day the king showed him the Princess Mary, then two years old, in her nurse's arms. "He drew near, knelt and kissed her hand, for that alone is kissed by any duke or noble of the land." Henry then said proudly to the envoy, *"Domine Orator, per Deum immortalem, ista puella nunquam plorat"*—this child never cries—to which Giustiniani replied, "Sacred Majesty, the reason is that her destiny does not move her to tears; she will even become Queen of France." These words pleased the king greatly.²

The twenty-five-year-old King Henry looked to hold his own against Francis I, the young new king of France, and Charles, duke of Burgundy, just sixteen, who had become king of Spain weeks before. Mary would increasingly become a pawn in their European rivalry.

Francis had triumphed in the latest conflict over Milan in Italy, and the warring kings had come to terms in the Treaty of Noyon. With neither side looking to England for an offensive alliance against the other, Thomas Wolsey, Henry's chief minister, sought to preserve England's status by becoming champion of peace. The Treaty of London, brokered by Wolsey in early October 1518, bound all the great powers to perpetual concord, to maintain peace and act together against any aggressor.[3] Sponsored by Pope Leo X, its declared aim was a European crusade against the Ottoman Turks, but for Henry and Wolsey it was a means of countering the growing threat of France. The treaty was underpinned by an Anglo-French rapprochement that hinged on a future marriage between Mary and the French dauphin, François, then just a few months old.[4] Although Mary was not to be delivered to France until she was sixteen and the dauphin fourteen, the betrothal sealed a new era of Anglo-French relations, which was to be celebrated the following year at a meeting of the two kings.

AT EIGHT O'CLOCK on the morning of Tuesday, October 5, 1518, Mary, just two and a half years old, was taken to her mother's chamber at Greenwich Palace in preparation for her betrothal. There her parents, the papal legates, Cardinal Wolsey and Cardinal Lorenzo Campeggio, the queen dowager of France, and numerous French dignitaries headed by the lord admiral, Guillaume Bonnivet, gathered to receive her. As Giustiniani described it, "all the court were in such rich array that I never saw the like either here or elsewhere."[5] Dressed "in cloth of gold, with a cap of black velvet on her head, adorned with many jewels," Mary was a vision of royal extravagance.[6] When Cuthbert Tunstall, the bishop of Durham, delivered his sermon in praise of marriage, she grew restless and was picked up and "taken in arms" by her lady mistress, Margaret Bryan.[7] Her betrothed, the six-month-old François, was spared the monotony of the ceremony, the lord admiral acting in his place.

After the vows were exchanged, Wolsey "placed on her finger a small ring in which a large diamond was set," leaving to Bonnivet, the proxy groom, the symbolic task of slipping it down over the second joint.[8] In spite of her young age, Mary did, it seems, know something of the meaning of the occasion. "Are you the Dauphin of France?" she was reported to have said to Bonnivet. "If you are, I wish to kiss you."[9] With the ceremony finally concluded, the party moved to the chapel for a celebratory Mass followed by a sumptuous banquet. The dancing continued long into the night, many hours after the young bride-to-be had been put to bed.

As a condition of the marriage alliance, the French had insisted that Mary be recognized as her father's heir. It was the first acknowledgment of her right to the throne.[10] At the time it seemed a relatively insignificant concession. Katherine was pregnant, and Henry held out great hope for the imminent birth of a son. But once again, to the "vexation of everyone,"[11] disappointment followed. On November 9, a month after the betrothal ceremonies, Katherine gave birth to a stillborn daughter. "Never had the kingdom desired anything so passionately as it had a prince," Giustiniani wrote. "Perhaps had the event taken place before the conclusion of the betrothal, that event might not have come to pass; the sole fear of this kingdom, that it may pass through this marriage into the power of the French."[12] By the beginning of 1519, Princess Mary, betrothed to the French dauphin, was the sole heir to the throne of England.

CHAPTER 4

A VERY FINE YOUNG
COUSIN INDEED

∴

IN 1519, THE HABSBURG-VALOIS STRUGGLE FOR EUROPEAN DOMI-nance imploded. Mary's cousin, nineteen-year-old Charles of Spain and Burgundy, became Holy Roman Emperor following the death of his grandfather. He was now the most powerful ruler in Christendom, heir to the vast territories of Spain, Burgundy, and the Netherlands and huge swaths of Germany. England held the balance of power. Francis needed English friendship to prevent French encirclement; Charles wanted English money and ships to suppress the Comuneros revolt, which had broken out in Castile against his rule. Seeking to maximize his advantage, Henry negotiated with both sides. While rumors circulated of a proposed marriage between Mary and her cousin the Emperor Charles, Henry sought to reassure Francis of his commitment to the Anglo-French match.

On Saturday, May 26, 1520, shortly before Henry's long-awaited meeting with the French king, Charles arrived in England on his way from Spain to the Low Countries. He landed at Dover and was conducted by Henry and Wolsey to Canterbury, where for the first time he met his aunt. Katherine "embraced him tenderly, not without tears." Their reunion had been "her greatest desire in the world."[1] For three days, amid lavish entertainment, Charles sought to undermine the marriage alliance between his cousin Mary and the Valois prince. On the twenty-ninth, Henry and Katherine set sail for France accompanied by a retinue of six thousand Englishmen and -women.

For just over three weeks, a temporary town, the Camp du Drap d'Or, or Field of the Cloth of Gold, stood on a no-man's-land between the English-held town of Guisnes and French-held Ardres.² Gold fountains flowed with claret; there were huge and elaborate pavilions and tents and a great temporary palace of classical design erected at the town's entrance. Together the two kings jousted, feasted, and celebrated the entente reached two years before. It was a spectacular meeting of two young and physically powerful monarchs, whose rivalry was at once political and intensely personal. It was the greatest and most conspicuous display of wealth and culture that Europe had ever seen.

While her parents feasted in France, Mary became the focus of royal attention, holding court at Richmond Palace. Her nursery had been expanded to become a more "princely" household, reflecting her status—albeit reluctantly acknowledged—as the king's sole heir. Head officers were appointed, and male servants, gentlemen, grooms, and valets were added to her original female staff. Lady Bryan was replaced as lady mistress by one of the most powerful and influential women in England: Mary's godmother, Margaret Pole, the countess of Salisbury—one of Katherine's most trusted and long-serving confidantes and a direct descendant of Edward IV's brother, George, duke of Clarence. It proved to be an inspired choice. Mary became devoted to her new governess and came to think of her as a "second mother."³

During this time privy councillors visited the young princess frequently and sent reports to her parents in France. As one letter explained, "We have sundry times visited and seen your dearest daughter the princess, who, God be thanked, is in prosperous health and convalescence; and like as she increaseth in days and years, so doth she in grace, wit and virtue."⁴ Another of June 13, 1520, described Mary as "right merry . . . and daily exercising herself in virtuous pastimes and occupations."⁵

As she was the betrothed wife of their dauphin, the French also monitored Mary's health and development. Queen Claude, Francis's wife, sent gifts of a jeweled cross "worth six thousand ducats" and a portrait of her son.⁶ Anxious to see that she was fit and well after a rumor of her death, Francis sent three gentlemen to visit Mary.⁷ On Saturday, June 30, the French delegation arrived by barge at Richmond and found Mary surrounded by a throng of lords, ladies, gentlemen, and gentlewomen, as befitted the heir to the throne and future queen consort of France.[8] As the envoys reported, she welcomed them "with most goodly countenance, proper communication and pleasant pastime in playing at the virginals, that they greatly marvelled and rejoiced the same, her young and tender age considered."[9] She was, of course, only four.

AFTER THE ANGLO-FRENCH entertainments were concluded, Henry rode to meet Charles V at Gravelines, Flanders, and returned with him to Calais the following day to begin negotiations. Meanwhile, Francis had taken advantage of the Comuneros revolt in Spain to reconquer Spanish Navarre. The emperor appealed to Henry for help under the Treaty of London, which had provided against such acts of aggression, and asked that he repudiate the French match and now accept him as a suitor for Mary. But Henry was keen to maintain his advantage and, though agreeing not to make any fresh treaty with the French, was reluctant to commit fully to an alliance with the emperor.

By the following year, Charles had made extravagant promises to secure an alliance, and Henry promised to declare war on France if the fighting continued until November and to mount a joint invasion within two years.[10] In these changed circumstances, Mary would be betrothed to her cousin the emperor.[11] Mary was five; Charles was twenty-one. He would have to wait eight years for Mary to be of marriageable age. As Henry acknowledged to his envoy, Cuthbert Tunstall, bishop of Durham, their agreement would "not prevent the Emperor from marrying any woman of lawful age before our daughter comes to mature years, as he will only be bound to take her if he is then at liberty." However, in order to win favorable terms from the emperor, "it is to be considered that she is now our sole heir and may succeed to the crown."[12] If Charles proved "intractable," Tunstall was instructed to warn him of what was likely to happen if the alliance was not concluded and the French marriage went ahead:

> If the match goes on between Mary and the Dauphin and he becomes King of France, and in her right, King of England, the navies of England and France will shut [the emperor] out of the seas. If he made his abode in Spain, the Low Countries will

be in danger, and the French King, having these two realms and the duchy of Milan, might do him great mischief in Naples and soon attain the monarchy of all Christendom. Whereas by this alliance the Emperor might get that power to himself, and put France in such perplexity as to be no longer able to trouble him.[13]

With both France and Spain seeking an English alliance, Mary was at the very center of European affairs. Katherine particularly favored the continuation of the Anglo-Spanish alliance inaugurated by her own betrothal to Prince Arthur thirty years before. When Charles Poupet de Lachaulx, the imperial ambassador, visited England in March 1522, Katherine was anxious to display her daughter's precocious abilities and would not let him leave until he had seen Mary dance. She "did not have to be asked twice" and performed with no hint of infant shyness, twirling "so prettily that no woman in the world could do better." Mary then played the virginals and "two or three songs on the spinet" with impressive accomplishment. As Lachaulx reported to Charles, "Indeed, sire, she showed unbelievable grace and skill and such self-command as a woman of twenty might envy. She is pretty and very tall for her age, just turned seven and a very fine young cousin indeed."[14]

It was exactly the response that Katherine had hoped for. Mary now chose Charles as her valentine and wore a golden brooch at her breast with "Charles" spelled out in jewels and owned another spelling out "the Emperour," which appears pinned to her bodice in a portrait miniature by Lucas Horenbout.[15] The marriage of her daughter to her nephew was a prospect that Katherine relished. As the imperial ambassador wrote to Charles, "her greatest desire, was to see you here and to receive you with the greatest honour and best cheer possible."[16]

ON MAY 26, CHARLES returned to England to celebrate the signing of the new treaty and his betrothal to Mary. He was met at Dover by Wolsey and a train of noblemen and conducted to Canterbury, where the king greeted him. Together they took the royal barge from Gravesend to Greenwich, arriving in the early evening. "At the hall door the Queen and the Princess and all the ladies received and

welcomed him . . . and the Emperor had great joy to see the Queen his
Aunt and especially his young cousin germain the Lady Mary."[17] Mary
was again expected to perform and impress. She danced and played the
virginals once more and won the praise of all those who looked on. As
one envoy reported, "she promises to become a handsome lady,
although it is difficult to form an idea of her beauty as she is still so
small."[18]

Little over a week later, Charles was formally received into the City
of London amid great pageantry. At London Bridge two giant figures
of Samson and Hercules had been erected, and at Leadenhall, Italian
merchants had constructed a genealogical tree showing their joint
ancestry. The two monarchs then moved to Windsor, where for a
month they jousted, hunted, and feasted before concluding a permanent treaty of peace and friendship that confirmed the Anglo-imperial
match.[19] Charles's negotiators had at first insisted that Mary be delivered to them the following year so that she could be trained as a lady of
the imperial court, but Wolsey had resisted. Mary would not go to the
Habsburg court in Brussels until she was twelve, the lawful age of
cohabitation, when she would become Charles's consort.[20] This fact
was to dominate the next four years of her life. She was to be trans-
formed as rapidly as possible into a Spanish lady, to be dressed "according to the fashion and manner of those parts," trained in Spanish
customs and politeness, and educated in a suitable manner.[21]

CHAPTER 5

THE INSTITUTION OF A CHRISTIAN WOMAN

∴

As concerning the bringing up of her, if he [King Henry, her father] should seek a Mistress for her to frame her after the manner of Spain, and of whom she might take example of virtue, he should not find in all Christendom a more mete than she now hath, that is to say, the Queen's grace, her mother, who is cometh of this house of Spain and who, for the affection she beareth to the Emperor, will nourish her, and bring her up as may be hereafter to his most contentment.[1]

—CUTHBERT TUNSTALL, BISHOP OF LONDON,
AND SIR RICHARD WINGFIELD, ENGLISH
AMBASSADORS TO THE EMPEROR, JULY 8, 1525

MARY WAS NOW TO BE EDUCATED AS THE FUTURE WIFE OF THE emperor and, if she remained sole heir to Henry's crown, queen of England. While it was a prospect that Henry was reluctant to accept, Katherine shared none of Henry's qualms about her daughter's right to succeed and the ability of women to govern. Her mother, Isabella, had ruled as queen of Castile and refused to yield to pressure to alter the Castilian laws that permitted her eldest daughter to succeed her. She had asserted her equality with Ferdinand in their roles as the "Catholic Kings" but had also acknowledged the importance of her role as dutiful wife and mother. For Katherine, female sovereignty was compatible with wifely obedience and there was no good reason why Mary should not succeed her father. Katherine was determined to prepare her daughter for rule.

In this she drew on her own education and experience. She consulted leading scholars and commissioned educational treatises to advise on Mary's program of instruction. Desiderius Erasmus, the great Dutch humanist, had produced the *Institutio Principis Christiani* (Institution of a Christian Prince) in 1516, but there was no similar guide for the education of a future queen regnant. Katherine requested the Spanish humanist Juan Luis Vives to write such a manual for the education of girls. As Vives wrote in his dedicatory letter of April 5, 1523, to his *De Institutione Feminae Christianae* (The Institution of a Christian Woman):

> Moved by the holiness of your life and your ardent zeal for sacred studies, I have endeavoured to write something for your Majesty on the education of the Christian Woman . . . your daughter Mary will read these recommendations and will reproduce them as she models herself on the example of your goodness and wisdom to be found within your home. She will do this assuredly, and unless she alone belies all human expectations, must of necessity be virtuous and holy as the offspring of you and Henry VIII, such a noble and honoured pair.[2]

While asserting that women should be properly educated, *De Institutione* was traditional in expecting women to be men's subjugated companions; their primary goals were virtue, domesticity, and chastity. Female education, Vives maintained, was preparation not for a public role but for the conventional occupations of wife and mother. As Vives explained, men would benefit from having educated spouses, as "there is nothing so troublesome as sharing one's life with a person of no principles." Since a woman "that thinketh alone, thinketh evil," it was recommended that Mary be kept away from the company of men and be surrounded at all times with "sad, pale and untrimmed" servants.

Two lists, one of "good" books—predominantly Spanish and French—the other of *libri pestiferi*—noxious books—were recommended for Mary's reading. Chivalric romances were to be avoided, as they were thought to incite women's imaginations and corrupt their minds, given their moral frailty. Instead, Mary should read the Bible, particularly the Gospels, Acts of the Apostles, and Epistles, every morning and evening, together with the works of the Church Fathers and writers such as Plato, Cicero, and Seneca.[3] Besides reading, Vives approved of the classical female recreations of spinning, needlework, and cooking, as all such activities put off the moral danger of idleness. He concluded that Mary should follow her mother in virtue, rather than her father to the throne.

But Vives's treatise lacked detail, and in October 1524, Katherine commissioned Vives to write a more specific curriculum of study for her seven-year-old daughter. The resulting *De Ratione Studii Puerilis* (On a Plan of Study for Children) was dedicated to the young princess herself. It set out rules for the proper pronunciation of Greek and Latin, emphasized the desirability of learning things by heart, and refined the earlier list of selected reading. Here the recommended books were much more oriented toward governance, perhaps reflecting Vives's tacit acknowledgment that Mary was destined to rule. She was to read Cicero, Seneca, Plutarch, and the dialogues of Plato, "particularly those which demonstrate the government of the commonwealth," together with Thomas More's *Utopia* and Erasmus's *Institutio Principis Christiani*.

Vives's curriculum did allow for a few stories for Mary's amusement, but they were carefully selected and focused heavily on the deeds of self-sacrificing women. Mary could read about the virtuous Roman matron Lucretia, who, after being raped by the son of Tarquin the Proud, stabbed herself to death; or about the patient Griselda, whose husband put her through endless trials to assure himself of her devotion. These were stories that taught "the art of life" and that Mary could "tell to others."[4] As Mary got older, Vives advised that Katherine revise her educational program more precisely: "Time will admonish her as to more exact details, and thy singular wisdom will discover for her what they should be."[5]

GIVEN KATHERINE's own intellect, much was anticipated of Mary. As Erasmus wrote to the queen in his *Christiani Matrimonii Institutio*, "Your qualities are known to us . . . we expect a work no less of your daughter Mary. For what should we not expect from a girl who is born of the most devout of parents and brought up under the care of such a mother?[6] Mary in fact proved to be a highly accomplished child. She was able to write a letter in Latin by the age of nine and at twelve translated the prayer of Saint Thomas Aquinas. Henry Parker, a literary noble, wrote in a later dedication to Mary, "I do well remember that scant you were twelve years of age but that you were so ripe in the Latin tongue, that rare doth happen to the woman sex, that your grace could not only perfectly read, write and construe Latin, but furthermore translate any hard thing of the Latin into our English tongue."[7]

But Mary would also receive an education for life and rule that went beyond the strictures of Vives's instruction. She proved to be precocious and talented and shared her father's love of music. When at the age of two she heard the Venetian organist Dionysius Memo playing at court, she ran after him calling "Priest, Priest" and refusing to stop until he agreed to play more.[8] By the age of four Mary was playing the virginals and would later win lavish praise for her lute playing. Like her parents, she liked to hawk and to hunt, and as a teenager she developed a love of gambling at cards: her privy purse accounts reveal numerous amounts lost in this way.[9] Mary developed her own style, loved fine clothes and jewelry, and, eager to please, would happily dance and perform at court as foreign ambassadors sued for her hand.

CHAPTER 6

GREAT SIGNS AND TOKENS OF LOVE

∴

Matters have gone so far, that the Queen sent her Confessor to me in secret to warn me of Henry's discontents. She is very sorry that your Majesty [Charles V] ever promised so much in this treaty, and she fears it may one day be the cause of a weakening of the friendship between you two.[1]

—LOUIS DE PRAET TO CHARLES V,
MARCH 26, 1524

IN THE SUMMER OF 1523, HENRY AND CHARLES EMBARKED ON THE "Great Enterprise," the joint invasion of France that they had agreed upon the year before. It proved to be a debacle. At the end of August, an English force of around 11,000 troops began a march toward Paris but was forced back by French resistance and severe weather. When Charles failed to open an offensive in France as he had promised, the Anglo-imperial alliance reached the breaking point. Mistrustful of his ally's fidelity, Henry began to consider the prospect of dissolving the marriage treaty with the emperor and began talks for a match between Mary and his sister's son, the young Scottish king, James V.[2] By the end of October it looked as if agreement were in sight. Wolsey sent word to Margaret that Henry would "find the means" to break Mary's engagement with Charles "in brief time" and then "conclude the marriage" between his daughter and "his dearest nephew, the young King of Scots."[3]

But the old alliances soon regained their appeal. On the morning of February 24, 1525, imperial troops decisively defeated the French army outside the walls of the city of Pavia. The French king was captured in battle and taken to Madrid in the custody of the emperor. Charles was in the ascendancy, and Henry now looked to revive the Anglo-imperial plans for the dismemberment of France.[4] "Now is the time," Henry declared to an ambassador from the Low Countries, "for the Emperor and myself to devise the means of getting full satisfaction from France. Not an hour is to be lost." Henry would receive the French Crown, which belonged to him "by just title of inheritance." In return he would hand Mary over to Charles when she came of age, without any guarantee as to "how she should be entreated and ordered touching her marriage."[5]

Katherine also began to petition Charles, appealing on the grounds of family loyalty. She lamented that she had heard nothing from him for a long time, choosing to attribute his silence to the "inconstancy and fickleness of the sea":

> Nothing indeed would be so painful to me as to think that your Highness had forgotten me, and therefore beg and entreat, as earnestly as I can, that your Highness be pleased to inform me of your health, and send me your orders, for love and consanguinity both demand that we should write to each other oftener.[6]

Katherine tried to reassure herself that "as long as our nephew keeps his promise to marry our daughter the alliance will remain unbroken; as long as the marriage treaty stands, he may be sure of England."[7]

IN APRIL, AT WOLSEY'S instigation, Mary sent Charles an emerald ring as a symbol of her "constancy." Accompanying it was a message that she sought "for a better knowledge to be had when God shall send them grace to be together, whether his Majesty doth keep constant and continent to her, as with God's grace she will." The envoys added that Mary's love for Charles was so passionate that it was confirmed by jealousy, "one of the great signs and tokens of love."[8]

Upon receiving the ring Charles put it on his little finger and ordered the ambassadors to say that he would wear it for the sake of the princess for the rest of his life.[9] Although his affection for Mary could not be doubted, Charles now looked to disavow her as his future bride. It was still five years before Mary could marry, and Charles was now in pursuit of another cousin, Isabella of Portugal, who was of marriageable age. He was anxious to be married at once so he could leave his new empress to rule Spain while he traveled to his other territories and sought to break off the English match by proposing unrealistic terms. He would raise an army for the invasion of France provided that Henry would pay for it and that Mary was handed over at once so that she might "learn the Castilian language and the manners of the people."[10] If Henry would not agree to his requests, Charles would demand to be released from the agreement.[11]

Henry refused, and Wolsey made his excuses. Mary would not be given up on account of "the tenderness of her age" and, given "the respect to be had to her noble person," it was "not meet as yet" that she "endure the pains of the sea, nor also to be brought up in an other air, that may be dangerous to her person." Henry agreed to break off the betrothal on condition that Charles made peace with France and pay his debts to England.[12] Within days the emperor signed a contract with Isabella of Portugal, whom he married in February of the following year.

The Anglo-Spanish alliance was at an end. To Katherine it was a personal affront, and she protested at her nephew's behavior: "I am sure I deserve not this treatment, for such are my affection and readiness for your Highness's service that I deserved a better reward."[13] For Mary, who had quickly become enamored of her Spanish cousin, it meant a painful rejection but the beginning of an attachment that would endure for the rest of her life.

CHAPTER 7

PRINCESS OF WALES

∴

ALTHOUGH MARY WAS COURTED BY THE RULING FAMILIES OF EUROPE, Henry remained reluctant to accept her as his successor and continued to hope for a male heir. But Katherine had not conceived since 1518. She was now forty and, as the Venetian ambassador observed, "past that age in which women most commonly were wont to be fruitful."[1] Rumors had circulated in Rome in 1514 that the "King of England meant to repudiate his present wife . . . because he is unable to have children by her."[2] Mary's birth had once given Henry reason to hope; now, with no prospect of an heir, he began to reflect on the consequences of his "childlessness."

On June 16, 1525, Henry's bastard son, Henry Fitzroy, the product of a brief affair with one of the queen's ladies, Elizabeth Blount, was recognized as the king's son and showered with titles and honors. He was installed as a Knight of the Garter and created earl of Nottingham, duke of Richmond, and duke of Somerset. This unprecedented double dukedom was then followed by his appointments as lord high admiral and warden general of the Scottish Marches and, two years later, by his investiture as lord lieutenant of Ireland. Not since the twelfth century had a king of England raised an illegitimate son to the peerage, and never had any subject held such a collection of offices and titles. Fitzroy was now given a great household and sent to Sheriff Hutton Castle in Yorkshire as the head of the King's Council of the North. Lorenzo Orio, the Venetian envoy, reported that "he is now next in rank to His Majesty, and might yet be easily by the King's means exalted to higher things."[3] Katherine was indignant and feared that Mary might be excluded outright from her inheritance. "No bastard," she complained, "ought to be exalted above the daughter of the Queen."[4]

But Henry had not yet resolved to prefer one child to another, and preparations were being made to enhance Mary's status. The nine-year-old was to be dispatched to the Welsh Marches, one of the most desolate and volatile areas of the kingdom, to preside over the Council of Wales and the Marches. While Henry stopped short of formally investing her with the title "princess of Wales" and thereby explicitly acknowledging her as his successor, Mary's appointment represented the revival of an association of the king's heir with the government of Wales that had begun under Edward, the firstborn son of Edward IV, and followed by Prince Arthur more than twenty years before.[5]

Though Katherine would mourn her daughter's absence, she would take comfort from the fact that the princess's status was at last being recognized.[6] She was now following the path of the heir to the throne.

ON AUGUST 12, 1525, Mary left Wolsey's manor, The More, near St. Albans, for the Marches, accompanied by a vast entourage dressed in her livery colors of blue and green. From Woburn, then to Reading, she reached Thornbury Castle in Gloucestershire on or about the twenty-fourth. Dozens of carts had been borrowed from local establishments to carry all the necessary household items and furnishings, ranging from "3 brass pots, one brazen pestle and mortar, a frying pan with a flesh hook and a chest with irons for keeping prisoners" to a throne for the Presence Chamber and all that was necessary to furnish the chapel at Thornbury, including standing candelabras, Mass books with golden covers, carved stands, kneeling cushions, and prayer stools.[7]

It was to be a court in miniature. Lord Ferrers and Lord Dudley headed the establishment as steward and chamberlain, respectively; Bishop John Voysey was appointed lord president of the Council, and Margaret Pole, the countess of Salisbury, who had been dismissed from Mary's service in 1521 when her son the duke of Buckingham had been executed for treason, was reappointed lady mistress. Beneath these head officers were three hundred other servants, including Mary's new schoolmaster, Richard Fetherstone.[8]

The king's instructions detailed precisely the expectations and duties of the household and Council and made provision for Mary's education, welfare, and pastimes. The main responsibility was placed with Margaret Pole, who was entrusted with "all such things as concern the person of the said princess, her noble education and training in all virtuous demeanour." Mary was to be treated as "so great a princess doth appertain." Ladies and gentlewomen were to remain in attendance of her and were to "use themselves sadly, honourably, virtuously and discreetly in words, countenance, gesture, behaviour and deed with humility, reverence, lowliness . . . so as of them proceed no manner of example of evil or unfitting manner or conditions, but rather all good and godly behaviour." She was to learn to serve God, to take "moderate exercise" in the "open air," in gardens, sweet and wholesome places, so as to "confer unto her health, solace and comfort" as her lady governess thought "most convenient." At some seasons she was to pass her time

at her virginals, or other instruments musical, so that the same be not too much, and without fatigacion or weariness to intend to her learning of Latin tongue or French. At other seasons to dance, and amongst the residue to have good respect unto her diet, which is mete to be pure, well-prepared, dressed and served, with comfortable, joyous and merry communication in all honourable and virtuous manner.

Her clothes, her chamber, and her body were to be kept "pure, sweet, clean and wholesome."[9]

With mother and daughter now apart, they maintained a correspondence, and Katherine resolved to remain closely involved in Mary's education, writing her:

Daughter,
I pray you think not that any forgetfulness hath caused me to
keep Charles [her messenger] so long here, and answered not to your
good Letter . . . the long absence of the King and you troubleth me.
My health is meetly good: and I trust in God, he that sent me the
last doth it to the best, and will shortly turn it to the first to come to

good effect. And in the meantime I am very glad to hear from You,
specially when they show me that you be well amended. I pray God
to continue it to his pleasure. As for your writing in Latin I am glad
that you shall change from me to Master Fetherstone, for that shall
do you much good, to learn by him to write right. But yet sometimes
I would be glad when you do write to Master Fetherstone of your own
editing when he hath read it that I may see it. For it shall be a great
comfort to me to see You keep your Latin and fair writing and all.
And so I pray You to recommend me to my Lady of Salisbury. At
Woburn this Friday night,

> *Your loving mother,*
> *Katherine the Queen.*[10]

MARY'S HOUSEHOLD WOULD become the center of a social elite and
of high courtly culture. Full royal ceremony was observed, with Mary
practicing the part of queen at the head of her own court. Every day at
least "two Gentleman Ushers, two Gentleman Waiters, two Yeoman
Ushers, twelve Yeomen and two Grooms" were to attend her in the
Presence Chamber, and more were to be added on "Sundays, Satur-
days and other principal seasons," when there "shall be access or
recourse of noblemen or other strangers repairing unto that court or
that it be as festival days or times or other things requisite to have be
great and honourable presence."[11]

Such numbers were expected to flock to Tewkesbury to pay homage
to the princess that John Voysey, the bishop of Exeter and lord president of the Council, anxiously wrote to Wolsey asking, on account of
the "great repair of strangers" anticipated, that "a ship of silver for the
almes dish" be sent to hold the princess's napkin, which afterward
would be filled with scraps to be distributed among the poor. Voysey
also inquired what provision would be made for the Twelfth Night
banquet entertainments and whether they should employ a "Lord of
Misrule," and requested that trumpets and a rebeck (a type of fiddle) be
sent to Thornbury.[12]

At the center of her own court, Mary began to learn the art of governance. Her French tutor, Giles Duwes, later wrote *An Introductory for*

to Learn to Read, to Pronouce, and to Speak French based on his time in the household in the Marches. In it he portrayed Mary as a princely ruler and her court as a center of literary patronage, educated conversation, and gentle manners. Mary features in a number of dialogues about piety, philosophy, and courtly love. In one, Duwes recalled an occasion when the young princess participated in the drawing of names on Valentine's Day. When Mary drew as her valentine her treasurer, Sir Ralph Egerton—an old man afflicted by gout—she insisted on calling him her "husband *adoptif.*" As his pretend wife, she criticized Sir Ralph for taking better care of his gout "than you do your wife." She could hardly believe "that the gout might withhold a good husband having some love to his wife" and begged him to teach her what "a good husband ought to teach his wife," that is, the definition of love.[13] She had just turned ten.

CHAPTER 8

PEARL OF THE WORLD

EVER SINCE CHARLES V HAD BROKEN OFF HIS BETROTHAL TO MARY, Wolsey had been in negotiations to revive an alliance with France. In March 1526, Francis had reentered his kingdom, having been in imperial captivity since the Battle of Pavia the previous year. By the terms of the Treaty of Madrid, which had secured Francis his freedom from imperial custody, he had handed over his two sons as hostages for the payment of his ransom and was contracted to marry Eleanor, the widowed queen of Portugal.

But Francis had no intention of keeping to these terms. As soon as possible, he told the English ambassadors, "I shall take off my mask."[1] Now seeking revenge, he joined a league formed at Cognac that comprised the pope, Venice, Milan, and Florence and looked to force the victorious imperial armies out of Italy. Wolsey, always hoping to enhance England's status by acting as the "peacemaker of Europe," sought an Anglo-French entente to compel Charles to moderate his settlement with Francis and prevent further war. Mary was once again to be used as a gambit for an alliance. As she was quickly learning, marriage was for political, not personal, ends. Mutual and sacred vows were made and unmade as the balance of power between England, France, and Spain dictated. As Nicholas von Schomberg, archbishop of Capua, wrote to the emperor, "in time of war the English make use of the princess as an owl, with which to lure birds."[2]

IN JULY, JOHN CLERK, bishop of Bath and Wells, was sent to France with instructions to renew marriage negotiations for a match between Mary and Francis's second son, Henry, duke of Orléans. Mary was, Clerk declared, "the pearl of the world" and "the jewel that his highness [Henry VIII] esteemed more than anything in earth."³ As the negotiations proceeded, Henry intervened with a proposal that he give up his ancient claim to France and join the League of Cognac, provided that Francis pay him a pension, cede Boulogne, and marry Mary himself.⁴ Francis, recently widowed, was only two years younger than Henry and a notorious womanizer. Yet for English interests the alliance made good sense. If Francis predeceased Henry and left children by Mary, the English and French succession would remain separate, as Francis already had two sons. If Henry died first, Francis could claim England through his wife. But his reign was likely to be short, given his age, and then the two kingdoms would become separate once more. At first Francis was skeptical of Henry's plan, but after the pope declared the match a *sancta conjunctio*—a holy union—Francis responded favorably to the proposal, seeing it as a valuable alliance against imperial designs.

The French king now proceeded to praise Mary's abilities, concluding that given "her education, her form and fashion, her beauty and virtue, and what father and mother she cometh of; expedient and necessary it shall be for me and for my realm that I marry her." He reassured the English ambassador, "I have as great a mind to her as ever I had to any woman."⁵ Francis wrote to Mary, addressing her as "high and powerful princess" and assuring her of his loyalty as her good brother, cousin, and ally.⁶ In February 1527, a legation left France for England to conclude the terms of an alliance.

ON APRIL 23, as the court celebrated the Feast of Saint George at Greenwich, Mary received the French visitors. She spoke to them in Latin, French, and Italian and entertained them on the virginals.⁷ The principal French ambassador, the marquess of Turenne, declared that he was impressed by her accomplishments but observed that she was "so thin, spare and small as to make it impossible for her to be married for the next three years."⁸ Francis's mother, Louise of Savoy, the queen regent, proposed that the marriage should take place at Calais in August, and after the solemnization, the king, her son, might "abide himself for an hour or less with the Princess," after which King Henry might carry her back again to England "unto such time as she should be thought [more] able."[9] Henry, however, refused to agree to either arrangement.

On April 30, "perpetual peace" was concluded between France and England: a pledge was made to declare war on Charles V if he refused to come to terms, and a French marriage between Mary and the French king, or his second son, the duke of Orléans, was agreed upon.[10] Mary was now betrothed to the House of Valois.

For two weeks, the Anglo-French festivities continued. These culminated on May 5 in a great court feast and a masque. A painted curtain was drawn back to reveal a stage, and Mary and seven ladies of the court emerged from a gold cave to the sound of trumpets. The princess was "dressed in cloth of gold, her hair gathered in a net, with a richly jewelled garland, surmounted by a velvet cap, the hanging sleeves of their surcoats being so long that they well nigh touched the ground." She looked radiant, wrote one observer; "her beauty in this array produced such an effect on everybody that all other marvellous sights previously witnessed were forgotten." She wore on her person "so many precious stones that their splendour and radiance dazzled the sight, in so wise as to make one believe that she was decked with all the gems of the eighth sphere."

Having descended from the cave, Mary and her ladies danced a ballet with eight lords. After the masque, festivities continued, with Mary dancing with her father at the heart of the revelry. Mary presented herself to Henry, who "took off her cap, and the net being displaced, a profusion of silver tresses as beautiful as ever seen on human head fell over her shoulders."[11] The evening entertainment culminated with the French ambassador dancing with Mary "and the King with Mistress Boleyn."[12]

CHAPTER 9

THIS SHEER CALAMITY

∴

ENRY MAINTAINED THAT IT WAS A QUESTION POSED BY THE bishop of Tarbes, one of the French envoys, in the spring of 1527 that first made him doubt the validity of his marriage to Katherine of Aragon and therefore Mary's legitimacy.[1] During the course of negotiations for the betrothal of Mary and the duke of Orléans, the bishop had inquired whether in fact Mary was so great a prospect after all. Had not Henry married his brother's widow? Was that marriage valid? Was Mary legitimate? The envoy's questions struck a resounding chord with the king. Having toyed with the idea of advancing his illegitimate son, Henry now settled on a more radical solution to the succession. The lack of a male heir, the successive failed pregnancies that had left the forty-two-year-old queen seeming dowdy and dumpy, and the allure of the twentysomething Anne Boleyn all contributed to Henry's mounting disillusionment with his Spanish wife.

Attractive and vivacious, Anne Boleyn had grown up in the household of Queen Claude, the first wife of the French king Francis I. She was, as one observer described, "beautiful, had an elegant figure and with eyes that were even more attractive."[2] On her return to England in the winter of 1521 she joined the queen's household as one of Katherine's ladies-in-waiting. Three years later Henry began his courtship of her. He had previously ended an affair with her sister Mary. Now he looked to install Anne as his "sole" mistress. But Anne refused. Henry grew increasingly infatuated, sending her gifts of jewelry and letters in which he declared his love and made promises that he would "cast off all others than yourself out of mind and affection and to serve you only."³ Still Anne resisted. Only if they were married would she give herself to him.

Henry now came to believe that his marriage to Katherine was contrary to divine law as stated in the Bible and that he was free to marry Anne. He looked to secure an annulment and cited Leviticus 20:21 to support his claim that in granting the dispensation for their marriage eighteen years before, Pope Julius II had breached the Word of God:

> If a man shall take his brother's wife, it is an impurity: he hath uncovered his brother's nakedness; they shall be childless.

On January 1, 1527, Henry and Anne secretly exchanged vows and pledged themselves to each other. It was at the Greenwich ball in May that they appeared in public for the first time. One moment the court was joyfully celebrating Mary's betrothal, the next she was all but forgotten, as all eyes and whispers turned to the subject of "mistress Boleyn." As Don Íñigo López de Mendoza, the new imperial ambassador, reported, the king was now "bent on divorce" and Wolsey was "scheming to bring it about."⁴ Mary's life was about to change forever.

TWELVE DAYS AFTER the ball, Wolsey summoned Henry to appear before a secret tribunal at his town palace at York to answer the charge of unlawfully cohabiting with his dead brother's wife. In the days that followed, evidence was presented against the marriage, and Wolsey and William Warham, archbishop of Canterbury, were called upon to make a judgment.⁵ It was a stage-managed trial, and the outcome seemed predictable. Yet on May 31, just when the verdict was to be delivered, Wolsey pronounced the case too difficult to call and referred it to a panel of learned theologians and lawyers.⁶ News had reached England that an imperial army in Italy had mutinied for want of pay and had sacked and pillaged Rome. Pope Clement VII had taken refuge in the Castel Sant'Angelo and was now effectively a prisoner of the emperor.⁷ Henry's divorce would be referred to Rome at just the time when the pope was at the mercy of Katherine's nephew.

Katherine had not been called to give evidence in the tribunal; she didn't even know it had taken place. It was not until June 22 that Henry went to her apartments to inform her of his intentions and to demand a formal separation. His conscience troubled him, he said; their marriage was invalid, and he was taking steps to have it annulled by the pope. He failed to mention his infatuation with Anne Boleyn, which was now an open secret. As Katherine began to cry, Henry lost his nerve: "all should be done for the best" he mumbled, and after begging her "to keep secrecy upon what he had told her," he beat a hasty retreat.[8]

But behind her tears the queen was "very stiff and obstinate." She confirmed that Arthur "did never know her carnally" and demanded counsel from both Henry's subjects and "strangers [foreigners]."[9] Wolsey immediately recognized the danger: Katherine was threatening to bring her nephew, the emperor, into the fight. "These were the worst points that could be imagined for the impeaching [preventing] of this matter . . . that she would resort to the counsel of strangers," and he "intended to make all the counsel of the world, France except, as a party against it."[10]

The queen hurriedly dispatched one of her Spanish servants, Francisco Felipez, to appeal to Charles to intervene. Henry ordered that Felipez be arrested, but the Spaniard eluded capture and reached the emperor at Valladolid at the end of July. Charles reacted quickly. He was shocked "to hear of a case so scandalous" and promised to "do everything in his power on her behalf." He told his ambassador in England, "We cannot desert the Queen, our good aunt, in her troubles and intend doing all we can in her favour." But, he added cautiously, "to this end, as the first step towards rendering help, it seems to us that this matter ought to be treated with all possible moderation, having recourse to kind remonstrances alone for the present."[11]

Charles wrote to Henry, asking that he halt the proceedings immediately, and to the pope, requesting that he revoke Wolsey's legateship and recall the case to Rome. He could not believe "that having, as they have, so sweet a princess for their daughter, [the King] would consent to have her or her mother dishonoured, a thing so monstrous of itself and wholly without precedent in ancient or modern history."[12] The fate of the king's marriage was not a merely personal affair but a public matter of European significance.

THE HUMANIST Juan Luis Vives, who had left England in May to spend the summer in the Netherlands, returned in late September to find Katherine "troubled and afflicted with this controversy that had arisen about her marriage." She "began to unfold . . . her calamity," weeping over her "destiny, that she should find him, whom she loved far more than herself, so alienated from her that he thought of marrying another; and this affected her with a grief the more intense as her love for him was the more ardent." She was unable to find out what Henry planned to do next, but the "report and common opinion was . . . that her cause was remitted to Rome."

Katherine instructed Vives to go to the emperor's ambassador, López, and ask the emperor on her behalf "that he would deal with the Pope that she might . . . be heard before his Holiness decided on her cause."[13] On October 26, López did as Katherine asked. "The divorce is more talked of than ever," he wrote to his master; "if therefore the Emperor really has the Queen's honour and peace of mind at heart, orders should be sent to Rome for a trusty messenger to bring us the Pope's decision."[14]

Cardinal Lorenzo Campeggio arrived in England on October 9 with orders from the pope to hear the case but to reach no decision.[15] He proposed that Katherine take vows of "perpetual chastity" and join a religious community, leaving Henry free to marry again without calling into question Mary's legitimacy or her claim to the throne. Katherine responded angrily: she would never take the veil as Campeggio had proposed and intended to "live and die in the estate of matrimony, into which God had called her, and that she would always be of that opinion and never change it." She held her husband's conscience and honor in "more esteem than anything in this world." She was, she said, the true and legitimate wife of the king and at the time of their wedding remained "intact and uncorrupted."[16] It was a protest she would make repeatedly for the next seven years.

Katherine would prove as defiantly committed to the legitimacy of her marriage as Henry was to its annulment. "She insists that everything shall be decided by [judicial] sentence," Campeggio reported.

"Neither the whole kingdom on the one hand, nor any great punishment on the other, although she might be torn limb by limb, should compel her to alter this opinion."[17]

AS THEIR MARRIAGE CRUMBLED and diplomats hurried between England and Rome, the king and queen continued to appear together in public at court. Mary lived as she had before her removal to the Marches, in houses adjacent to her parents, and regularly visiting them at court. With the outbreak of the plague in May 1528, the royal family, Henry, Katherine, and Mary, came together at Wolsey's house at Tyttenhanger, near St. Albans in Hertfordshire. For the twelve-year-old Mary, it was precious time spent with both her parents. In what is the earliest of her letters known to have survived, she thanked Wolsey for arranging for all of them to be together, telling him "I have been allowed for a month to enjoy, to my supreme delight, the society of the King and Queen my parents."[18]

It was but a temporary reprieve. Increasingly Henry would leave Katherine for days at a time to visit Anne. In advance of the Christmas festivities of 1528, Henry "lodged [his mistress] in a very fine lodging, which he has prepared for her close by his own." And, as Cardinal Jean du Bellay, the French diplomat, remarked, "Greater court . . . is paid to her everyday than has been to the Queen for a long time."[19] It was the way of things to come. But if Katherine knew all this, she chose to turn a blind eye. Perhaps she hoped that Henry's affection for Anne would wane. Certainly she took comfort in the fact that, as she confided to Mendoza, Henry continued "to visit her, and they dine and sleep together."[20]

ON MAY 31, 1529, the public trial of the king's marriage was held in the Parliament Chamber of the Dominican Friary of London, Blackfriars.[21] Both parties were required to answer their summons on Friday, June 18, but though Henry sent proxies, Katherine unexpectedly appeared in person. She entered the chamber accompanied by four bishops and "a great company" of ladies and gentlewomen. Then, "sadly and with great gravity," she read out a written statement protesting the cardinal's jurisdiction to hear the case.[22] The court was adjourned to consider her appeal and was reassembled on the Monday morning. Katherine arrived first, followed by Wolsey, Campeggio, and finally the king himself. Henry spoke briefly, asking for a quick decision "to determine the validity or nullity of his marriage, about which he has from the beginning felt a perpetual scruple." Wolsey spoke next, assuring the court, and in particular Katherine, that the case would be judged fairly. After Campeggio rose to formally reject Katherine's protestation and reassert the judges' jurisdiction, the court crier called, "Katherine, queen of England, come into court!"

Once again Katherine rejected the authority of the court and appealed directly to Rome: how could she, a foreigner, expect justice in England? She then turned to Henry. Though her address was public and in the austere setting of Campeggio's court, her words were intimate and imploring. Why did he now raise these scruples? she asked; "it was not the time to say this after so long silence."

In the face of Katherine's personal appeal, Henry was forced to respond. He had, he said, remained silent only because of "the great love he had and has for her"; he desired more than anything else that the marriage should be declared valid. Her appeal to Rome was unreasonable, "considering the Emperor's power there," but she had "the choice of prelates and lawyers." England was "perfectly secure for her," and that was where the case should be decided.[23] Suddenly the queen left her dais, walked across the courtroom, and knelt down at the king's feet. Twice Henry tried to raise her up, but she continued to kneel. Then, as Campeggio reported, "in the sight of all the court and assembly," she spoke "in broken English."

[She begged] him to consider her honour, her daughter's and his; that he should not be displeased at her defending it, and should consider the reputation of her nation and relatives, who will be seriously offended; in accordance with what she had said about his goodwill, she had throughout appealed to Rome, where it was reasonable that the affair should be determined, as the present place was open to suspicion and because the cause is already [begun] at Rome.[24]

Katherine had turned Henry's protestations of love against him. How could he, if he was so keen for their marriage to be declared valid, object to her appeal to Rome? Katherine got to her feet, curtsyed to the king, and left the court ignoring calls for her to return.[25]

On July 31, Campeggio announced that the pope had adjourned the court.[26] While Henry immediately began petitioning for the court to be reconvened, Katherine and the Habsburgs urged Pope Clement to return a favorable verdict. And so events proceeded: high politics and diplomacy in London and Rome conducted alongside the personal reality of a marriage unraveling.

CHAPTER 10

THE KING'S GREAT MATTER

∴

The Queen writes that such are the King's disappointment and passion at not being able to carry out his purpose that the Cardinal will inevitably be the victim of his rage.[1]

—MENDOZA TO THE EMPEROR,
JULY 25, 1529

WITH THE DIVORCE CASE REFERRED TO ROME, THERE SEEMED little prospect of Henry securing a favorable judgment. By the Treaty of Cambrai, Francis, Charles, and the pope had come to terms and ended French military efforts in Italy. France could no longer be used to put pressure on the emperor. While in Charles's custody, the pope had promised the emperor "not to grant unto any act that might be preparative, or otherwise, to divorce to be made to the King and Queen."[2]

It signaled Wolsey's fall from favor. He had failed in his efforts to free the pope from Charles's domination and to secure the annulment that Henry demanded. In his dispatch of September 1, the new imperial ambassador, Eustace Chapuys, reported that "the affairs of the Cardinal are getting worse and worse every day." Henry had banned him from receiving foreign ambassadors and prevented his coming to court. As the envoy continued in cipher, "the cause of this misunderstanding between the King and the Cardinal can be no other than the utter failure of the measures taken in order to bring about the divorce."[3] By October, Wolsey had been charged with *praemunire*, the illegal exercise of papal authority in England, in his role as legate. On the twenty-second, having resigned the lord chancellorship to the

lawyer and accomplished humanist Sir Thomas More, Wolsey acknowledged his offenses and placed himself and his possessions into the
king's hands.

Anticipating that the verdict from Rome would be hostile, Henry
now embarked on an English solution to the annulment. Letters "of
great importance," as the accounts of Sir Brian Tuke, the master of the
posts, record, were sent to Henry's ambassadors in Rome, instructing
them to inform the pope that neither he nor any other Englishman
could be summoned to a Roman court because by ancient custom and
privileges of the realm no one could be "compelled to go to law out of
the Kingdom."[4] Over the next four years, under the stewardship of
Thomas Cromwell, Parliament gradually eroded Rome's power in
England: first to pressure the pope to make concessions, then to fashion
a homemade settlement. By 1533, Henry would be the supreme head of
the English Church and married to his new wife, Anne Boleyn.

AS THE CAMPAIGN against the Church reached a crescendo, relations between Henry and Katherine broke down irrevocably, with
Mary remaining the only bond between them. In March 1531, Henry
"dined and resorted to the Queen as he was accustomed, and diminished nothing of her estate, and much loved and cherished their daughter the Lady Mary, but in no ways would he come to her bed."[5] Mary
lived in the midst of all this: sometimes at a distance in adjacent royal
houses, at other times at court. At Christmas the previous year, Henry,
Katherine, and Mary had been together; but Anne Boleyn remained a
constant, tormenting presence. On Christmas Eve, Katherine directly
challenged Henry about his relationship with Anne. His behavior was
a personal affront to her: he was setting a scandalous example. Henry's
response was curt: there was nothing wrong in his relationship with
Anne, and he intended to marry her whatever Katherine or the pope
might say.[6]

Anne was becoming equally bold. In conversation with one of
Katherine's ladies-in-waiting, she declared that "she wished all the
Spaniards were at the bottom of the sea" and added that "she cared not
for the Queen or any of her family, and that she would rather see her
hanged than have to confess that she was her Queen and mistress."[7]

Katherine now wrote to the emperor that she believed Anne alone stood in the way of a reconciliation with her husband and if she—that "woman [Henry] has under his roof"—were out of the way, their marriage might have a chance. Her husband's behavior displayed "not the least particle of shame."[8]

For Mary, separation from her father was proving hard to bear, and she continually petitioned to see him. In July 1530, she wrote asking to be allowed to visit him before he left for four months of hunting. On this occasion Henry agreed. He traveled to Richmond, where Mary was staying, and spent the whole day with her, "showing her all possible affection."[9] Suspicious of Mary's influence over her father, Anne Boleyn sent two servants to report on their conversation.[10] The following summer, Henry visited Mary again at Richmond "and made great cheer with her," speaking of her as he had when she was a young child, as a great "pearl."[11]

Such visits became more infrequent as Henry's views became increasingly colored by those of Anne. As Chapuys surmised, the king's apparent reluctance to see Mary was "to gratify the lady [Anne] who hates her as much as the Queen, or more so because she sees the King has some affection for her."[12] Chapuys believed that Anne was constantly scheming to have Mary moved as far away from court, and her father, as possible.[13] The child who had once bound the royal couple together was now used by Henry to pry them apart. The king demanded that Katherine choose between his company and that of Mary. He made it clear that if she visited the princess she might be forced to stay with her permanently and lose what little claim she had on Henry's companionship.[14] Desperate not to enrage Henry, Katherine "graciously replied that she would not leave him for her daughter, nor for anyone else in the world."[15] It was a painful and ultimately futile gesture of wifely loyalty.

AT THE END of May, a further attempt was made to force Katherine to submit to Henry's will on the divorce. A delegation of some thirty privy councillors was sent to see her in her Privy Chamber at Greenwich. Once again they made their case on behalf of the king, and once again Katherine's response was robust:

I say I am his lawful wife, and to him lawfully married and by
the order of the holy Church I was to him espoused as his true
wife, although I was not so worthy, and in that point I will abide
till the court of Rome which was privy to the beginning have
made thereof a determination and final ending.[16]

The king would not approach Katherine again on the matter.

Henry and Anne left court for several weeks, leaving Katherine
behind.[17] It marked the beginning of their public separation, though
Katherine did not at first realize it. She sent a messenger to inquire
about her husband's health, as was usual when they were apart, "and to
signify the regret she had experienced at not having been able to see
him before his departure for the country." Could he not at least have
bid her farewell? Henry's reply was cruel and to the point. "He cared
not for her adieux," he replied; "he had no wish to offer her the consolation of which she spoke or any other; and still less that she should
send to him or to inquire as to his estate." He was "angry at her because
she had wished to bring shame on him by having him publicly cited."[18]
To both Katherine and the emperor's ambassador, it was obvious who
was responsible: it "must have been decreed by her [Anne]."[19]

Mary and her mother stayed at Windsor, hunting and moving
between royal residences. When Henry and Anne were ready to
return, the king sent orders that his daughter should go to Richmond
and the queen, banished from court, to Wolsey's former residence, The
More in Hertfordshire.[20] It was the last time mother and daughter
would see each other, though at the time neither realized it. Their separation would, it was hoped, force Katherine to accept a repatriation of
the trial back to England. But, as Chapuys predicted, Katherine would
never agree, "whatever stratagems may be used for the purpose."[21]
Now, without her mother's comfort and support, the fifteen-year-old
Mary would have to grow up alone.

Shortly after parting from her mother, Mary became unwell with
sickness and stomach pains.[22] She wrote to the king that "no medicine
could do her so much good as seeing him and the Queen, and desired
his licence to visit them both at Greenwich." Chapuys reported that
"this has been refused her, to gratify the lady, who hates her as much as
the Queen, or more so, chiefly because she sees the King has some

affection for her."[23] It is likely that Mary's illness was the onset of menstruation, with recurrent pains and melancholy exacerbated by distress and anxiety. It was a condition from which she would suffer repeatedly.

IN THE SUMMER of 1531, Mario Savorgnano, a wealthy Venetian, visited England from Flanders. His praise of Henry's warm welcome and impressive physique and intellect was tempered by criticism of his private mores. His wish to divorce his wife "detracts greatly from his merits, as there is now living with him a young woman of noble birth, though many say of bad character, whose will is law to him, and is expected to marry her." Having visited the queen, Savorgnano went to Richmond Palace to see Mary. The Venetian waited in the Presence Chamber

> until the Princess came forth, accompanied by a noble lady advanced in years, who is her governess, and by six maids of honour. We kissed her hand and she asked us how long we have been in England, and if we had seen their Majesties, her father and mother, and what we thought of the country; then she turned to her attendants, desiring them to treat us well, and withdrew into her chamber.
>
> This princess is not very tall, has a pretty face, and is well proportioned, with a beautiful complexion and is fifteen years old. She speaks Spanish, French and Latin besides her own mother English tongue, which is well grounded in Greek, and understands Italian, but does not venture to speak it. She sings excellently and plays on several instruments, so that she combines every accomplishment.[24]

Mary was acknowledged as a highly accomplished European princess. But in the years that followed such talents would be overshadowed by the need for courage and self-preservation. She would be forced to grow up quickly.

CHAPTER 11

THE SCANDAL OF CHRISTENDOM

∴

Though the Queen has been forbidden to write or send messages to the King, she sent one the other day . . . a gold cup as a present, with honourable and humble words; but the King refused it, and was displeased with the person who presented it . . . it was sent back to the Queen. The King has sent her no present, and has forbidden the Council and others to do the same, as is usual. He used to send New Year's presents to the ladies of the Queen and Princess, but this has not been done this year. Thus they will lower the state of both, unless there is speedy remedy. He has not been so discourteous to the Lady, who has presented him with certain darts, of Biscayan fashion, richly ornamented. In return, he gave her a room hung with cloth of gold and silver, and crimson satin with rich embroideries. She is lodged where the Queen used to be and is accompanied by almost as many ladies as if she were Queen.[1]

—CHAPUYS TO CHARLES V,
JANUARY 4, 1532

IT WAS BUT A MATTER OF TIME BEFORE KATHERINE'S POSITION as Henry's wife was entirely usurped, and steps were now taken to overcome clerical resistance. On May 15, 1532, the English clergy surrendered their last remaining independent legislative power: all new clerical legislation would now be submitted to the king. It was in direct breach of Magna Carta and of the coronation oath by which Henry had sworn that the Church in England would remain free. The following day, Thomas More resigned as lord chancellor in protest. Three months later, another staunch defender of the pope was lost with the death of the eighty-two-year-old William Warham, archbishop of Canterbury. Within weeks, Thomas Cranmer, an erstwhile supporter of the king's cause and ex-chaplain of the Boleyn family, was consecrated as his successor.

Henry now began to talk openly about the prospect of his remarriage. Anne Boleyn was made marchioness of Pembroke with a landed income of £1,000 a year. It was an unprecedented step: never before had a peeress been created in her own right. When Anne asked to have Katherine's jewels, the queen declared that she would never willingly give them up to "a person who is the scandal of Christendom."[2] When Henry sent a direct command, Katherine was forced to relinquish them.

As Henry took the last steps to repudiate Katherine and challenge the power of the pope and the emperor, he moved to shore up his alliance with France, concluded two years before. On June 23, a treaty of mutual aid was signed by which each party promised to send aid to the other if Charles invaded. An attack on England constituted an attack on France, and Henry knew that Charles would not be able to confront both.[3] Henry now prepared for a personal meeting with Francis designed to reenact the Field of the Cloth of Gold, to showcase Anglo-French amity and demonstrate to Charles and the pope the strength of their alliance.[4] On October 11, Henry and Anne Boleyn set sail for France with an entourage of more than two thousand.[5] For ten days the two kings feasted and jousted amid elaborate tents and pageantry. For now, at least, Henry had an ally and a means of applying pressure on the pope.[6]

Henry and Anne's six-week sojourn proved momentous. While they were away, Anne finally submitted to Henry's lustful advances and their relationship was consummated. By the end of December she was pregnant. They were married on January 25 in a secret ceremony presided over by Archbishop Cranmer. The formal dissolution of Henry's first marriage now became a priority. Katherine realized that time was running out. She wrote again to her nephew Charles:

> Though I know that Your Majesty is engaged in grave and important Turkish affairs . . . I cannot cease to importune you

about my own, in which almost equal offence is being offered to
God. . . . The prospective interview between the two kings, the
companion the King now takes everywhere with him, and the
authority and place he allows her to have cause the greatest
scandal and the most widespread fear of impending calamity.
Knowing the fears of my people, I am compelled by my conscience to resist, trusting in God and Your Majesty, and begging
you to urge the Pope to pronounce sentence at once.[7]

Chapuys also made an urgent appeal on Katherine's behalf to the
emperor:

The Queen begs once more for the immediate decision of her
case . . . she takes upon herself full responsibility for all the consequences, and assures Your Majesty that there need not be the
slightest danger that war will follow. She believes that if His
Holiness were to decide in her favour the King would even now
obey him, but even should he fail to do so, she will die compara-
tively happy, knowing that the justice of her cause has been
declared, and that the Princess, her daughter, will not lose her
right to the succession.[8]

ON APRIL 5, 1533, the Convocation of English Bishops ruled that
Pope Julius II's dispensation allowing Henry to marry Katherine had
been invalid, "the same Matrimony to be against the law of God," and
therefore "hath divorced the King's Highness from the noble Lady
Katherine."[9] The Act in Restraint of Appeals decreed that England was
now an empire, "governed by one Supreme Head and King" and subject to no outside authority.[10] There was now nothing to stop Henry
from marrying Anne.

On May 23, Thomas Cranmer pronounced the marriage of Henry
and Katherine to be null and void. It marked the failure of Katherine's
long battle to save her twenty-four-year marriage. A week after
Cranmer passed judgment, the visibly pregnant Anne Boleyn rode
through the City of London to be anointed and crowned at
Westminster Abbey. Chapuys recorded that along the procession route

no one cried "God save the Queen!" and the "people, though forbidden on pain of death to call Katherine Queen, shouted it loud."[11]

Katherine was ordered to surrender the title of queen; her household was reduced in status, and workmen removed her arms from the walls of Westminster Hall and from the royal barge.[12] She was now the dowager princess of Wales, the widow of Prince Arthur. Lord Mountjoy, her lord chamberlain, at Ampthill Castle in Bedfordshire, was ordered to inform her of her demotion. Katherine rejected the title of princess dowager outright: she was and would always be the king's wife and the mother of his legitimate heir.[13] Henry's patience had run out. Katherine was to move to Buckden in Huntingdonshire, a remote palace of the bishops of Lincoln. The arrangement amounted to house arrest. She was forbidden to leave without the king's permission and prevented from seeing her daughter.

As Henry anticipated the birth of what he hoped would be his longed-for son, he began to harden his attitude toward his daughter as well. He forbade her to write or send messengers to Katherine, though Mary begged him to change his mind. He might, she suggested, "appoint someone next to her person to give evidence that her messages to her mother are only in reference to her health" and proposed that her own letters and those of her mother first pass through the king's hands, but Henry refused.[14]

When Mary was officially told of her father's remarriage in April, she displayed her developing self-preservation: she was "at first thoughtful" and then, "as the very wise person that she is, dissembled as much as she could and seemed even to rejoice at it. Without alluding in the least to the said marriage, and without communicating with any living soul, after her dinner the princess set about writing a letter to her father." On receiving the letter, Henry was "marvellously content and pleased, praising above all things the wisdom and prudence of his daughter."[15] As the imperial ambassador remarked, "As to the Princess, her name is not yet changed, and I think that they will wait until the Lady had a child."[16] For the time being Mary would be left alone.

Mary was a young woman caught between estranged parents and a new, hostile stepmother. Her mother, her role model, meanwhile, cast herself increasingly as martyr. In a letter to the emperor, the deeply troubled Katherine declared, "In this world I will confess myself to be

the King's true wife and in the next they will know how unreasonably I
am afflicted."[17] But as Chapuys said of Katherine, "wherever the King
commanded her, were it even into the fire she would go."[18] Though
mother and daughter were forbidden to communicate with each other,
they sent letters secretly through trusted servants and the imperial
ambassador. On April 10, Chapuys wrote of how Anne openly boasted
that "she would have the princess for her lady's maid; but that is only to
make her eat humble pie, or to marry her to some varlet, which would
be an irreparable injury."[19] There was now an air of foreboding. Anne
knew that both Mary and Katherine were held in great popular affection and that the majority of English people regarded Mary as "the true
princess."

BY APRIL 1533, the imperial ambassador believed England was on
the brink of civil war, and he implored Charles to invade:

> Considering the great injury done to Madame, your aunt, you
> can hardly avoid making war now upon this King and kingdom,
> for it is to be feared that the moment this accursed Anne sets her
> foot firmly in the stirrup she will try to do the Queen all the
> harm she possibly can, and the Princess also, which is the thing
> your aunt dreads most . . .
>   I hear that the King is about to forbid everyone, under pain
> of death, to speak in public or private in favour of the Queen.
> After that he will most likely proceed to greater extremities
> unless God and Your Majesty prevent it.[20]

But Charles was preoccupied with the danger of the Turks in Hungary
and the Mediterranean, the unrest in Germany, the intrigues in Italy,
and the vengeful attitude of France.[21] Though committed in his support
of Katherine, the emperor was not prepared to risk war with England;
it was a private matter, and Henry had given him no pretext to intervene.[22]

CHAPTER 12

THE LADY MARY

∴

AT THREE IN THE AFTERNOON OF SEPTEMBER 7, 1533, THE CHILD that Henry had gone to such lengths to have legitimized was delivered. The king's physicians and astrologers had predicted that it would be a boy, and letters written in advance announced the birth of a "prince."

They had to be hastily altered. Anne had been delivered of a girl. As the imperial ambassador reported gleefully, "God has forgotten him entirely, hardening him in his obstinacy to punish and ruin him."[1] She was christened three days later at the Church of the Observant Friars at Greenwich and her name and titles proclaimed by the Garter King of Arms:

> God of his infinite goodness, send prosperous life and long to the High and mighty Princess of England, Elizabeth.[2]

For some, however, like Chapuys, she would always be "the Concubine's little bastard," the living symbol of England's breach with Rome.

Within a week of Elizabeth's birth, Mary's chamberlain, Sir John Hussey, received instructions "concerning the diminishing of her high estate of the name and dignity of the princess." Mary was to cease using the title immediately; her badges were to be cut from her servants' clothing and replaced with the arms of the king.[3] She was now to be known only as "the Lady Mary, the King's daughter": she was a bastard and no longer acknowledged as the king's heir.

Incredulous, Mary immediately wrote to her father:

*This morning my chamberlain came and showed me that he had
received a letter from Sir William Paulet, comptroller of your
household . . . wherein was written that "the lady Mary, the King's
daughter, should remove to the place aforesaid"—the leaving out of
the name of princess. Which, when I heard, I could not a little marvel,
trusting verily that your grace was not privy to the same letter, as
concerning the leaving out of the name of princess, forasmuch as I
doubt not in your goodness, but that your grace doth take me for his
lawful daughter, born in true matrimony. Wherefore, if I were to say to
the contrary, I should in my conscience run into the displeasure of God,
which I hope assuredly your grace would not that I should.*

    *And in all other things your grace shall have me as, always, as
humble and obedient daughter and handmaid, as ever was child to
the father . . .*

               *By your most humble daughter
               Mary, Princess.*[4]

She had signed herself "Princess." Henry's response was immediate. A deputation led by the earl of Oxford was sent to visit her at the king's manor at Beaulieu (New Hall), in Essex, with a clear message:

The King is surprised to be informed, both by Lord Hussey's letters and his daughter's own . . . that she, forgetting her filial duty and allegiance, attempts, in spite of the commandment given . . . arrogantly to usurp the title of Princess, pretending to be heir-apparent, and encourages others to do the like declaring that she cannot in conscience think she is the King's lawful daughter, born in true matrimony, and believes the King in his own conscience thinks the same.

To prevent her "pernicious example" spreading, the earls were commanded to make clear "the folly and danger of her conduct, and how the King intends that she shall use herself henceforth, both as to her title and her household." She has "worthily deserved the King's high displeasure and punishment by law, but that on her conforming to his will he may incline of his fatherly pity to promote her welfare."[5]

In spite of the threats, Mary stood her ground.[6] When the delegation left, she wrote to her father, telling him that "as long as she lived she would obey his commands, but that she could not renounce the titles, rights and privileges which God, Nature and her own parents had given her." Compliance for Mary would mean acknowledging her own illegitimacy and the invalidity of her mother's marriage, and that she would not do.

ON DECEMBER 10, three months after her birth, Elizabeth was taken from court to Hatfield in Hertfordshire, a house some seventeen miles from London. Although there was "a shorter and better road . . . for great solemnity and to insinuate to the people that she is the true Princess," she was carried through the City accompanied not only by her new household but also by a distinguished escort of dukes, lords, and gentlemen.[7]

The following day, Thomas Howard, duke of Norfolk, was sent to Beaulieu to inform Mary that her father desired her "to go to the Court and service of [Elizabeth], whom he named Princess."[8] Mary responded that "the title belonged to herself and no other." Norfolk made no answer, declaring "he had not come to dispute but to accomplish the King's will." When Mary was told that she would be allowed to take very few servants with her, Margaret Pole—her longtime governess and godmother, who had been in Mary's entourage since the princess was three—asked if she might continue to serve Mary at her own expense and pay for the whole household. Her request was refused.[9] Henry wanted Mary, like Katherine, to be separated from those she trusted to encourage her submission. As Chapuys surmised, Pole would have prevented them from

> executing their bad designs, which are evidently either to cause her to die of grief or in some other way, or else to compel her to renounce her rights, marry some low fellow, or fall prey to lust, so that they may have a pretext and excuse for disinheriting her and submitting her to all manner of bad treatment.[10]

Mary was to be isolated in a household under the stewardship of Anne Boleyn's uncle and aunt, Sir John and Lady Anne Shelton.[11] Such was to be the princess's humiliation: she was to be little more than a servant—"lady's maid to the new bastard," as the imperial ambassador described it[12]—and prisoner.

As she prepared for her departure, Mary copied a protest, drafted for her by Chapuys, that declared that nothing she might do under compulsion should prejudice her status as princess:

> My lords, as touching my removal to Hatfield, I will obey his grace, as my duty is, or to any other place his grace may appoint me; but I protest before you, and all others present, that my conscience will in no wise suffer me to take any other than myself for princess, or for the King's daughter born in lawful matrimony; and that I will never wittingly or willingly say or do aught, whereby any person might take occasion to think that I agree to the contrary. Nor say I this out of any ambition or proud mind, as God is my judge. If I should do otherwise, I should slander the deed of my mother, and falsely confess myself a bastard, which God defend I should do, since the pope hath not so declared it by his sentence definitive, to whose final judgement I submit myself.[13]

On arriving at Hatfield, the duke of Norfolk asked her "whether she would not go and pay her respects to the Princess?" She responded that she "knew no other Princess in England except herself and the daughter of my Lady Pembroke [Anne Boleyn] had no such title." She might call her only "sister," as she called the duke of Richmond, Henry Fitzroy, "brother." As the duke departed, Mary requested that he should carry to the king the message that the princess, his daughter, begged his blessing. Norfolk refused, and Mary "retired to weep in her Chamber," which, Chapuys noted, "she does continually."[14]

Mary, like her mother, was now under house arrest. She was forbidden to walk in the garden or the public gallery of the house or attend Mass at the adjoining church lest the neighboring populace see her and cheer for her. Henry reproached Norfolk for going about his task "too softly" and "resolved to take steps to abate the stubbornness and pride" of the princess.[15]

Mary's resolve would prove hard to break; such were her love and commitment to Katherine. With the tenacity worthy of any Tudor, she determined to be as difficult as possible. For days she remained in her chamber, "the worst lodging of the house" and a place "not fit for a maid of honour."[16] She would eat a large breakfast to avoid having to eat dinner in the hall and often pleaded sickness as an excuse to have supper brought to her chamber. As soon as Anne Boleyn came to hear of this, she quickly stepped in, instructing her aunt that if Mary continued to behave in this way she was to be starved back into the hall, and if she tried to use the banned title of princess she was to have her ears boxed "as the cursed bastard."[17]

Over the next two years at Hatfield, Lady Anne Shelton would be repeatedly reprimanded for not being harsh enough and for showing Mary too much respect and kindness. Whenever Mary protested, she was punished: by the confiscation first of her jewels and then of almost everything else. By February 1534, she was "nearly destitute of clothes and other necessaries" and was compelled to ask her father for help. But even then she remained defiant: the messenger was instructed to accept money or clothing if they were offered, "but not to accept any writing in which she was not entitled princess."[18] Such was the hostility toward Mary that Sir William Fitzwilliam, treasurer of the king's household, was able to say with impunity of the king's daughter that if she would not be obedient, "I would that her head was from her shoulders, that I might toss it here with my foot," at which point, according to two witnesses, he "put his foot forward, spurning the rushes."[19]

CHAPTER 13

SPANISH BLOOD

∴

AROUND THE TIME MARY JOINED THE INFANT ELIZABETH'S HOUSE-hold, she received a letter in secret from her mother. It was an extraordinary epistle, written in the most exceptional circumstances, born of Katherine's concern for her daughter's welfare.

> Daughter,
> I heard such tidings today that I do perceive (if it be true) the time is
> very near when Almighty God will prove you; and I am very glad of
> it for I trust he doth handle you with a good love. I beseech you,
> agree of His pleasure with a merry heart; and be sure that, without
> fail, He will not suffer you to perish if you beware to offend Him. I
> pray you, good daughter, to offer yourself to Him. . . . And if this
> lady [Shelton] do come to you as it is spoken, if she do bring you a
> letter from the King, I am sure in the self same letter you shall be
> commanded what you shall do. Answer with few words, obeying the
> King, your father, in everything, save only that you will not offend
> God and lose your own soul; and go no further with learning and
> disputation in the matter. And wheresoever, and in whatsoever,
> company you shall come, observe the King's commandments.
>   But one thing I especially desire you, for the love that you do owe
> unto God and unto me, to keep your heart with a chaste mind, and
> your body from all ill and wanton company, [not] thinking or
> desiring any husband for Christ's passion; neither determine yourself
> to any manner of living till this troublesome time be past. For I dare
> make sure that you shall see a very good end, and better than you can
> desire. . . . And now you shall begin, and by likelihood I shall follow.

I set not a rush by it; for when they have done the uttermost they can, then I am sure of the amendment . . . we never come to the kingdom of Heaven but by troubles. Daughter wheresoever you come, take no pain to send unto me, for if I may, I will send to you,

Your loving mother,
Katherine the Queen.[1]

It is the suggestion of a shared martyrdom that stands out. If matters did not improve on Earth, they would do so, Katherine reassured her daughter, in Heaven. The letter enshrined many of what would become Mary's guiding principles, not just for the next few torturous months but for the rest of her life: to dedicate her life to God, to remain chaste, and to accept struggles with good grace. Accompanying the letter, Katherine sent two books: *De Vita Christi* and Saint Jerome's letters to Paula and Eustochium, women who lived austere lives and dedicated themselves to God.

Katherine was then at Buckden. In mid-January, Chapuys reported that she had not "been out of her room since the Duke of Suffolk was with her [in mid-December], except to hear mass in a Gallery. She will not eat or drink what her new servants provide. The little she eats in her anguish is prepared by her chamberwomen, and her room is used as her kitchen."[2] Katherine was convinced that Henry and Anne were seeking to poison her. She trusted only the imperial ambassador, referring to him in correspondence as "My Special Friend."[3] Katherine continued to beseech the emperor that the pope do her justice. She and Mary were imprisoned "like the most miserable creatures in the world."[4] Charles accused Henry of mistreating them, but the king remained unmoved; "there was no other princess except his daughter Elizabeth, until he had a son which he thought would happen soon."[5] Still Henry hoped for a male heir.

ALTHOUGH MARY LOVED and respected Henry as her father, she refused to submit to his will as king, and at the vulnerable age of seventeen, this meant painful rejection. In January, when Henry visited the household at Hatfield, Mary was ordered to stay in her chamber.

Instead, Thomas Cromwell and the captain of the Guard were sent to
Mary to urge her to renounce her title. Mary responded that she had
already given her answer and it was useless trying to persuade her otherwise. She still craved her father's favor, however, and begged for permission to see him and kiss his hand. When she was refused yet again,
she went out onto the terrace at the top of the house as her father prepared to leave. As he was mounting his horse he spotted her and, seeing her on her knees with her hands together, bowed and touched his
cap.[6] Mary would not see him again for more than two and a half years.

Upon his return to court, Henry explained that he had refused to
see Mary on account of her obstinacy, which "came from her Spanish
blood." But when the French ambassador mentioned how "very well
brought up" she was, "the tears came into his [Henry's] eyes and he
could not refrain from praising her."[7]

Anne continued to resent Henry's clear affection for his elder
daughter and persisted in conspiring against her. When she heard of
Mary's defiance, she railed that "her answers could not have been made
without the suggestion of others" and complained that Mary was not
being kept under close enough surveillance.[8] When Anne went to visit
her daughter at Hatfield in March, she wasted no time in humiliating
her. She "urgently solicited" Mary to visit her and "honour her as
Queen," saying that it "would be a means of reconciliation with the
King, and she would intercede with him for her." Mary replied that
"she knew no other Queen in England except her mother" but that if
Anne would do her that favor with her father she would be much
obliged. Enraged, Anne departed, swearing that "she would bring
down the pride of this unbridled Spanish blood."[9]

According to a source close to Chapuys, Anne had been heard to
say more than once that as soon as Henry was out of the country, leaving her as regent, she meant to use her authority to have Mary killed,
"either by hunger or otherwise," even if she, Anne, was "burnt alive
for it."[10]

CHAPTER 14

HIGH TRAITORS

∴

ON MARCH 24, 1534, POPE CLEMENT VII PASSED FINAL SENTENCE on the marriage of Henry and Katherine. It "was and is valid and canonical."[1] Katherine's cause had triumphed, but it was a hollow victory and had come too late to alter events. A week later, the Act of Succession received royal assent, endorsing exactly what the pope's sentence had rejected. Thomas Cranmer decreed in favor of Henry's marriage to Anne, and the succession was now transferred to Henry's male heirs by Anne or any subsequent wife. In default of a male heir, the throne would pass to Elizabeth. Mary was excluded from the succession. An oath to the act's contents was to be sworn by all the king's subjects, with refusal to swear treated as high treason:

> If any person or persons . . . do, or cause to be procured or done, any thing or things to the prejudice, slander, disturbance or derogation of the said lawful matrimony solemnised between your Majesty and the said Queen Anne, or to the peril, slander . . . the issues and heirs of your highness being limited to this Act . . . then every such person and persons . . . for every such offence shall be adjudged high traitors.[2]

On April 20, the Henrican regime made a very public display of its intent when Elizabeth Barton, known as "the Holy Maid of Kent," and five Carthusian priests met their deaths at Tyburn, a village just outside the boundaries of London. Tied to wooden planks, they were dragged behind horses through the streets of the city for the five-mile journey from the Tower of London. Barton, a nun famous for her prophecies, had made clear her sympathy to the cause of Katherine of Aragon and had foretold plagues and disaster if the divorce went ahead. She declared that by marrying Anne, Henry had forfeited his right to rule: in God's eyes he was no longer king, and the people should depose him. Among the charges made against her was that she had declared that "no man should fear" taking up arms on Mary's behalf and that "she should have succour and help enough, that no man should put her from her right that she was born unto."[3]

Barton had been used by opponents of the divorce, particularly by a number of monks of the Observant and Carthusian orders, who circulated accounts of the nun's prophecies. Now they were all to be made an example of. Elizabeth Barton died first, followed by her "accomplices," who, as priests, suffered all the penalties of the law of treason. The monks were hanged in their habits until they lost consciousness, then revived so that they could watch as they were castrated and disemboweled. Their entrails were burned in front of them and then each body was quartered and beheaded.[4]

On the same day the citizens of London were required to make the Oath of Succession.[5] The executions were intended as a warning to those who opposed the king's policies and reforms. Barton's head was impaled on a railing at London Bridge, and the heads of her followers were placed on the gates of the city.[6]

AS THE ACT OF Succession was passed, Thomas Cromwell, the king's principal secretary and chief minister, made a note to "send a copy of the act of the King's succession to the Princess Dowager and the Lady Mary, with special commandment that it may be read in their presence and their answer taken."[7] Commissioners were sent to Katherine at Buckden and directed to beseech her to have, above all, "regard for her honourable and most dear daughter the Lady Princess. From whom . . . the King's highness . . . might also withdraw his princely estimation, goodness, zeal and affection, [with] no little regret, sorrow and extreme calamity."[8]

In response to this clear threat made against her daughter, Katherine reiterated that Mary "was the King's true begotten Child, and as God had given her unto the King, as his daughter, to do with her as shall stand with his pleasure, trusting to God that she will prove an honest woman."[9] After refusing to sign the oath, Katherine told the commissioners, "If any one of you has a commission to execute this penalty upon me, I am ready. I ask only that I be allowed to die in the sight of the people." Weeks later, she was moved from Buckden to Kimbolton in Huntingdonshire, another gloomy fortified manor house, with thick walls and a wide moat.[10]

Meanwhile, Mary stood firm. As Chapuys described it, "Some days ago the King asked his mistress's [aunt], who has charge of the Princess, if the latter had abated her obstinacy, and on being answered 'No,' he said there must be someone about her who encouraged her and conveyed news from the Queen her mother." Lady Shelton suspected one of the maids of the household, who in turn was quickly dismissed. "The Princess has been much grieved at this," Chapuys reported, "for she was the only one in whom she had confidence, and by her means she had letters from me and others."

Faced with Mary's intransigence and realizing that he could get his way "neither by force nor menaces," Henry changed tack and began to beg her to "lay aside her obstinacy" on the promise that she would be rewarded with "a royal title and dignity." But Mary refused to yield: "God had not so blinded her as to confess for any kingdom on earth that the King her father and the Queen her mother had so long lived in adultery, nor would she contravene the ordinance of the Church and make herself a bastard." As the ambassador explained, "She believes firmly that this dissimulation the King uses is only the more easily to attain his end and cover poison, but she says she cares little, having full confidence in God that she will go straight to Paradise and be quit of the tribulations of this world, and her only grief is about the troubles of the Queen her mother."[11]

WHEN EMPEROR CHARLES V complained once more to Henry about his ill-treatment of Mary and Katherine, the king responded scathingly, "It is not a little to our marvel that, touching the fact, either the Emperor, or any of his wise council learned, or other discreet person would in anything think us, touching our proceeding therein, but that which is godly, honourable and reasonable."[12]

But the ill-treatment continued. By the middle of May, Katherine's household and Mary's remaining servants were made to swear to the act. Several men and women were committed to the Tower charged with holding private conversations with the Lady Mary and styling her "Princess." Of these, Lady Anne Hussey, formerly one of Mary's gentlewomen, was interrogated on August 3.[13] Questions were asked about her contact with Mary "since she lost the name of princess." Did she know that the Lady Mary was justly declared by law not to be a princess and yet she had called her so? Had she received any messages or tokens from the Lady Mary? She had, she explained, visited Mary only once since the king had discharged her from the lady's service the previous Whitsuntide. Hussey admitted that she had inadvertently addressed Mary as "Princess" twice, not from any wish to disobey the law but from having long been accustomed to doing so. She also confessed that she had received a present from Mary and that she had sent Mary secret notes and received tokens from her in return. After signing a confession and begging forgiveness, Hussey was released.[14]

The conditions of Mary's house arrest grew more restrictive. She received fewer and fewer visitors, and those who did visit her were heavily scrutinized and reported to the Privy Council. Often when people came to pay their respects to the infant Elizabeth, Mary was locked in her room and the windows were nailed shut. In February 1534, as she walked along a gallery, she was spotted by some local people, who called out to her as their princess and waved their caps, after which she was watched more closely.[15] Lady Shelton continued to torment Mary, saying that if she were Henry she would throw her out of the house for disobedience and that "the King is known to have said that she would make her lose her head for violating the laws of his realm."[16]

CHAPTER 15

WORSE THAN A LION

∴

IN FEBRUARY 1535, TWO WEEKS BEFORE HER NINETEENTH BIRTH-day, Mary fell "dangerously ill" with pain in her head and stomach. It was feared she had been poisoned. Few had forgotten Anne Boleyn's threats against her.

Henry was reported to be "as much grieved at her sickness as any father could be for his daughter"; he sent his own physician, Sir William Butts, and instructed Chapuys to choose one or two others to visit her. Their presence was to be strictly controlled: they were not to speak to Mary unless other people were present and then in no language other than English for fear that she would use them to convey messages to the emperor.[1]

Butts informed the king that Mary's illness was partly caused by "sorrow and trouble." He advised that she should be sent to her mother, arguing that it would be both less expensive and better for her health and that if anything did happen to her, the king would be free from suspicion. But Henry did nothing. It was a "great misfortune," he declared, that she was so stubborn, as she "took away from him all occasion to treat her as well as he would."[2]

When Katherine learned of her daughter's condition, she asked Chapuys to petition the king to reconsider. She had "grave suspicion" about the cause of Mary's ill health and insisted that "there is no need of any person but myself to nurse her . . . I will put her in my own bed where I sleep, and watch her when needful."[3] But Henry again did nothing. He blamed Katherine for Mary's "obstinacy and disobedience," asserting that "although sons and daughters were bound to some obedience towards their mothers, their chief duty was to their fathers." He believed that if Mary had the comfort of her mother, "there would be no hope of bringing her to do what he wanted, to renounce her lawful and true succession."[4] In this trial of wills, he hoped to break Mary's resolve by starving her of affection and blunt the threat that she and her mother represented. "The Lady Katherine," Henry declared, "is a proud, stubborn woman of high courage. If she took it into her head to take her daughter's part, she could quite easily take the field, muster a great army, and wage against me a war as fierce as any her mother Isabella ever wages in Spain."[5] It was a grudging acknowledgment of Katherine's resolve and her mighty political lineage.

Henry did agree that Mary could be moved to a house nearer Kimbolton, where her mother's doctor, Miguel de la Soa, could attend her, but on condition that Katherine did not attempt to see her. Writing to Cromwell, Katherine offered her thanks:

> Mine especial friend, you have greatly bound me with the pains, that you have taken in speaking to the King my Lord concerning the coming of my daughter with me. . . . As touching the answer, which has been made you, that his Highness is contented to send her to some place near me, for as long as I do not see her; I pray you, vouchsafe to give unto his Highness mine effectual thanks for the goodness which he showeth unto his daughter and mine, and for the comfort that I have thereby received . . . you shall certify that, if she were within one mile of me, I would not see her.

Katherine had wanted Mary to be brought to her, she said, as a "little comfort and mirth" would "undoubtedly be half a health unto her," explaining "I have proved the like by experience, being diseased of the same infirmity." Both mother and daughter suffered from "deep melancholy."

Katherine told Cromwell that she did not understand how Henry could distrust them or why he would not allow mother and daughter to be together:

> Here have I, among others, heard that he had some suspicion of the surety of her. I cannot believe that a thing so far from reason

should pass from the royal heart of his highness; neither can I think that he hath so little confidence in me. If any such matter chance to be communed of, I pray you say unto his highness that I am determined to die (without doubt) in this realm; and that I, from henceforth, offer mine own person for surety, to the intent that, if any such thing should be attempted, that then he do justice of me, as of the most evil woman that ever was born.[6]

Mary received word through Lady Shelton that the king now regarded her as his "worst enemy." She had already succeeded in turning most of the Christian princes of Europe against him, and he believed "her conduct was calculated to encourage conspiracy."[7] Cromwell openly lamented the fact that, by their very existence, Katherine and Mary were preventing good relations between England and the Holy Roman Empire. If Mary were to die, it would do far less harm than good, as the immediate result would be a treaty of mutual goodwill between Henry and Charles.[8] If only God had "taken them to himself," Cromwell cursed, no one would have questioned Henry's marriage to Anne or the right of their daughter to succeed him; the possibility of internal revolt and war with the emperor would never have arisen.[9]

By early January 1535, Henry was losing patience. Mary was told that she must take the oath and "on pain of her life she must not call herself Princess or her mother Queen but that if ever she does she will be sent to the Tower."[10]

THE ACT OF SUPREMACY, passed in November 1534, authorized the king to assume the Supreme Headship of the Church and repudiated any "foreign laws or foreign authority to the contrary." Another act established an oath of obedience to the king, which involved a renunciation of the power of any "foreign authority or potentate"—that is, the pope—as well as an endorsement of the Boleyn marriage and the succession. Moreover, by the Treasons Act it was now treasonable, either by overt act or by malicious "wish, will or desire, by words or in writing," to do harm to Henry, Anne, or their heirs, to deprive the king of his titles (including supreme head) or to call him heretic, tyrant, or usurper.[11] To deny the royal supremacy, even to fail to acknowledge it, was high treason. The stakes had risen.

The first victims of the new treason laws were John Fisher, bishop of Rochester, and the humanist and former lord chancellor Thomas More; both were high-profile opponents of the royal divorce and supporters of Katherine and Mary. They were condemned for refusing to swear to the Act of Succession and for their denial of Henry as supreme head of the English Church. As he faced the block on Tower Hill in June 1535, Fisher addressed the gathered crowd: "Christian people, I am come hither to die for the faith of Christ's Catholic Church."[12]

Once he was dead, his naked corpse was displayed at the site of the execution, as Henry had demanded, and his head put on a spike. Nine days later, More's sentence of a traitor's death was commuted from disembowelment to beheading in deference to his former office. He was butchered on July 6 with one stroke of the ax. His corpse was taken to the Chapel Royal of St. Peter ad Vincula within the Tower, where it was interred; his head was parboiled and impaled on a pole on London Bridge.[13]

News of the executions shocked Europe. In Italy the bishop of Faenza described his horror on reading that the English king had caused "certain religious men" to be "ripped up in each other's presence, their arms torn off, their hearts cut out and rubbed upon their mouths and faces."[14] Meanwhile, Anne Boleyn urged Henry to mete out punishment to the real traitors, as Chapuys recounted: "She is incessantly crying after the King that he does not act with prudence in suffering the Queen and the Princess to live, who deserved death more than all those who have been executed and that they were the cause of all."[15]

Fearing for their lives, Mary wrote to the emperor, pleading for immediate intervention, while Katherine addressed the pope.

Most Holy and Blessed Father,

I have for some time ceased from writing to Your Holiness, though my conscience has reproached me for my silence. . . . [Now] once more . . . I do entreat you to bear this realm especially in mind, to remember the King, my lord and husband, and my daughter. Your Holiness knows, and all Christendom knows, what things are done here, what great offence is given to God, what scandal to the world, what reproach is thrown upon your Holiness. If a remedy be not applied shortly, there will be no end to ruined souls and martyred saints. . . . I write frankly to your Holiness, as one who can feel with me and my daughter for the martyrdom of these good men, whom, it comforts me to hope, we may follow in their sufferings though we cannot imitate their lives. . . . We await a remedy from God and from Your Holiness. It must come speedily or the time will be past![16]

Through a letter to Chapuys, Mary urged her cousin Charles to take action:

Now more than ever those services on your part are urgently required, considering the miserable plight and wretched conditions of affairs in this country, which is such that unless His Majesty, the Emperor, for the service of God, the welfare and repose of Christendom, as well as for the honour of the King, my father, takes pity on these poor afflicted creatures, all and everything will go to total ruin and be irretrievably lost. For the Emperor to apply a prompt remedy, as I hope and trust he will, it is necessary that he should be well and minutely informed of the state of affairs in this country. . . . I would dare to ask this favour of you, that you dispatch forthwith one of your men, an able one . . . to the Emperor, and inform him of the whole and beg him, in the name of the Queen, my mother and mine, for the honour of God, and the considerations above mentioned, to take this matter in hand, and provide a remedy for the affairs of this country.[17]

Mary was now desperate to escape England. A servant of the imperial ambassador who visited her at Eltham reported that "she thinks of nothing else than how it may be done, her desire for it increasing every day."[18] Chapuys had raised the prospect frequently over the previous two years, but then the immediate danger had receded and plans had not developed further. This time it was different: Mary felt the danger to be greater than ever. She sent word to Chapuys, "begging him most urgently to think over the matter, otherwise she considered herself lost, knowing they wanted only to kill her."[19]

Suspicious of Mary's intentions, Henry ordered that armed watches be kept around every house Mary stayed at and troops were placed at every seaport within a day's ride of these residences. On November 6, Chapuys wrote that according to Gertrude Blount, marchioness of Exeter, the king "has lately said to some of his most confidential councillors that he would no longer remain in the trouble, fear and suspense he had so long endured on account of the Queen and Princess" and that they "should see, at the coming Parliament, to get him released therefrom, swearing most obstinately that he would wait no longer."[20] All talk was of imminent martyrdom. Weeks later the imperial agent Dr. Pedro Ortiz wrote of the likelihood that Katherine and the princess would be "sentenced to martyrdom which she [Katherine] was ready to receive in testimony of the Holy Faith, as the Cardinal of Rochester and other holy martyrs have done."[21] Mary would, Chapuys feared, be made an example of, "to show that no one ought to disobey the laws" and that Henry meant to fulfill what "had been foretold of him; that is, that at the beginning of his reign he would be as gentle as a lamb, and at the end, worse than a lion."[22]

CHAPTER 16

SUSPICION OF POISON

∴

My most dear lord, King and husband,

*The hour of my death now drawing on, the tender love I owe you
forceth me, my case being such, to commend myself to you, and to put
you in remembrance with a few words of the health and safeguard of
your soul, which you ought to prefer before all worldly matters, and
before the care and pampering of your own body, for the which you
have cast me into many calamities and yourself into many troubles.
For my part, I pardon you everything, and I wish to devoutly pray
God that He will also pardon you.*

*For the rest, I commend unto you our daughter Mary, beseeching you to
be a good father unto her, as I have heretofore desired. . . . I forgive you
myself, and I pray God to forgive you. . . . I make this vow, that mine eyes
desire you above all things.*[1]

AT TWO IN THE AFTERNOON OF FRIDAY, JANUARY 7, 1536, KATHERINE
of Aragon died in her chamber at Kimbolton Castle. She was fifty
years old. She had suffered with "pain in her stomach" for several
months and had begged Henry to allow Mary to visit her.[2] Yet mother
and daughter, separated for four years, were not to be granted the solace of a final meeting.

But Eustace Chapuys was given permission to visit. He arrived at
Kimbolton on Sunday, the second, seeking to console Katherine as she
prepared to die and to assure her, albeit falsely, that "the King was sorry
for her illness."[3] For several hours each day he sat with Katherine, and
they talked of the events of the previous years. Katherine thanked the

ambassador for his good services and expressed regret as to "her misfortune and that of the princess," and for the "delay of remedy by which
all good men had suffered." Chapuys reassured her that the mounting
tide of heresy had not arisen because of her defiance, as she feared, but
that God sent such trials "for the exaltation of the good and the confusion of the wicked." In response to the ambassador's words, "she
showed herself very glad, for she had previously had some scruple of
conscience because the heresies had arisen from her affair." Her nephew
"could not have done better," given the "great affairs which had hindered him," and she declared it was "not without its advantages as the
Pope now upon the death of the Cardinal of Rochester and other disorders, intended to seek a remedy in the name of the Holy See."[4]

The visit of the ambassador comforted Katherine, and for a while
after she rallied a little. She managed to sleep; "her stomach retained
her food" and, "without any help, [she] combed and tied her hair, and
dressed her head"; but then her health deteriorated once more.[5] At
dawn on Friday the seventh, she heard Mass, dictated her final letters
to Charles and Henry, and prayed "that God would pardon the King
her husband for the wrong that he had done her."[6] Having received
Extreme Unction, she spent her last hours in calm reflection. By the
early afternoon she was dead.

Later that day Sir Edmund Bedingfield, Katherine's steward, wrote
to Cromwell, informing him of her death and detailing the arrangements that were to be made for the preparation of her body: "the groom
of the chandlery here can cere [disembowel and embalm] her . . . and,
further, I shall send for a plumber to close the body in lead."[7] Having
embalmed the body, the chandler declared that her organs were sound,
except for the heart, which was black all through and had "some black
round thing which clung closely to the outside."[8] It was most likely a
cancerous tumor, but her physician, Soa, concluded that she had been
poisoned.

Katherine had been taken ill "about five weeks ago," according to the
imperial ambassador. "The attack was renewed on the morrow of
Christmas Day. It was a pain in the stomach, so violent that she could
retain no food." He continued, "I asked the physician several times if
there was any suspicion of poison. He was afraid it was so, for after she
had drunk some Welsh beer she had been worse, and that it must have

been a slow and subtle poison."[9] Katherine's supporters needed little persuading.

ACCORDING TO CHAPUYS, Henry greeted the news of Katherine's death with great jubilation. "You could not conceive," read his dispatch, "the joy that the King and those who favour the concubinage have shown at the death of the good Queen." That Sunday, Henry attended Mass in the Chapel Royal dressed entirely in yellow, signifying joy, except for a white feather in his cap. After dining, he went to Anne's apartments, "where the ladies danced and there did several things like one transported with joy." The ambassador continued, "From all I hear the grief of the people at this news is incredible, and the indignation they feel against the King, on whom they lay the blame of her death, part of them believing it was by poison and others by grief; and they are the more indignant at the joy the King has exhibited."[10]

Yet Henry was celebrating more than the demise of a former wife; Katherine's death had a far greater significance. On hearing the news he shouted, "God be praised that we are free from all suspicion of war!"[11] With the principal source of enmity between them removed, Henry believed the threat of war with the emperor had ended. He added a postscript to Cromwell's dispatch to the ambassadors in France to that effect: now that "the Emperor has no occasion to quarrel," they were to keep themselves "more aloof" and less ready to accede to the French king's requests.[12] Chapuys told the emperor:

> Cromwell was not ashamed in talking with one of my men, to tell him you had no reason to profess so great grief for the death of the Queen, which he considered very convenient and advantageous for the preservation of friendship between you and his Majesty, his master; that henceforth we should communicate more freely together, and that nothing remained but to get the Princess to obey the will of the King, her father.[13]

Katherine's death had altered Charles's position in relation to England. He was not bound to Mary as he had been to her mother, and now, as he resumed hostilities with France, he looked once again to court English favor. He wrote to Chapuys at the end of February that "a renewal of amity might be more easily effected now . . . with some suitable provision for the princess than during the Queen's life." It would be a means to "abate the insolence of Francis" and win time for Mary.[14]

Mary's status and welfare were, as they would always be, secondary to Habsburg strategic interests. Charles was not prepared to remain estranged from England over her disinheritance or ill-treatment, and he was soon in more pressing need of Henry's goodwill. In the spring of 1536, Francis invaded Savoy, triggering an imperial invasion of Provence. Both sides now sought an English alliance. Henry, who had risked war to be rid of Katherine, had apparently been absolved.

FOUR DAYS AFTER Katherine's death, Lady Shelton went to Mary and "most unceremoniously without the least preparation" told her that her mother was dead. That evening Mary requested that Katherine's physician and apothecary be allowed to visit her so she might hear of her mother's final hours and of the manner of her death.[15] As Charles told Isabella, his wife, Mary was "inconsolable at the loss she has sustained, especially when she thinks of her father's past behaviour towards herself, and the little favour she can expect for the future."[16] It was feared she would "die of grief" or with Katherine out of the way, Anne Boleyn might hasten "what she has long threatened to do, viz. to kill her."[17]

But Anne's intentions were far from clear. Although she had celebrated when informed of Katherine's death, rewarding the messenger with a "handsome present," thereafter she "frequently wept, fearing that they might do with her as with the good Queen."[18] Ironically, Katherine had been Anne's best protection. Henry was not likely to question his second marriage while his first wife was still alive. Fearing that Henry's affection was declining, Anne sought to be reconciled with Mary as a means of securing her own favor. She instructed Lady Shelton to tell Mary that "if she would lay aside her obstinacy and obey her father," Anne would be "the best friend in the world to her, like another mother, and would obtain for her anything she liked to ask and that if she wished to come to court Mary would be exempted from holding the tail of her gown." But Mary would not be swayed. As Lady Shelton informed Anne, she would "rather die a hundred times than change her opinion or do anything against her honour and conscience."[19]

By the new year, Anne knew that she was pregnant again, and, with her confidence renewed, she changed tack. Lady Shelton, Mary's governess, was instructed to ease the pressure, not to "further move the lady Mary to be toward the King's Grace otherwise than it pleases herself."[20] Anne felt sure she knew Mary's fate: "If I have a son, as I hope shortly," she wrote menacingly, "I know what will happen to her."[21]

Mary now raised once more with Chapuys the prospect of fleeing to the imperial court in Brussels. If she had something to drug the women with, she told him, she might easily escape and pass under Lady Shelton's window and then find some means to break or open the garden gate.[22] As the ambassador reported, "She is so eager to escape from all her troubles and dangers that if he were to advise her to cross the Channel in a sieve she would do it." Chapuys advised caution. Mary was then at Hunsdon, forty miles from Gravesend, from which she could be taken to Flanders. Any escape plan would necessitate her riding through many villages and towns, and she would be at high risk of discovery or capture. For now it was simply too hazardous an undertaking, and he recommended that she wait until Easter, when she would be moved again, hopefully to somewhere more convenient from which to escape.

In the meantime, Chapuys told Mary she should continue in the semiseclusion of mourning and, if approached by the king's officers, beg them to leave her in peace to grieve for her mother. If pressed, she might tell them she was thinking of entering a convent when she reached full age to stun them into indecision.[23] Mary was becoming increasingly hysterical, he added; "she is continually asking [me to] beg the Emperor to hasten the remedy, which she fears will be too late for her, for which reason she is daily preparing herself for death."[24]

CHAPTER 17

THE RUIN OF THE CONCUBINE

∴

O N JANUARY 26, TWO WEEKS AFTER HER DEATH, KATHERINE OF Aragon's coffin was taken in procession, amid chaplains, gentlemen, ladies, and maids, on the nine-mile journey from the chapel at Kimbolton to Peterborough Cathedral. Three days later, Mass was said and a sermon preached by John Hilsey, the bishop of Rochester. He claimed that "in the hour of death" Katherine had acknowledged "that she had not been Queen of England."[1] In death, Henry claimed that Katherine had submitted to him as she had refused to in life. She was buried as a princess dowager and not as a queen:

> The right excellent and noble princess the Lady Katherine, daughter of the right high and mighty Prince Ferdinand, late King of Castile, and wife to the noble and excellent Prince Arthur, brother to our Sovereign Lord, Henry the 8th.[2]

On the day of Katherine's burial, Anne Boleyn was delivered of a stillborn son. Four days earlier, Henry had fallen badly from his horse during a joust, and Anne claimed the shock had brought on the miscarriage. As Chapuys reported, much to Henry's "great distress" the fetus "seemed to be a male child which she had not borne three and a half months."[3]

Gertrude Courtenay (née Blount), marchioness of Exeter, and her husband, the marquess, who was the honorific head of the Privy Chamber and Henry's first cousin, reported that Henry had shared with someone "in great confidence, and as if it were in confession" his doubts about Anne. "He had made this marriage," he said, "seduced by witchcraft and for this reason he considered it null; and that this was evident because God did not permit them to have any male issue."

He now believed that he might take another wife.[4] He had been "making much of a lady of the Court, named Mistress Semel [Seymour], to whom, many say, he [Henry] has lately made great presents."[5] Jane Seymour, the twenty-five-year-old daughter of a Wiltshire gentleman, had formerly been in the service of Katherine of Aragon and was now the focus of the king's affection. As for Anne, "her heart broke when she saw that he loved others."[6]

IN EARLY FEBRUARY, Mary changed residence. The imperial ambassador reported that the princess was well and "better accompanied on her removal and provided with what was necessary to her than she had been before." Her father had put "about 100,000 crowns" at her disposal to distribute in alms. It had been rumored that the king meant "to increase her train and exalt her position." But, as Chapuys wrote, this had been before Anne's miscarriage:

> I hope it may be so, and that no scorpion lurks under the honey. I think the King only waited to summon the said Princess to swear to the statutes in expectation that the concubine would have had a male child, of which they both felt assured. I know not what they will do now.[7]

Mary's supporters, including the marquess and marchioness of Exeter; Lord Montague (the son of Margaret Pole); Sir Nicholas Carew, the master of horse; and the imperial ambassador sought to capitalize on Anne Boleyn's loss of favor and looked toward restoring Mary as the rightful heir to the throne. Jane Seymour's sympathy for Mary was well known. Two years before, she had sent to Mary to "tell her to be of good cheer, and that her troubles would sooner come to an end than she supposed, and that when the opportunity occurred she would show herself her true and devoted servant."[8]

On April 29, it was reported that Sir Nicholas Carew was promoting

Jane Seymour and communicating with Mary, telling her "to be of good cheer, for shortly the opposite party would put water in their wine."[9] Carew and his allies at court coached Jane as to how she should behave to secure the king's affection, urging her "that she must by no means comply with the King's wishes except by way of marriage."[10] When, in March, Henry sent her a letter and "a purse full of sovereigns," Jane returned them unopened and, falling to her knees, begged that Henry "consider that she was a gentlewoman of good and honourable parents, without reproach" and that if he "wished to make her some present in money she begged it might be when God enabled her to make some honourable match."[11] As Gertrude Courtenay, the marchioness of Exeter, put it, "Henry's love and desire . . . was wonderfully increased."[12] It was claimed that "[Anne] and Cromwell were on bad terms, and . . . some new marriage for the King was spoken of."[13] Now, with the king looking to marry once more, Cromwell sought to bring about Anne Boleyn's downfall.

EASTER WEEK PROVED to be of fateful consequence. Two public rows—the first between Anne and Mark Smeaton, one of the queen's musicians, the other between Anne and Sir Henry Norris, the chief gentleman of the king's Privy Chamber—gave Cromwell the excuse he needed. The conversations had suggested that they were infatuated with the queen and desired the king's death. By the afternoon of Sunday, March 30, Henry had been told of the exchanges and had angrily confronted Anne. They both attended the May Day jousts as planned, but as soon as the tournament was over, Henry left for his town palace, Whitehall, formerly York Place, accompanied by Henry Norris. As Edward Hall's chronicle related, "of this sudden departing many men mused, but most chiefly the Queen." George Constantine, Norris's servant, reported, "[The king] had Mr Norris in examination and promised him his pardon in case he would utter the truth." Yet "whatsoever could be said or done, Mr Norris would confess no thing to the King."[14] The following day he was sent to the Tower, where Smeaton was already imprisoned. After four hours of torture and interrogation, Smeaton confessed to adultery with the queen.

On May 2, Anne and her brother, George, Viscount Rochford,

were taken by river to the Tower. To Henry, Anne was now an "accursed and poisoning whore" who had conspired to kill Katherine and Mary, Henry Fitzroy, and the king himself.[15] Two days later there were further arrests of members of the Privy Chamber: Sir William Brereton, Sir Francis Weston, and Sir Richard Page, together with the poet Sir Thomas Wyatt. A grand jury indicted all the accused, except Wyatt and Page, on charges of having committed adultery with the queen. At their trial days later, all except Smeaton pleaded innocent, yet all were found guilty and sentenced to death for high treason "upon presumption and certain indications," but, Chapuys noted, "without valid proof and confession."[16]

Two days later Anne and Rochford stood trial in the Tower before a crowd of two thousand spectators. Anne was "principally charged with . . . having cohabited with her brother and other accomplices," that there was "a promise between her and Norris to marry after the King's death, which it thus appeared they hoped for," and that she "had poisoned [Katherine] and intrigued to do the same to [Mary]." The ambassador continued, "These things, she totally denied, and had a plausible answer to each."[17] It made little difference; each member of the jury declared her guilty, and the duke of Norfolk, Anne's uncle, who was presiding as lord high steward, pronounced the sentence. The usual punishment for a traitoress was being burned alive, yet, "because she was Queen, Norfolk gave judgement that she should be burnt or beheaded at the King's pleasure."[18]

On Monday, May 17, the men condemned to death for high treason were executed. On the nineteenth, at eight in the morning, Anne was led out to the scaffold on Tower Green. Henry had decreed that she should be beheaded, not burned, and granted her one final "mercy": that she be beheaded by a French executioner's sword rather than an ax, as was the English fashion. Foreigners were prevented from attending the execution, and large crowds were discouraged by the delaying of the death from the usual hour. Anne begged the people to pray for the king, "for he was a good, gentle, gracious and amiable prince."[19] With one swing of the sword she was dead. She was buried in the Chapel Royal of St. Peter ad Vincula within the Tower.

The day before her execution, Anne asked Lady Kingston, the wife of the lieutenant of the Tower, to go to Hunsdon and on her behalf kneel before Mary and beg her pardon for all the wrongs she had done her.[20] On her way to the scaffold, as Antoine Perrenot, Cardinal Granvelle wrote to Chapuys, "the Concubine declared that she did not consider herself condemned by divine judgement, except for being the cause of the ill-treatment of the Princess, and for having conspired her death."[21] Two days after Anne's execution, Thomas Cranmer pronounced her marriage with Henry to have been invalid. Elizabeth, like Mary, now became a bastard. The love affair that had wreaked such havoc was over.

> The joy shown by this people every day, not only at the ruin of the Concubine, but at the hope of the Princess Mary's restoration, is inconceivable, but as yet, the King shows no great disposition towards the latter; indeed he has twice shown himself obstinate, when spoken to on the subject by his Council.[22]

On the day of Anne Boleyn's death, Henry VIII was betrothed to Jane Seymour. They were married ten days later in the queen's closet at Whitehall.[23] "She is," Chapuys told Antoine Perrenot, the emperor's minister, "the sister of a certain Edward Seymour, who has been in the service of his Majesty [Charles V]"; while "she [herself] was formerly in the household of the good Queen [Katherine]." The ambassador described Jane as being "of middle stature, and no great beauty; so fair that he would call her rather pale than otherwise." Her personal motto was "Bound to obey and serve."[24] On Whitsunday, June 4, she was formally proclaimed queen.[25]

For most of the three years that Anne Boleyn had been queen, Mary had lived in fear of death. Now, with a new stepmother whose patrons were Mary's leading supporters at court, there was hope of a return to favor and to the line of succession. Even before Anne's execution, Jane had, much to Henry's annoyance, begged for Mary's restoration, but Henry had resisted. "She was a fool," he declared, and "ought to solicit the advancement of the children they would have between them, and not any others." Jane was not deterred: "in asking for the restoration of [Mary as] Princess, she conceived she was seeking the rest and tranquillity of the King, herself, her future children, and the whole realm."[26]

Over the Easter holidays, April 14 to 17, Chapuys, supported by Cromwell, made overtures for a settlement between Henry and Charles V and a renewal of their earlier alliance. Three proposals were made: that Charles broker a reconciliation between Henry and the pope; that in default of male issue, "we would," as Henry recounted, "legitimate our daughter Mary, in such degree, as in default of issue by our most dear and entirely beloved wife the Queen, she might not be reputed unable to some place in our succession"; and that Henry help Charles against the Ottoman Turks and against the anticipated French assault on Milan.[27] But when, on the eighteenth, Chapuys was summoned for an audience, Henry dismissed each of the proposals and instead unleashed an attack on the emperor's fidelity. Charles would not "have acquired the Empire or enjoyed Spain without him" but had "treated him with neglect . . . tried to get him declared schismatic and deprived of his kingdom"; and he had not kept his promise "not to make peace with the King of France" until Charles had obtained for Henry the crown of France. As Chapuys reported, the "Chancellor and Cromwell appeared to regret these answers, and in spite of the King's gestures to them that they should applaud him, neither of them would say three words."

The next day, the whole of the King's Council was assembled for three or four hours, and, as Cromwell told Chapuys, "there was not one of them but remained long on his knees before the King to beg him, for the honour of God, not to lose so good an opportunity of establishing a friendship so necessary and advantageous." However, no one could change the king's mind: "he would sooner suffer all the ills in the world than confess tacitly or expressly that he had done you any injury, or that he desired this friendship."[28] He again made it clear that he would not tolerate interference from Charles:

As to the legitimisation of our daughter Mary, if she will submit to our grace, without wrestling against the determination of our laws, we will acknowledge her and use her as our daughter; but we would not be directed or pressed herein, nor have any other order devised for her entertainment, than should proceed from the inclination of our own heart being moved by her humility, and the gentle proceedings of such as pretend to be her friends.[29]

For Henry, to give Mary back her rights without terms was tantamount to submitting to the pope, to humbling himself before the emperor, and to climbing down in the eyes of his enemy, the king of France, and that he would never do.

CHAPTER 18

MOST HUMBLE AND
OBEDIENT DAUGHTER

:·:

Master Secretary,
I would have been a suitor to you before this time,
to have been a means for me to the King's Grace, my father,
to have obtained his Grace's blessing and favour; but I
perceived that no body durst speak for me, as long as that
woman lived, which now is gone, whom I pray our Lord of his
great mercy to forgive. Wherefore, now she is gone, I am the bolder
to write to you, as she which taketh you for one of my chief friends.
And therefore I desire you for the love of God to be a suitor
for me to the King's Grace, to have his blessing and licence
to write unto his Grace, which shall be a great comfort to me,
as God knoweth; who have you evermore in his holy keeping.
Moreover I must desire you to accept mine evil writing. For I
have not done so much this two year and more, nor could
not have found the means to do it at this time, but my Lady
Kingston's being here.

At Hunsdon, the 26th of May.
By your loving friend,
Marye.[1]

AFTER THE FALL OF ANNE BOLEYN, MARY HOPED SHE MIGHT REGAIN
her father's favor. She had waited at Hunsdon to be summoned to
court, but when no word came she wrote to Cromwell asking him to
intercede with Henry now that "that woman" was dead.

Four days later, Mary wrote again, thanking him for leave to write to the king and assuring him that "you shall find me as obedient to the King's Grace, as you can reasonably require of me." She trusted that this would be enough to withdraw her father's displeasure and permit her to "come into his presence."² Cromwell had been enlisted as mediator between Henry and Mary as Jane Seymour pressed for reconciliation. The king, however, remained determined that Mary submit. The price of his restored favor would be her complete subjugation to his will.

On June 1, Mary addressed a letter to Henry directly. In "as humble and lowly a manner, as is possible for a child to use to her father," she begged for forgiveness:

> I beseech your Grace of your daily blessing, which is my chief desire in the world. And in the same humble ways [ac] knowledging all the offences that I have done . . . I pray your Grace, in the honour of God, and for your fatherly pity, to forgive me them; for the which I am sorry, as any creature living; and next unto God, I do and will submit me in and all things to your goodness and pleasure to do with me whatsoever shall please your grace.

She prayed God to send him a prince, "whereof," she declared, "no creature living shall more rejoice or heartier pray for continually than I," and signed herself "Your grace's most humble and obedient daughter and handmaid, Mary."³

After she had been granted leave to write to him, Mary had assumed that her father had forgiven her and withdrawn his "dreadful displeasure." Yet her letter met with no response. She had submitted to her father "next unto God," but this was not enough. She wrote again, begging to receive some sign of his favor and to be called into his presence, but again there was no reply.⁴ On the tenth she drafted another letter, this time sending a copy to Cromwell. In it she declared herself "most humbly prostrate before your noble feet, your most obedient subject and humble child, that hath not only repented her offences hitherto, but also decreed simply from henceforth and wholly next to Almighty God, to put my state, continuance and living in your gracious mercy."⁵ As Mary added in her dispatch to Cromwell:

> I trust you shall perceive that I have followed your advice and counsel, and will do in all things concerning my duty to the King's Grace (God and my conscience not offended) for I take you for one of my chief friends, next unto his Grace and the Queen. Wherefore, I desire you, for the passion which Christ suffered for you and me, and as my very trust is in you, that you will find such means through your great wisdom, that I be not moved to agree to any further entry in this matter than I have done. But if I be put to any more (I am plain with you as with my great friends) my said conscience will in no ways suffer me to consent thereunto.⁶

Cromwell's letter does not survive, but his disapproval is clear from Mary's reply. He had taken exception to her qualified response and, enclosing a draft for her guidance, instructed her to write again to the king and to send him a copy:

> *Good Master Secretary,*
>   *I do thank you with all my heart, for the great pain and suit you have had for me, for the which I think myself very much bound to you. And whereas I do perceive by your letters, that you do mislike mine exception in my letter to the King's Grace, I assure you, I did not mean as you do take it. For I do not mistrust that the King's goodness will move me to do anything which should offend God and my conscience. But that which I did write was only by the reason of continual custom. For I have always used, both in writing and speaking, to except God in all things.*
>   *Nevertheless, because you have exhorted me to write to his Grace again, and I cannot devise what I should write more but your own last copy, without adding or [di]minishing; therefore I do send you by this bearer, my servant, the same, word for word; and it is unsealed, because I cannot endure to write another copy.*

For the pain in my head and teeth hath troubled me so sore
these two or three days and doth yet so continue, that I have
very small rest, day or night.

> *Your assured bounden loving friend*
> *during my life,*
>
> > *Marye.*[7]

Mary copied Cromwell's draft "word for word" and then addressed the king once more. Having begged "in my most humble and lowly manner" for his "daily blessing" and permission to come into his presence, she continued:

I have written twice unto your highness, trusting to have, by some
gracious letters, token or message, perceived sensibly the mercy,
clemency and pity of your Grace, and upon the operation of the
same, at the last also to have attained the fruition of your most noble
presence, which above all worldly things I desire: yet I have not
obtained my said fervent and hearty desire, nor any piece of the same
to my great and intolerable discomfort I am enforced, by the
compulsion of nature, eftsones to cry unto your merciful ears, and
most humbly prostrate before your feet.

She signed off by petitioning for "some little spark of my humble suit and desire" and praying God

to preserve your Highness, with the Queen, and shortly to send you
issue, which shall be gladder tidings to me than I can express in
writing. . . . Your most humble and obedient daughter and
handmaid, Marye.[8]

The king's response was direct and unequivocal. Within days he sent a delegation of councillors, headed by the duke of Norfolk, to visit Mary at Hunsdon to demand that she take the oath of allegiance and make a complete submission. The councillors condemned her for her earlier refusal to obey as a "monster in nature," a freakish departure from the natural obedience of a daughter toward her father. Any other man, they declared, would have sent her away, but, given Henry's "gracious and divine nature," he was willing to withhold his displeasure if Mary would now submit to him. Would she accept all the laws and statutes of the realm? Would she accept Henry as supreme head of the Church and repudiate the jurisdiction of the bishop of Rome? Would she acknowledge that her mother's marriage was invalid and accept all the laws and statutes of the realm?

Her answer to each was no. She was willing to obey her father in all matters except those that injured her mother, her present honor, or her faith, and in this she was steadfast. Norfolk angrily declared that "so unnatural" was she to oppose the king's will that "they could scarcely believe she was his bastard, and if she were their daughter, they would beat her and knock her head so hard against the wall that it made it as soft as a baked apple." She was a traitoress and "should be punished." They left, instructing Lady Shelton to keep her under constant surveillance, day and night, and to make sure she spoke to no one.[9]

Cromwell had pledged that he would secure Mary's submission, and he now feared for his own life. He confided to Chapuys that "he considered himself a dead man" for having represented Mary as "penitent and obedient."[10] Writing to Mary, he chastised her over her position:

> Knowing how diversely and contrarily you proceeded at the late being of his Majesty's counsel with you, I am both ashamed of that I have said, and likewise afraid of that I have done; in so much that what the sequel thereof shall be God knoweth.

He continued:

> Thus with your folly you undo yourself, and all that hath wished you good. . . . Wherefore, Madam, to be plain, as God is my witness . . . I think you the most obstinate and obdurate woman all things considered, that ever was, and one that so preserving, well deserveth the reward of malice in extremity of mischief, or at least that you be both repentant for your ingratitude and miserable unkindness, and ready to do all things that you be bound unto by your duty of allegiance.

He commanded her to sign the articles required and warned that if she refused he would "take leave" of her forever and desire her "never to write or make mean unto me hereafter. For I will never think you other than the most ungrateful, unnatural, and most obstinate person living, both to God and your most dear and benign father."[11] Mary still refused. It was the very apogee of her resistance. She had become a traitor to the king and his laws. Henry now insisted that she should be treated as such, as should her allies.

IN JUNE, THE MARQUESS of Exeter and Sir William Fitzwilliam were dismissed from the Privy Council as "suspected persons." Weeks later, Sir Anthony Browne and Sir Francis Bryan, two gentlemen of the Privy Chamber, were arrested and interrogated over their support of Mary.[12] Henry believed that such individuals were encouraging the princess in her defiance.[13] The examinations of Browne and Bryan implicated Sir Nicholas Carew, who had been in correspondence with the princess, and Thomas Cheney and John Russell, both gentlemen of the Privy Chamber. Bryan deposed that the rest of his "fellows of the Privy Chamber" were rejoicing at the fall of Anne and advancing Mary's claim should Jane Seymour fail to give Henry a son.[14] He claimed further that since the king's divorce they had been working against Anne Boleyn, supporting Katherine and Mary, liaising with Charles V, and working in defense of the traditional religion.[15] They were all now placed in the Tower along with Lady Anne Hussey, the wife of Mary's chamberlain.

The danger to Mary was now as great as it had been during the months before her mother's death. According to Ralph Morice, Thomas Cranmer's old secretary, Henry "fully purposed to send the lady Mary his daughter unto the Tower, and there to suffer as a subject, by cause she would not obey unto the laws of the realm in refusing the bishop of Rome's authority and religion."[16] Judges were commanded to proceed with a legal inquiry into Mary's treachery and sentence her as willfully defiant of the king's authority. Unwilling to use the legal system against her, they gave Mary one final chance. She was to be sent a document entitled "Lady Mary's Submission," detailing all points the king required her to agree to.[17] If she refused to sign those articles, legal proceedings would begin and she would be charged with treason.

Mary sent word to Chapuys, begging his counsel. He told her that "if the King persisted in his obstinacy, or she found evidence that her life was in danger, either by maltreatment or otherwise," she should "consent to her father's wish." He assured her that this was what the emperor wanted and that "to save her life, on which depended the peace of the realm, and the redress of the great evils which prevail here, she must do everything and dissemble for some time."

ON THURSDAY, JUNE 22, under threat of death, Mary signed the formal statement required of her. In "The confession of me the Lady Mary made upon certain points and articles under written," she acknowledged the illegitimacy of her mother's marriage, her own bastard status, and her father's Supreme Headship of the Church of England:

> First, I confess and [ac]knowledge the King's Majesty to be my Sovereign Lord and King, in the imperial Crown of this realm of England, and do submit myself to his Highness, and to all and singular laws and statutes of this realm, as becometh a true and faithful subject to do . . .
>
> (SIGNED)   *"MARY"*

> I do recognise, accept, take, repute and [ac]knowledge the King's Highness to be supreme head in earth under Christ of the Church of England, and do utterly refuse the Bishop of Rome's pretended authority, power and jurisdiction within this realm heretofore usurped . . .
>
> (SIGNED)   *"MARY"*

> I do freely, frankly . . . recognise and acknowledge that the marriage, heretofore had between his Majesty, and my mother, the late Princess dowager, was, by God's law and Man's law, incestuous and unlawful.[18]
>
> (SIGNED)   *"MARY"*

In one stroke she had been compelled to betray the memory of her mother and the Catholic faith of her childhood. She had signed away all that her mother had resisted until her death; all that Mary herself had clung to and fought so hard to defend. It was in this moment of total and agonizing submission that the seeds of Mary's future defiance were sown.

CHAPTER 19

INCREDIBLE REJOICING

∴

*Most humbly, obediently and gladly lying at the feet of your
most excellent majesty, my most dear benign father and sovereign
lord, I have this day perceived your gracious clemency and merciful
pity to have overcome my most unkind and unnatural proceedings
towards you and your most just and virtuous laws; the great and
inestimable joy whereof I cannot express. . . . I shall daily pray
to God, whom eftsoons I beseech to send you issue, to his honour
and the comfort of the whole realm, From Hunsdon, the 26th
of June,*

*Your grace's most humble and
obedient daughter and handmaid,
Marye.*[1]

MARY'S CAPITULATION WAS GREETED WITH "INCREDIBLE REJOICING"
at court. Restored to favor, she was acknowledged as the king's daughter once more and offered a sumptuous new wardrobe and a choice of
servants.[2] Cromwell returned to Hunsdon with "a most gracious letter" from the king and, "kneeling on the ground," begged Mary's pardon for his former harsh conduct.[3]

Three weeks later, Mary journeyed to Hackney for a secret reunion
with her father. It was their first meeting for five years. She had been a
young teenager when Henry last saw her, and she was now a woman of
twenty. Chapuys wrote that the kindness shown by the king to the
princess was "inconceivable, regretting that he had been so long separated from her." He showed her "such love and affection, and such
brilliant promises for the future that no father could have behaved better towards his daughter."[4] Jane Seymour gave Mary a diamond ring

and Henry 1,000 crowns for her "many pleasures."[5] They spent one night together and parted on Friday, July 7, with Henry promising that she would be brought to court to take her place immediately after the queen.

Yet beneath the veneer of reconciliation there were, as Chapuys observed, "a few drachmas of gall and bitterness mixed with the sweet food of paternal kindness."[6] Before returning to court, Mary was forced to write to the emperor and his sister, Mary of Hungary, regent of the Netherlands, confirming her submission to her father as head of the Church; her acknowledgment of the statutes declaring her mother's marriage unlawful; and her decision to freely renounce her right to the throne.[7] For Henry it was a means of emphasizing his victory over the emperor. According to Chapuys, he had told the princess "that her obstinate resistance to his will had been encouraged and strengthened by the trust she had in you; but that she ought to know that your majesty could not help or favour her in the least as long as he [the king] lived."[8] Henry gave Mary a ring to celebrate her obedience. On one side was a relief of Henry and Jane, on the other a picture of Mary. The Latin inscription read:

> Obedience leads to unity, unity to constancy and a quiet mind, and these are treasures of inestimable worth. For God so valued humility that he gave his only son, a perfect exemplar of modesty, who in his obedience to his divine father, taught lessons of obedience and devotion.[9]

Mary's submission had cost her dearly. As Chapuys warned the emperor, "this affair of the princess has tormented her more than you think"; she had "escaped from the greatest danger that ever a princess was in, and such as no words can describe."[10] She now asked Chapuys to obtain a secret papal absolution, "otherwise her conscience could not be at perfect ease."[11]

> The princess is every day better treated, and was never at greater liberty or more honourably served than now . . . she has plenty of company, even of the followers of the little Bastard, who will henceforth play her court. Nothing is wanting in her except the

name and title of Princess, for all else she will have more fully than before.[12]

On June 30, 1536, just days after Mary's submission, a new Act of Succession was introduced into the House of Lords. Yet neither Mary's legitimacy nor her position as heir was restored. The succession was conferred instead on the heirs of Jane Seymour or, as the act declared, "any subsequent wife." Both of Henry's first marriages were declared invalid, and Elizabeth was stripped of the title of princess and removed from the line of succession. Henry was granted unprecedented powers to nominate whomever he pleased as his successor, irrespective of illegitimacy, should he have no children with the queen.[13] He might have intended to promote his bastard son Henry Fitzroy, duke of Richmond, but three weeks later, just after Parliament was dissolved, Richmond died, probably of tuberculosis. "Few are sorry," wrote Chapuys to Perrenot de Granvelle, "because of the Princess."[14]

Those who wished for a return to the old order in England now looked to Mary's influence to bring it about. "It is to be hoped," the ambassador wrote to the empress Isabella, "that through the Princess's means, and through her great wisdom and discretion she may hereafter little by little bring back the King, her father, and the whole of the English nation to the right path."[15]

In October there was unrest in Lincolnshire, and over the following weeks rebellion spread across the northern counties. Under the leadership of the lawyer Robert Aske, the rebels, some forty thousand in number, demanded the return of the "old faith"; the restoration of the monasteries ransacked in the dissolution of the past year; the return of the old religion; and "that the Lady Mary may be made legitimate and the former statute therein annulled."[16] Among the rebels were Lord Hussey, Mary's old steward, and Lord Darcy, who had for many months been petitioning Charles V to intervene in England. As Aske related in his subsequent examination, "both he and all the wise men of those parts much grudged, seeing that on the mother's side she came from the greatest blood in Christendom." The statute declaring her illegitimacy would "make strangers think." It was "framed more for some displeasure towards her and her friends than for any just cause, while in reason she ought to be favoured in this realm rather than otherwise."[17]

When news reached Rome of the rebellion, Pope Paul III appointed
Reginald Pole cardinal and commissioned him as *legate a latere* to go to
England and raise support for the rebels.[18] Pole was a cousin of the
king and a son of Margaret Pole, countess of Salisbury, Mary's godmother and former governess. He had left England in 1532 following
Henry's break with Rome and in 1536, in answer to Henry's request for
his views, had sent him the treatise *De Unitate Ecclesiae* (In Defense of
the Unity of the Church). The tract had turned Pole from Henry's pro-
tégé into his bitterest enemy. In it he appealed to the nobility of
England and the emperor to take action, and he called on Henry to
repent for having broken with Rome. He warned that the king would
not get away with repudiating Mary and that among "such a number of
most noble families" any disruption of the succession would lead to
sedition.[19] By the time Pole left for England, the rebellion had been put
down. Henry demanded Pole's extradition from France as a traitor and
to have the cardinal "by some means trussed up and conveyed to
Calais" and then to England.[20]

MARY WAS TO SPEND Christmas at court for the first time in years.
On December 22, Henry, Jane, and Mary rode from Westminster
through the City of London to Greenwich, preceded by the mayor and
aldermen of the city. In Fleet Street, four orders of friars stood in copes
of gold, "with crosses and candlesticks and censers to cense the King
and Queen as they rode by." The choir of St. Paul's, the bishop of
London, and two priests from every parish church in London stood
outside St. Paul's to watch the royal procession.[21] "The like sight,"
Richard Lee wrote to Lady Lisle, formerly a maid of honor to Jane
Seymour and wife of Arthur Plantagenet, "hath not been seen here
since the Emperor's being here [in 1522]." He noted the presence of
Chapuys, "the ambassador to the Emperor," with the royal party,
which "rejoiced every man wondrously."[22]

In April, the Privy Council recommended that Mary and Elizabeth
be "made of some estimation" and since Mary was the elder, "and more
apt to make a present alliance than the other," it "might please the King
to declare her according to his laws" so that she might be more attrac-

tive as a bride, as a means of ensuring that the king "may provide himself of a present friend."[23] Although Charles pressed for a match with Dom Luis of Portugal, the young brother of the king of Portugal, the advice was not taken. Jane was pregnant, and Henry was optimistic that it would be a son. Any negotiation for a betrothal would now depend on public recognition of Mary's illegitimacy.

CHAPTER 20

DELIVERANCE OF A GOODLY PRINCE

∴

Right trust and well beloved, we greet you well. And forasmuch
as by the inestimable Goodness and grace of Almighty God we be
delivered and brought in child bed of a Prince conceived in most
Lawful Matrimony between my lord the King's Majesty and us,
doubting not but that for the love and affection which ye bear
unto us and to the common wealth of this Realm the Knowledge
thereof should be joyous and glad tidings unto you, we have
thought good to certify you of the same.[1]

—JANE SEYMOUR TO CROMWELL,
OCTOBER 12, 1537

AT TWO IN THE MORNING OF FRIDAY, OCTOBER 12, 1537, JANE
Seymour gave birth to a son at Hampton Court. Born on the Feast of
Saint Edward the Confessor, he was named after the royal saint.

By eight o'clock Te Deums had been sung in every parish church in
London; bonfires were lit, and the firing of the Tower guns continued
well into the evening.[2] Messengers were dispatched around the country
and to courts across Europe proclaiming the birth. "Here be no news,
but very good news," wrote Thomas Cromwell to Sir Thomas Wyatt,
the ambassador to Spain, who had been imprisoned after the fall of
Anne Boleyn. "It hath pleased Almighty God of his goodness, to send
unto the Queen's Grace deliverance of a goodly Prince, to the great
comfort, rejoice and consolation of the King's Majesty, and of all us his
most humble, loving and obedient subjects."[3] Finally Henry had a
legitimate male heir.

Anticipation of the birth had been growing since the spring. On May 23, Jane's pregnancy was made known at court, and four days later a Te Deum was celebrated at St. Paul's upon the "quickening" of her child.[4] The king added a nursery to the building works at Hampton Court in preparation for the queen's confinement, and Mary was summoned to attend on the queen.[5] On Sunday, September 16, Jane took to her chamber, where she remained for three weeks before going into a prolonged and arduous thirty-hour labor. A solemn procession was made at St. Paul's "to pray for the Queen that was then in labour of child."[6] On the following morning, Jane was safely delivered. As news of the birth rang out from the bells of St. Paul's, Henry hurried back from Esher in Surrey, to which he had been forced to move on account of the plague, to begin a round of celebratory banquets.[7]

Three days after the birth, Mary stood as godmother at the font in the newly decorated Chapel Royal at Hampton Court as Thomas Cranmer, archbishop of Canterbury, performed the rites of baptism over the infant prince.[8] Although the plague limited the size of the retinues coming to court, it was a lavish ceremony. Some three or four hundred courtiers, clerics, and foreign envoys formed the midnight procession from the queen's chamber to the chapel. After the prince had been baptized and confirmed, the heralds proclaimed him "Edward, son and heir to the King of England, Duke of Cornwall, and Earl of Chester." Amid a torchlit procession, Mary led her four-year-old sister, Elizabeth, back to the queen's apartments for the giving of the baptismal gifts.[9] Mary presented a golden cup, which she gave, along with £30, to Edward's nurse, midwife, and cradle rockers. Great fires were lit on the streets of London, and bells rung across the country.

WITH THE REJOICING barely over, Jane fell seriously ill with "a natural lax"—heavy bleeding.[10] The week of celebrations ended with a general procession at St. Paul's for "the health of the Queen," and the Chapel Royal was filled with courtiers praying for her safety. By the evening of the twenty-fourth, her condition had worsened and she received Extreme Unction. She died in the early hours of the morning of puerperal fever, having suffered a massive hemorrhage and contracted

septicemia. Henry withdrew to Windsor, where, as the chronicler
Edward Hall recorded, "he mourned and kept himself close and secret
a great while."[11] Writing to Francis I in acknowledgment of the French
king's congratulations on Edward's birth, Henry described how
"Divine Providence . . . hath mingled my joy with the bitterness of her
who brought me this happiness."[12]

In the days immediately following the queen's death, Mary was too
grief-stricken—"accrased"—to take part in the initial obsequies, and
the marchioness of Exeter had to take her place.[13] But as she gathered
her composure, she appeared as chief mourner at dirges and Masses in
the Chapel Royal, accompanied by her ladies. On November 8, she
rode behind the coffin at the head of the funeral cortege, her steed covered in black trappings, as the procession made its way from Hampton
Court to Windsor. Upon the coffin was an effigy of Jane in robes of
state, a crown upon her head and a scepter in her right hand. Four days
later, she was buried between the stalls and altar of St. George's
Chapel. Above the vault the Latin inscription heralded her as a phoenix, her personal emblem, which in death had brought life:

> HERE A PHOENIX LIETH, WHOSE DEATH
> TO ANOTHER PHOENIX GAVE BREATH:
> IT IS TO BE LAMENTED MUCH,
> THE WORLD AT ONCE N'ER KNEW TWO SUCH.[14]

In a letter of condolence, Cuthbert Tunstall, bishop of Durham,
reminded Henry that though God had taken his queen, Henry should
not forget "our most noble Prince, to whom God hath ordained your
Majesty not only to be father, but also as the time now requireth, to
supply the room of a mother also."[15]

Edward spent his first Christmas with Henry at Greenwich and was
with him again in May 1538 at the royal hunting lodge at Royston,
where the king "solaced all his day with much mirth and joy, dallying
with him in his arms . . . and so holding him in a window to the sight
and great comfort of all the people."[16]

But it was Mary, then twenty-two, who would be most involved in
Edward's early upbringing. She would be his most frequent family
visitor. Residing for much of the time at Hampton Court, she was just a

barge ride across the river from her brother's nursery at Richmond. She visited him in November 1537 and in March, April, and May the following year.[17] As Jane Dormer, one of Mary's gentlewomen, later noted, when Mary came to see him "he took special content in her company . . . he would ask her many questions, promise her secrecy, carrying her that respect and reverence, as if she had been his mother." She would offer him advice "in some things that concerned himself, and in other things that touched herself; in all showing great affection and sisterly care of him."[18]

Lady Lisle visited all the royal children at Hampton Court in November. "His grace [Edward]," she wrote to her husband, "is the goodliest babe that ever I set mine eye upon. I pray God to make him an old man, for I think I should never weary of looking on him. . . . I saw also my Lady Mary and my Lady Elizabeth."[19] Edward was acknowledged as the king's heir, and the rivalry between Mary and Elizabeth abated. All three siblings were now brought together under one roof.

CHAPTER 21

THE MOST UNHAPPY LADY
IN CHRISTENDOM

∴

The King . . . is little disposed to marry again, but some of his Council have thought it mete for us to urge him to it for the sake of his realm.[1]

AS HENRY MOURNED THE DEATH OF JANE SEYMOUR, THE FRENCH king and the emperor agreed upon a truce and began peace talks mediated by the pope. Now, with the growing threat of a Catholic offensive against him, the search for a new wife for Henry and a husband for Mary was used in an effort to forge an alliance that would keep France and the empire apart. "Since the King [Francis I] my brother, has already so great an amity with the Emperor, what amity should I have with him?" asked Henry. "I ask because I am not resolved to marry again unless the Emperor or King prefer my friendship to that which they have together."[2]

Offers of marriage alliances were made to the empire and France for a match between Mary and either Dom Luis of Portugal or the duke of Orléans. Henry considered the prospect of marriage with the dowager duchess of Milan and for a time with Mary of Guise, though Henry delayed too long and in May she was betrothed to King James V of Scotland, thereby renewing the "Auld Alliance" between France and Scotland. At Nice in June, Charles and Francis came to terms, signing a ten-year truce, and some months later they pledged themselves to cooperate against the enemies of Christendom. Henry now moved to secure his position at home and look for new friends abroad.

Though publicly reconciled, Henry still regarded Mary and her supporters with suspicion. In the summer of 1538, Cromwell sent her a letter of warning. She had taken some "strangers" into her house. The incident had been relayed to the king in such a way to put her trustworthiness in doubt.[3] Mary responded, "I fear it hath been reported to the worst, nevertheless I will promise you, with God's help, from henceforth to refrain [from] it so utterly that of right none shall have cause to speak of." She assured Cromwell that she would not lodge anyone in her house again and added that she would rather endure physical harm than lose even the smallest part of the king's favor.[4]

Amid renewed fears of war, Henry sought to alienate Mary from the emperor and draw her more securely to him. At the end of August 1538, she was instructed to complain to the imperial ambassadors, Chapuys and Mendoza, about the emperor's failure to conclude the Portuguese alliance and the miserable terms he had offered. Cromwell wrote to Mary outlining the supposed grievances that she was to present to the ambassadors when they visited her at Havering. Upon their arrival on the twenty-sixth, Mary dutifully protested about the "dissimulation" employed by the ambassadors, the offer of a miserly "dower," and the emperor's failure to show her the cousinly kindness and friendship she expected of him. "She was a woman only and could not help saying these things." But "after so many overtures and fine words, nothing had been concluded."[5]

Later Mary made clear her real feelings. She told Chapuys that she held the emperor in high esteem, as a "father and mother," and "was so affectionately attached" to him "that it seemed almost impossible to her to have such an affection and love for a kinsman." She did not believe what her father said about him, and she stood ready to do whatever he asked of her in the issue of marriage.[6] Fearing for her safety, the ambassador raised again the prospect of escape. Mary was hesitant: "It might happen," she said, that her father "might hereafter show greater consideration for her, or cause her to be more respected and better treated than she had been until now." If that were the case, "she would much prefer remaining in England and conforming herself entirely to her father's commands and wishes."

When quizzed by Cromwell on her meeting with the ambassadors, Mary displayed some political astuteness, saying only that they had reiterated the emperor's support for her and had urged her to remain "in the obedience and goodwill of my father."

HENRY NOW TOOK action against the old Catholic families of royal Plantagenet blood, the Poles, Nevilles, and Courtenays, who had long been objects of suspicion for their loyalty to Katherine of Aragon and Mary. Reginald Pole had denounced Henry's tyranny and heresy in the bitterest terms and, according to reports by the emperor's agents, had hoped that the unrest in England might lead to "his marrying the princess himself."[7] As John Wroth wrote in a letter to Lord Lisle, who was in Calais on May 18, "Pole intended to have married my old lady Mary and betwixt them both should again arise the old doctrine of Christ."[8] It was such a union, or a rising in support of Mary against Edward's succession, that the regime particularly feared.

In late August 1538, Sir Geoffrey Pole, the younger brother of Reginald, was arrested for treason and imprisoned in the Tower. Under interrogation he implicated his elder brother Henry Pole, Lord Montague; Sir Edward Neville, Montague's brother-in-law; and Henry Courtenay, marquess of Exeter—the king's cousin—in an alleged conspiracy that sought to deprive the king of his supremacy and marry Mary to Reginald Pole. By November 4, Exeter, his wife, Gertrude, and their twelve-year-old son, Edward, were committed to the Tower. Soon after, the elderly countess of Salisbury was interrogated and her house searched. She was convicted without trial of aiding and abetting her sons Henry and Reginald and of having "committed and p[er]petrated div[er]se and sundry other detestable and abominable treasons" and was imprisoned also.[9] On Monday, December 9, Montague, Sir Edward Neville, and Exeter were tried and, having received unanimous guilty verdicts—on the basis of remarks such as "I like well the proceedings of Cardinal Pole"—were executed at Tower Hill.[10]

Two days after Christmas, Reginald Pole set out again secretly from Rome to rally the Catholic powers against "the most cruel and abominable tyrant" the king of England.[11] In the Pact of Toledo in January 1539, Charles and Francis agreed to make no further agreements with England. It seemed that a crusade, termed the "Enterprise of England," was about to begin.[12] The pope was determined to "chastise the irreverence and extravagance of the King of England."[13] Counties were mustered, defenses were strengthened, and the country prepared for war. Meanwhile, diplomatic overtures were made to the Schmalkaldic League of German princes and any other rulers opposed to Charles or the pope.

On New Year's Eve, Sir Nicholas Carew, a onetime royal favorite, was apprehended and questioned. A letter had allegedly been found at the home of the marchioness of Exeter that implicated him in the treason for which the marquess had been executed earlier in the month. Carew was tried and convicted on February 14, 1539, and beheaded on Tower Hill three weeks later. For Mary, the execution of so many of those who had supported her and her mother served as a sharp reminder of her father's capacity for vengeance and cruelty. As Chapuys reflected, "It would seem that they want to leave her as few friends as possible."[14]

WITH RENEWED FEARS of war against him, Henry was keen to secure alliances among the Lutheran princes in Germany. In mid-January 1539, the English ambassador Christopher Mont was sent to the duke of Saxony to discuss the prospect of a double match between Henry and the duke of Cleves's eldest daughter, Anne, and between Mary and the young duke of Cleves himself.[15] Cromwell instructed Mont to make clear that although Mary was "only the King's natural daughter"—meaning she was not of "princely status"—she was "endowed, as all the world knows, with such beauty, learning and virtues, that when the rest was agreed, no man would stick for any part concerning her beauty and goodness."[16]

Though the negotiations for a marriage with Mary and the young duke of Cleves came to nothing, by the autumn an alliance had been secured between Henry and Anne, the sister of Duke William of Cleves. The duke was a natural ally for Henry: a committed Habsburg opponent yet not a Lutheran. Agreement was reached in October, and, as negotiations continued for a match with Mary and another of the German princes, Anne of Cleves began her journey to England.

Meanwhile, Thomas Wriothesley, the earl of Southampton, was

sent to Mary to instruct her that she should entertain the prospect of marriage with the Lutheran Duke Philip of Bavaria, who was in England in advance of Anne of Cleves's arrival.[17] Mary responded that although she knew the matter was of "great importance," she "would wish and desire never to enter that kind of religion, but to continue still a maid during her life," although she "committed herself to his majesty, her benign and merciful father." On December 22, she agreed to meet the duke in the gardens of Westminster Abbey. Speaking partly in German with an interpreter and partly in Latin, the duke declared his intention to take Mary as his wife, if it were agreeable to her, and was bold enough to kiss her.[18] When he left England in the new year, Duke Philip believed he would soon be returning to marry the princess. The French ambassador, Charles de Marillac, expected the wedding to take place within "ten or fifteen days," and in December a draft treaty was drawn up.[19]

By January, word reached Rome that Mary had already married "without the advice or knowledge of the Emperor." Chapuys sought desperately to learn if rumors of her marriage to a Lutheran duke were true. They were not. For Henry the negotiations had never been intended as anything more than a ploy to strengthen his hand against the emperor at a time when he feared a Catholic crusade against him.

Steps were also taken to suppress popular heresy and to appease conservatives at home. In the Parliament of 1539, the Act of Six Articles was passed, intended to head off the rising tide of heresy. It reaffirmed the Catholic doctrine of transubstantiation, with denial punishable by death by burning; rejected Communion in both kinds for the laity; required priests to remain celibate; and advocated the continued use of private Masses and auricular confession. Since the break with Rome, only John Lambert, an Anabaptist and one of Europe's most radical heretics, had been burned for heresy. The passing of the Six Articles was intended to reassure Europe's Catholic rulers that Henry, despite the schism, was fundamentally orthodox and they need not respond to the pope's calls for a crusade against him.

In any event, no invasion came. The pope withheld the promised bull and recalled Cardinal Pole to Rome.[20] France was unwilling to take action without a commitment from Charles, and the emperor, faced with the threat of the Ottoman Turks and the Lutherans in Germany and deteriorating relations with France, was not prepared to act against England.[21] Instead, negotiations for an English alliance and a marriage with Mary were reopened with both sides.[22] Yet as Marillac, the French ambassador, observed, "The King will not marry [his daughter] out of England, lest the crown of England should be claimed for her as legitimate by the Church and not of those born since the withdrawal of obedience to the Holy See, like the prince."[23] Moreover, as Henry made clear to Marillac, "I love my daughter well, but myself and honour more." He would not declare Mary legitimate and refused to allow the invalidity of his first marriage to be doubted.[24]

Mary, then twenty-six, expressed her situation to one of her chamberwomen, an informant of Marillac. "It was folly to think that they would marry her out of England, or even in England," she said, "for she would be, while her father lived, only Lady Mary, the most unhappy Lady in Christendom."[25]

CHAPTER 22

FOR FEAR OF MAKING A
RUFFLE IN THE WORLD

∴

ON DECEMBER 27, 1539, ANNE OF CLEVES ARRIVED IN ENGLAND. "The day," the duke of Suffolk reported to Cromwell, "was foul and windy, with much hail [that blew] continually in her face."[1] She journeyed to Canterbury and then to Sittingbourne and Rochester, where she remained for New Year's Eve. The following day, a party of six gentlemen went unannounced into Anne's chamber at Rochester. All were disguised, yet one was the king. He had been scheduled to meet Anne formally at Blackheath on January 3, but curiosity had gotten the better of him.[2] "How ye liked the Lady Anne?" Cromwell asked the king on his return to Greenwich. "Nothing so well as she was spoken of," Henry replied, adding, "if [he] had known as much before as [he] then knew, she should not have come within this realm." He now asked his minister, "What remedy?" To which Cromwell responded, "I know none, he was very sorry therefore."[3]

The twenty-four-year-old was not the beauty that Hans Holbein's portrait, sent to England before her arrival, had portrayed. Henry immediately questioned her virginity, observing that she had the fuller figure expected of an older woman rather than the slender figure of a maid. He believed she was already married to François, heir to the Duchy of Lorraine, to whom she had been betrothed at the age of twelve.

The marriage was postponed while Cromwell investigated whether the Lorraine match had been properly broken off. Two days later, with assurances from the Cleves ambassadors, Henry reluctantly resumed preparations for the wedding. Francis I and Charles were celebrating the New Year together in Paris, and Henry needed to maintain the alliance with the German princes. As he later declared, "If it were not . . . for fear of making a ruffle in the world—that is, to be a means to drive her brother into the hands of the Emperor, and the French King's hands, being now together, I would never have married her."[4]

When Anne made a solemn declaration before the Privy Council "that she was free from all contracts," Henry urgently petitioned his chief minister. "Is there none other remedy," he questioned, "but that I must needs, against my will, put my neck in the yoke?" Cromwell hurried away without offering a reply.[5] Within a few months the cost of Cromwell's blunder would become clear.

AT EIGHT IN the morning on Tuesday, January 6, 1540, the Feast of the Epiphany, Thomas Cranmer, archbishop of Canterbury, celebrated the marriage of Henry and Anne of Cleves in the Chapel Royal at Greenwich. Both Mary and Elizabeth attended the service.[6] The next morning, Cromwell visited the king in the Privy Chamber. "How liked the Queen?" he asked, to which Henry replied, "Surely, as ye know, I liked her before not well, but now I like her much worse. For I have felt her belly and her breasts, and thereby, as I can judge, she be no maid." The king continued, "[The] which struck me so to the heart when I felt them that I had neither will nor courage to proceed any further in matters. . . . I have left her as good a maid as I found her."[7]

For the next six months, despite repeated efforts, the marriage remained unconsummated. As Henry explained to his physician, "He found her body in such sort disordered and indisposed to excite and provoke any lust in him. Yea, [it] rather minister[ed] matter of loathsomeness unto [him], that [he] could not in any wise overcome that loathsomeness, nor in her company be provoked or stirred to that act."[8] Now he lamented the fact that he would never have any more children for "the comfort of the realm, if he should continue in marriage with this lady." Cromwell responded that "he would do his utmost to comfort and deliver his Grace of his affliction."[9]

By the summer, Henry had decided to sever his ties with the

German princes and to seek an annulment. He could afford to break
the alliance. The Franco-imperial entente had become strained, and
another phase in the Habsburg-Valois conflict had begun. Some weeks
before, he had started an affair with one of Anne's maids, Katherine
Howard, a niece of the duke of Norfolk. "The King is," the French
ambassador reported, "so amorous of her that he knows not how to
make sufficient demonstrations of his affection." He "caresses her more
than he did the others" and lavished her with jewels.[10]

As Henry's infatuation with Katherine grew, his calls for a divorce
from Anne became more strident. The leading religious conservatives,
Norfolk and Bishop Stephen Gardiner, saw an opportunity to install a
queen supportive of their cause and effecting the downfall of their
great enemy, Thomas Cromwell. As Marillac wrote, "The King, wishing by all possible means to lead back religion to the way of truth,
Cromwell, as attached to the German Lutherans, had always favoured
the doctors who preached such erroneous opinions and hindered those
who preached the contrary." Having been recently warned that he was
working "against the intention of the King and of the acts of Parliament," Cromwell had "betrayed himself."[11]

When letters from the Lutheran lords of Germany were found in
his house, the chief minister's fate was sealed. "The King was thereby
so exasperated against him that he would no longer hear him spoken
of, but rather desired to abolish all memory of him as the greatest
wretch ever born in England."[12]

AT 3 P.M. ON SATURDAY, June 10, 1540, Cromwell was arrested in
the Council Chamber by the duke of Norfolk. His goods were seized
and confiscated, and he was sent to the Tower, charged with heresy
and treason and of plotting to marry Mary.[13] He had lost Henry's confidence, and the king had disavowed him.

From the Tower Cromwell wrote to Henry protesting his innocence and begging for mercy, signing himself "with the heavy heart
and trembling of your Highness's most heavy and most miserable prisoner and poor slave."[14] He was condemned on June 29 as "the most
false and corrupt traitor, deceiver and circumventor against your royal

person and the imperial crown of this realm that had ever been known in your whole reign." Cromwell was paying the price for the failed match, for his reformist inclinations, and for the rise in ascendancy of the conservative Howard family. He was kept alive only to recount all that he knew about the king's marriage to Anne of Cleves and of Henry's conversations with him as to the nonconsummation of the marriage.

On June 24, Anne of Cleves was ordered to go to Richmond Palace, ostensibly to avoid an outbreak of the plague.[15] The convocation of the clergy was instructed to examine the king's marriage after doubts had been raised about its validity. The investigation concluded that Anne had been precontracted to the prince of Lorraine, that the king had wed her against his will, and that the whole nation desired the king to have more heirs. On the twenty-fifth, the king's commissioners visited Anne and informed her that her marriage was invalid.[16] She consented without protest, agreeing to the divorce proceedings and confirming that the marriage had not been consummated.[17] Her acquiescence was rewarded: she was endowed with lands to the value of £4,000 annually and Richmond and Bletchingley manors, and was thereafter known as "the old Queen, the King's sister." On July 9, the convocation found their marriage to have been unlawful given its nonconsummation, her precontract with the duke of Lorraine, and the fact that Henry had acted under compulsion. Four days later, Parliament confirmed the verdict and Henry was declared free to remarry.

On July 28, Cromwell was finally taken to the scaffold on Tower Green. Maintaining his innocence to the end, he denied that he had supported heretics but accepted the judgment of the law. He knelt, prayed, and, laying his head on the block, "patiently suffered the stroke of the ax," it taking a number of attempts to remove his head. Two days later, three well-known reformers, Robert Barnes, William Jerome, and Thomas Garret, were burned as heretics at Smithfield. At the stake, Barnes utterly denied his guilt: he was condemned to die, "but wherefore I cannot tell."[18] The others made similar declarations. On the same day, three defendants of the old faith were put to death: Edward Powell; Richard Fetherstone, Mary's former schoolmaster; and Thomas Abel, Katherine of Aragon's chaplain, were hanged, drawn, and quartered for treason. All had refused to acknowledge the Act of Supremacy. The heretics and traitors were dragged facedown on sheep hurdles through the streets of London, a heretic and a papist strapped to each.[19] The king would not tolerate opposition of any kind. A major inquisition for heresy now began.

CHAPTER 23

MORE A FRIEND THAN
A STEPMOTHER

∴

On JULY 28, 1540, THREE WEEKS AFTER THE ANNULMENT OF HIS
marriage to Anne of Cleves, Henry married his fifth wife, Katherine
Howard, at Oatlands Palace in Surrey.¹ She was the nineteen-year-old
niece of Thomas Howard, duke of Norfolk. By November, Marillac
was writing to the French king, "The new Queen, has completely
acquired the King's Grace and the other [Anne of Cleves] is no more
spoken of than if she were dead."²

Yet Anne was "loved and esteemed" by the people and, having
readily accepted her new status as the "King's sister," was welcomed at
court. She arrived at Hampton Court on January 3 and was admitted to
the queen's presence. "Lady Anne approached the Queen with as much
reverence and punctilious ceremony as if she herself was the most
insignificant damsel about Court . . . all the time addressing the Queen
on her knees." Katherine "received her most kindly, showing her great
favour and courtesy." The king then entered the room and, "after making a very low bow to Lady Anne, embraced and kissed her." They all
sat down to supper at the same table with "as good a mien and countenance and look[ed] as unconcerned as if there had been nothing between
them," as the two queens danced and drank together.³

Relations between Mary and Katherine Howard were initially
fraught. The new queen was a cousin of Anne Boleyn and five years
younger than Mary. On December 5, Chapuys told the emperor's sister
that the queen had tried to remove two of Mary's attendants because
she believed that the princess was showing less respect to her than to

her predecessors. Mary's behavior evidently improved, as it was soon reported that she had "found means to conciliate" Katherine and "thinks her maids will remain."[4] Though they were too different in temperament and too similar in age to ever be close, relations began to settle down. "A week ago," on May 17, the imperial ambassador reported, "the King and Queen went . . . to visit the Prince [at Waltham Holy Cross in Essex] at the request of the [Lady Mary], but chiefly at the intercession of the Queen herself." It proved a successful visit, and "upon that occasion" the king granted Mary "full permission to reside at Court, and the Queen has countenanced it with a good grace."[5]

But ever present were reminders of her father's vengeance and the price Mary might pay for her perceived disloyalty. The following year, sixty-eight-year-old Margaret Pole, the woman whom Mary had referred to as her "second mother," was taken to the scaffold on the slope of Tower Hill. She had been attainted in 1539 without ever having been tried. At seven in the morning of May 27, 1541, she was brought out to die. She commended her soul to God, prayed for the king, and requested to be remembered to the "Princess Mary." She then placed her head on the block. In the absence of the usual Tower executioner, "a wretched and blundering youth . . . literally hacked her head and shoulders to pieces."[6]

> Thinking now in his old days, the King felt after sundry troubles of mind which have happened unto him by marriages, to have obtained such a jewel [Katherine] for womanhood and very perfect love towards him . . . and showed outwardly all virtue and good behaviour.[7]

Yet unbeknown to the king, Katherine had had relationships before she was married, when she had been part of the household of her stepgrandmother the dowager duchess of Norfolk: first in 1536, when she was fourteen, with her music teacher, Henry Manox, and then two years later with Francis Dereham, a kinsman of her uncle the duke of Norfolk. Upon becoming queen, Katherine resumed her illicit liaisons. Dereham returned to court as her private secretary, and Thomas Culpepper, a gentleman of the king's Privy Chamber, began regularly meeting with her in her chamber. By October 1541, Cranmer, the arch-bishop of Canterbury, learned of Katherine's continuing behavior, and, on November 2, he presented Henry with a written statement of allega-tions. The king was initially disbelieving, but after Manox and Dereham were questioned, he was forced to accept the fact of Katherine's adultery.

Five days later, at Hampton Court, Katherine was interrogated by her uncle, Norfolk, and Cranmer. At first she denied the allegations, but then she admitted the truth. In a letter of confession to the king, she begged for his mercy, describing her relationships with Manox and Dereham and explaining why she had not told him before they were married: "I was so desirous to be taken unto your grace's favour and so blinded with the desire of worldly glory that I could not, nor had grace, to consider how great a fault it was to conceal my former faults from your Majesty."[8]

In January, Katherine and Lady Rochford, her lady of the bed-chamber, who had arranged illicit meetings, were declared guilty of treason. On February 10, Katherine was moved from Syon to the Tower, passing first beneath London Bridge, where the heads of Dereham and Culpepper, executed the previous year, were still dis-played. Two days later, Sunday the twelfth, she was told to prepare herself for death. According to Chapuys, "she asked to have the block brought in to her so that she might see how to place herself, which was done, and she made trial of it."[9] Early the following morning, her prep-arations complete, Katherine knelt at the scaffold and her head was struck off.[10]

"This King has wonderfully felt the case of the Queen his wife," Chapuys wrote. "He has certainly shown greater sorrow and regret at her loss than at the faults, loss or divorce of his preceding wives."[11] By April, it was reported that, since learning of his late wife's conduct, he had "not been the same man" and was often to be found "sad, pensive and sighing."[12]

Following Katherine Howard's execution, Mary enjoyed far greater favor and presided over court feasts as if she were queen. As a New Year's gift Henry presented her "with rings, silver plate, and other jew-els" among which were "two rubies of inestimable value."[13] However, during those months, the princess suffered repeatedly from chronic ill health, linked to anxiety, depression, and irregular menstruation, although the symptoms varied widely from one episode to the next. In March and April, she had a "strange fever" that brought on heart palpitations and so afflicted her that at times "she remained as though dead."[14] On April 22, Chapuys told the queen of Hungary, "the princess has been seriously ill, and in danger of her life."[15] Yet Mary recovered and on December 17 was summoned to court for the Christmas festivities "with a great number of ladies . . . they work day and night at Hampton Court to finish her lodging."[16] Chapuys reported that the king "spoke to her in the most gracious and amiable words that a father could address to his daughter."[17]

ON JULY 12, 1543, Mary and Elizabeth attended their father's sixth wedding, in the queen's Privy Closet at Hampton Court. As Thomas Wriothesley, secretary of the Privy Council, reported to the duke of Suffolk:

> The King's Majesty was married on Thursday last to my Lady Latimer, a woman in my judgement, for virtue, wisdom and gentleness, most mete for his Highness, and sure I am his Majesty had never a wife more agreeable to his heart than she is. Our Lord send them long life and much joy together.[18]

It was a small ceremony with some twenty people in attendance, presided over by Stephen Gardiner, bishop of Winchester.[19] Henry's bride, the twice-married Katherine Parr, a former member of Mary's household, had come to the king's attention during Mary's frequent visits to court. Katherine had long-standing connections with the princess. Her mother, Maud, had been one of Katherine of Aragon's ladies-in-waiting, and she had been named after the queen, who stood as godmother at her baptism. It was soon apparent that Katherine Parr, only four years older than Mary, was to be "more a friend than a stepmother." She sought to improve relations between Mary and her father, and soon Chapuys was reporting, "The King continues to treat her [Mary] kindly, and has made her stay with the new Queen, who behaves affectionately towards her."[20] Mary and Katherine were both learned women, and, despite Katherine's evangelical sympathies, they enjoyed a close relationship and studied together.

In 1544, under Katherine Parr's influence, Mary took up the translation of *Erasmus's Paraphrases on the Four Gospels*. The scholar Nicholas Udall was the editor of the book, Katherine funded its publication, and Mary was one of the translators. Ill health prevented Mary from finishing work on the book, and her chaplain, Francis Mallet, eventually completed it. In a letter of September 20, Katherine inquired as to whether Mary wished it "to go forth to the world (most auspiciously) under your name, or as the production of an unknown writer?" adding, "You will, in my opinion, do a real injury if you refuse to let it go down to posterity under the auspices of your own name, since you have undertaken so much labour in accurately translating it for the great good of the public and would have undertaken still greater (as is well known) if the health of your body had permitted." She continued, "I do not see why you should repudiate that praise which all men justly confer on you."[21] In his preface to the *Paraphrases*, Udall paid tribute to "the most noble, the virtuous, the most witty, and the most studious Lady Mary's grace," calling her "a peerless flower of virginity."[22]

Based at court, Mary thrived in the favor of an intelligent and benevolent queen. When in February 1544 a ball was held during the visit of the Spanish grandee the duke of Nájera, Mary danced elegantly, dressed extravagantly in a gown of gold cloth under a robe of violet velvet with a coronal of large precious stones on her head. As Nájera described her:

> The princess Mary has a pleasing countenance and person. It is said of her that she is endowed with very great goodness and discretion, and among other praises, I heard of her is this, that she knows how to conceal her acquirements; and certainly this is no small proof of prudence, since the real sage, who is aware of the extent of knowledge, thinks his own learning of too low an estimate to be boasted of, whilst those who have only a superficial acquaintance with learning exhibit the contrary, as they pride themselves in proportion to their acquirements and with-

out imparting their knowledge, allow no one to be learned but themselves. The princess is much beloved throughout the kingdom, that she is almost adored.[23]

Despite being twenty years younger than Mary, Edward was fiercely protective of his elder sister. Writing to his stepmother, the six-year-old urged her to keep a careful eye on the princess: "preserve her, therefore, I pray you, my dear sister Mary," from all the "wiles and enchantments of the evil one" and "beseech her to attend no longer to foreign dances and merriments which do not become a most Christian princess."[24] At the same time he praised Mary, telling her, "I like you even as a brother ought to like a very dear sister, who hath within herself all the embellishments of virtue and honourable station." In the same way that he "loved his best clothes most of all, though he seldom wore them," he explained, "so he wrote seldom to her, but loved her most."[25]

CHAPTER 24

THE FAMILY OF HENRY VIII

⁖

His Majesty therefore thinketh convenient before his departure beyond the seas that it be enacted by his Highness with the assent of the lords spiritual and temporal and the commons in this present Parliament . . . that in case it shall happen the King's Majesty and the said excellent Prince his yet only son Prince Edward and heir apparent to decease without heir of either of their bodies lawfully begotten . . . then the said Imperial Crown . . . shall be to the Lady Marie the King's Highness' daughter and to the heirs of the body of the Lady Marie lawfully begotten . . . and for default of such issue the said Imperial Crown . . . shall be to the Lady Elizabeth the King's second daughter and to the heirs of the body of the Lady Elizabeth lawfully begotten.[1]

IN FEBRUARY 1544, PARLIAMENT PASSED A NEW AND RADICAL ACT of Succession. The previous law, passed in 1536 following Henry's marriage to Jane Seymour, had bastardized both Mary and Elizabeth and settled the succession on any son born of Seymour or "by any other lawful wife."[2] Yet now, as Henry visibly aged and the six-year-old Edward remained his sole heir, a real uncertainty hung over the Tudor succession. As the new act declared, "It standeth in the only pleasure and will of Almighty God whether the King's Majesty shall have any heirs begotten and procreated between his Highness and his . . . most entirely beloved wife Queen Katherine" or whether "the said Prince Edward shall have issue of his body lawfully begotten."[3] Although still regarded as illegitimate, Mary, and then Elizabeth, were placed in the line of succession after Edward and his heirs.

On June 26, the royal children came together with their father at Whitehall for a lavish reception—a *voyde*—at which wine and sweet-meats were served. It was the first public outing of the reconciled royal family.[4] The reunion was commemorated in the portrait known as *The Family of Henry VIII*, painted by an unknown artist. The picture is dominated by Henry, sitting on his throne between his son and heir, the six-year-old Prince Edward, and, to emphasize the line of dynastic succession, Edward's mother, the long-since-dead Jane Seymour. On the left stands Mary, on the right Elizabeth. Both are dressed similarly, with Mary distinguishable only by being the taller sister. Despite having played a part in brokering the reconciliation between Henry and his children, Katherine Parr is omitted from the scene. This was more than just a family portrait, however; it was to commemorate the political settlement enshrined in the Act of Succession. This was the Tudor family as Henry had decreed it: the king's heirs in degree of precedence. It would shape the English monarchy for the rest of the century.

WITH THE SUCCESSION settled, Henry looked to recapture the glories of his youth by going to war with France. The emperor and the French king had resumed hostilities, and both sovereigns once again began to compete for Henry's favor. Chapuys reported that the French "now almost offer the English carte blanche for an alliance," and he advised that England must, at whatever cost, be secured for the imperial interest.[5] Henry would indeed make a secret treaty with the emperor, in February 1543, that provided for a joint invasion of France within two years.

But Henry first needed to secure the northern border by mounting a campaign against Scotland. At Solway Moss in November 1542, the English inflicted a humiliating defeat on the Scots. Three weeks later King James V died, leaving the kingdom to his week-old daughter, Mary. Henry then sought to subdue Scotland in advance of his invasion in France, and in July 1543 a treaty of peace and dynastic union was signed at Greenwich with Prince Edward betrothed to Mary, queen of Scots.[6] But within five months, the entente had broken down as the Scots reaffirmed their alliance with the French.

Preparations were now made for war on two fronts: with Scotland

and with France. While the emperor sought to make Francis relinquish his claim to Milan and support the German princes, Henry looked to force him to abandon the cause of Scottish independence. In May 1544, 14,000 troops were sent to Scotland, and a month later, an English force of some 40,000 men invaded France. On July 11, Henry, despite his greatly expanded girth and swollen, ulcerated legs, left Whitehall for France.[7] In his absence, Katherine Parr was appointed regent of England, to rule the country in the name of the king as Katherine of Aragon had done some thirty years before. She managed the five-man council that Henry had appointed to assist her and oversaw the supply of men and money for the war. Writing to Henry's council, Katherine adopted the full royal style: "Right trusty and right well-beloved cousins, we greet you well." She signed herself "Katherine the Queen." In letters to Henry she used the submissive tone of a royal wife "by your majesty's humble obedient servant."[8] She was a model of wifely queenship.

As Katherine governed from Hampton Court, Mary was with her, and later Edward and Elizabeth too. Both stepdaughters witnessed a woman governing and imposing her authority on her male councillors. It would prove formative for both.

ON JULY 14, HENRY arrived in Calais, ready for the planned siege of Boulogne, which began five days later. After weeks of laying siege, the Council wrote to Katherine on August 4, informing her that "Yesterday, the battery began, and goes lustily forward, and the walls begin to tumble apace." They anticipated that Boulogne must fall shortly.[9] Six weeks later, the town surrendered and Henry entered in triumph. Yet on the same day the emperor, who sought to concentrate his efforts on Germany, had concluded a treaty with the French at Crépy and abandoned England. Henry was left to fight Francis alone. The French king now pledged "to win as much as the Englishmen had on this side of the sea," to capture a town on England's southeast coast that could be exchanged for Boulogne, and to send troops into Scotland for an invasion of the north.

On May 31, 1545, a French expeditionary force landed at Dumbarton in Scotland, and on July 19, a French invasion fleet of more than two hundred ships entered the Solent. Fires were lit across England, raising the alarm.[10] In the skirmishes that followed, Henry's warship the *Mary Rose* was sunk with the loss of 500 men. Two days later, 2,000 French troops landed at Bembridge on the Isle of Wight and burned several villages before being forced to retreat. English shipping in Portsmouth harbor was attacked and the towns of Newhaven and Seaford were sacked until the French forces were driven back across the English Channel. The following day Henry ordered processions throughout the realm and prayers to be said to intercede for victory.[11]

"We are in war with France and Scotland," warned Bishop Gardiner;

> we have enmity with the bishop of Rome, have no assured friendship here, and have received from the Lansgrave, chief captain of the Protestants, such displeasure that he has cause to think us angry with him. Our war is noisome to our realm and to all our merchants that traffic throughout the Narrow Seas. . . . We are in a world where reason and learning prevail not and covenants are little regarded.[12]

By September, as both sides sued for peace, negotiations were revived with the emperor. On October 23, Bishops Gardiner and Thomas Thirlby were commissioned to present a three-pronged plan: Charles V would marry Mary, Edward the emperor's daughter, and Elizabeth his son, Philip. Charles did not respond favorably.[13] It was clear that Henry was seeking better relations with the emperor merely to secure a stronger negotiating position with France, and the proposals came to nothing.

IN MAY 1546, the ailing Eustace Chapuys prepared to leave England after sixteen years as ambassador. On May 4 he went to the palace of Westminster to bid farewell to the queen and Mary. Katherine expressed her desire that the friendship between England and Spain be maintained. "She . . . begged me affectionately, after I presented to your majesty her humble service, to express explicitly all I had learned here of the good wishes of the King towards you." Mary, meanwhile, thanked him for the emperor's "good wishes towards her," and, "in default of her power to repay your Majesty in any other way, she said she was bound to pray constantly to God for your Majesty's health and prosperity."

At a final audience, Chapuys and Henry spoke about future relations between England and France. Henry "observed that he would very much prefer a settled peace to a truce . . . but, after all, if your Majesty would aid him, in accordance with the treaty, he did not care very much either." The king stressed "the importance of the treaty of friendship . . . that I would report very fully and use my best endeavours, in every way, to induce your Majesty to declare against the French."[14]

Finally, on June 7, 1546, French and English commissioners signed a peace treaty in which it was agreed that Boulogne would be returned to France in eight years' time on payment of 2 million crowns. In the hope of exploiting the new accord, the pope sent an envoy to England, Gurone Bertano, to propose terms for Henry's reconciliation to Rome. Pope Paul had hoped that the prodigal son might now submit to papal primacy, but Bertano's overtures were firmly rebuffed.[15]

CHAPTER 25

DEPARTED THIS LIFE

∴

Sir, I am confused and apprehensive to have to inform your Majesty that there are rumours here of a new Queen, although I do not know why, or how true it may [be].[1]

—AMBASSADOR FRANÇOIS VAN DER
DELFT TO THE EMPEROR,
FEBRUARY 27, 1546

IN FEBRUARY 1546, A PLOT WAS HATCHED TO DESTROY THE QUEEN. Her evangelical beliefs and her growing influence over the king had made her enemies among the religious conservatives at court. With Henry's deteriorating health, and his temper growing ever shorter, he became increasingly irritated by Katherine's debates with him over religion. "A good hearing it is," he retorted to Bishop Gardiner, "when women become such clerks; and a thing much to my comfort, to come in mine old days to be taught by my wife."[2] Seeing an opportunity to gain the ascendancy at court and halt the progress of religious reform, Gardiner and his fellow conservatives moved to convince Henry that Katherine was to be feared.[3] Gardiner murmured to the king that the queen's views were heretical under the law and that he,

with others of his faithful councillors, could, within a short time, disclose such treasons cloaked with this heresy that His Majesty would easily perceive how perilous a matter it is to cherish a serpent within his own bosom.[4]

Gardiner secured Henry's agreement for Katherine to be investigated for heresy and for treason. Her chief intimates, the ladies Herbert, Lane, and Tyrwhitt, were to be questioned and their closets searched for anything that might incriminate the queen.[5]

In the spring, Anne Askew, a young Lincolnshire gentlewoman who held evangelical opinions and who associated with Lady Hertford and Lady Denny, both high-ranking women at court, was taken to the Tower. There she was interrogated in an attempt to extract information that could be used against Katherine. Did not the ladies of the court share her opinion? Could she not name "a great number of my sect"? She conceded nothing. She was put on the rack and tortured and, refusing to implicate anyone, was revived and racked again. The lieutenant of the Tower would not perform the second torture, so her interrogators, the chancellor of the Court of Augmentations and the lord chancellor of England, "threw off their gowns" and became "tormentors themselves." As a gentlewoman, Askew should have been protected against torture, and the Council was "not a little displeased" when news of the racking spread. So desperate were the conservatives to implicate the queen that the lord chancellor of England himself had broken the law.

On July 16, 1546, Askew's broken body was carried on a wooden chair and she was bound to the stake, together with Nicholas Belenian, a priest from Shropshire, and John Adams, a tailor. All were accused of heresy for refusing to accept the Real Presence in the Eucharist, as the Act of Six Articles had decreed.

Although Askew failed to incriminate Katherine, Gardiner managed to procure evidence regarding the discovery of forbidden religious books and a warrant of arrest was issued. Katherine was warned by her physician, Thomas Wendy, of the action to be taken against her and advised to submit before Henry; she should "somewhat . . . frame and conform herself to the King's mind." If she would do so and "show her humble submission unto him . . . she should find him gracious and favourable unto her."

Fearing that she faced the same fate as her predecessor, Katherine took Wendy's advice and acquiesced to the king, protesting her weakness as a woman and the God-given superiority of men: "Must I, and will I, refer my judgement in this, and all other cases, to your Majesty's wisdom, as my only anchor, Supreme Head and Governor here in earth, next under God." Henry relented. "Is it even so, Sweetheart? And tend your arguments to no worse end? Then perfect friends we are now again, as ever at any time heretofore."⁶

When Chancellor Wriothesley arrived the following day with a detachment of the guard to arrest the queen, Henry berated him as a "Knave! Arrant knave, beast! And fool!" and ordered him to "*avaunt* [leave]" his "sight."

THE COLLAPSE OF the plot against Katherine Parr signaled the end of the conservatives' brief period of ascendancy. With Henry's health deteriorating rapidly, the Seymour faction, led by Edward's uncle Edward Seymour, earl of Hertford, acted to destroy its enemies, the Howards and Bishop Gardiner, and take control of the government. "Nothing is done at court," reported the newly arrived van der Delft, "without their intervention and the Council mostly meets at Hertford's house. It is even asserted that the custody of the Prince and government of the realm will be entrusted to them; and this misfortune to the house of Norfolk may have come from that quarter."⁷

Mary, meanwhile, was untouched by these shifts of power and remained in relative peace at court as Henry continued to show her every sign of favor. One of the last entries in the king's accounts is the purchase of a horse for Mary, "a white grey gelding."⁸

On December 12, Thomas Howard, the foremost peer of the realm, and his eldest son, Henry Howard, earl of Surrey, were arrested on grounds of treason and sent to the Tower. Surrey, a descendant of Edward III, had boasted of his Plantagenet blood and declared that when Henry died, his father would be "metest to rule the prince." He had planned, it was alleged, to disband the Council, depose the king, seize the young Prince Edward, and display his own heraldry as the royal arms and insignia, an indication of his ambition for the throne. It was upon this last charge that he was tried and found guilty of high treason.⁹

Meanwhile his father, Norfolk, was questioned and imprisoned in the Tower. On January 12, he confessed that he had "offended the King in opening his secret counsels at divers times to sundry persons to the peril of his Highness . . . [and] concealed high treason, in keeping secret the false acts of my son, Henry, Earl of Surrey, in using the arms of St Edward the Confessor, which pertain only to kings."[10] Surrey was executed on January 19 on the scaffold at Tower Hill. A week later Thomas Howard was attainted without trial and awaited execution.

ON THE EVENING of December 26, Henry ordered his will to be brought to him. He wanted to make some changes to the list of executors. "Some he meant to have in and some he meant to have out." The crown would go directly to Edward and any lawful heirs of his body and in default to Mary "upon condition that she shall not marry without the written and sealed consent of a majority" of Edward's surviving Privy Council. In the event of Mary's childless death, Elizabeth would succeed. The succession would then be conferred on the Grey and Clifford families, descendants of Henry's younger sister, Mary.[11] Sixteen executors were to act as Edward's councillors until he reached the age of eighteen. They included Edward Seymour, the earl of Hertford; John Dudley, the earl of Warwick; Sir William Paget, the royal secretary; and Sir Anthony Denny, chief gentleman of the Privy Chamber. Stephen Gardiner, bishop of Winchester, was excluded, and Katherine's position as regent was revoked. Instead, the voices of all the executors were to be equal and decisions were to be taken by majority vote.

Though he had suffered for some time from ulcerated legs, obesity, and gout, Henry's health had declined rapidly since the New Year and he remained confined to the Privy Chamber with a high fever. On January 10, the French ambassador, Odet de Selve, wrote to Francis I that "neither the Queen nor the Lady Mary could see him."[12] His doctors had known that death was approaching but for fear of punishment had held back from telling him. Sir Anthony Denny finally volunteered to inform the king of his imminent demise. He was "to a man's judgement not like[ly] to live." He should, Denny advised, now "prepare himself to death."

"Yet is the mercy of Christ able," Henry asked, "to pardon me all my sins, though they were greater than they be?" He ordered that Archbishop Cranmer be sent for to hear his confession, first declaring that he would "sleep a little." He woke an hour later, "feeling feebleness to increase upon him." By the time the archbishop arrived, Henry was unable to speak. So when Cranmer asked him his faith and assured him of salvation, he urged him to "give some token with his eyes or with his hand, that he trusted in the Lord." Henry squeezed his hand and wrung it "as hard as he could."[13]

By two in the morning of January 28, 1547, Henry was dead. He was fifty-six. Apothecaries, surgeons, and wax chandlers were immediately summoned to "do their duties in spurging, cleansing, bowelling, searing, embalming, furnishing and dressing with spices the said corpse." The body was wrapped in fine linen and velvet and tied with silk cords before the plumber and carpenter cased the corpse in lead. The coffin was then laid out in the middle of the Privy Chamber at Whitehall, watched over by Henry's chaplains and gentlemen.[14]

For three days the king's death was not made public and was kept secret from all except Henry's councillors. Life at court continued without interruption. Henry's meals were brought into the great hall as usual to the sound of trumpets; Parliament remained in session, and those who requested audiences with the king were told that he was indisposed. As van der Delft wrote to the emperor, "I learn from a very confidential source that the King, whom may God receive His Grace, had departed this life, although not the slightest signs of such a thing were to be seen at court."[15] The imperial ambassador subsequently wrote that Mary had been very displeased with Edward Seymour because "he did not visit her or send to her for several days after her father's death."[16] Only when Edward's succession was secure would Mary be told of Henry's passing.

Finally, on the morning of January 31, the tearful Lord Chancellor Wriothesley announced Henry's death to the dumbstruck Parliament, and a section of his will, dealing with the succession of the crown, was read out.[17] Meanwhile, on the twenty-eighth, the day of the king's death, Edward Seymour, the new king's uncle, and Sir Anthony Browne, master of the king's horse, had ridden with a force of 300 mounted troops from London to Hertford Castle to inform Edward of his father's death and pay homage to him as the new king.[18]

PART TWO

A King's Sister

THE KING IS DEAD,
LONG LIVE THE KING

∴

Edward VI, by the grace of God King of England, France, and
Ireland, defender of the faith and of the Church of England and
also of Ireland in earth the supreme head, to all our most loving,
faithful, and obedient subjects, and to every of them, greeting.
    Where it hath pleased Almighty God, on Friday last past in
the morning to call unto his infinite mercy the most excellent high
and mighty prince, King Henry VIII of most noble and famous
memory, our most dear and entirely beloved father, whose soul
God pardon; forasmuch as we, being his only son and undoubted
heir, be now invested and established in the crown imperial of
this realm.[1]

—PROCLAMATION OF KING EDWARD VI,
WESTMINSTER, JANUARY 31, 1547

AT THREE IN THE AFTERNOON OF MONDAY, JANUARY 31, 1547, nine-year-old King Edward VI entered the City of London to take possession of his kingdom. Guns fired from ships on the Thames as the nobility of the realm accompanied the boy king to his lodgings.[2]

The following day the Privy Council gathered in the Presence Chamber, where Edward sat in a chair of estate, and Henry's will was read out. The executors announced that it had been "agreed with one assent and consent" that Edward Seymour, the king's uncle, should be "preferred in name and place before others" and become lord protector. This was not as Henry had decreed. The sixteen executors were to have formed a regency council with all men having equal status; now Seymour emerged as the foremost councillor. Two weeks later, amid a general granting of lands and titles, Seymour would become duke of Somerset. "There was none so mete . . . in all the realm as he," the House of Lords declared.[3]

Having sworn oaths to the king, his councillors cried together, "God save the noble King Edward!" Edward thanked them heartily and doffed his cap.[4] He would remain in the Tower for the next three weeks until after his father's funeral had taken place and preparations had been made for his own coronation. From there he wrote letters of condolence to his stepmother Katherine Parr and this to his sister Mary, then thirty-one, who remained in the dowager queen's household:

> Natural affection, not wisdom, instigates us to lament our dearest father's death. For affection thinks she has utterly lost one who is dead; but wisdom believes one who lives with God is in happiness everlasting. Wheretofore, God having given us such we ought not to mourn our father's death, since it is his will, who works all things for good . . . so far as lies in me, I will be to you a dearest brother, and overflow with all kindness.[5]

On Wednesday, February 2, between eight and nine at night, Henry's body was moved from the Privy Chamber to the Chapel Royal at Whitehall. Ten days later it was taken to Windsor in a gilded chariot pulled by seven horses, all bedecked in black velvet. The roads had been cleared and widened to allow the easier passage of the procession, which stretched over four miles. In front were 250 poor men, dressed in mourning gowns and carrying torches, followed by gentlemen bearing the king's standards and heralds with the king's helmet, targe (sword) shield, and coat of arms. Upon the coffin, draped in cloth of gold and blue velvet, was a life-size, lifelike effigy of King Henry, a scepter of gold in his right hand, in his left the ball of the world with a cross. On his head rested the imperial crown, and around his neck was the collar of the Garter.[6] According to one observer, it "looked exactly like that of the King himself . . . just as if he were alive."[7] Behind the coffin rode the king's chief mourner, the marquess of Dorset, constable of England, and the king's guard, all in black, their halberds pointing to the ground.

The procession reached Syon, the former Bridgettine house on the banks of the Thames in Middlesex, at two in the afternoon. There, after Masses were said, the corpse remained overnight. One account describes how, at Syon, "the leaden coffin being cleft by the shaking of the carriage, the pavement of the church was wetted with his [Henry's] blood." When plumbers later came to solder the coffin, they saw a "dog creeping, and licking up the King's blood."[8]

At seven the following morning, the procession resumed its slow progress to Windsor. Funeral knells were rung, and townspeople lined the route through each town it passed. Finally the gilded chariot arrived at the chapel of the Order of the Garter, where the coffin was placed in a hearse thirty-five feet tall and covered with tapers and candles. The next morning, February 15, Henry's burial took place. Stephen Gardiner preached the funeral sermon, and sixteen yeomen of the Guard lowered the coffin into the vault next to that of Jane Seymour, just as Henry's will had instructed.[9]

As Edward Hall wrote in his chronicle, "The late King was buried at Windsor with much solemnity, and the officers broke their staves, hurling them into the grave. But they were restored to them again when they came to the Tower."[10] With Henry laid to rest, Edward's reign could be formally inaugurated.

AT ONE IN THE afternoon of Saturday, February 19, Edward left the Tower, dressed in white velvet and cloth of silver embroidered with precious stones, to ride on horseback through the city to Westminster.[11] Before him went an ordered procession: his messengers walking side by side; his gentlemen, chaplains, esquires of the body, and nobles; and his councillors, each paired with a foreign ambassador. The marquess of Dorset walked ahead of the young king, bearing the sword of state. Bringing up the rear were the gentlemen and grooms of the Privy Chamber, the pensioners, and the Guard.[12]

Along the route were pageants celebrating Edward's arrival, many echoing those that had greeted the last boy king, Henry VI, on his entry into London in 1432.[13] Edward was heralded as "a young King Solomon," charged with "rebuilding the Temple"—that is, continuing his father's reformation.[14] In one pageant, a phoenix, representing Edward's mother, Jane Seymour, emerged from an artificial Heaven of suns, stars, and clouds to be met by a crowned golden lion (Henry). Two angels then crowned their offspring; the phoenix and the old lion vanished, leaving the cub to rule on his own. The highlight of the pageantry, in nine-year-old Edward's eyes, was an acrobat who "came sliding down" a rope strung from the uppermost part of the steeple of St. Paul's to an anchor in the garden of the dean's house. The tumbler stood up, kissed Edward's foot, then walked back up the rope, "tumbling and casting himself from one leg to another."[15] By the time the procession reached Westminster, it was nearly six in the evening, five hours after it had set off from the Tower.[16]

Early the following day, noblemen were summoned to accompany the king to Westminster Abbey and attend the coronation.[17] Edward was taken by barge to Whitehall and dressed in a robe of crimson velvet, "furred with powdered ermines throughout." At the abbey a scaffold seven stairs tall had been erected, on top of which was set the throne, a white chair covered with damask and gold. Two cushions had been placed on the seat, one of cloth of tissue, the other black velvet embroidered with gold, upon which the diminutive boy king would sit.

Edward was not the youngest king to be crowned; Henry VI had been just eight at his coronation in 1429. However, his would prove to be the most radical English coronation in its thousand-year history. He would be the first monarch to be anointed "Supreme Head of the English Church," and though the coronation would broadly follow the *Liber Regalis*—the Book of Kingship—which had dictated the ceremony for kings since 1375, there would be some significant departures.[18]

The week before, the Council had announced its decision, "upon mature and deep deliberation," that the "old observances and ceremonies [should] be corrected" on account of the king's "tender age" and so that they might conform to the "new laws of the realm," particularly concerning the supremacy and abolition of papal authority. A new king would traditionally swear to confirm laws and liberties that had been granted to people by kings before him and to observe "such laws as . . . shall be chosen by your people."[19] This was drastically altered. It was now left to the king to decide which laws and liberties he would obey. The clause ensuring the protection of the liberties of the clergy was entirely omitted, and the final part of the oath was rewritten: the people, not the king, now had to consent to the new laws.

As Thomas Cranmer, the archbishop of Canterbury, explained in his sermon, the oaths Edward had sworn were not to "be taken in the bishop of Rome's sense," and the clergy had no right to hold kings to account ("to hit your Majesty in the teeth").[20] Although Edward was to be anointed, Cranmer made clear that this was "but ceremony." He was king "not in respect of the oil which the bishop useth, but in consideration of their power which is preordained . . . the King is yet a perfect monarch notwithstanding, and God's anointed, as well as if he was inoiled." Edward had come to the throne "fully invested and established in the crown imperial of this realm."[21]

Now the young king was called upon to do his princely duty:

Your Majesty is God's vice-regent and Christ's vicar within your own dominions, and to see, with your predecessor Josiah, God truly worshipped, and idolatry destroyed; the tyranny of the bishops of Rome banished from your subjects, and images removed. These acts be signs of a second Josiah, who reformed the church of God in his days.[22]

Edward was to model himself on the young biblical King Josiah and purge the land of idols. The coronation was an opportunity to showcase the Protestant aspirations of the new regime.

With the oaths made and litanies sung, Edward was anointed and crowned with the crown of Edward the Confessor, the imperial crown—styled as such since the reign of Henry V—and a third crown made especially for his small head.[23] Normally the imperial crown was not part of the crowning ritual; its inclusion here emphasized the imperial status of the king and echoed the triple crowning of the pope.

The spurs, orb, and scepter were then presented to the young king and Te Deums were sung as the lords spiritual and temporal paid him homage.

Recalling the coronation in his journal, Edward noted only that he had sat next to his uncle Edward Seymour and Archbishop Thomas Cranmer and that he had worn "the crown on his head."[24]

CHAPTER 27

FANTASY AND NEW FANGLENESS

∴

THE EMPEROR AND PAPAL CURIA DID NOT IMMEDIATELY RECOG-
nize the new king. In the eyes of Catholic Europe, Edward was illegitimate and Mary the lawful heir. Charles returned Edward's greetings
without explicitly acknowledging his title. "We went no further than
this with regard to the young King," he explained to Ambassador van
der Delft, "in order to avoid saying anything which might prejudice
the right that our cousin the Princess might advance to the throne."[1]

Similarly, Charles's sister, Mary of Hungary, regent of the Netherlands, wrote to van der Delft, "We make no mention at present of the
young prince, as we are ignorant as yet whether or not he will be rec-
ognised as King. . . . We likewise refrain from sending you any letters
for our cousin, the Princess Mary, as we do not yet know how she will
be treated."[2] Meanwhile, the French, always keen to drive a wedge
between English and imperial interests, claimed that the emperor
planned to make war on the English in support of Mary's claim.[3] As it
was, Mary accepted her brother as Henry's rightful heir and made no
challenge.

In his will, Henry had confirmed Mary in her right to the succession and granted her and Elizabeth a yearly income of £3,000 "in
money, plate, jewels and household stuff" and, upon their marriage, a
dowry of £10,000 each. But amid the general sharing of lands, titles,
and estates among the regency councillors, aimed at securing their support for the new regime, Mary received a much more generous provision. She was granted lands and estates in East Anglia and the Home
Counties valued at £3,819 18s. 6d.[4] Most of her endowment consisted of
properties in Norfolk, Suffolk, and Essex, including Hunsdon and

Beaulieu (New Hall), where she had spent much of her time, and Kenninghall in Norfolk, the home of the Catholic Thomas Howard, duke of Norfolk, before his attainder on the eve of Henry's death. In all, Mary received thirty-two principal manors and a number of minor ones, which were later exchanged for Framlingham Castle in Suffolk.

Now thirty-one, Mary was one of the wealthiest peers in England and a significant regional magnate. She could choose her own household personnel and surrounded herself with Catholic men local to her estates, such as Sir Francis Englefield, Sir Robert Rochester, and Rochester's nephew Edward Waldegrave, who shared her commitment to the faith. Many of the women she chose, such as Jane Dormer, Eleanor Kempe, and Susan Clarencius, had been in her service and would remain with her for many years. Mary's household would become a bastion of Catholic loyalty. Ordinances were drawn up at Kenninghall providing for religious services. Particular importance was attached to the observance—by all her servants—of Matins, Mass, and Evensong. "Every gentleman, yeoman and groom not having reasonable impediment" was to be at the services every day.[5] To be in Mary's service was to live as a Catholic. Service and sanctity were inextricably bound together.

IN APRIL 1547, Mary left Katherine Parr, with whom she had remained since her father's death, and journeyed north to her new estates. Within weeks, Katherine had rekindled her relationship with her old love Thomas, Lord Seymour of Sudeley, and in May they were secretly married. Seymour sought to win Mary's approval, but she responded with thinly veiled disapproval, declaring that "being a maid," she was "nothing cunning" about "wooing matters." Henry was "as yet very ripe in her own remembrance," and she found it "strange news": "it standeth lest with my poor honour to be a meddler in this matter, considering whose wife her grace was of late."[6]

Initially relations between Mary and the Edwardian regime were distinctly amicable. The lord protector, Somerset, had previously been in the service of the emperor at the imperial court, and Anne, duchess of Somerset, formerly in the household of Katherine of Aragon.[7] Mary addressed her as "my good gossip" and "my good nann" and signed off a letter to her "your assured friend to my power, Mary."[8] As Christmas approached, Edward wrote to Mary, inviting her to spend the festive period with him and Elizabeth at court:

> *Right dear and right entirely beloved sister,*
>
> *We greet you well. And whereas our right dear and right entirely beloved sister, the Lady Elizabeth, having made suit to visit us, hath sithence [since] her coming desired to remain with us during all this Christmas Holydays, like as we cannot but take this her request in thankful part, so would we be glad, and should think us very well accompanied, if we might have you also with us at the same time.*

However, Edward concluded with the suggestion that if Mary's health was not good, she might postpone her visit to another occasion "when both the Time and your Health shall better suffer."[9]

ALTHOUGH THE NEW evangelical establishment was determined to overturn Henry's Act of Six Articles, at first it proceeded cautiously. Negotiations for peace with France had ended with the French king's death at the end of March, and in April Charles had defeated the German Protestants at Mühlberg. England was diplomatically isolated; it was not a good time to champion religious reform. But such prudence was short-lived, and the government was keen to press ahead with the process of reformation.

On July 31, 1547, new Church "Injunctions" were issued in the king's name and a general visitation ordered for the whole Church. Though the wording on the Mass was cautious and conservative—"of the very body and blood of Christ"—it was ordered that "abused" images be destroyed, processions abolished, the ringing of bells and use of rosary beds condemned, and the lighting of candles on the altar forbidden.[10] The same year *The Book of Homilies,* which set out the Lutheran doctrine of justification by faith alone, was written by Cranmer and issued to be read in all churches. A translation of Erasmus's *Paraphrases* on the Gospels—which Mary had had a role in translating under the sponsorship of Katherine Parr—was also to be placed in every church. Within three months, each parish was to possess the Bible in English. Sermons were to be preached regularly and priests instructed to recite the Lord's Prayer, creed, and Ten Commandments in English. When Bishops Edmund Bonner and Gardiner protested against the Injunctions, they were imprisoned. It was the prelude to further change. In Edward's first Parliament, which opened on November 4, 1547, the Act of Six Articles and Treasons Act were repealed. Marriage was made legal for the clergy, and the laity were to receive Communion in both kinds.

As the practices of the "old religion" came under attack, Mary made her Catholic devotion stridently clear, hearing up to four Masses every day in her chapel at Kenninghall.[11] In a dispatch of October 4, 1548, Jehan Dubois, the imperial secretary, described how Mary had just returned from Norfolk, where she had inspected her estates "and was much welcomed in the north country and wherever she had the power to do it she had Mass celebrated."[12] Mary wrote to Somerset, protesting at the "fantasy and new fangleness" and declaring that the Henrican religion had been established by parliamentary statute and it was illegal to defy it. Her father, she claimed, had left the realm in "Godly order and Quietness," which the Council was now disrupting with innovations.[13] No change should be made to the religious settlement imposed by the Act of Six Articles until the king came of age and was old enough to make his own decisions about religion. Somerset professed astonishment at Mary's attitude, believing that her words could not have "proceeded from the sincere mind of so virtuous and wise a lady, but rather by the setting on and procurement of some uncharitable and malicious persons." Henry had, Somerset continued, died before he had achieved all that "he purposed to have done" in religion.[14]

AS THE ACT OF Uniformity made its way through Parliament in January 1549, making the Book of Common Prayer the only legal form of worship, confrontation between Mary and the Edwardian government seemed inevitable. While maintaining doctrinal conservatism, the book represented a significant break with the past. The number of saints' days was reduced; only plain vestments were to be worn by the priest; and the Latin Mass was to be said in English and was now described ambiguously as "the supper of the Lord and the holy communion commonly called the mass."[15] The Elevation of the Host was abolished and the Catholic doctrine of the sacrifice of the Mass omitted.

When van der Delft visited Mary in late March, she complained bitterly of the changes brought about in the kingdom and of her private distress, saying she would rather give up her life than her religion. Once again she looked to the emperor for protection against the law that was shortly to come into effect. She explained how "in these miserable times," Charles was her "only refuge."[16]

Days later Mary addressed a letter directly to the emperor:

We have never been in so great necessity and I therefore entreat your Majesty, considering the changes that are taking place in the kingdom, to provide, as your affairs may best permit, that I may continue to live in the ancient faith and in peace with my conscience.

She feared that, except by way of his Majesty, the emperor, she would "not be permitted to do so, judging by what has been settled in Parliament," and she reaffirmed her commitment "that in life and death I will not forsake the Catholic religion of the Church our mother."[17]

Charles was determined that he would "suffer no pressure to be put upon her [Mary], our close relative, or allow religious innovations to cause them to assume a different and less suitable manner towards her."[18] He ordered his ambassador to obtain a written assurance,

in definite, suitable and permanent form, that notwithstanding all new laws and ordinances made upon religion, she may live in the observance of our ancient religion as she has done up to the present, so that neither the King nor Parliament may ever molest her, directly or indirectly by any means whatever.[19]

His dispatch to his ambassador on June 8 underlined his position:

With regard to the Princess our cousin, the Protector and all other worthy people must understand that, her near kinship to us and close affinity, the perfect friendship we have always felt and feel for her, make it impossible that we should ever desist from our endeavours to save her from molestation in the free practice and observance of her faith . . . the Protector's answer that the Princess must obey the laws of the realm, is too bare and harsh to our cousin, the King's own sister . . . neither we nor our brother, the King of the Romans, nor any of the relatives of the Princess could tolerate such attempts, as the Protector might well suppose.[20]

Under instruction from the emperor, van der Delft went to Somerset to try to get a guarantee of Mary's freedom of worship. Somerset made it clear that "it was not in his power to act against the laws passed by Parliament" and that the ambassador had "asked for something dangerous to the kingdom":

If the King and his sister, to whom the whole kingdom was attached as heiress to the crown in the event of the King's death, were to differ in matters of religion, dissension would certainly spring up. Such was the character of the nation . . . he [Somerset] hoped the Lady Mary would use her wisdom and conform with the King to avoid such an emergency and keep peace within the realm.[21]

Keen to preserve his good relationship with the emperor, Somerset was conciliatory. Though he could not act against statute and would not grant a formal dispensation for Mary to be immune from the laws, he made it clear that he had no intention of inquiring into the worship of her household until the king came of age.[22] Many on the Privy Council, however, disagreed, and they demanded that Mary submit to the law.

CHAPTER 28

ADVICE TO BE CONFORMABLE

∴

ON JUNE 9, 1549, THE DAY THE FIRST ENGLISH PRAYER BOOK became law, Mary celebrated Latin Mass in her chapel at Kenninghall amid incense, candles, and the chiming of bells. In doing so she publicly signaled her opposition to the religious changes and defied Edward's authority as king. The Privy Council responded swiftly. In a letter dated June 16, Mary was given "advice to be conformable and obedient" to the law: Mass was no longer to be celebrated in her house. Her comptroller, Robert Rochester, and her chaplain, Dr. John Hopton, were summoned to court to receive further instructions.[1]

A week later, addressing Somerset and the rest of Edward's Council, Mary responded directly to their charges:

> My Lorde, I perceive by the letters which I late received from you, and all of the king's Majesty's council that you be all sorry to find so little conformity in me touching the observation of his Majesty's laws; who am well assured that I have offended no law, unless it be a late law of your own making, for the altering of matters in religion which in my conscience, is not worthy to have the name of a law, both for the King's honour's sake, the wealth of the realm . . . and (as my conscience is very well persuaded) the offending of God, which passes all the rest.

She would not change her practices and would obey only her father's laws, and she trusted that the Council would "no more to trouble and unquiet" her with "matters touching her conscience." She excused from obedience the two men whose presence the Council had demanded: Hopton because of his ill health, Rochester because "the chief charge of my house resteth upon his travails."[2] In a subsequent letter to Somerset and the Privy Council, she expressed her anger and disappointment: "For my part I assure you all, that since the King my father, your late master and very good Lord died I never took you for other than my friends; but in this it appeareth co[n]trary."[3]

Days later, Lord Rich, the lord chancellor, and Sir William Petre, the first secretary, were sent to visit Mary at Kenninghall. Their brief was to challenge the points she had made in her previous letter, to induce her to comply with the new regulations, and to make her servants aware of the danger of disobeying the law.[4] In their "Remembrance for certain matters appointed by the Council to be declared to Dr Hopton to the Lady Mary's Grace for Answer to her former letter," the Privy Council rebuffed her objections point by point, yet Mary remained immovable and resistant to any such pressure.[5] She was determined to defend her servants' rights to the free practice of their religion. She described her staff as "worthy people, ready to serve their King after their God to the whole extent of their power"; they were "as her own kin" whom she would stand by. When Rochester and Hopton were instructed that they must persuade their mistress to conform, they explained that they would not and could not. Rochester protested that "it was nowise suitable that a servant should act otherwise than in obedience to his mistress's orders, and discharge of his domestic duties," while Hopton declared that "he was the Lady Mary's servant and obeyed her orders in her own house."[6]

As in years before, Mary gave the emperor a powerful hold over English politics, with the threat of war hanging over the country.[7] Sir William Paget was to be sent to the imperial court to "renew and make fast the amity with the Emperor" and make a formal proposition of marriage for Mary and the Infante Dom Luis of Portugal, the emperor's brother-in-law and a longtime suitor for Mary's hand. Rich and Petre were to ask Mary to draft, in her own hand, a letter of recommendation introducing William Paget to ensure that he gained the emperor's favor. Mary took the opportunity to defend her household. She would write the letter, but if the councillors spoke to her servants as they had threatened, she would add an account to the emperor of how she was being treated in religious matters.[8] The commissioners departed with "soft words having made no declaration or inhibition to her servants."[9]

When Paget arrived at the imperial court in late July, Charles expressed "great astonishment" at the pressure that had been put on Mary to accept the changes in religion. He stressed that, even if she were inclined to accept the reforms, he would do his "utmost to dissuade her, our close relative; for we and those to our blood would grieve exceedingly if she were to change." He repeated his request for an assurance "in writing or otherwise, that she should not be included in the regulations made by Parliament about religion or be kept in suspense on the matter."[10]

THE DAY AFTER the Prayer Book was introduced at Sampford Courtenay in Devon, local villagers petitioned the priest to defy the government. As John Hooker described it in his contemporary account of the rebellion, the priest "yielded to their wills and forthwith ravessheth [clothed] himself in his old popish attire and sayeth mass and all such services as in times past accustomed."[11] The news spread; a considerable force of Cornishmen angry at the religious changes gathered at Clyst St. Mary near Exeter. "We will," the manifesto of the western rebels demanded, "have the mass in Latin, as was before"; "we will have holy bread and holy water made every Sunday, psalms and ashes at the times accustomed, images set up again in every church, and all other ancient, old ceremonies used heretofore by our mother the Holy Church." The rebels insisted that the Act of Six Articles of 1539 be reintroduced until Edward came of age and described the new Prayer Book as a "Christmas game."[12]

There was violence too in Hertfordshire, Essex, Suffolk, and Norfolk, as the rural poor protested against the economic hardships brought about by Somerset's policy of land enclosure. Fences were pulled down and deer killed, and chaos engulfed the countryside. In Norfolk, rebels led by Robert Kett called for all bondmen to be free and emphasized that Thomas Howard, the third Duke of Norfolk, who had been imprisoned in 1547, "had used much more extremity than his Ancestors did towards them." Since many of the rebellions occurred in East Anglia, near Mary's estates, suspicion naturally fell on Mary.

On July 18, the Council warned her that certain of her servants were reported to be "chief in these commotions." One of her staff had been active among the rebels at Sampford Courtenay in Devon, and another, Thomas Poley, was declared to be "a captain of the worst sort assembled in Suffolk."¹³ Men spoke of her complicity and of her plan to overthrow the present rulers of England. In a letter to the secretary of state, William Cecil, Sir Thomas Smith disguised his accusations not only by writing in Latin but also by referring to Mary in the masculine form: "Marius and the Marians; the fear which torments me to the point of destruction."¹⁴

Mary replied immediately, denying all charges made against her. The uprisings, she countered, "no less offend me, than they do you and the rest of the Council." As for her chaplain being at Sampford Courtenay, "I do not a little marvel; for, to my knowledge, I have not one chaplain in those parts." Poley had remained in her household, she claimed, and "was never doer amongst the commons, nor came in their company."¹⁵

IN THE MIDST of rebellion and as the French king declared war, Mary was able to continue to flout the law. As Somerset noted, "whereas she used to have two masses said before, she has three said now since the prohibitions and with greater show."¹⁶ The government needed to maintain the imperial alliance, and it was considered prudent that for now, Mary be left alone to practice her religion. "If she does not wish to conform," Somerset reasoned, "let her do as she pleases quietly and without scandal."¹⁷

Yet as Edward wrote to Mary in August:

> We have somewhat marvelled, and cannot but still marvel very much, what grounds or reasons have or do move you to mislike or refuse to follow and embrace that which, by all the learned men of our realm, hath been so set forth, and of all our loving subjects obediently received; and knowing your good nature and affection towards us, we cannot think any other matter in this your refusal than only a certain grudge of conscience, for

want of good information and conference with some goodly and well learned men for remedy.[18]

Mary would receive corrective instruction. Such men would be chosen and sent to her, after which it was expected that her attitude would improve. Both the king and the lord protector clung to the hope that in time Mary would come to embrace the religious reforms.

Mary's conscience had driven her into a position of direct opposition to the government. The girl who had been broken down and forced to yield her soul and the honor of her mother in fear of her father was now a mature woman of thirty-three. She was a landed magnate with a following of her own and the support of Emperor Charles V. Her brother, the king, was a child. She would not succumb again.

CHAPTER 29

THE MOST UNSTABLE MAN
IN ENGLAND

∴

MATTERS IN THIS REALM ARE RESTLESS FOR CHANGE," VAN der Delft wrote on September 15, 1549. Somerset's handling of the rebellions and the continuing war with France and Scotland had lost him the confidence of the nobility and gentry. "The people are all in confusion, and with one common voice lament the present state of things."[1]

It was the beginning of the end of Somerset's protectorate. Dudley and the conservative nobles, Thomas Wriothesley, earl of Southampton, and Henry FitzAlan, earl of Arundel, were plotting against him and the country was drawing close to civil war. Matters came to a head on Saturday, October 5, when Somerset issued a proclamation commanding men to come to Hampton Court "in most defensible array" with harness and weapons, to defend the king against "a most dangerous conspiracy."[2] Dudley and his supporters immediately took up arms riding through the city, their retinues following behind "attending upon them in new liveries to the great wondering of many."[3] Letters were sent to other members of the nobility across the country, ordering them to ignore Somerset's proclamation and repair to London armed. Somerset moved Edward to Windsor as chaos engulfed the capital. Four days later, faced with overwhelming opposition among the ruling elite, Somerset surrendered. On October 14, he was arrested and sent to the Tower, charged with treason.

Dudley and his allies had asked Mary to support the coup against Somerset, but on the advice of the emperor she had declined to get involved. "As for certain councillors' machinations against the Protector, it does not for the present seem opportune that such an important change take place in England," wrote Charles; "it would be exceedingly hazardous for the Lady Mary to take any share in such proceedings."[4] There now developed a struggle for power on the Council, raising hopes among Mary's Catholic supporters. Van der Delft cautiously rejoiced, for "religion could not be in a worse state, and that therefore a change must be for the better, and that it was not made by the enemies of the old religion."[5] Wriothesley reassured the ambassador that Mary would be allowed to hear Mass, saying "those who have molested her will do so no more, and even though they were to begin afresh she has many good servants of whom I hold myself to be one."[6]

How they were deceived. Dudley emerged as leader of the government and lord president of the Council and, despite earlier indications of conservative sympathies, soon became a supporter of more evangelical reform. Mary was to come under renewed pressure to conform to the new religious practices. By the end of October, a proclamation announced that the government would "further do in all things, as time and opportunity may serve, whatsoever may lend to the glory of God and the advancement of his holy word."[7] When van der Delft visited Mary early the following year, she told him she considered Dudley to be "the most unstable man in England" and that the conspiracy against the protector had "envy and ambition as its motives." She was anxious and fearful of what lay ahead: "You will see that no good will come of this move, but that it is punishment from Heaven, and may be only the beginning of our misfortunes." It was for this reason, she declared, that she wished herself "out of the kingdom."[8]

IN DECEMBER, EDWARD once more invited Mary and Elizabeth to spend Christmas at court. He wanted all three siblings to be together for the festivities, but Mary suspected a trap.

They wished me to be at court so that I could not get the mass celebrated for me and that the King might take me with him to hear their sermons. I would not find myself in such a place for anything in the world. I will choose a more convenient time to go and pay my duty to the King, when I need not lodge at court, for I have my own establishment in London. I shall stay for four or five days only, and avoid entering into argument with the King my brother who, as I hear, is beginning to debate the question of religion . . . as he is being taught to do.[9]

Mary made her excuses on the ground of ill health. It was a wise decision. On Christmas Day, the king and Council, heavily influenced by Dudley, publicly pledged to further the reformation. In a letter written in the king's name to the bishops, Dudley challenged those "evil disposed persons" who, since the "apprehension" of the duke of Somerset, "have bruited abroad that they should have again their old Latin services, their conjured bread and water, with such like vain and superstitious ceremonies, as if the setting forth of the said book had been the act of the Duke only." The bishops were commanded to order the clergy to gather up all service books besides the Book of Common Prayer and to "deface or destroy them," and send to prison anyone who refused to obey. Further, "excommunication or other censures of the Church" were to be imposed on any layman who refused the new Communion service.[10] By late January, pressure was mounting on Mary once more. England had signed a peace treaty with France, at the cost of Boulogne, and the necessity to appease Charles V receded.

Yet Mary continued to say Mass and keep a strict Catholic household, its daily routine based around the Mass. As van der Delft described the situation following a visit to Kenninghall:

It is a pleasure to see how well kept and well ordered is her household in the observance of our ancient religion. Her servants are well to do people and some of them men of means and noblemen too whose boast is to be reputed her servants, and by these means they continue to practise the said religion and hear God's service . . . six chaplains . . . say mass in her presence every day.

Mary was now "more than ever afraid that the Council would attempt to disturb her."[11] She wrote to Charles, declaring that she trusted in his goodness and regarded him as her father in "spiritual and temporal matters." She then asked him what she must do: "Our kingdom is daily approaching nearer to spiritual and material ruin, and matters grow worse day by day."[12] She had heard that her household servants would in future be excluded from all Catholic services held under her roof, and soon she would be ordered to conform to the Act of Uniformity. The emperor again demanded an assurance from England that his cousin "should be permitted to continue in her observance of the ancient religion, and in the enjoyment of the same liberty that had been hers at the time of the death of the late king her father."[13]

Mary now waited for the ax to fall, "being neither summoned nor visited by the Council." Meanwhile, Elizabeth, who had conformed to the statutes, remained in high favor. As van der Delft observed, "It seems that they have a higher opinion of her for conforming with the others and observing the new decrees, than of the Lady Mary who remains constant in the Catholic faith."[14]

CHAPTER 30

WHAT SAY YOU, MR AMBASSADOR?

∴

They are wicked and wily in their actions, and
particularly malevolent towards me, I must not wait
till the blow falls.[1]

—MARY TO VAN DER DELFT,
MAY 2, 1550

AT THE END OF APRIL 1550, MARY SUMMONED VAN DER DELFT TO
her residence at Woodham Walter Manor, near Maldon in Essex.
She was in despair and had resolved to leave the country. "If my
brother were to die," she told the ambassador, "I would be far better out of the kingdom, because as soon as he were dead, before the
people knew it, they would despatch me too." She feared what was to
come:

> When they send me orders forbidding me the mass, I shall
> expect to suffer as I suffered once during my father's lifetime;
> they will order me to withdraw thirty miles from any navigable
> river or sea-port, and will deprive me of my confidential ser-
> vants, and having reduced me to the utmost destitution, they
> will deal with me as they please. But I will rather suffer death
> than stain my conscience. . . . I am like a little ignorant girl, and
> I care neither for my goods nor for the world, but only for
> God's service and my conscience. I know not what to say; but if
> there is peril in going and peril in staying, I must choose the
> lesser of two evils. . . . I would willingly stay were I able to live

and serve God as I have done in the past; which is what I have always said. But these men are so changeable that I know not what to say. What say you, Mr Ambassador?[2]

Mary, then thirty-four, had been contemplating escape for some time. In September the previous year, before Somerset's fall, she had sent the emperor a ring and a message that she wished to flee England and seek refuge with him.[3] Charles had responded cautiously, declaring it a matter in which Mary "should not be encouraged" because of the difficulties of getting her out of the realm and the cost of supporting her at the imperial court.[4] Now, faced with her continued persecution and her ever-shriller protests, Charles cautiously agreed to support her in her wish, "for we have the best of reasons and have done all we could do to protect our cousin's person and conscience." He had held back as long as possible from "this extreme measure" but agreed it had "now become imperative to resort to because of the attitude adopted in England."[5]

It was arranged that Mary's escape should coincide with a change of imperial ambassador in mid-May. Van der Delft had been in England for six years, and his recall would not cause suspicion. Once he had formally taken leave, his ship would be diverted to waters off the Essex coast for long enough to meet a boat bringing Mary from Maldon. But with the plan set, fear of renewed popular unrest led to extra watches being placed on the roads near Woodham Walter. There was no chance of her passing unrecognized; another scheme had to be devised.[6]

On the evening of Monday, June 30, 1550, three imperial warships arrived off the coast near Maldon under the command of a Dutchman, Cornelius Scepperus, admiral of the imperial fleet. The next day, Jehan Dubois, secretary to the imperial embassy in London, rowed ashore disguised as a grain merchant. The plan, devised over the previous months, would see Mary escape under cover of darkness from Woodham Walter to the sea two miles away. She would then be rowed out to the waiting ships and taken to the Low Countries and the court of Charles's sister, the regent Mary of Hungary.

In the early hours of July 2, Dubois arrived in Maldon, but there was no one to meet him. He sent an urgent, detailed dispatch to Robert Rochester, one of Mary's senior household officers:

> Sir . . . I arrived here this morning in a six-oared boat. Yesterday I sent my brother, Peter Marchant, to announce in this town that we had brought the corn, and were coming with the next tide; and this I did in order that you might the sooner be advised of my arrival. However, as far as I know, there was nobody there to take the corn or receive the said Peter. Therefore I am obliged to write now to point out to you that there is danger in delay, especially as M. Scepperus is now coming to Stansgate with a warship, and near Harwich there are three other ships waiting and moreover four larger ships are out to sea. Consider therefore whether we must not hurry. There is yet another reason as well: the water will not be as high tomorrow night as tonight, and will be lower every night until next moon, and we now have the advantage that the tide serves our purpose late at night and towards morning, that is, about two o'clock. By that hour or immediately afterwards all ought to be here, so that we may be on our way while the tide is still rising . . . I will sell my corn at once, and be ready tonight. Please let me know your intentions. . . . I must add that I see no better opportunity than the present one; and this undertaking is passing through so many hands that it is daily becoming more difficult, and I fear it may not remain secret. However I will yield to a better opinion, and I pray God to inspire you now; for the Emperor has done all he could.

Hours later, Dubois and Rochester met on the pretext of trading grain. Though Dubois expected them to confirm the final details of the plan, Rochester called the whole scheme into question. He said he thought Mary's imminent flight was unnecessary, as she would be "in no way molested before the end of the Parliament that was to meet the following Michaelmas at the earliest," at which point she would have the advantage of being at her house at St. Osyth, also in Essex, which had a garden from which it was easy to reach the open sea. It was, he argued, simply too dangerous for Mary to attempt her escape with a watch posted on every road near Maldon. "If you understand me," Rochester explained, "what I say is not that my Lady does not wish to go, but that she wishes to go if she can." Dubois demanded clarification. "The thing was now a question of Yes or No." A decision had to be made. The men of Harwich had seen their ships, and it would not be long before the Council was informed of their presence.

That evening Dubois rode in secret to visit Mary. Rochester voiced his concerns again, and the imperial secretary grew frustrated. "The whole business was so near being discovered that it was most improbable that it could be kept secret." Rochester replied, "For the love of God, do not say that to my Lady! She is a good woman and really wants to go; but neither she nor you see what I see and know. Great danger threatens us!" As Mary stowed her possessions into hop sacks, she expressed fear as to "how the Emperor would take it if it turned out to be impossible to go now." She would not be ready until the day after next. On Friday morning, just after the watch retired, she would leave her house on the pretext of going "to amuse herself and purge her stomach by the sea."

As the plan was agreed, word came that the bailiffs of Maldon wished to impound Dubois's boat on suspicion that it was associated with the warship at Stansgate. According to Dubois, Mary started to panic, asking "What shall we do? What shall become of me?" She feared "how the Emperor would take it if it turned out impossible to go now, after I have so often importuned his Majesty on the subject." Dubois urged that they should take Mary immediately, but Rochester declared that it would be impossible: the watch was going to be doubled that night and men would be posted on the church tower. At this point Mary became hysterical, repeatedly shrieking "But what is to become of me?" It was decided that Rochester would contact her again within ten or twelve days with an exact date when they would be ready to put the plan into action. But no further attempt was made. Dubois suspected "that the Comptroller had made out the situation at Maldon to be more dangerous than it was in reality."[7]

To have fled would have been to gamble. If Edward died when Mary was abroad, she would have no hope of succeeding. If she stayed, she might be deprived of her household and be left to face dangers alone. There was both "peril in going and peril in staying." Having set the plan into motion, Mary procrastinated, then changed her mind. She accepted that to win her rightful throne and restore Catholicism, she needed to be in England. She resolved to stay and fight.

CHAPTER 31

AN UNNATURAL EXAMPLE

∴

The Lady Mary sent one of her servants to me today to tell me that a publication was recently made in that part of the country where she lives, forbidding, as she hears, chaplains or others to say mass or officiate at all in her house according to the rites of the ancient religion, under certain heavy penalties both civil and criminal. She requested therefore that I should remonstrate with the Council on the first opportunity and declare that she demanded and would persist in her demand to live according to the ancient religion, in virtue of what had passed in this matter. She requested me also to inform your Majesty and the Queen [Dowager of Hungary].[1]

—AMBASSADOR JEHAN SCHEYFVE TO
THE EMPEROR, JULY 26, 1550

WITH THE ESCAPE PLAN ABORTED, MARY PREPARED TO LEAVE Woodham Walter and sent her chaplain, Francis Mallet, ahead to Beaulieu to arrange Mass for her arrival. When Mary was delayed, Mallet performed the service anyway with many of her household servants in attendance. The incident gave the Council the pretext it had been looking for. Orders were dispatched for Mallet's arrest, and Mary was summoned to court. Again she refused to attend, claiming ill health—"being the fall of the leaf"—and petitioned the Council to rethink the enforcement of the statutes.[2] The Council responded that the dispensation regarding Mary's freedom of worship had been made to the imperial ambassador

for his sake and for your own also, that it should be suffered and
winked at, if you had the private mass used in your own closet
for a season, until you might be better informed, whereof there
was some hope, having only with you a few of your Chamber,
so that for all the rest of your household the service of the realm
should be used, and none other. Further than this the promise
exceeded not.[3]

Mary made a fresh appeal to the emperor, who instructed Scheyfve
to secure unconditional assurances. As he added in his dispatch, "You
will persist in your request at all costs. Give them plainly to understand
that if they decide otherwise, we will not take it in good part, or suffer
it to be done."[4]

BY CHRISTMAS, MARY had run out of excuses to avoid attending
court and all three Tudor siblings gathered for the reunion, postponed
from the previous year. Edward, now twelve, rebuked Mary for hearing Mass in the chapel. She continued to argue that he was not yet old
enough to make up his own mind about religion. He demanded her
obedience, she resisted, and both were reduced to tears. Writing later
to the Privy Council, she blamed its members for turning her brother
against her:

When I perceived how the King, whom I love and honour above
all things, as by nature and duty bound, had counselled against
me, I could not contain myself and exhibited my interior
grief. . . . I would rather refuse the friendship of all the world
(whereunto I trust I shall never be driven), than forsake any
point of my faith.[5]

But though Edward protested that he thought "no harm of her," he
remained determined that she submit. He would "inquire and know all
things." On January 17, 1551, Mary received letters from the Privy
Council ordering that Mass must no longer be heard in her household.
While claiming her "general health and the attack of catarrh in the
head" did not permit her to answer their points "in detail, sentence by

sentence," she vehemently disputed the assertion that no promise had been made to Charles V as to the practice of the Mass:

> God knows the contrary to be true: and you in your own consciences (I say to those who were then present) know it also . . . you accuse me of breaking the laws and disobeying them by keeping to my own religion; but I reply that my faith and my religion are those held by the whole of Christendom, formerly confessed by this kingdom under the late King, my father, until you altered them with your laws. To the King's majesty, my brother, I wish prosperity and honour such as no King ever enjoyed . . . but to you, my lords, I owe nothing beyond amity and goodwill. . . . Take this as my final answer to any letters you might write to me on matters of religion.

Once again she emphasized her poor health in an attempt to bring the confrontation with the king to an end: "were you to know what pain I suffer in bending down my head to write," she said, he would "not wish to give me occasion to do it. My health is more unstable than that of any creature and I have all the greater need to rejoice in the testimony of pure conscience."[6]

A week later Edward wrote, advising Mary that he would see that his laws were obeyed:

> *Dear and well-beloved sister,*
>
> *We have seen the letters recently sent to you by our*
> *Council, together with your answer thereto, concerning the*
> *matter of certain chaplains of your household, who have committed a*
> *breach of our laws by singing mass. We have heard their*
> *good and suitable admonitions, and your fruitless and wayward*
> *misunderstanding of the same. We are moved to write to you*
> *these presents, that where the good counsel of our Councillors have*
> *failed to persuade, the same advice given by us may haply produce*
> *some effect. After giving all due consideration to the matter, it*
> *appears to us to stand as follows: that you, our nearest sister, in*
> *whom by nature we should place reliance and our highest esteem,*
> *wish to break our laws and set them aside deliberately and of your*

own free will; and moreover sustain and encourage others to commit a
like offence. . . .

   . . . it appears by your letters that you have persuaded yourself
that you may continue in your erring ways in virtue of a promise
which you claim to have received, though we truly know that the said
promise was not given with the intention you Lend to it. My sister,
you must learn that your courses were tolerated when our laws were
first promulgated, not indeed as a permission to break the same, but
so that you might be inclined to obey them, seeing the love and
indulgence we displayed towards you. We made a difference between
you and our subjects, not that all should follow our ordinances, and
you alone disregard them, but in order that you should do out of love
for us what the rest do out of duty. The error in which you persist is
twofold, and each part of it so great that for the love we bear to God
we cannot suffer it, but you must strive to remedy it; nor can we do
otherwise than desire you to amend your ways, for the affection we
bear you . . . knowledge was offered to you, and you refused it.

Mary would be permitted to "speak frankly" and would be listened
to, provided she agreed to abide by Edward's response. As for the second part of her offense—"the transgression of our laws"—Edward
made it clear that he would not tolerate the abuse of his office as king:

We have suffered it until now, with the hope that some improvement
might be forthcoming, but none has been shown, how can we suffer it
longer to continue? . . . Your near relationship to us, your exalted
rank, the condition of the times, all magnify your offence. It is a
scandalous thing that so high a personage should deny our
sovereignty; that our sister should be less to us than any of our other
subjects is an unnatural example; and finally, in a troubled republic,
it lends colour to faction among the people.

He summed up his position in a postscript written in his own hand:
"Sister, consider that an exception has been made in your favour this
long time past, to incline you to obey and not to harden you in your
resistance." He could not "say more and worse things because my duty
would compel me to use harsher and angrier words. But this I will say

with certain intention, that I will see my laws strictly obeyed, and those who break them shall be watched and denounced."[7]

Mary was stunned. Replying two days later, she declared that his words, accusing her of being "a breaker of your laws" and "inciting others to do the same," had caused her "more suffering than any illness even unto death." She had been promised free expression of her faith and implored him to command his ambassador in Brussels to learn from the emperor "the truth concerning the said promise" so that he could see that she was guilty of no offense. She beseeched him "for the love of God to suffer me to live as in the past" and reiterated that rather than offend him and her conscience she would "lose all that I have left in the world, and my life too."[8]

The same day Mary sent another hastily written letter to Francesco Moronelli, a former servant of van der Delft, who had traveled in secret to meet her at Beaulieu months before. At the time she had made him promise that if she were ever in trouble he would travel to Flanders to tell the emperor's ministers that help was urgently needed. That moment had now arrived.

> *Francisco, you must make great haste concerning the message,*
> *for since your departure I have received worse and more dangerous*
> *letters than ever before from the King himself, written in haste*
> *the 3rd of February.*
> *[Postscript]: I request and command you to burn this note directly*
> *after you have read it.*[9]

Charles again made representations to the Privy Council through Scheyfve, but Edward remained firm. In March, to affirm his determination, he summoned Mary to court. No further disobedience would be tolerated.[10]

CHAPTER 32

NAUGHTY OPINION

∴

O N MARCH 15, 1551, MARY ARRIVED IN LONDON, RIDING TO HER house at St. John's, Clerkenwell. Fifty knights and gentlemen in velvet coats and chains of gold rode before her; some four hundred gentlemen and ladies followed behind. As Henry Machyn the London diarist recorded, each carried a "pair of beads of black"—a rosary. It was a dramatic display of Catholic defiance and the scale of Mary's power and support.[1] By the time she reached the gates of the city, there were more than four hundred people in her train. It was, in Machyn's assessment, the greatest demonstration of loyalty in living memory: "The people ran five or six miles out of town and were marvellously overjoyed to see her, showing clearly how much they love her."[2]

The following day, Mary was met unceremoniously at the court gate at Whitehall and led into the Presence Chamber, where the young king and his Council waited to receive her. She was charged with disobedience and ordered to obey. In his journal, Edward described the meeting:

> The Lady Mary my sister came to me at Westminster, where after salutations she was called with my Council into a chamber, where was declared how long I had suffered her Mass [against my will; *crossed out*], in hope of her reconciliation and how now, being no hope, which I perceived by her letters, except I saw some short amendment, I could not bear it. She answered that her soul was God['s], and her faith she would not change, nor dissemble her opinion with contrary doings. It was said I constrained not her faith, but willed her [not as a King to rule;

inserted] but as a subject to obey. And that her example might breed too much inconvenience.[3]

When Edward warned her of the dangers of continuing to practice the old religion, Mary put it to him again that he was not yet old enough to be making decisions, assuring him "Riper age and experience will teach Your Majesty much more yet." This time Edward snapped back, "You also may have somewhat to learn. None are too old for that." Mary reasoned that even if there had been no assurance to hear Mass, she hoped that, as her brother, he "would have shown her enough respect to allow her to continue in the observance of the old religion, and to prevent her from being troubled in any way." Did he want "to take away her life rather than the old religion, in which she desired to live and die?" Edward responded that "he wished for no such sacrifice."

The meeting broke up unresolved. Mary left beseeching Edward not to listen to those who spoke ill of her, "whether about religion or anything else," and assuring him that he would always find her his obedient sister, something, Edward replied, "he had never doubted."[4]

Soon after Mary's visit to court, two prominent Catholics, Sir Richard Morgan and Sir Clement Smith, were summoned before the Council, accused of having heard Mass two or three days earlier in the princess's house at St. John's, Clerkenwell.[5] Days later, Sir Anthony Browne was questioned about the same offense and admitted that he had heard Mass "twice or thrice at the New Hall, and Romford, as my Lady Mary was coming hither about ten days past, he had heard mass."[6] All three men were imprisoned in Fleet Prison on Farringdon Street.[7] Some weeks later Francis Mallet, Mary's principal chaplain and almoner, was arrested. He was condemned for reoffending and for persuading others to embrace his "naughty opinion" and imprisoned in the Tower.[8]

Mary immediately wrote to the Council, claiming that "he [Mallet] did it by my commandment . . . none of my chaplains should be in danger of the law for saying mass in my house" and asking them to "set him at liberty."[9] The Council rejected her appeal: "To relieve him would take the fault upon yourself; we are sorry to perceive your grace so ready to be a defence to one that the King's law doth condemn."[10]

❧

ON MARCH 19, Charles V threatened war if Mary were not given freedom of worship. Edward noted the event in his journal: "The Emperor's ambassador came with a short message from his master, of war if I would not suffer his cousin, the princess, to use her mass. To this no answer was given at this time."[11]

Meanwhile, a diplomatic row broke out at the imperial court in Brussels between Charles and the resident English ambassador, Sir Richard Morison, an outspoken evangelical, who argued on behalf of the English government that envoys to Brussels should have the right to exercise their evangelical beliefs. With Jehan Scheyfve continuing to assert that a promise had been made that Mary "might freely retain the ancient religion in such sort as her father left it in this realm . . . until the King should be of more years,"[12] diplomatic relations reached a crisis point. Edward insisted that he would not give way on a matter "that touched his honour as head of the family." He would "spend his life, and all he had, rather than agree and grant to what he knew certainly to be against the truth."[13] The bishops Thomas Cranmer, Nicholas Ridley, and John Ponet instead advised the king that "to give licence to sin was to sin; to suffer and wink at it for a time might be borne." The Council now feared that the emperor might take action as he had threatened and that the whole realm might be in peril. They persuaded Edward to send Nicholas Wotton, dean of Canterbury, to the imperial court to try to reason with the emperor. He was instructed to make it clear that no assurance or promise had ever been made by the king regarding Mary's right to hear Mass but that he was only "to spare the execution of the laws for a time, until he saw some proof of her amendment."

As pressure came to bear on Mary once more, the emperor challenged Wotton:

> Ought it not to suffice you that ye spill your own souls, but that ye have a mind to force others to lose theirs too? My cousin, the Princess, is evil handled among you; her servants plucked from her, and she still cried to leave Mass, to forsake her religion in which her mother, her grandmother, and all her family, have lived and died. I will not suffer it.

Wotton replied that Mary had been well treated when he left England and he had heard of no change, but the emperor insisted:

Yes by St. Mary . . . of late they handle her evil and therefore say you hardly to them, I will not suffer her to be evil handled by them. I will not suffer it. Is it not enough that mine aunt, her mother, was evil entreated by the King that dead is, but my cousin must be worse ordered by councillors now.

Though Mary had "a King to her father, and hath a King to her brother, she is only a subject and must obey the law," Wotton countered. "A gentle law I tell you!" snorted the emperor. Wotton then asked if Sir Thomas Chamberlain, English ambassador to Mary of Hungary, might be permitted to have the service of the Book of Common Prayer in his house, at which Charles exploded, "English service in Flanders! Speak not of it. I will suffer none to use any doctrine or service in Flanders that is not allowed of the Church." He ended the audience by saying that if Mary were not allowed her Mass, he would provide her with a remedy. And as Charles made clear: "We would rather she had died ten years ago than see her waver now; but we believe her to be so constant that she would prefer a thousand deaths rather than renounce her faith. If death were to undertake her for this cause, she would be the first martyr of royal blood to die for our holy faith, and for this earn glory in the better life."[4] The emperor had raised the prospect that Mary might be sacrificed as a Catholic martyr.

CHAPTER 33

MATTERS TOUCHING MY SOUL

∴

O N SUNDAY, AUGUST 9, 1551, TWENTY-FOUR LORDS OF THE PRIVY Council met at Richmond, as Edward noted in his journal, to "commune of my sister Mary's matter." It was agreed that "it was not mete to be suffered any longer." In July a new Anglo-French alliance had been concluded, with Edward betrothed to Henry II's daughter Elizabeth. Dudley now felt confident to confront the issue of Mary's disobedience.[1] Mary's senior household officers, Robert Rochester, Francis Englefield, and Edward Waldegrave, were all summoned before the Council at Hampton Court to receive instructions ordering the princess to conform.[2] Upon their return to Mary's residence, Copped Hall, near Epping in Essex, on Saturday the fifteenth, Mary forbade them to speak with her chaplains or her household and required them to return to London with a personal letter to the king:

> I have by my servants received your most honourable letter, the contents whereof do not a little trouble me, and so much the more for that any of my said servants should move or attempt me in matters touching my soul. . . . Having for my part utterly refused heretofore to talk with them in such matters, trusted that your Majesty would have suffered me, your poor humble sister . . . to have used the accustomed Mass, which the King your father and mine, with all his predecessors did evermore use; wherein also I have been brought up from my youth, and thereunto my conscience doth not only bind me, which by no means will suffer me to think one thing and do another, but also the promise made to the Emperor, by your Majesty's Council, was

an assurance to me that in so doing I should not offend the laws, although they seem now to qualify and deny the thing.

Mary maintained that although the letter was signed by Edward's hand, it was "nevertheless in my opinion not your Majesty's in effect," and she restated her belief that "it is not possible that your Highness can at these years be a judge in matters of religion." She petitioned him "to bear with me as you have done, and not to think that by my doings or example any inconvenience might grow to your Majesty or your realm . . . rather than to offend God and my conscience, I offer my body at your will, and death shall be more welcome than life with a troubled conscience."[3] When the household officers arrived back in London, they were each commanded separately to return to Mary and do what had been asked of them. They all refused, Rochester and Waldegrave saying that they would rather endure any punishment and Sir Francis Englefield declaring that he could find it "neither in his heart nor his conscience to do it."[4]

ON AUGUST 28, the lord chancellor, Lord Rich; Sir Anthony Wingfield, comptroller of the king's household; and Sir William Petre were sent to Mary at Copped Hall with instructions from the king:

> His Majesty did resolutely determine it just, necessary and expedient that her Grace should not any ways use or maintain the private mass or any other manner of service than such as by the law of the realm is authorised or allowed.[5]

Mary treated their authority with contempt. She would hear no service than that left by her father, though when the king came of age and maturity of judgment he would find her conforming to his laws. Her chaplains might do as they wish, but if they read the new service she would leave her own house. Again Mary stated that she was prepared to die for her faith:

> First she protested that to the King's Majesty she was, is and ever will be his Majesty's most humble and most obedient

subject and poor sister, and would most willingly obey all his commandments in any thing (her conscience saved); yea, and would willingly and gladly suffer death to do his Majesty good, but rather than she will agree to use any other service than was used at the death of the late King her father, she would lay her head on a block and suffer death.[6]

Mary lamented, "You give me fair words, but your deeds will always be ill towards me."

The commissioners then called the chaplains and the rest of the household and gave them "straight commandment upon pain of their allegiance, that neither the priests should from henceforth say any Mass or other Divine Service than that which is set forth by the laws of the realm." As their subsequent report to the Council stated, "Her chaplains, after some talk, promised to obey all the King's Majesty's commandment signified by us." As the men were leaving, Mary called out that she needed her comptroller, Robert Rochester, to be returned to her, adding that since his departure "I take the account myself of my expenses, and how many loaves of bread be made a bushel of wheat . . . my father and mother never brought me [up] with baking and brewing, and to be plain with you I am weary of mine office, and therefore, if my Lords will send my officer home they shall do me pleasure."[7] But the Council ignored Mary's plea and sent Englefield, Waldegrave, and Rochester first to the Fleet and then to the Tower.

With the situation at a deadlock, security around the princess was tightened. Edward recorded in his journal that "pinnaces were prepared to see that there should be no conveyance overseas of the Lady Mary, secretly done." Meanwhile, the lord chancellor, the lord chamberlain, the vice chamberlain, and Secretary Petre "should see by all means they could whether she used the mass, and if she did that the laws should be executed on her chaplains."[8]

IN OCTOBER 1551, Henry II of France declared war on Charles V with the intention of recapturing Italy and securing European supremacy. The renewal of Habsburg-Valois hostilities brought an increased fear of imperial intervention in England. Mary of Hungary,

Charles's sister, was certain that England would join France in the war and so proposed an invasion of England to gain a strong port from which to defend the Netherlands and to place Mary on the throne.[9]

With her fortune ever tied to events in Europe, pressure eased on Mary. When Mary of Guise, the dowager queen of Scotland, visited Edward for several days in October, Mary was invited to court "to accompany and entertain" her, while Edward sent his own message, that he would enjoy the pleasure of Mary's company. Once again Mary pleaded ill health to avoid being put under religious pressure by her brother.[10] Over the next few months the conciliatory overtures continued. In March 1552, Rochester, Englefield, and Waldegrave were released from the Tower and returned to Mary's household. Two months later, Mary rode through London to St. John's "with a goodly company of gentlemen and gentlewomen" and went by barge to Greenwich to visit her brother.[11]

In April, Edward had written in his chronicle, "I feel sick of the measles and the smallpox." He made a quick recovery, but by the winter of 1552 he was seriously ill once more, his body racked by a hacking cough. It was clear that the king was suffering from "consumption"—tuberculosis. The Council made no further overt attempts to suppress Mary's Masses. With Edward's health deteriorating, it was prudent to conciliate one who stood so near to the throne.

CHAPTER 34

MY DEVICE FOR THE SUCCESSION

∴

THE YEAR 1552 SAW THE CLIMAX OF THE EDWARDIAN REFORMATION. In the Second Book of Common Prayer and Forty-two Articles, the Real Presence in the Eucharist was rejected outright; altars were stripped from churches throughout the country and replaced by Communion tables; and images were whitewashed.[1] The long-term survival of the new Protestantism was, however, under threat. By the terms of Henry VIII's will, Mary was Edward's heir, but it was clear that she would halt the process of reformation and restore Catholicism. It was a prospect that Edward would not countenance. He needed to overturn his father's will and the parliamentary statute of 1544 that had decreed Mary his successor.

On February 10, 1553, Mary rode to court along Fleet Street, accompanied by more than two hundred lords and ladies. She was met on the outskirts of the city by John Dudley and knights and gentlemen, who escorted her to the gates of Whitehall. There she was "more honourably received and entertained with greater magnificence" than ever before, "as if she had been Queen of England."[2] But for several days, Edward could not see her, having contracted a "feverish cold." Following Mary's visit, the fifteen-year-old's health deteriorated further, though his decline was concealed from both his sisters. Mary heard falsely that he was better and sent a letter giving thanks for his recovery and praying "with long continuance in prosperity to reign."[3] It would be her final contact with her brother.

Among the Council there was a growing sense of fear that the king would soon die. His doctors believed he had a "suppurating tumour" of the lung, exacerbated by a hacking cough and a fever. "The sputum which he brings up is livid, black, fetid and full of carbon; it smells beyond measure; if it is put in a basin of water it sinks to the bottom. His feet are swollen all over. To the doctors all these things portend death, and that within three months, except God of His great mercy spare him."[4]

Writing at the end of May, Scheyfve described how Dudley, who had become duke of Northumberland in October, "and his party's designs to deprive the Lady Mary of the succession to the crown are only too plain. They are evidently resolved to resort to arms against her, with the excuse of religion among others."[5] By mid-June, it was obvious that Edward did not have long to live. Another successor needed to be found.

In early spring, Edward had drawn up in his own hand "My Device for the Succession" by which he sought to direct the succession and, specifically, disinherit his sisters. Mary and Elizabeth were excluded on the grounds that they were both bastards. The line of succession was transferred to the family of Edward's cousins the Greys—the male heirs of Frances Grey, duchess of Suffolk, the daughter of Henry VIII's sister Mary, and the male heirs of her eldest daughter, Lady Jane Grey.[6] Women were, Edward determined, unfit to rule in their own right and through marriage might subject the realm to foreign domination. Edward was relying on a yet-unborn male heir. It was a last-ditch attempt to avert a female succession.

On May 21, Lady Jane Grey was married to Guildford Dudley, Northumberland's son. But within days, Edward's health deteriorated rapidly. There would be no time for Jane to become pregnant. Edward was forced to overcome his misogyny and, in his own hand, to alter his device. Whereas originally he had left the crown to the "Lady Jane's heirs male" he edited the text and changed it to "Lady Jane and her heirs male."[7] The Protestant Lady Jane was preferred as Edward's successor to the throne.

Three weeks later, Sir Edward Montagu, the lord chief justice, and other senior lawyers of the King's Bench were summoned to the king's bedside at Greenwich. To make the succession legal, they were required to draw up letters patent to give legal effect to the terms of the revised "device." Montagu refused, declaring he would not be involved with any changes to the succession and asserting that letters patent could not overturn statute; Parliament needed to meet. There was, he warned, "the danger of treason." He suggested a compromise: Mary should be allowed to succeed if she pledged to "make no religious change." Northumberland and Edward were furious. The plan was sharply rejected.[8] As Edward explained, neither Mary nor Elizabeth was acceptable as his heir:

> I am convinced that my sister Mary would provoke great disturbances after I have left this life, and would leave no stone unturned, as the proverb goes, to gain control of this isle, the fairest in all Europe, my resolve is to disown and disinherit her together with her sister Elizabeth, as though she were a bastard and sprung from an illegitimate bed. . . . Therefore, to avoid the kingdom being weakened by such shame, it is our resolve, with the agreement of our noblemen, to appoint as our heir our most dear cousin Jane . . . for if our sister were to possess the kingdom (which Almighty God prevent) it would be all over for the religion whose fair foundation we have laid.
>
> For indeed my sister Mary was the daughter of the King by Katherine the Spaniard, who before she was married to my worthy father had been espoused to Arthur, my father's elder brother, and was therefore for this reason alone divorced by my father. But it was the fate of Elizabeth, my other sister, to have Anne Boleyn for a mother; this woman was indeed not only cast off by my father because she was more inclined to couple with a number of courtiers rather than reverencing her husband, so mighty a King, but also paid the penalty with her head— a greater proof of guilt. Thus in our judgment they will be undeservedly considered as being numbered among the heirs of the King our beloved father.

Lady Jane, by contrast, would support "the religion whose fair foundation we have laid."[9]

Finally, confronted by Edward's frail figure, the judges relented and agreed to help the king draw up his will.[10] The letters patent were countersigned by Edward in six places and then by more than a hundred signatories, including judges, peers, nobles, and other dignitaries.

Edward made his final appearance at the window at Greenwich Palace on Saturday, July 1. It was clear to all that death was little more than hours away. "He was doomed, and that he was only shown because the people were murmuring and saying he was already dead, and in order that his death, when it should occur, might the more easily be concealed."[11]

THE FRENCH NOW urged Northumberland to commit to war against Charles in return for their support for Jane's accession; the situation in England had turned to their advantage.[12] With Edward in poor health in the spring of 1553, both rulers had sent ambassadors to England. Antoine de Noailles represented the French king, and Simon Renard, who would become the resident ambassador, came as part of a three-man embassy from Brussels. The emperor's mission, as Charles outlined in instructions drawn up on June 23, was to "preserve our cousin's [Mary's] person from danger, assist her to obtain possession of the Crown, calm the fears the English may entertain of us, defeat French machinations and further a good understanding between our dominions and the realm of England."[13]

Noailles feared that Northumberland had made a deal with Charles V to hand over Mary to be married, possibly to his eldest son, "a thing which is more to be feared than a thousand others which might happen in this affair."[14] In desperation he presented the Council with further "honest and fine offers" from Henry II, pledging his military support. Northumberland thanked him, saying that he hoped for the support of French troops "when the occasion presents itself," and a letter was sent to the French court, stating, "We shall never forget this great friendship in so difficult times, although we doubt not but that the estate and power of this realm shall, by God's goodness, prevail against all manner of practices or attempts either by the Emperor or any other, either foreign or outward enemies whatsoever the same be."[15]

A year earlier, Henry II had extended the frontiers of France almost to the Rhine by seizing the bishoprics of Metz, Toul, and Verdun. His great ambition was to win back the last English territory in France, Calais. An alliance with England would tilt the balance of power decisively in favor of either Henry or the emperor. For the French, it would provide a base from which to launch an invasion of the Netherlands, while for the emperor it would mean the encirclement of France and security of the sea route between Spain and the Low Countries. England now stood as a potential battleground between the Habsburg and Valois kings.

AS EDWARD LAY on his deathbed, struggling to breathe, Northumberland took the first steps to execute the plan. He needed to ensure that Mary did not become suspicious of his intentions for the succession and sought to lull her into a false state of security, regularly sending her news of the king's health and promising that if he should die she would be queen with his assistance. At first Mary believed him, but then she learned the truth. On or about July 1, her closest advisers told her of Northumberland's deceit.

Mary acted swiftly. She feigned ignorance and tricked the duke into thinking he could get possession of her whenever he pleased. She was then staying at Hunsdon in Hertfordshire, no more than twenty miles from his grasp. Yet her household servants had already formulated a plan for her escape. She had been summoned to Edward's bedside, but on July 3 she received a tip-off from a spy at court that the king's end was near. On the night of the fourth, she fled with six attendants, four men and two women. The pretext was the illness of her physician, Rowland Scurloch, which forced her to move household for risk of infection. Through the night Mary and her party traveled, riding north through Hertfordshire to Sawston Hall in Cambridgeshire, the home of Sir John Huddleston, a local Catholic gentleman. At first light, Mary rose, heard Mass, and then set out once again. There would be perilous consequences for Huddleston's loyalty to the princess: when Northumberland's men arrived the following day and realized that Mary had fled, they burned his house to the ground.

Instructions were hurriedly dispatched to lieutenants and justices across the country, notifying them of Mary's escape and ordering them to prepare to muster troops at an hour's notice and to maintain continual watch:

These shall be to signify unto you that the Lady Mary being at Hunsdon is suddenly departed with her train and family toward the sea coast at Norfolk, upon what occasion we know not, but as it is thought either to flee the realm or to abide there some foreign power . . .

Wherefore to avoid the danger that may ensue to the state and to preserve the realm from the tyranny of foreign nations which by the said Lady Mary's ungodly pretenses may be brought into this realm to the utter ruin and destruction of the same, we have thought good to require and charge you, not only to put yourselves in readiness after your best power and manner for the defence of our natural country against all such attempts, but likewise exhort you to be ready upon an hour's warning with your said power to repair unto us. . . . From Greenwich, the 8th of July.[16]

From Sawston, Mary rode the next twenty-eight miles virtually nonstop. Finally she reached Hengrave Hall, the seat of the earl of Bath, just outside Bury St. Edmunds. There she rested briefly before continuing on to Euston Hall, where she was met by the dowager Lady Burgh. When she had been informed of the king's death on the previous day, the sixth, she had reacted with cautious suspicion: the messenger, Robert Reyns, had been sent by Sir Nicholas Throckmorton, a gentleman of Edward's Privy Chamber who was known for his Protestant sympathies. Whatever the truth, the message had made flight more urgent. Mary hurried on to her seat at Kenninghall, Norfolk, where the news of the king's death was confirmed.

CHAPTER 35

FRIENDS IN THE BRIARS

∴

The 10. of July, in the afternoon, about 3. of the clock, Lady Jane was conveyed by water to the Tower of London, and there received as Queen. After five of the clock, the same afternoon, was proclamation made of the death of King Edward the sixth, and how he had ordained by his letters patents bearing the date the 21. of June last past that the Lady Jane should be heir to the Crown of England, and the heir males of her body, &c.[1]

As LADY JANE GREY WAS PROCLAIMED QUEEN, "NO ONE SHOWED any sign of rejoicing, and no one cried 'Long live the Queen' except the herald who made the proclamation and a few archers who followed him."[2] As the Genoese merchant Baptista Spinola continued, "for the hearts of the people are with Mary, the Spanish Queen's daughter."[3] One young man, Gilbert Potter, who had shouted out that Lady Mary was the rightful queen, was arrested and sent to Cheapside, where his ears were nailed to the pillory and then cut off.[4]

All hope of Mary's accession looked to have been lost. The Armory, Treasury, and Great Seal were all under the control of the duke of Northumberland, and with Lady Jane in possession of the Tower, the capital seemed to be secure. Warships had been dispatched to the Thames, and "troops were stationed everywhere to prevent the people from rising in arms or causing any disorder."[5] Mary had neither soldiers nor sufficient funds; she was an isolated figure in East Anglia, surrounded only by her household servants. The ambassadors sent by the emperor were pessimistic about her safety. Believing Northumberland had secured French support, they feared nothing could be done to prevent Jane's accession and considered Mary's chances "well-nigh impossible."[6]

But Mary was determined to proclaim herself queen, a resolution the ambassadors believed was fraught with danger. "All the forces of the country are in the Duke's hands, and my Lady has no hope of raising enough men to face him, nor means of assisting those who may espouse her cause."[7] They sent agents to advise her not to issue a proclamation but to wait to see if any support was forthcoming.[8] Now only the English people could put Mary on the throne.

ON JULY 9, MARY wrote to Jane's Council from Kenninghall, demanding that it renounce Jane and recognize her as queen, as her father's will had decreed:

> You know, the realm and the whole world knoweth; the rolls and records appear by the authority of the King our said father, and the King our said brother, and the subjects of this realm; so that we verily trust that there is no good true subject, that is, can, or would, pretend to be ignorant thereof.

Mary made it clear that she knew of the plot against her:

> We are not ignorant of your consultations, to undo the provisions made for our preferment, nor of the great bands, and provisions forcible, wherewith ye be assembled and prepared—by whom, and to what end, God and you know, and nature cannot but fear some evil.

She called upon them to display their loyalty to her "just and right cause" and declared that she was ready to pardon them in the hope of avoiding bloodshed and civil war.[9]

After presenting the dispatch to the Privy Council, Mary's messenger, Thomas Hungate, was sent to the Tower. The Council replied in a letter of the same day, addressed to "my Lady Mary" and criticizing "your supposed title which you judge yourself to have." They asserted that Jane was queen of England by the authority of letters patent executed by the late king and endorsed by the nobility of the realm. They reminded her that by an act of Parliament she was illegitimate and unable to inherit and urged her to submit with assurances that "if you will for respect be quiet and obedient as you ought, you shall find us all and several [ready] to do any service that we, with duty, may be glad with you to preserve the common state of this Realm."[10] Meanwhile, circulars hurriedly drafted by Northumberland were sent to justices of the peace, ordering them to "assist us in our rightful possession of this kingdom and to extirp, to disturb, repel and resist the fained and untrue claim of the Lady Mary bastard."[11]

The duke of Suffolk, Jane's father, was nominated to lead an army of reinforcements to East Anglia to capture Mary, though Jane "with weeping tears made request to the whole Council that her father might tarry at home in her company," and Northumberland declared that he would lead the charge himself.[12] On the evening of July 13, three carts rumbled out of the Tower, laden with "great guns and small; bows, bills and spears." Before he left, Northumberland bade the Council farewell: "Well, since ye think it good, I and mine will go, not doubting of your fidelity to the Queen's Majesty, which I leave in your custody," not to leave them your "friends in the briars, and betray us." They were fighting for "God's cause" and for "fear of papistry's re-entrance" into the realm.[13]

The following morning, Northumberland set out from Durham Palace with munitions, artillery, field guns, and more than 6,000 men. The imperial ambassadors wrote to Charles V, "We believe that my Lady will be in his hands in four days' time unless she has sufficient force to resist."[14] Yet as he rode eastward Northumberland noted, "The people press to see us, but not one sayeth God speed us."[15]

Within days Richard Troughton, bailiff of South Witham, Lincolnshire, who was attempting to win support for Mary in Lincolnshire, had submitted a petition to the Privy Council stating that Northumberland had poisoned King Edward and would now "go about to destroy the noble blood of England." He was confident that "over a hundred thousand men would rise" in support of Mary, believing "her grace should have her right, or else there would be the bloodiest day . . . that ever was in England."[16]

CHAPTER 36

TRUE OWNER OF THE CROWN

∴

This attempt should have been judged and considered one of Herculean rather than womanly daring, since to claim and secure her hereditary right, the princess was being so bold as to tackle a powerful and well-prepared enemy, thoroughly provisioned with everything necessary to end or to prolong a war, while she was entirely unprepared for warfare and had insignificant forces.[1]

—ROBERT WINGFIELD, *VITA MARIAE*

FOR FIVE DAYS MARY STAYED AT KENNINGHALL, RALLYING FRIENDS and supporters among the East Anglian gentry and commons. The core of her support was her household. Many, like Robert Rochester and Edward Waldegrave, had served her throughout Edward's reign and had consistently defended her and her right to hear the Catholic Mass. Now they moved to defend her right to the throne. As Robert Wingfield, an East Anglian gentleman, wrote, they "did not hesitate to face an untimely death for their Queen." Each played an important role in mobilizing members of the local gentry and their tenants. The first gentlemen to arrive at Kenninghall, Sir Henry Bedingfield, Sir John Shelton, and Sir Richard Southwell, were from the same group of conservative East Anglian magnates as the men in Mary's household. The arrival of Southwell and Henry Radcliffe, earl of Sussex, with money, provisions, and armed men would greatly expand Mary's meager forces. Southwell was a knight, the wealthiest of his rank in Norfolk, and his commitment did much to raise the morale of Mary and her supporters.

On July 12, with her forces growing, Mary moved southeast to another of her principal houses, Framlingham Castle in Suffolk, the ancient seat of the Howard family. It was far larger than Kenninghall and, as the strongest castle in the area, an ideal place from which to defend against, or indeed engage, a determined enemy. Built by the old duke of Norfolk, it had come into her possession only a few months before. Now it would witness Mary's stand against the might of central government. As she journeyed to Framlingham, many of the local gentry and justices, together with a crowd of country folk, gathered in the deer park adjacent to the castle to await her arrival. "A great concourse of people were moved by their love for her to come and promise to support her to the end and maintain her right to the Crown, bringing money and cattle as their means enabled them."[2]

Finally, at eight in the evening, she arrived. Her standard was unfurled and displayed over the gate tower. It was a defiant gesture on the eve of what looked to be imminent conflict. Northumberland was said to have had 3,000 men and the whole of the royal armory to draw on. Mary's forces and supplies were thin in comparison. Again she sent a desperate appeal to the imperial ambassadors: "She saw destruction hanging over her" unless she received help. But the emperor believed Mary's chances of coming to the throne to be "very slight," and he sent nothing.[3]

For a number of days Mary's fate hung in the balance. In many towns it was a confused picture of shifting and changing allegiances. In Ipswich, Sir Thomas Cornwallis, the sheriff of Norfolk and Suffolk, together with Thomas, Lord Wentworth, and other prominent Suffolk men, initially declared for Jane, on July 11. But then one of Mary's servants, Thomas Poley, arrived in the town's marketplace and proclaimed Mary "hereditary Queen of England." It was only then that Cornwallis saw where the sympathies of the people lay and declared for Mary. As Wingfield described it, the public outcry against Jane was so great that Cornwallis actually stood "in grave peril of his life." Although a lifelong religious conservative, Cornwallis, like many other East Anglian gentry, had bet against Mary, given Jane's access to superior military resources. Yet they too had underestimated the popular support for Mary. At Framlingham, Cornwallis humbly prostrated himself before her and begged her pardon. For Cornwallis, as for many others, factors other than faith or principle led him to declare for Mary.

In Norwich, where the town authorities had on July 11 refused to open the gates to Mary's messengers, saying that they did not yet know for certain that the king was dead, they not only proclaimed her the following day but also sent men and arms. Gradually events began to swing in Mary's favor. A squadron of five ships of the late king, laden with soldiers and weaponry, had been forced into the safety of Orwell harbor by bad weather. The crews mutinied against their officers for disowning Mary and put themselves under the command of Mary's ardent supporter Sir Henry Jerningham. Many others flocked to Mary's side. Henry Radcliffe arrived at Framlingham with a cohort of horsemen and foot soldiers. He was followed by John Bourchier, earl of Bath, another noble figure, who also arrived with a large band of soldiers including Sir John Sulyard, knight of Wetherden, and Sir William Drury, knight of the shire for Suffolk. All leading figures in East Anglia, they, together with Sir Thomas Cornwallis, were important gains that would prove crucial to Mary's success. Yet one figure eluded her. To secure her position in eastern Suffolk, Mary needed to win the support of Thomas, Lord Wentworth, a prominent and respected nobleman. She sent two of her servants, John Tyrell and Edward Glenham, to Nettlestead to negotiate with him. She warned that forsaking her cause would lead to the perpetual dishonor of his house. He paused and reflected. Finally he declared for Mary. It was a great coup. Wentworth arrived at Framlingham on the fifteenth, clad in splendid armor and with a large military force of gentlemen and tenants.

It was just in time. Northumberland was en route to Bury St. Edmunds, just twenty-four miles from Framlingham. Five hundred men were appointed to guard Mary within the walls of Framlingham Castle. Mary was focused and resolute. She summoned her household council, ordered her field commanders to prepare her forces for battle, and issued a proclamation asserting her authority, making clear her defiance:

> We do signify unto you that according to our said right and title we do take upon us and be in the just and lawful possession of

the same; not doubting that all our true and faithful subjects will
so accept us, take us and obey us as their natural and liege sovereign lady and Queen.[4]

Now, as her army mustered, Mary declared that she was "nobly and
strongly furnished of an army royal under Lord Henry, Earl of Sussex,
her Lieutenant General, accompanied by the Earl of Bath, the Lord
Wentworth, and a multitude of other gentlemen." She condemned
Northumberland, that he "most traitorously by long-continued treason
sought, and seeketh, the destruction of her royal person, the nobility
and common weal of this realm," and finished with a rallying cry:

> Wherefore, good people, as ye mindeth the surety of her said
> person, the honour and surety of your country, being good
> Englishmen, prepare yourselves in all haste with all power to
> repair unto her said armies yet being in Suffolk, making your
> prayers to God for her success . . . upon the said causes she
> utterly defyeth the said duke for her most errant traitor to God
> and to the realm.[5]

Within days an unskilled and disorganized mob had been turned
into a disciplined army, obedient to order and eager to meet the enemy.
On the twentieth, Mary rode down from the castle to review her
troops. Standards were unfurled and her forces drawn up in battle
order; helmets were thrown high in the air as shouts of "Long live our
good Queen Mary!" and "Death to the traitors!" rang out across the
Suffolk countryside. Mary dismounted and for the next three hours
inspected her troops on foot.

SINCE NORTHUMBERLAND'S departure from London, the privy
councillors had begun to waver in their support for Jane as queen,
"being deeply rooted in their minds, in spite of these seditions, a kind
of remorse, knowing her [Mary] to be, after all the daughter of their
King Henry VIII."[6] By the eighteenth, their resolve had crumbled.
Ships' crews off Yarmouth had deserted, and rumors had spread that
Sir Edmund Peckham, treasurer of the Mint and keeper of the king's

privy purse, had fled with the monies to Framlingham. Now a proclamation was drawn up offering a reward for the arrest of Northumberland: £1,000 in land to any noble, £500 to any knight, and £100
to any yeoman bold enough to lay his hand on the duke's shoulder and
demand his surrender.[7]

The following day, a dozen or so privy councillors, including the
earls of Bedford, Pembroke, Arundel, Shrewsbury, and Worcester, and
Lords Paget, Darcy, and Cobham, broke out of the Tower, which had
been locked, and rendezvoused at Pembroke's house, Baynard's Castle.
There they took the final step. In a speech before the Council, Arundel
declared:

> This Crown belongs rightfully, by direct succession, to My
> Lady Mary lawful and natural daughter of our King Henry
> VIII. Therefore why should you let yourselves be corrupted and
> tolerate that anybody might unjustly possess what does not
> belong to him? . . . [8]
>
> If by chance you should feel somehow guilty proclaiming
> now our Queen My Lady Mary, having acclaimed Jane only a
> few days ago, showing such quick change of mind, I tell you this
> is no reason to hesitate, because having sinned it befits always to
> amend, especially when, as in the present circumstances, it
> means honour for your goodselves, welfare and freedom for our
> country, love and loyalty to his King, peace and contentment for
> all people.[9]

At five or six in the evening of the twentieth, as Arundel and Paget
set out to pledge their fidelity to Mary at Framlingham and petition for
pardon on behalf of the whole Council, two heralds and three trumpeters rode from Baynard's Castle to the Cross at Cheapside. With the
streets full of Londoners, the heralds announced that Mary was
queen.[10] "There was such shout of the people with casting up of caps
and crying, 'God save Queen Mary,' that the style of the proclamation
could not be heard, the people were so joyful, both man, woman and
child."[11] For two days all the bells in London, "which it had been
decided to convert into artillery," rang; money was "cast a-way," and
there were banquets and bonfires in the streets.[12] "It would be impossible

to imagine greater rejoicing than this," the imperial ambassadors reported.[13]

> From a distance the earth must have looked like Mount Etna. The people are mad with joy, feasting and singing, and the streets crowded all night long. I am unable to describe to you, nor would you believe, the exultation of all men. I will only tell you that not a soul imagined the possibility of such a thing.[14]

Upon hearing the news, Northumberland, then at Cambridge, was forced to admit defeat. He threw his cap into the air and acknowledged Mary as queen. The coup attempt was over. That evening the earl of Arundel arrived to arrest Northumberland in the queen's name.[15]

PART THREE

A Queen

CHAPTER 37

MARYE THE QUENE

DAYS BEFORE SHE WAS TO BE CROWNED AT WESTMINSTER ABBEY, Mary called together her Council for an impromptu and improvised ceremony. Ensconced in the Tower of London, she had been preparing for the coronation to come, rehearsing the oaths and changes of clothes and regalia and pondering the responsibilities of office. Kneeling before her councillors, Mary spoke of how she had come to the throne and what she considered to be her duties as queen. It was her solemn intention to carry out the task God had given her "to His greater glory and service, to the public good and all her subjects' benefit." She had entrusted "her affairs and person" to her councillors and urged them to be faithful to the oaths they had sworn and to be loyal to her as their queen. Mary remained on her knees throughout. So "deeply moved" were her councillors that "not a single one refrained from tears. No one knew how to answer, amazed as they all were by this humble and lowly discourse unlike anything ever heard before in England, and by the Queen's great goodness and integrity."[1] It was an astonishing sight, yet these were extraordinary times: a woman was now to wear England's crown.

THE FIRST QUEEN to rule England was a small, slightly built woman of thirty-seven. With her large, bright eyes, round face, reddish hair, and love of fine clothes, she cut a striking figure, though one marked by age and ill health.[2] She suffered bouts of illness, heart palpitations, and headaches, was exceedingly shortsighted, and was prone to melancholy. Although for most of her adult life she had known neither security nor happiness, she was regarded as "great-hearted, proud and magnanimous." Highly educated and intelligent, well versed in languages, and quick of wit and understanding, her frequent acclamation was "In thee, O lord, is my trust, let me never be confounded. If God be for us, who can be against us?"[3]

Mary had secured the throne against the odds. It was a victory, Wingfield wrote, "one of Herculean rather than womanly daring."[4] A female accession had been a prospect her father had gone to great lengths to avoid, but on Edward's death all the plausible candidates for the English throne were female. In default of male heirs, Edward had had to accept Lady Jane Grey as his Protestant successor. Yet Mary had managed to win support across the religious spectrum as the rightful Tudor heir. Notably it was a victory won without direct foreign aid; the English people had put Mary on the throne. The anonymous author of "The Legend of Sir Nicholas Throgmorton" put into the mouth of his hero the sentiments of many:

> *And though I lik'd not the Religion*
> *Which all her life Queen Mary had professed,*
> *Yet in my mind that wicked Motion*
> *Right heirs for to displace I did detest.*[5]

Her victory was widely celebrated. She was as popular as any English sovereign who had ascended the throne before her, and her triumph was one of the most surprising events of the sixteenth century.[6] She had preserved the Tudor dynasty, and now both the French king and the emperor sought to ingratiate themselves with her.

"This news," wrote Charles V to his ambassadors, "is the best we could have had from England and we render thanks to God for having guided all things so well . . . [you will] offer our congratulations on her happy accession to the throne, telling her how great was our joy on hearing it." The emperor now sought to justify his lack of intervention: "You may explain to her that you were instructed to proceed very gradually in your negotiation, with the object of rendering her some assistance, and that we were hastily making preparations, under cover of protection of the fisheries, to come to her relief."[7]

Meanwhile the French, who had conspired with Northumberland, were now forced to declare their belief in Mary's legitimacy and deny their part in the coup.[8] Many Englishmen believed that France had been set to invade in support of Northumberland. As Noailles reported, "You could not believe the foul and filthy words which this nation cries out every day against our own."[9] Henry II now feared that England might join the war on the emperor's side and sought to emphasize Charles's lack of support for Mary in the July crisis. "In all her own miseries, troubles and afflictions," wrote the French ambassador, "as well as in those of the Queen her mother, the Emperor never came to their assistance, nor has he helped her now in her great need with a single man, ship or penny."[10]

AS BELLS ACROSS the country rang out the news of her victory, Mary left Framlingham to begin her slow and triumphant progress toward London.[11] Along the route and at her various stopping places, she received the homage of her subjects. At Ipswich she was met by the bailiffs of the town, who presented her with "eleven pounds sterling in gold," and by some young boys, who gave her a golden heart inscribed with the words "The Heart of the People."[12] Having spent two days in Ipswich, Mary moved to Colchester, where she stayed at the home of Muriel Christmas, a former servant of her mother, Katherine, and then journeyed to her residence Beaulieu in Essex. There she was presented with a purse of crimson velvet from the City of London, filled with half sovereigns of gold, "which gift she highly and thankfully accepted, and caused the presenters to have great cheer in her house."[13] From Beaulieu she rode on to Wanstead, east of London, where she was joined by her sister, Elizabeth, who had ridden from the Strand to meet her, accompanied by countless gentlemen, knights, and ladies.[14]

Leaving Wanstead on the third, Mary began her journey into the city, stopping en route at Whitechapel at the house of one "Mr Bramston," where she "changed her apparel."[15] As Wingfield described the occasion:

Now indeed her retinue reached its greatest size . . . nothing was left or neglected which might possibly be contrived to decorate the gates, roads and all places on the Queen's route to wish her joy for her victory. Every crowd met her accompanied by children, and caused celebrations everywhere, so that the joy of that most wished for and happy triumphal procession might easily be observed, such were the magnificent preparations made by the wealthier sort and such was the anxiety among the ordinary folk to show their goodwill to their sovereign.[16]

CHAPTER 38

THE JOY OF THE PEOPLE

⁖

AT SEVEN IN THE EVENING OF AUGUST 3, 1553, MARY ENTERED the City of London, accompanied by gentlemen, squires, knights, and lords, the king's trumpeters, heralds, and sergeants at arms with bows and javelins.

She was dressed in a gown of purple velvet, its sleeves embroidered in gold; beneath it she wore a kirtle of purple satin thickly set with large pearls, with a gold and jeweled chain around her neck and a dazzling headdress on her head. Her mount, a palfrey, was richly trapped with cloth of gold.[1] As the imperial ambassadors reported, "her look, her manner, her gestures, her countenance were such that in no event could they be improved."[2] Behind her rode Sir Anthony Browne, "leaning on her horse, having the train of her highness' gown hanging over his shoulder," followed by her sister, Elizabeth, the Duchess of Norfolk, the Marchioness of Exeter, and a "flock of peeresses, gentlewomen and ladies-in-waiting, never before seen in such numbers."[3] It was a spectacular display of dynastic unity, of power and authority: the first formal appearance of England's queen regnant. According to one estimate, some ten thousand people accompanied the new queen into the capital.

Mary was met at Aldgate by the lord mayor and aldermen of London. Kneeling before her, the lord mayor presented the scepter of her office as a "token of loyalty and homage" and welcomed her into the city. She returned the scepter to the lord mayor with words "so gently spoken and with so smiling a countenance that the hearers wept for joy."[4] Mace in hand, the lord mayor joined the cavalcade next to the earl of Arundel, who bore the sword of state. At St. Botolph's Church, a choir of a hundred children from Christ's Hospital, all dressed in blue with red caps on their heads and sitting on a great stage covered with canvas, sang choruses of welcome.[5]

All along the procession route the streets had been swept clean and spread with gravel so that the horses would not slip; the buildings had been decorated with rich tapestries, and spectators crowded onto roofs, walls, and steeples. As the procession moved through Aldgate, trumpets sounded from the gate's battlements. Lining the streets through Leadenhall to the Tower were the guilds of London, all wearing their livery hoods and furs, all paying homage to their new queen. Wherever the queen passed, placards declared, *"Vox populi, vox Dei"*—"The voice of the people is the voice of God."[6] The streets thronged "so full of people shouting and crying 'Jesus save her grace,' with weeping tears for joy, that the like was never seen before," reported the chronicler Charles Wriothesley.[7] The imperial ambassadors agreed: The "joy of the people" was "hardly credible," "the public demonstrations" having "never had their equal in the kingdom."[8]

With cannons sounding from every battlement "like great thunder, so that it had been like to an earthquake," Mary arrived at the Tower. There the lord mayor took his leave and Mary was met by Sir John Gage and Sir John Brydges, constable and lieutenant of the Tower, respectively, standing in front of rows of archers and arquebusiers. Kneeling on the green before the Chapel Royal of St. Peter ad Vincula within the Tower precinct were Edward Courtenay, who had been prisoner since the age of nine and whose father, the marquess of Exeter, had been beheaded in 1538; the aged Thomas Howard, duke of Norfolk, still under sentence of death since the last months of Henry VIII's reign; and the deprived bishops of Winchester and Durham, Stephen Gardiner and Cuthbert Tunstall. In the name of all the prisoners, Bishop Gardiner congratulated Mary on her accession. "Ye are my prisoners!" exclaimed the queen. Raising them up one by one, she kissed them and granted them their liberty. Courtenay and Norfolk were restored to their rank and estates, the deprived bishops to their sees. Then, as her standard was raised above the keep, Mary entered the Tower.[9] "The people . . . are full of hope," wrote the imperial ambassadors, "that her reign will be a godly, righteous and just one, and help to establish her firmly on the throne."[10]

NOW IN POSSESSION of her kingdom, Mary could begin the task of governing. She had won the throne at Framlingham with a small council of her household officers, including Robert Rochester, Edward Waldegrave, and Henry Jerningham, together with figures such as the earls of Sussex and Bath, who had arrived in the early days of the coup. All were of proven loyalty, but few had political experience. Then, as Mary journeyed to London, she had been besieged with apologies and pledges of fidelity from the Edwardian councillors who had been so closely involved with Edward's Protestant reforms and who had, just days before, conferred the crown on Lady Jane Grey. Some had displayed reluctance in agreeing to Northumberland's plan, but all had eventually signed Edward's "Device for the Succession." Though Mary doubted their loyalty and their motives, most upon their submission were restored to royal favor.

To her existing council of household servants, Mary appointed experienced men such as Sir William Petre, Lord William Paget, the earls of Arundel and Pembroke, Sir John Mason, and Sir Richard Southwell. The earl of Arundel became lord steward; William Paulet, the marquess of Winchester, retained his office of high treasurer. By the time Mary reached the Tower, she had a Privy Council, a hybrid of trust and experience, of some twenty-five members.

Mary also appointed to her Privy Council men who had suffered for their views and faith under the previous regime, including those she had freed from the Tower. Stephen Gardiner was appointed to the Privy Council the day after his release and three weeks later became lord chancellor. Though he had been principal adviser to Henry VIII in the king's divorce from Katherine of Aragon, he had become increasingly conservative in his religious views during Edward's reign and had developed a hatred for Northumberland after being imprisoned in 1551. As far as Mary was concerned this sufficiently redeemed him, though he would never come to enjoy the queen's full confidence. Yet Mary's political pragmatism was resented by many of the councillors. "Discontent is rife," the imperial ambassadors reported on August 16, "especially among those who stood by the queen in the days of her adversity and trouble, who feel they have not been rewarded as they deserve, for the conspirators have been raised in authority."[11] Although their commitment to Mary varied, they all shared a fundamental loyalty to the Tudor regime.

In all, Mary's Privy Council numbered some forty councillors. While it was among these men that a core group formed to govern and administer the realm, it was as much in the halls and corridors of the royal household, in whispered conversations and secret meetings with the queen, that decisions were made and policies formed. Unlike the Privy Council, the upper echelons of the royal household were an exclusive preserve of trusted Catholic loyalists whom Mary relied upon. Members of Mary's "princely affinity of proven loyalty" replaced all those who had acted against her in the succession crisis. Sir Henry Jerningham, who had been in Mary's service since 1533, became vice chamberlain and captain of the Guard; the long-serving Robert Rochester became comptroller of the household; Edward Waldegrave, master of the great wardrobe; and Sir Edward Hastings, master of the horse. John de Vere, the earl of Oxford, whose defection to Mary in the succession crisis had proved decisive, recovered the "hereditary" position of lord great chamberlain from the marquess of Northampton.

THE ACCESSION OF a queen regnant necessitated changes in the monarch's private apartments. The male servants of Edward's entourage were replaced by female attendants, many of them long-serving servants from her princely household, such as Jane Dormer, Mary Finch, Frances Waldegrave, Frances Jerningham, and Susan Clarencius, who became chief lady of the Privy Chamber. Their positions close to the queen gave these women a measure of influence, especially in the early months of the reign, a fact that was of concern to the emperor. "If you have an opportunity of speaking to her without her taking it in bad part," he instructed Renard, "you might give her to understand that people are said to murmur because some of her ladies take advantage of their position to obtain certain concessions for their own private interest and profit."[12]

But it was Simon Renard, building on Mary's familial ties and attachment to the emperor, who would enjoy an unprecedented role as secret counselor and confidant. From the start, Mary had expressed her uncertainty as to how to "make herself safe and arrange her affairs," and, as the ambassadors reported, "still less did she dare to speak of them to anyone except ourselves. She could not trust her Council too much, well knowing the particular character of its members."[13] Just a few hours after the imperial ambassadors' first public audience, on July 29, and within days of her accession, the queen sent all three ambassadors word that one or two of their number might go to her privately in her oratory, "entering [by] the back door to avoid suspicion."[14] The task was delegated to Renard, who from then on acted as a secret counselor, advising and admonishing Mary as to decisions to be made and actions taken. He quickly won the queen's trust and confidence and was frequently consulted by her in secret, when none of her English advisers was present. On religion Renard told her:

> not to hurry . . . not to make innovations nor adopt unpopular policies, but rather to recommend herself by winning her subjects' hearts, showing herself to be a good Englishwoman wholly bent on the kingdom's welfare, answering the hopes conceived of her, temporising wherever it was possible to do so.[15]

Huddled under a cloak, Renard would slip quietly in through the back door of the queen's privy apartments. She would encourage him to come in disguise and under cover of darkness.

> Sir, If it were not too much trouble for you, and if you were to find it convenient to do so without the knowledge of your colleagues, I would willingly speak to you in private this evening. . . . Nevertheless, I remit my request to your prudence and discretion. Written in haste, as it well appears, this morning, 13 October. Your good friend, Mary.[16]

To consult an ambassador as though he were a secret counselor upon the domestic affairs of the kingdom was a highly unusual step for a monarch to take. But from her earliest days Mary had pledged herself to the emperor. On July 28, when the imperial ambassadors had journeyed to meet Mary at Beaulieu, she had declared that "after God, she desired to obey none but" her cousin Charles, "whom she regarded as a father."[17] After her accession, she wrote thanking him for his congratulations, adding, "May it please your Majesty to continue in your goodwill towards me, and I will correspond in every way which it may please your Majesty to command, thus fulfilling my duty as your good and obedient cousin."[18] It was a sign of things to come.

CHAPTER 39

CLEMENCY AND MODERATION

∴

A WEEK BEFORE MARY'S CEREMONIAL ENTRY INTO LONDON, JOHN Dudley, the duke of Northumberland, and his accomplices, Sir John Gates and Sir Thomas Palmer, were brought back to London under heavy guard.[1] Despite a proclamation ordering citizens to allow the prisoners to pass by peacefully, the mounted men at arms struggled to hold back the large crowds.[2] As they made their way to the Tower from Shoreditch, Londoners filled the streets to watch, throwing stones and calling out "Death to the traitors!" and "Long live the true queen!" Pausing at Bishopsgate, the earl of Arundel made Northumberland take off his hat and scarlet cloak to make him less conspicuous among the group of prisoners. For the rest of the journey to the Tower, he rode bareheaded through the streets, his cap in his hand.[3]

Two weeks later the duke was tried and condemned to death. During his time in the Tower he was assailed by remorse for his sins, begging to be pardoned and professing his adherence to Catholicism: "I do faithfully believe this is the very right and true way, out of which true religion you and I have been seduced this xvj years past, by the false and erroneous preaching of the new preachers."[4] His apostasy did not save him. He went to the block with Gates and Palmer in front of a huge crowd on August 22.[5]

None of the other July rebels was executed, and both Lady Jane Grey and her husband, Guildford Dudley, remained in the Tower in honorable imprisonment. The emperor urged Mary to act against them, but she "could not be induced to consent that she should die."[6] Jane had written a long confession explaining that she had known nothing of the plan to declare her queen until three days before she was taken to the Tower and had never given any consent to the duke's intrigues and plots. Upon the proclamation of Mary's accession, she had, she claimed, gladly given up the royal dignity as she knew the right belonged to Mary.[7] Mary acknowledged her submission and showed a spirit of temperance toward her. Her mother, the duchess of Suffolk, was a long-standing acquaintance and had spent Christmas with Mary the previous year. "My conscience," Mary declared to the ambassador, "will not permit me to have her put to death."[8]

On July 31, upon the petition of his wife, Frances, Mary released the duke of Suffolk from the Tower, even though he had been strongly implicated in Northumberland's coup to place Jane on the throne. As Renard reported, "many who judge her actions impartially, praise her clemency and moderation in tempering the rigour of justice against those who plotted her death and disinheritance, in staying their punishment, and, moreover, in forgiving their misdeeds and extending her grace and mercy to them."[9]

FIVE DAYS AFTER Mary had taken possession of the Tower and a month after the king's death, the coffin of the late Edward VI was carried from Whitehall to Westminster Abbey. Mary had initially expressed her intention to have him buried "for her own peace of conscience" according to the "ancient ceremonies and prayers" of the Catholic Church, fearing that if she "appeared to be afraid" it would make her subjects, particularly the Lutherans, "become more audacious" and "proclaim that she had not dared to do her own will."[10] But in a confidential memorandum, Renard advised caution: if Mary inaugurated her reign in this fashion, she would "render herself odious and suspect." Burying Edward, who had lived and died a Protestant, with Catholic rites might "cause her Majesty's subjects to waver in their loyal affection."[11] Mary agreed to compromise. On August 9, while Mary and her ladies heard a Requiem Mass for the repose of his soul in a private chapel in the Tower, Edward was buried in the abbey in a Protestant service conducted by Thomas Cranmer, the archbishop of Canterbury.[12]

Outside the Tower, there was evidence that religious change had

Henry VIII by unknown artist c. 1520: THE YOUNG HENRY IN THE EARLY YEARS OF HIS REIGN.

Portrait of Katherine of Aragon: MARY'S MOTHER PICTURED C. 1525 WHEN HENRY'S AFFECTION WAS BEGINNING TO WANE AND SHE WAS CONSIDERED TO BE PAST THE AGE OF CHILDBEARING.

The Family of Henry VIII by Horenbolt: THE PAINTING COMMEMORATES THE RESTORATION OF MARY AND ELIZABETH TO THE LINE OF SUCCESSION. MARY IS ON THE RIGHT, ELIZABETH ON THE LEFT, WHILE EDWARD AND JANE SEYMOUR STAND NEXT TO HENRY. KATHERINE PARR, HENRY'S WIFE AT THE TIME WHO WAS CHILDLESS, IS NOT PICTURED.

Lord Cromwell, Wearing the Order of St. George, by Hans Holbein: THE KING'S CHIEF MINISTER, WHO BROKERED MARY'S RECONCILIATION WITH HER FATHER IN 1536.

Princess Mary: THIS PORTRAIT MINIA-TURE WAS PAINTED AT THE TIME WHEN MARY WAS BETROTHED TO THE EMPEROR CHARLES V. THE LETTERS OF HER BROOCH SPELL OUT "THE EMPEROUR." THE PORTRAIT WAS ALMOST CERTAINLY INTENDED AS A GIFT FOR CHARLES.

The Emperor Charles V on Horseback in Muhlberg by Titian: MARY'S COUSIN, UPON WHOM SHE RELIED THROUGHOUT HER LIFE AS HER "SECOND FATHER."

Michaelmas Plea Roll (1553):
MARY AS A TRIUMPHANT QUEEN
HAVING WON THE THRONE IN
JULY 1553. SHE IS PICTURED IN
THE FULL PANOPLY OF
A QUEEN REGNANT.

*Mary Tudor curing
the King's Evil:*
MARY IS PICTURED
HERE PERFORMING
THE ROYAL TOUCH
TO HEAL THOSE
SUFFERING FROM
THE "KING'S EVIL"
(SCROFULA) AND
DEMONSTRATING
THAT SHE WAS
INVESTED WITH
THE TRADITIONAL
QUASI-PRIESTLY
POWER OF MALE
MONARCHS.

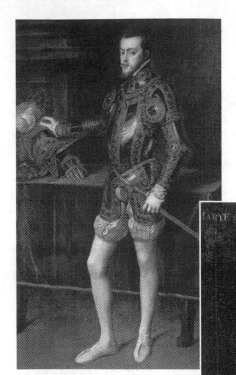

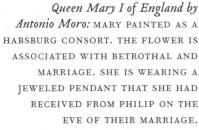

Queen Mary I of England by Antonio Moro: MARY PAINTED AS A HABSBURG CONSORT. THE FLOWER IS ASSOCIATED WITH BETROTHAL AND MARRIAGE. SHE IS WEARING A JEWELED PENDANT THAT SHE HAD RECEIVED FROM PHILIP ON THE EVE OF THEIR MARRIAGE.

King Philip II by Titian c. 1550.

Michaelmas Plea Roll (1556): THE KING AND QUEEN PICTURED TWO YEARS AFTER THEIR WEDDING. PHILIP ASSUMES THE DOMINANT POSITION ON MARY'S RIGHT WHILST A CROWN FLOATS BETWEEN THE TWO, SUGGESTING SHARED ROYAL POWER.

Simon Renard by Giacomo Antonio Moro c. 1553: THE IMPERIAL AMBASSADOR UPON WHOM MARY DEPENDED AS HER CHIEF CONFIDANT DURING THE FIRST YEAR OF HER REIGN.

Philip II and Mary I by Hans Eworth c. 1558.

Cardinal Reginald Pole, Archbishop of Canterbury: MARY'S COUSIN AND THE SON OF HER FORMER GOVERNESS, REGINALD POLE ABSOLVED ENGLAND FROM ITS SCHISM WITH ROME. MARY RELIED HEAVILY ON HIM IN PHILIP'S ABSENCE DURING THE LATTER PART OF HER REIGN.

"*A Lamentable Spectacle of three women, with a sely infant brasting out of the Mothers Wombe, being first taken out of the fire, and cast in agayne, and so burned together in the Isle of Garnesey,*" *from Foxe's* Book of Martyrs (1563).

The Burning of Thomas Cranmer, Archbishop of Canterbury, from Foxe's Book of Martyrs (1563): IT HAD BEEN MORE THAN TWENTY YEARS SINCE CRANMER HAD PRONOUNCED THE MARRIAGE OF MARY'S PARENTS TO BE INVALID AND HAD MARRIED HENRY TO ANNE BOLEYN. MARY NEVER FORGAVE HIM.

Queen Mary I by Hans Eworth: A PORTRAIT OF A MAGNIFICENT QUEEN. SHE
LOVED TO DRESS EXTRAVAGANTLY AND KNEW THE IMPORTANCE OF
DISPLAYING A STRIKING IMAGE OF ROYAL MAJESTY. MARY IS AGAIN PICTURED
WITH THE PENDANT JEWEL THAT SHE HAD RECEIVED FROM PHILIP.

The signature of Mary I.

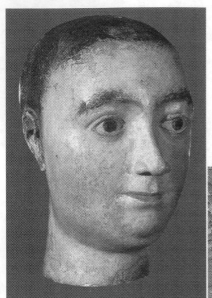

The head of Mary's funeral effigy, displayed at Westminster Abbey.

The tomb of Mary and Elizabeth at Westminster Abbey: ELIZABETH'S BODY WAS MOVED HERE BY JAMES I, THREE YEARS AFTER HER DEATH, BUT MARY'S PRESENCE IS BARELY ACKNOWLEDGED.

already begun. Even before Mary had reached London, altars and crucifixes had started to reappear in the city's churches, and Matins and
Evensong were being recited "not by commandment but by the devotion of the people." As the chronicler Wriothesley described, at St.
Paul's "the work that was broken down of stone, where the high altar
stood, was begun to be made up again with brick." And on Saint
Bartholomew's Day, August 24, a Latin Mass was said there.[13]

But amid such demonstrations of enthusiasm for the old religion,
violent disturbances erupted across London. On Sunday, August 13,
during a sermon at St. Paul's Cross, Gilbert Bourne, chaplain to the
bishop of London, was "pulled out of the pulpit by vagabonds" and
"one threw his dagger at him."[14] The following Sunday, crowds there
were met by the captain of the Guard and more than two hundred
guardsmen to protect the preacher. Defamatory pamphlets exhorting
Protestants to take up arms against Mary's government littered the
streets. "Nobles and gentlemen favoring the word of God" were asked
to overthrow the "detestable papists," especially "the great devil"
Stephen Gardiner, bishop of Winchester.[15] A number of leading
Protestant figures, including John Bradford, the prebendary of St.
Paul's, and John Rogers, the canon of St. Paul's, were arrested, and
leading reformist bishops such as John Hooper, bishop of Worcester
and Gloucester, and Hugh Latimer, bishop of Worcester, were imprisoned some weeks later. In September, Thomas Cranmer, the archbishop of Canterbury, was imprisoned for treason for his role in Lady
Jane's attempted coup.

In mid-August, as violence and alarm spread, Mary issued her first
proclamation, intended to avoid "the great inconvenience and dangers"
that had arisen in times past through the "diversity of opinions in questions of religion":

> Her Majesty being presently by the only goodness of God settled
> in the just possession of the imperial crown of this realm and
> other dominions thereunto belonging, cannot now hide that reli-
> gion which God and the world knoweth she hath ever professed
> from her infancy hitherto, which her majesty is minded to
> observe and maintain for herself by God's grace during her time,
> so doth her highness much desire and would be glad the same

were all of her subjects quietly and charitably embraces. And yet
she doth signify unto all her Majesty's said loving subjects that of
her most gracious disposition and clemency her highness mind-
eth not to compel any her said subjects thereunto unto such time
as further order by common assent may be taken therein.

Mary called on her subjects "to live in quiet sort and Christian charity"
and told them that further religious change would be settled by
"common consent," by act of Parliament.[16] In the midst of popular
unrest and fear of change, Mary had responded with moderation and
pragmatism.

YET WHILE MARY publicly temporized, she made secret steps
toward restoring Catholicism. In August, she addressed a private letter
to Pope Julius III, petitioning him to remit all the ecclesiastical censures against England that had been imposed when Henry broke with
Rome. As she wrote to Henry Penning, the pope's chamberlain, she
had "always been most obedient and most affectionate towards the
Apostolic See and his Holiness had no more loving daughter than herself." She declared that within a few days she "hoped to be able to show
it openly to the whole world" and would first need to "repeal and annul
by Act of Parliament many perverse laws made by those who ruled
before her."[17]

On learning of Mary's accession, the pope had appointed as cardinal and papal legate Reginald Pole, the son of Mary's former governess
Margaret Pole, in order to arrange the reconciliation of England to the
Catholic Church. Pole began petitioning for an immediate and unconditional return to Roman obedience, for "The Queen, or at least
England, was assuredly [ship]wrecked when she threw herself over-
board . . . into the sea of this century." As he had "drawn a picture of
the danger; her Majesty will judge whether it is time to deliberate, or
rather to act as ordained and prescribed by divine and human counsel."[18] With Parliament summoned for the beginning of October, Pole
demanded that the issue of papal supremacy and monastic property be
quickly resolved and on August 10 launched a series of exhortations to
the queen, begging her to end the schism without delay.

Yet Mary had come to realize the scale of her task. On September 11, she wrote to the cardinal of Imola, informing him that no legatine mission should be sent until the time was more propitious. She was aware of the dangers of introducing religious changes before they could be sanctioned by Parliament. For now she dissembled, maintaining that she did not want to coerce people into going to Mass. As Mary declared to Renard, "she had so far found no better expedient than to leave each free as to the religion he would follow. . . . If some held to the old, and others to the new, they should not be interfered with or constrained to follow any other course until the coming Parliament should decide by law."[19] There was, however, one notable exception.

WITHIN TWO WEEKS of Mary's entry into London, Renard reported that he had raised with the queen the presence at court of the Lady Elizabeth, who might, out of "ambition or being persuaded thereunto, conceive some dangerous design and put it to execution, by means which it would be difficult to prevent, as she was clever and sly."[20] Writing to Mary in late August, the imperial ambassadors, M. de Courrières, M. de Thoulouse, and Renard, advised her "not to be too ready to trust the Lady Elizabeth" and urged her

> to reflect that she now sees no hope of coming to the throne, and has been unwilling to yield about religion. . . . Moreover, it will appear that she is only clinging to the new religion out of policy, in order to win over and make use of its adepts in case she decided to plot. A mistake may perhaps be made in attributing this intention to her, but at this stage it [is] safer to forestall than to be forestalled and to consider all possible results; for there are clear enough indications.[21]

Aware of such suspicions against her and "perceiving that the Queen did not show her as kindly a countenance as she could wish," Elizabeth asked Mary for a private audience. They met at the beginning of September at Richmond, in one of the galleries of the palace; Mary was accompanied by one of her ladies, Elizabeth by one of her maids. Falling on her knees before the queen, Elizabeth wept, saying she knew the queen was "not well disposed towards her, and she knew no other cause except religion." She begged for understanding. She acted out of ignorance, not obstinacy: she had never been taught the doctrine of the ancient religion. She asked for books so that "having read them she might know if her conscience would allow her to be persuaded; or that a learned man might be sent to her, to instruct her in the truth."

Glad to see such "good resolves," Mary granted her request.[22] Meanwhile, as she had promised, Elizabeth attended Mass in the Chapel Royal on September 8, the Feast of the Nativity of the Blessed Virgin. It was clearly under duress. She had tried to excuse herself on grounds of ill health and had complained loudly of a stomachache all the way to church.[23] It was a rerun of the earlier clashes between Mary and Edward, when he had implored her to submit to his authority and accept the Protestant changes. But unlike Mary, Elizabeth had no desire to be a martyr.

No one, least of all Mary, was fooled by Elizabeth's display of compliance. Within days the imperial ambassadors were reporting that "last Sunday the Lady Elizabeth did not go to mass," adding "the Queen has sent us word that she has half-turned already from the good road upon which she had begun to travel."[24] Mary continued to press Elizabeth as to the purity of her motives, questioning whether she really believed, as Catholics did, "concerning the holy sacrament," or whether she "went to mass in order to dissimulate, out of fear or hypocrisy." Elizabeth replied that she was contemplating making a public declaration "that she went to mass and did as she did because her conscience prompted and moved her to it, that she went of her own free will and without fear, hypocrisy or dissimulation."[25]

Although she continued to doubt Elizabeth's sincerity, Mary allowed her sister to remain at court and to attend her coronation. But underlying tensions remained. Within weeks Renard reported that Mary was considering barring her from the succession on account of her "heretical opinions and illegitimacy, and characteristics in which she resembled her mother." As Anne Boleyn "had caused great trouble in the kingdom," she feared her daughter might do the same "and particularly that she might imitate her mother in being a French partisan." She told Renard that it "would burden her conscience too heavily to allow a bastard to succeed."[26] Mary increasingly suspected that Elizabeth went to Mass only "out of hypocrisy; she had not a single servant or maid of honour who was not a heretic, she talked every day with heretics and lent an ear to all their evil designs."[27]

Finally, in early December, Elizabeth asked for permission to leave court. The sisters parted on affectionate terms. Mary gave her a coif of rich sables, and en route to Hatfield, Elizabeth stopped to write to Mary asking her for copes, chasubles, chalices, and other ornaments for her chapel. The queen ordered all these things to be sent to her, "as it was for God's service and Elizabeth wished to bear witness to the religion she had declared she meant to follow."[28]

CHAPTER 40

OLD CUSTOMS

∴

As to the establishment of the Queen upon her throne, the preparations for the coronation are going forward apace for the first of October.[1]

—IMPERIAL AMBASSADORS TO THE
EMPEROR, SEPTEMBER 9, 1553

ROM THE EARLIEST WEEKS OF HER REIGN, PLANS WERE PUT into place for Mary's coronation.[2] Fabrics and cloth were purchased and delivered, clothing was made ready, the nobility was summoned, and triumphal pageants were composed. By mid-September, the citizens of London had begun decorating the city; arches, scaffolds, and scenery for the pageants were erected and painted, and wooden rails were installed along the coronation procession route to hold back the crowds.[3] At Westminster Abbey a great stage had been constructed for the crowning, and banners hung all around. It was as it had been for countless coronations before.

Yet amid the following of "old customs" there existed unease.[4] Though everyone had resolved to make the ceremonies "very splendid and glorious," the manner and form of the ceremony were uncertain. There were no precedents for the crowning of a queen regnant, let alone a Catholic bastard.[5] The fourteenth-century guide *Liber Regalis* and the "Little Device," first used for the coronation of Richard III, outlined only the procession and ceremony of a queen consort. And after weeks of religious unrest and plotting in the capital, there were fears of further violence.

As Renard reported, "arquebusers, arrows and other weapons were being collected in various houses," giving rise to fears that during the coronation procession "some attempt might be made against [the Queen's] person."[6] A number of former Edwardian councillors called for unprecedented change, arguing that the coronation should be postponed until after Parliament had met and confirmed Mary's legitimacy.[7] The imperial ambassadors believed that such "novelty" was intended to "cast doubts upon and put in question the Queen's right to the throne, to render her more dependant on [her] council and Parliament than she should be [and] bridle her so that she cannot marry a foreigner." It was a proposal born of the fears raised by accession of the country's first female sovereign, and one that Mary rejected outright.[8]

The coronation had been set for October 1, a Sunday, according to tradition. Although the 1552 Act of Uniformity remained in force and Mary was to be crowned supreme head of the Church, the coronation ceremony was to proceed as a full Catholic Mass. Recognizing the potential illegitimacy of the ceremony, Mary requested that Pole, the papal legate, absolve her and her bishops on the day of the coronation so that they might be able to say Mass and administer the sacraments without sin.[9] Moreover, concerned that the oils to be used in the anointing, which had been consecrated by an Edwardian minister, "may not be such as they ought," she asked the imperial ambassadors to write to the bishop of Arras, Charles's chief minister in Brussels, to secretly prepare specially consecrated oil for her anointing.[10] The conservative Bishop Gardiner, recently freed from the Tower, was chosen to perform the rite in place of Thomas Cranmer, archbishop of Canterbury, who remained imprisoned. With the amendments made, all was ready for the pageantry to begin.

ON THURSDAY, September 28, Mary departed St. James's Palace for Whitehall, accompanied by her sister, Elizabeth, now heir apparent, and their former stepmother Anne of Cleves. At Westminster, Mary boarded her barge and was escorted down the Thames to the Tower by the lord mayor, the aldermen of London, and the companies, their boats festooned with banners and flying streamers.[11] As the flotilla approached the Tower, a salute was fired. At the Watergate, Mary thanked the city officials, and then, amid a cacophony of trumpets, musicians, singers, and the pounding of cannon, she entered the Tower.[12]

On Saturday, the eve of the coronation, a symbolic chivalric ritual dating back to the fourteenth century was performed. Fifteen young nobles were created knights of the bath. A ceremony of naked bathing, shaving, and prayer marked their coming of age as warriors.[13] It was a male rite of passage, an exercise in chivalric kingship, and a means of rewarding loyalty and service to the Crown. Many of those given the honor were those of Mary's servants who had acted in her defense in the succession crisis, men such as Sir Henry Jerningham and Robert Rochester. Not for the last time, Mary's gender necessitated the redefining of ritual as the lord steward, the earl of Arundel, deputized in Mary's place. On Saturday morning the chosen gentlemen plunged naked into a wooden bath in the chapel of the Tower before reemerging to kiss Arundel's shoulder.

At three that afternoon, as guns fired from the ramparts and bells rang from the churches all around, Mary departed the Tower for the coronation procession. The event, another tradition dating from the reign of Richard II, was an opportunity for Londoners to see their sovereign before the coronation the following day. First, the queen's messengers rode out from the courtyard of the Tower, followed by trumpeters, esquires of the body, the knights of the bath, heralds, bannerets, and members of the council and clergy, some in gold, some in silver, their horses covered in plate. Then, in rank order, came the Garter knights, the rest of the nobility, the foreign ambassadors, each paired with an Englishman, merchants, soldiers, and knights; behind them the queen's personal entourage, the earl of Sussex, her Chief Server, carrying the queen's hat and cloak; and "two ancient knights with old-fashioned hats, powdered on their heads, disguised," representing, as was traditional, the dukes of the former English territories of Normandy and Guienne. Gardiner and Paulet followed with the seal and mace; the lord mayor in crimson velvet carrying the golden scepter; the sergeants at arms; and the earl of Arundel bearing Mary's sword.[14]

Then came Mary herself, riding in an open litter pulled by six horses in white trappings almost to the ground. Official accounts describe her as "richly apparelled with mantle and kirtle of cloth of gold . . . all things thereunto appertaining, according to the precedents."[15] Mary was dressed as a queen consort. On her head she wore a gold tinsel cloth and a jeweled crown, which was described as being "so massy and ponderous that she was fain to bear up her head with her hands."[16] Around Mary's litter rode four ladies on horseback: Edward Courtenay's mother, the marchioness of Exeter; and the wives of the duke of Norfolk, the earl of Arundel, and Sir William Paulet. Next came the carriage carrying Elizabeth and Anne of Cleves; then lines of peeresses, ladies, and gentlewomen, some in chariots, some on horseback, and the royal henchmen dressed in the Tudor colors of green and white.[17]

For a mile and a half, the grand procession wound its way through the graveled streets of London. The aldermen of the city stood within the rails; behind them the multitudes, "people resorted out of all parts of the realm, to see the same, that the like have not been seen before."[18] The procession was, Renard reported, "a memorable and solemn one, undisturbed by any noise or tumult."[19]

From the Tower to Temple Bar, Mary was greeted by an array of civic pageantry. At Fenchurch Street, Genoese merchants had created a triumphal arch decorated with verses praising Mary's accession: as she passed, a boy dressed as a girl and carried on a throne by men and "giants" delivered a salutation.[20] At Cornhill, the Florentines paid tribute to Mary's triumph over Northumberland's forces by invoking an image of Judith, the Israelite heroine, saving her people from Holofernes, the Assyrian leader, and of Tomyris, who had led her people to victory against the all-conquering Cyrus. In the pageant, an angel clothed in green, trumpet in hand, was strung up at the highest point between four gigantic "pictures." As the angel put the trumpet to his mouth, a trumpeter hidden within the pageant "did sound as if the noise had come from the angel, to the great marvelling of many ignorant persons."[21] In Cornhill and Cheap, the conduits ran with wine and pageants were performed in which people stood singing verses in praise of their queen.

At St. Paul's, Mary was addressed by the recorder of London and the chamberlain before being presented with a purse containing a thousand marks of gold, a gesture of goodwill "which she most thankfully received."[22] At the school in St. Paul's churchyard, the playwright John Heywood, sitting under a vine, delivered an oration in Latin and English; and at the dean of St. Paul's Gate, choristers held burning tapers that gave off "most sweet perfumes."[23] At Ludgate, minstrels played and children sang songs of joy. Then, passing through Temple Bar by early evening, Mary finally reached Whitehall and took leave of the lord mayor. The following day she would be crowned queen of England.

CHAPTER 41

GOD SAVE QUEEN MARY

.·.

AT ELEVEN IN THE MORNING ON SUNDAY, OCTOBER 1, 1553, MARY proceeded to the south transept of Westminster Abbey for her coronation. It was a sight not seen before and combined elements of both precedent and novelty. The queen, dressed as a male monarch in traditional state robes of crimson velvet, walked beneath a canopy borne by the barons of the Cinque Ports; the duke of Norfolk carried the crown, the marquess of Winchester the orb, and the earl of Arundel the ball and scepter. Before her, in pairs, walked an ordered procession of gentlemen, knights, and councillors, headed by the bishop of Winchester and ten others, all with miters on their heads and crosses in their hands.¹

In the center of the abbey a raised walkway led to the royal stage and then steps to a higher plinth bearing the coronation chair. It had seated every monarch at coronations since Edward the Confessor more than five hundred years before. Now, for the first time, it would seat a queen regnant. Two noblemen led Mary to each corner of the dais so the congregation might see her. To this assembly Gardiner made his address:

> Sirs, Here present is Mary, rightful and undoubted inheritrix by the Laws of God and man to the Crown and Royal Dignity of this realm of England, France and Ireland, whereupon you shall understand that this day is appointed by all the peers of this land for the consecration, injunction and coronation of the said most excellent Princess Mary; will you serve at this time and give your wills and assent to the same consecration, unction and coronation?

The gathered throng answered as one: "Yea, yea, yea! God save Queen Mary!"

Mary went before the altar and, as she lay facedown on a velvet cushion, prayers were said over her. From the side of the stage she listened to the sermon of George Day, bishop of Chichester, on the subject of the obedience owed to a monarch. Then, kneeling in front of the altar, Mary prepared to make her oaths, pledging to defend her subjects, maintain peace, and administer justice throughout the realm. She had feared that the oath would be tampered with so that in some way she would be called upon to condone the new religion, and she therefore added the words "just and licit laws" to the traditional form. "Will ye grant to keep to the people of England and others your realms and dominions, the *just and licit* laws and liberties of this realm and other your realms and dominions?" Mary was asked.[2] Then, lying prostrate before the high altar, the choirs sang "Veni Creator Spiritus."

After the choir quieted, Mary moved to a curtained traverse at the left-hand side of the altar, accompanied by some of her ladies. Here she made her first change of clothing in preparation for her anointing. This, the most solemn part of the ceremony, was intended to mark the monarch with the indelible stigma of divine majesty. Her mantle of crimson velvet was removed, and she returned to the altar in a simple petticoat of purple velvet. She lay again before the altar, a pall held over her by four knights of the Garter, and she was anointed by Bishop Gardiner on her shoulders, breast, forehead, and temples with the holy oil and chrism secretly obtained from Flanders.[3] Returning to the traverse dressed in her robes of state, Mary was led to the altar, where she received the ornaments, her symbols of power: the sword, the scepter, and the orbs. She was crowned with the crown of Edward the Confessor, the imperial crown of the realm, and with another specially made for her, a vast yet simply designed crown with two arches, a large fleur-de-lis, and prominent crosses. The choir then burst into a Te Deum.[4]

Mary was crowned in a fashion similar to her male predecessors: "girt with a sword as when one is armed a knight, and a King's sceptre was placed in one hand, and in the other a sceptre wont to be given to queens, which is surmounted by doves."[5] Finally, the crimson mantle furred with ermine was fastened on her shoulders. Arrayed in her regalia, Mary was seated in Saint Edward's Chair, where she received the nobles, led by Gardiner, who paid homage to her as queen.[6]

At four that afternoon Mary emerged from the abbey as queen of England. Carrying the orb and scepter, which "she twirled and turned in her hand," she proceeded back along the carpeted path to Westminster Hall for a ceremonial dinner. Gardiner sat to her right, Elizabeth and Anne of Cleves to her left, though at a distance.[7] Four swords were held before her as she ate, and according to custom she "rested her feet on two of her ladies."[8] The earl of Derby, high steward of England, and the duke of Norfolk, high marshal, rode around the hall on chargers trapped with cloth of gold, overseeing the banquet and maintaining order. After the second course, the banquet was interrupted by a horseman, the queen's champion, Sir Edward Dymocke, who entered dressed in bright armor, ostrich plumes in his helmet, with a surcoat of armorial bearings. He read out a challenge: "Whosoever shall dare to affirm that this Lady is not the rightful Queen of this Kingdom I will show him the contrary, or will do him to death" and threw down his glove.

Returning to the queen, he proclaimed that seeing that "none was found who dared to gainsay him or take up his glove, he hailed her as the true and rightful Queen."[9]

CHAPTER 42

INIQUITOUS LAWS

∴

FOUR DAYS AFTER HER CORONATION, MARY OPENED HER FIRST Parliament. As she looked on from her throne, Bishop Gardiner, the lord chancellor, made his opening address in which he "treated amply of the union with religion," demonstrating how many disadvantages had befallen the realm owing to its separation. "Parliament," he declared, "was assembled by her Majesty and the Council to repeal many iniquitous laws against the said union, and to enact others in favour of it."[1]

In one of its first acts, Parliament declared that the marriage of Mary's parents, Katherine of Aragon and Henry VIII, had been valid and that Mary was therefore legitimate. The queen's title was vindicated from "the corrupt and unlawful sentence" that had divorced her father and mother and from subsequent laws that had declared her illegitimate. It was what Mary had fought for since the years of her adolescence. Finally she had restored her mother's memory and confirmed her own legitimacy.

Next came the repeals of the Edwardian religious legislation that had pronounced on the Prayer Book, the sacraments, and married priests, thereby restoring the Church settlement to that of the final years of her father's reign. All offenses defined as treasonable during Henry and Edward's reigns were repealed, and the law was taken back to its basic definition of 1352, with evidence of guilt now lying once more in action against the monarch rather than in a denial of the royal supremacy.

To make the bills acceptable to the House of Commons, all allusion to the pope had to be avoided. Holders of monastic and chantry lands, whatever their doctrinal beliefs, feared that a return to Rome would threaten the property that they had received following the dissolution of the monasteries during the 1530s. Writing to Pole, Mary explained that the Commons would not hear of "the abolishing, specially of the law that gave the title of the supremacy of the Church in the realm of the crown, suspecting that to be an introduction of the Pope's authority into the realm, which they cannot gladly hear of."[2]

Although the bill was eventually passed, it demonstrated that though Parliament was willing to restore church services and religious ceremonies to the pattern of the 1540s, it was not prepared to sanction the abolition of the Supreme Headship and the return of papal authority in the realm. The Commons would not sacrifice their property and revenue from ex-monastic lands; these would need to be safeguarded before a return to Rome could be achieved.[3] "There is difficulty about religion, the Pope's authority and the restitution of Church property," Renard explained, "so much so that a conspiracy has been discovered among those who hold that property either by the liberality of the late Kings Henry and Edward, or by purchase, who would rather get themselves massacred than let go." Renard's message to the emperor was clear: "The majority of Parliament refuses to admit the Pope's authority or to come back into the fold."[4]

Mary was forced to curb her zeal; for now she would remain supreme head of the Church. As she wrote to Pole on November 15:

This Parliament was to make a full restoration [of obedience], but we now need another in three or four months. You will hear that all Edward's statutes about religion have been annulled, and the state of religion put back where it was at the time of the death of King Henry, our father of the most pious memory.

Yet Pole still pushed for an immediate and full restitution: "He [God] destroyed the government that displeased Him without any human action, and gave power to a virgin, who trusted in Him," he railed, yet Mary "thinks that temporal matters should be taken care of first. She must not be so ungrateful . . . nothing more neglectful than putting off religion to the end. Her impudent councillors must not intimidate her." And he implored Mary, "[God] did not give you such great courage so that you might become fearful as Queen."[5] In a subsequent letter he told her, "You have given your enemies good argument that you [are] schismatic, since [you] have taken Parliament's authority for most important confirmation of your claim." It was "no excuse" that some of Parliament had proved resistant. Her adversaries could say that she was "no better than Northumberland" with regard to obedience. "You look weak now," he ended; "these acts establish schism."[6]

Despite Pole's insistence, Mary knew she could not move too fast. Yet she dared not show "the intent of her heart in this matter," given the opposition expressed.[7] On the day that Parliament rose, a dead dog with a shaved crown, representing a tonsured priest, a rope about its neck, was slung through the windows of the Queen's Presence Chamber.[8] Mary was indignant and warned Parliament that "such acts might move her to a kind of justice further removed from justice than she would wish."[9]

AS OF DECEMBER 20, religious services were to be conducted and sacraments administered as they had been in the last years of Henry VIII's reign. It marked the beginning of restoration and reform. Although Mary did not use the title, she did use her authority as supreme head to press for reform. In royal articles of March 1554, she ordered the strict observance of the traditional ceremonies and the repression of "corrupt and naughty opinions, unlawful books, ballads, and other pernicious and hurtful devices." Married priests were to be deprived, all processions were to be conducted in Latin, all "laudable" ceremonies were to be observed, and "uniform" doctrine was to be set forth in homilies.[10]

The restoration of the Mass and of Catholic ceremonies demanded the return of all that the Edwardian government had had stripped out of the churches. In articles designed for the visitation of his diocese in the autumn, Edmund Bonner, bishop of London, outlined a program of reconstruction to be adopted by bishops. The articles specified what his church now required, and parishioners were ordered to return property still in their possession:

Whether the things underwritten (which are to be found at the cost of the parishioners) be in the church: it is to wit, a legend, an antiphoner, a grail, a psalter, an ordinal to say or solemnize divine office, a missal, a manual, a processional, a chalice, two cruetts, a principal vestment with chasuble, a vestment for the deacon and sub-deacon, a cope with the appurtenances, it is to wit an amice, alb, girdle, stole and fannon, the high altar with apparel in the front and parts thereof, three towels, three sur-plices, a rochet, a cross for procession with candlesticks, a cross for the dead, an incenser, a ship or bessel for frankincense, a lit-tle sanctas bell, a pix with an honest and decent cover, and a veil for the Lent, banners for the Rogation week, bells and ropes, a bier for the dead, a vessel to carry holy water about, a candle-stick for the paschal taper, a font to christen children with cover-ing and lock and key, and generally all other things, which after the custom of the country or place, the parishioners are bound to find, maintain and keep?"

Bonner's investigation was minute in its detail, from issues of dress to clerical residence and morality. But it also focused specifically on seeking out heresy. He wanted to know about the doctrine taught by the clergy, about seditious or heretical books in circulation, and about priests who administered any sacraments in English. In addition, Bonner wanted the names of any laity who, at the moment of consecra-tion, "do hang down their heads, hide themselves behind pillars, turn away their faces, or depart out of the church," any who "murmured, grudged or spoke against" the Mass, the sacraments, or ceremonies, and any who "made noise, jangled, talked or played the fool in church."¹² He demanded the names of any circulating "slanderous books, ballads or plays, contrary to the Christian religion." He wanted to know about any who refused to take part in rituals such as proces-sion on Sunday, and issuing of the pax, and any who had eaten flesh on the traditional fasts or vigils. Pictures on the walls of churches were to be removed that "chiefly and principally do tend to the maintenance of carnal liberty" by attacking fasting, good works, celibacy, or the ven-eration of the Blessed Sacrament.¹³

Gradually, signs indicating the return to Catholicism were visible across the country. In November 1553, Saint Katherine's image was carried around the steeple at St. Paul's on her patronal feast day, and on Saint Andrew's Day there was "a general procession . . . in Latin with *ora pro nobis*."[14] As Machyn recorded in his diary, "The viii day of December was [the] procession at [St.] Paul's. When all was done my lord of London [Bonner] commanded that every parish church should provide for a cross and a staff and cope to go to the procession every Sunday, Wednesday and Friday, and pray unto God for fair weather through London."[15]

Outside London, Robert Parkyn, a Yorkshire priest, described how

it was joy to hear and see how these carnal priests (which had led their lives in fornication with their whores and harlots) did lower and look down when they were commanded to leave and forsake their concubines and harlots and to do open penance according to the Canon Law . . . all old ceremonies, laudably used before-time in the holy Church was then revived, daily frequented and used.[16]

The process of Catholic revival, resisted by some but welcomed by many, had begun.

CHAPTER 43

A MARRYING HUMOR

∴

So as to restore the succession and continue the line, they [the Council] considered it necessary for the good of the kingdom that the Queen should enter into an alliance, and marry; and the sooner the better, because of the state of her affairs and her years.[1]

—RENARD TO THE EMPEROR,
OCTOBER 5, 1553

UPON MARY'S ACCESSION THERE WAS GENERAL EXPECTATION THAT she would marry. No one expected a woman to rule alone. It was important that she have an heir to ensure a Catholic succession and someone to assist her in government.[2] Mary now accepted the need to marry: "I have lived a virgin, and I doubt not, with God's grace, to live still. But if, as my ancestors have done it might please God that I should leave you a successor to be your governor."[3] At thirty-seven Mary would have to wed quickly if she were to stand any chance of conceiving.

Despite the contemporary belief that a queen needed a consort, there was also apprehension. It was assumed that a husband would exercise power. Under English law not only would a woman's property, titles, and income pass to her husband upon marriage, but she would also cede governance of her person. For Mary, any prospective bridegroom had to be of royal blood and a good Catholic.

English hopes came to focus on the twenty-five-year-old Edward Courtenay, a great-grandson of Edward IV. His father, the marquess of Exeter, had been executed by Henry VIII in 1538; his mother, Gertrude Courtenay (née Blount), the marchioness of Exeter, remained one of

Mary's most trusted intimates. Chief among his supporters was the lord chancellor, Stephen Gardiner, who had spent a number of years imprisoned with Courtenay in the Tower. Although Gardiner was supported by almost all the other privy councillors, Mary quickly made it clear that she had no intention of marrying Courtenay or any other of her own subjects. Dom Luis of Portugal, the brother of King Juan, who had been suggested as a husband many times over the previous years, now renewed his overtures. Maximilian, the son of the emperor's brother, Ferdinand, also emerged as a possible candidate; while Charles V intrigued for a match between Mary and his own son, Philip, prince of Spain.

The prospect of Mary's marriage was of great importance in the struggle between the Houses of Habsburg and Valois. If Charles could succeed in establishing his son, Philip, upon the throne of England as Mary's husband, the sea route between Spain and the Netherlands would be secured, the Netherlands themselves would be saved from falling into the clutches of the king of France, as they seemed likely to do, and France would be encircled.[4] Moreover, it would provide a counterweight against the intended marriage of the French dauphin to Mary, queen of Scots.

To the French an Anglo-Habsburg marriage was deeply alarming and had to be prevented. As Noailles wrote to the French king, the queen's marriage would be "to the great displeasure of all, with perpetual war against your Majesty, the Scotch and her own subjects, who will unwillingly suffer the rule of a foreigner." He continued, "It was a perpetual war against the King [of France] that the Emperor wished her to espouse rather than his son."[5] The final outcome of the long struggle between Habsburg and Valois seemed to depend on developments in England: at stake was the hegemony of Europe.

IT WAS ON JULY 29, at his first private audience with the queen at Beaulieu in Essex, that Simon Renard raised the question of the queen's marriage. The emperor, he declared, was mindful of the fact that a "great part of the labour of government could with difficulty be undertaken by a woman" and urged her to "entertain the idea of marriage and fix on some suitable match as soon as possible."[6]

Mary had told Renard that she had never thought of marrying before she was queen and "as a private individual she would never have desired it, but preferred to end her days in chastity." Katherine of Aragon, in one of her last letters, had urged her daughter "not thinking or desiring any husband for Christ's passion."[7] However, as she now occupied "a public position," Mary was determined to follow the emperor's advice and said she would "choose whomsoever you might recommend." At his second audience two weeks later, Renard reopened the subject by mentioning Mary's duty to the nation and implying that a foreigner would best help her fulfill the obligation. At this Mary laughed "not once but several times, whilst she regarded me in a way that proved the idea to be very agreeable to her."[8]

Meanwhile, Charles wrote to his son, Philip, that he was "glad to see our cousin in the place that is hers by right, to strengthen her position and to aid the restoration of Catholicism." He told him he was contemplating marrying the English queen himself, as he had some thirty years before: "I am sure that if the English made up their minds to accept a foreigner they would more readily accept me than any other, for they have always shown a liking for me." But ill and aged, Charles had no real intention of marrying Mary. As his letter continued, he wondered whether Philip might be a better choice. He asked his son "to consider it privately and keep the matter a close secret."[9]

A month later, Philip, who had been in negotiations for a possible match with the Infanta Maria of Portugal, finally responded to his father's letter: "All I have to say about the English affair is that I am rejoiced to hear that my aunt has come to the throne . . . as well as out of natural feeling as because of the advantages mentioned by your Majesty where France and the Low Countries are concerned." He continued, "As your Majesty feels as you say about the match for me, you know that I am so obedient a son that I have no will other than yours, especially in a matter of such high import."[10]

Awaiting further instructions from Brussels as to the advancing of Philip's suit, Renard questioned Mary about Edward Courtenay and the "common rumour" that she was to marry him. Mary was adamant that she "knew no one in England with whom she would wish to ally herself" and asked whether the emperor had yet selected "a suitable person." Renard responded that it would be much easier for the emperor to advise if "she could inform him of her inclinations." Mary had expressed her desire for someone "middle aged"; Renard had mentioned several Catholic princes, but she had responded that she "was old enough to be their mother."[11]

On October 10, Renard knelt before Mary and formally offered the hand of Prince Philip. He assured her that "if age and health had permitted," the emperor would "have desired no other match, but as years and infirmity" rendered him "a poor thing to be offered to her," he could think of no one dearer or better suited than Philip, "who was of middle age, of distinguished qualities, and of honourable and Catholic upbringing."

Philip was twenty-six, eleven years Mary's junior. She was the granddaughter of Ferdinand and Isabella; he was their great-grandchild. He had already been married to his cousin Infanta Maria of Portugal, who had died in childbirth in July 1545. Their son, Don Carlos, was now nine years old. For Mary the prospect of marriage to Philip represented her imperial destiny, a chance to join the family that she had long since relied on for support and protection. Moreover, it would put England at the center of European politics.

Mary was thrilled, calling it a "greater match than she deserved." But, she said, "she did not know how the people of England would take it." She also expressed fears about what the marriage would entail; "if he were disposed to be amorous, such was not her desire, for she was of the age your Majesty knew of, and had never harboured thoughts of love." She would, however, "wholly love and obey him to whom she had given herself, following the divine commandment and would do nothing against his will." But, if he wished to "encroach in the government of the kingdom, she would be unable to permit it, nor if he attempted to fill posts and offices with strangers, for the country itself would never stand such interference."[12] Mary would attempt to separate her duties as Philip's wife and her responsibilities as queen, as her grandmother Isabella had before her.[13]

For a month the court was an agitated ferment of secret meetings, hushed conversations, and exaggerated rumor. William Paget and Renard lobbied councillors in favor of Philip, and Gardiner pressed the claims of Courtenay. On October 20, Gardiner and a number of Mary's trusted household servants approached her to speak of the

English candidate. As Mary told Renard, because their actions were "dictated by whole-hearted affection and devotion to her service," she could not "take the advice of such trusty counsellors in bad part."[14] Gardiner had stressed that "the country would never abide a foreigner; Courtenay was the only possible match for her"; Francis Englefield added "that his highness had a kingdom of his own he would not wish to leave to come to England and that his own subjects spoke ill of him." Edward Waldegrave argued that if the queen "wedded his Highness the country would have to go to war with the French."

But Mary begged them all to "lay aside their private considerations" and to "think of the present condition of affairs, the French plottings, the marriage of the French Dauphin with the Queen of Scotland, what benefit the country could look for were she to marry Courtenay, and what profit might accrue to it if she chose a foreigner."

Robert Rochester and other of the household servants were given letters from the emperor in which he feigned to care for their opinions "as to what alliance would be best for her [Mary] and the country," suggesting that he would be guided by their advice. Meanwhile, by intrigues, bribes, and promises, and drawing on a web of agents and informants, Noailles sought to make the idea of a Spanish alliance hateful to the people of England. When Henry II heard rumors of the impending betrothal, his "countenance was sad, his words few, and his dislike of the match marvellously great." Speaking to the English ambassador, Nicholas Wotton, the French king remarked that "a husband may do much with his wife" and that it would be hard for Mary, as for any woman, "to refuse her husband anything that he shall earnestly require of her."[15]

FINALLY, ON THE EVENING of Sunday, October 29, Mary sent again for Renard. He found her in her chamber alone, save for Susan Clarencius, her trusted lady-in-waiting. The room was barely lit. A lamp shone in one corner, its glow illuminating the Holy Sacrament, which stood on the altar before them. It was a momentous decision for Mary, both as a woman and as a queen. Her Council and even most of her trusted household servants opposed the match; it could be expected that the country would too. Ever since the emperor's letter had arrived, she had not slept. Instead she woke, weeping and praying for guidance. Now all three knelt before the sacrament, singing "Veni Creator Spiritus"—"Come, Holy Spirit, eternal God." Rising to her feet, Mary announced her decision. She had, she declared, been inspired by God to be Prince Philip's wife. "She believed what I have told her of his Highness's qualities," Renard explained, "and that your Majesty would ever show her kindness, observe the conditions that would safeguard the welfare of the country, be a good father to her as you had been in the past and more, now that you would be doubly her father and cause his highness to be a good husband to her." Now that her mind had been made up, "she would never change but love him perfectly and never give him cause to be jealous."[16]

Two days later Mary hastily wrote to Renard, revealing her anxious excitement:

> *Sir: I forgot to ask you one question the other night: that is to say, are you quite sure that there has never been any contract concerning marriage between the Prince and the daughter of Portugal, for there was much talk to that effect? I request you to write me the truth, on your faith and conscience, for there is nothing else in the world that could make me break the promise I made to you, so may God of His grace assist me! I also pray you to send me your advice as to how I shall broach this matter to the Council, for I have not yet begun to do so with any of them, but wish to speak to them before they speak to me.*
>
> *Written in haste, this All Saints Eve,*
> *Your good friend, Mary,*
> *Queen of England.*[17]

CHAPTER 44

A SUITABLE PARTNER IN LOVE

∴

In the beginning of November was the first notice among
the people touching the marriage of the Queen to the King of
Spain.[1]

—RESIDENT OF THE TOWER
OF LONDON, 1553

ON NOVEMBER 16, 1553, MARY FACED A DEPUTATION OF SOME
twenty members of the Commons seeking to dissuade her from marrying Philip. She had postponed the meeting for three weeks, claiming ill
health; now she could delay no more. As Sir John Pollard, the speaker
of the Commons, put it, it would displease the people to have a foreigner as the queen's consort. If Mary died childless, her husband
would deplete the country of money and arms. He might decide to
remove Mary from the kingdom "out of husbandly tyranny," and if he
were left a widower with young children, he might try to usurp the
crown for himself.[2] Instead, the speaker argued, it would be better for
the queen to marry an Englishman. Mary listened to Pollard's long
speech with exasperation. As she later told Renard, his discourse had
been "so confused, so long-winded and prolific of irrelevant arguments," that she had found it irritating and offensive.

Finally, when Pollard had finished and without waiting for the
chancellor to answer on her behalf, Mary rose to address the assembly.
She thanked it for encouraging her to marry but, as she went on, she
said that she did not appreciate the idea that it should attempt to choose
"a companion" for her "conjugal bed." As she declared, "I now rule

over you by the best right possible, and being a free woman, if any man
or woman of the people of our realm is free, I have full right and sufficient years to discern a suitable partner in love"—both someone she
could love and someone who would be to the benefit and advantage of
the realm. It was, she told them,

> entirely vain for you to nominate a prospective husband for me
> from your own fancy, but rather let it be my free choice to select
> a worthy husband for my bridal bed—one who will not only
> join with me in mutual love, but will be able with his own
> resources to prevent an enemy attack, from his native land.[3]

She warned that "if she were married against her will she would not
live three months and she would have no children." Her affairs had
been conducted by divine disposition, and she would pray to God to
counsel and inspire her in her choice of husband, "who would be bene-
ficial to the kingdom and agreeable to herself . . . for she always
thought of the welfare of her kingdom, as a good princess and mistress
should."[4] Her riposte was so extraordinary that Pollard was rendered
speechless and the deputation retired.

Mary suspected that Gardiner had inspired the speaker's words
and afterward challenged him directly. "She would never marry
Courtenay," she told him; "she never practiced hypocrisy or deceit,
and had preferred to speak her mind, and she had come near to being
angry on hearing such disrespectful words."[5] Mary asked him crossly,
"Is it suitable, that I should be forced to marry a man because a
bishop made friends with him in prison?" Courtenay was, she said, of
"small power and authority," and, given the intrigues of the French
and the poverty of the kingdom, would not be the most desirable
match.

Gardiner tearfully admitted that he had spoken with Pollard but
now accepted that "it would not be right to try to force her in one
direction or another." He now swore to "obey the man she had chosen."[6] The Commons' petition proved futile; Mary had already made
her decision. On the day after Parliament was dissolved, her betrothal
was made public.

MARY'S REBUTTAL OF the Commons' challenge enhanced her authority. Never before had a Tudor ruler flaunted popular opinion, as expressed by Parliament, so openly. In the face of the Commons' delegation, Mary had claimed the right to marry whomever she wished. By maintaining that she would marry as God directed her, "to his honour and to our country's good," she argued that her private inclination and the public welfare were compatible. But many within and outside the court remained discontented. As one contemporary observed, "This marriage was not well thought of by the Commons, nor much better liked by many of the nobility."[7]

At end of the year, Mary wrote to Henry II, assuring him that her marriage to Philip would not alter her desire for amicable relations with France. Henry was not convinced. He told Sir Nicholas Wotton "that he clearly saw that she was allying herself with the greatest enemy he had in the world, and he knew marital authority to be very strong with ladies. He had not thought she would choose a match so odious to him."[8] As Renard reported, the French ambassador "is plotting openly against the alliance, and has spoken to several councillors and nobles to whom he has rehearsed all imaginable disadvantages," spreading fears that England would be forced into war against France and that the country would become ever more subject to Spanish rule.[9]

When the imperial delegation arrived in the City of London to sign the marriage treaty on January 2, 1554, it was received coldly. The people, "nothing rejoicing, held down their heads sorrowfully." As the retinue rode through the capital, "boys pelted them with snowballs; so hateful was the sight of their coming in to them."[10]

Henry, meanwhile, instructed his ambassador:

If you see that the Queen is resolved to marry the Prince of Spain and also that there is likelihood that Courtenay has the will and means to upset the apple-cart, you may say still more confidently that you are sure that for such a great benefit to the realm [of England] I would not deny my favour either to him or to the other gentlemen who know the evil which the marriage could bring to the realm and would like to oppose it. However, since things are as they are, you must act prudently and with great caution.[11]

On December 1, Mary wrote to the emperor:

> I would begin this letter by offering my excuses for not having written before . . . and would repeat in detail all my conferences with your Majesty's ambassador, were it not that your letters show that he has omitted nothing, so I feel sure that he has explained all and freed me of the necessity.
>
> He assures me that he has sent you accounts of the progress of the marriage negotiations he has conducted with me, telling you of my reply and professions of goodwill and affection for the Prince, my good cousin; the reasons founded on my zeal for my kingdom's welfare, towards which I have the duty your Majesty is aware of, that moved me to give my consent; my belief in the Prince's excellent qualities, and confidence that your Majesty will ever remain my good lord and father, and will offer terms in accordance. He also avers that he has not forgotten to transmit to your Majesty my most humble and affectionate thanks for the honour you have done me by proposing so great an alliance, for the mindfulness of my kingdom and myself and constant care for all my interests and concerns.[12]

As a token of the new accord, Charles had sent Mary "a large and valuable diamond"—"in witness of the fact," he told his ambassadors, "that beyond our old friendship and in respect for her position, we now consider her as our own daughter in virtue of this alliance." Their union saw the climax of Mary's long-standing relationship with the emperor and the revival of the Anglo-Spanish entente established by Mary's mother on her marriage to Prince Arthur, fifty-three years earlier.

On January 14, the terms of the treaty were officially proclaimed at Westminster "to the lords, nobility, and gentlemen" by the lord chancellor. As Gardiner explained, Mary had made her decision to wed Philip "partly for the wealth and enriching of the realm, and partly for friendship and other weighty considerations."[13] They should, he continued, "thank God that so noble, worthy, and famous a prince" would "humble himself as in this marriage to take upon him rather as a subject than otherwise; and that the Queen should rule all things as she doth now; and that there should be of the counsel no Spaniard."[14]

It did little to allay fears. After Gardiner's declaration of the terms of the marriage treaty, one chronicler described how the news was "very much misliked . . . almost each man was abashed, looking daily for worse matters to grow shortly after."[15]

CHAPTER 45

A TRAITOROUS CONSPIRACY

∴

The King of France . . . is fitting out his best ships, so that before Easter arrives there shall be such a tumult in England as never was seen.[1]

—RENARD TO THE EMPEROR,
DECEMBER 11, 1553

IN LATE NOVEMBER 1553, A GROUP OF CONSPIRATORS, LED BY SIR Thomas Wyatt, a Kentish gentleman and the son of the poet of the same name; Sir James Croft, the head of a Marches family; and Sir Peter Carew, a soldier and Devonshire landowner, met to discuss the overthrow of the Marian government. Their plan would see a four-pronged rising in Kent, the Midlands, the Southwest, and the Welsh Marches, followed by a march on London. Mary would be deposed and the Spanish marriage thwarted; Elizabeth and Edward Courtenay would be married and both placed on the throne.

The rising was timed for Palm Sunday, March 18, to coincide with the start of Philip's journey to England. It was a scheme backed by the French in what was a final attempt to thwart the Spanish marriage. As Henry II wrote dismissively, the conspirators "have to do only with a woman who is badly provided with good counsel and men of ability, so it should be easy for them to guard against discovery if they are prudent enough and have blood in their nails."[2]

By the new year reports had spread of a "traitorous conspiracy" fostered by "certain lewd and ill-disposed persons."[3] Sir Peter Carew's return to Devon during the Christmas festivities raised suspicions, which seemed to be confirmed when he failed to obey a summons to attend the Privy Council.[4] On January 18, Renard informed Mary that a French fleet was assembling off the Normandy coast and pressed her to take immediate steps to protect herself.[5] Mary ordered that troops be raised and an oath of loyalty be administered to each member of the royal household "in order to ascertain the real feelings of each one." As the oath requesting "obedience and fidelity to his Highness" was read out, "all raised their hand." The same was done with the mayor, magistrates, aldermen, and men of law of the city, who "did not openly show any opposition."[6] Circulars were sent out across the country with copies of the treaty's provisions and orders to proclaim them, "lest rebels be inspired under the pretence of misliking this marriage, to rebel against the Catholic religion and divine service within this our realm, and to take from us that liberty which is not denied to the meanest woman in the choice of husband."[7]

On the twenty-first, Courtenay confessed his role in the affair to Gardiner. As Renard reported in a letter to the emperor, Courtenay had been approached by certain individuals who had sought to influence him "where religion and the marriage were concerned." However, "he had never paid any attention to them." Three days later, the details were revealed and the plot began to unravel.[8] The rebels were forced into action two months earlier than expected. Three of the anticipated risings failed. Carew fled to France, and the duke of Suffolk, who was to have led the rising in Leicestershire just weeks after he was pardoned for his support of Northumberland's coup, was arrested and taken to the Tower. Sir Thomas Wyatt, meanwhile, succeeded in raising a substantial force in Kent.

ON THURSDAY, JANUARY 25, Wyatt raised his standard at Maidstone with 3,000 men and issued a proclamation declaring the realm to be in imminent danger. He appealed to the townsmen to "join with us," maintaining that he meant the queen no harm "but better counsel and councillors" to preserve liberty against the Spaniards.[9] He declared he had taken up arms solely for the love of his country, fearing that the Spanish match would reduce the realm to slavery, and called upon "every good Englishman" to help him. The Spaniards had "already arrived at Dover," he said, and were "passing upward in

London, in companies of ten, four and six, with harness and arqubus-
ers, and marions, with matchlight."[10] By Thursday the twenty-fifth,
Wyatt had taken Rochester for the rebels.

The queen was at Whitehall when she heard of Wyatt's proclamation, and a band of citizens was quickly drawn together under the command of the eighty-year-old Thomas, duke of Norfolk.[11] On Sunday,
the twenty-eighth, Norfolk set out for Rochester with a detachment of
the Guard and five hundred city whitecoats, accompanied by one of the
queen's heralds.

Upon reaching Wyatt's forces, the herald pronounced that all rebels
who would desist from their purpose would be pardoned. With great
shouts the rebels declared "they had done nothing whereof they should
need any pardon." A commander with the city whitecoats, Captain
Alexander Brett, addressed his men, telling them, "Masters, we go
about to fight against our native countrymen of England and our
friends in a quarrel unrightful and partly wicked"; the rebels were
assembled to prevent Englishmen from becoming "slaves and villeins,"
to protect against Spanish designs "to spoil us of our goods and lands,
ravish our wives before our faces, and deflower our daughters in
our presence." Many of the whitecoats deserted, proclaiming "We are
all Englishmen!" and expressing fear at the prospect of rule by the
Spaniards.[12]

Norfolk and the remnant of his forces retreated to London. One
chronicler wrote, "You should have seen some of the guard come
home, their coats torn, all ruined, without arrows or string in their
bow, or sword, in very strange ways."[13]

The desertion of the city whitecoats threw into question the loyalty
of the whole of the capital. Wyatt's forces were rumored to be near,
moving along the banks of the Thames toward Blackheath and
Greenwich. Guns were set at each of the city gates, and a watch was
kept day and night. The queen sent privy councillors Sir Edward
Hastings and Sir Thomas Cornwallis to establish the cause of the com-
motion. If it was a question of the Spanish marriage, they were to point
out that it was the duty of true subjects to sue by petition and not by
force. If the rebels would lay down their arms, Hastings and Cornwallis
were to offer to negotiate.[14]

They encountered Wyatt at Dartford, but he dismissed their conciliatory overtures, declaring that he would not lay down arms before he had secured control of queen and capital, and proceeded to march on London. "I am no traitor," he declared, "and the cause whereof I have gathered the people is to defend the realm from our overrunning by Strangers; which follows, this Marriage taking place."[15]

The Privy Council was divided as to how to protect the queen's person. Mary had been urged to withdraw to Windsor or the Tower but chose to remain at Westminster with a guard of 500 men, well armed and with all the necessary provision for defense. "She even asked to go and fight herself; that however was not permitted to her."[16] Instead she put her faith in Londoners to defend her. On the thirty-first a further proclamation was issued, condemning Wyatt and his company as "rank traitors."[17] The livery companies were informed that 2,000 men were needed for the defense of the city, and every householder was instructed to "raise for his family . . . on pain of death" and arm immediately for the defense of London "and not elsewhere at their peril."[18]

MEANWHILE, MARY took the initiative. At three in the afternoon of February 1, she ordered her horse to be brought to her and rode with her armored guard, heralds, trumpeters, and Council and a company of ladies along the Strand, through Ludgate to the Guildhall, "addressing the people as she went with wonderful good nature and uncommon courtesy."[19] There, beneath the cloth of estate and with scepter in hand, she gave a stirring speech to rally London to her cause, her voice, as one ambassador later described, "rough and loud almost like a man's so that when she speaks she is always heard a long way off."[20]

I am come in mine own person to tell you what you already see and know, I mean the traitorous and seditious assembling of the Kentish rebels against us and you. Their pretence (as they say) is to resist a marriage between us and the prince of Spain . . . by their answers, the marriage is found to be the least of their quarrel; for, swerving from their former demands, they now arrogantly require the governance of our person, the keeping of our town, and the placing of our councillors. What I am loving subjects, ye know your Queen, to whom, at my coronation, ye promised allegiance and obedience, I was then wedded to the realm, and to the laws of the same, the spousal ring whereof I wear here on my finger, and it never has and never shall be left off.

She was the rightful and true inheritor of the English Crown, she said. She was her father's daughter and the kingdom's wife. She told them:

I cannot tell how naturally a mother loveth her children, for I never had any, but if the subjects may be loved as a mother doth her child, then assure yourselves that I, your sovereign lady and your Queen, do earnestly love and favour you. I cannot but think you love me in return; and thus, bound in concord, we shall be able, I doubt not, to give these rebels a speedy over-throw.

She now addressed the subject of her marriage:

I am neither so desirous of wedding, nor so precisely wedded to my will, that I needs must have a husband. Hitherto I have lived a virgin, and I doubt not, with God's grace, to live still. But if, as my ancestors have done, it might please God that I should leave you a successor to be your governor, I trust you would rejoice thereat; also, I know it would be to your comfort. Yet, if I thought this marriage would endanger any of you, my loving subjects, or the royal estate of this English realm, I would never consent thereto, nor marry while I lived. On the word of a Queen I assure you, that if the marriage appear not before the court of Parliament, nobility and commons, for the singular benefit of the whole realm, then I will abstain—not only from this, but from any other.

She finished:

Good and faithful subjects, pluck up your hearts, and like true men stand fast with your lawful prince against these rebels both our enemies and yours, and fear them not, for I assure you that I fear them nothing at all.²¹

She was loudly cheered. Londoners rallied to her defense, throwing their caps into the air. So eloquent was her speech that people cried out that they would live and die in her service and that Wyatt was a traitor.²² It was inspired rhetoric. Her queenship, which had lacked precedent, was defined in these moments with clarity, conviction, and originality. She had pledged herself to her country in entirely feminine terms but with an invocation of motherhood that was strong and resolute. It was an extraordinary moment. Hearts and minds were won over. "God save Queen Mary and the prince of Spain!" cried the crowd.

William Herbert, earl of Pembroke, was appointed as chief captain and general against Wyatt, and preparations were made for the defense of the capital. The following day, Candlemas, the inhabitants of London were "in harness."²³ Five hundred peasants were said to have deserted Wyatt on the night of the queen's speech alone.

ON SATURDAY, February 3, Wyatt reached Southwark and set up two cannon against London Bridge. Finding the bridge's drawbridge up and defended strongly against him, he laid siege for three days, waiting in vain for the bridge to be opened. There were a number of anxious days as the loyalty of the queen's subjects hung in the balance. When Wyatt heard that the lord warden, Thomas Cheney, was pursuing him and that George Neville, Lord Abergavenny, along with Pembroke and Edward, Lord Clinton, intended to cut off his retreat and attack him from three sides, he broke camp. On Tuesday the sixth, he headed for Kingston, where he crossed the river during the night.

The climax came the following day, Ash Wednesday, as Londoners received news that Wyatt was upon them. By the early hours of the morning volunteers had been armed and called to rendezvous at Charing Cross. The musters were summoned immediately. "Much noise and tumult was everywhere; so terrible and fearful at the first was Wyatt and his armies coming to the most part of the citizens, who were seldom or never wont before to have or hear any such invasions to their city."[24] But the queen would not let the guns of the Tower be turned against the rebels, lest innocent citizens in Southwark be caught in the fire.

Earlier that morning Mary's councillors had awakened her and urged her to flee by boat. She immediately requested Renard. He advised her to stay, arguing that if she fled she risked losing her kingdom. If London rose, the Tower would be lost, the heretics would throw religious affairs into confusion and kill the priests; Elizabeth would be proclaimed queen, and irremediable harm would result. The Council was divided; some pleaded with her to depart, others to stay. But Mary ignored their words of despair. She remained at Whitehall Palace in Westminster, praying, as some of her ladies wailed, "Alack, alack! We shall all be destroyed this night."

Troops were mustered, trenches dug, artillery was positioned, and three squadrons of cavalry and 1,000 infantry were drawn up.[25] Mary ordered Pembroke to lead out his infantry at first light and Lord Clinton, commander of the cavalry, to send a detachment of horse against Wyatt's troops while they were disorganized and fatigued by their march. The queen's main forces waited at Charing Cross. It was known that the rebels planned to pass through the area in the hope of gathering more sympathizers or splitting the queen's forces before attacking Whitehall.

By nine in the morning, Wyatt was mustering his forces in Hyde Park, within six miles of Westminster and St. James's. Again Mary was urged to flee, but again she refused and sent word that "she would tarry there [Westminster] to see the uttermost." So great was her determination that "many thought she would have been in the field in person."[26]

At around midday, Wyatt led his forces down St. James's, past Temple Bar, and along Fleet Street, passing citizens armed at their doors. The mayor and aldermen stood paralyzed "as men half out of their lives."[27] Wyatt found Ludgate barred against him with cannon. He retreated toward Charing Cross and was attacked by the queen's soldiers at Temple Bar. By five in the afternoon, Wyatt was captured and taken by boat to the Tower. Altogether, forty people were killed in the fighting in London, only two of them the queen's men.

Celebrations were held across the capital

for the good victory that the Queen's grace had against Wyatt and the rebellious of Kent, the which were overcome, thanks be unto God, with little bloodshed, and the residue taken and had to prison, and after where divers of them put to death in divers places in London and Kent, and procession everywhere that day for joy.[28]

As in July 1553, the citizens of London had shown that they were not prepared to support a usurper against their rightful queen. Mary had triumphed over the rebels. A fortnight of fear, panic, and danger had passed.

Though Mary had displayed clemency with the Northumberland conspirators on her accession, this time she could show no mercy. Stephen Gardiner used his Lenten sermon at court on February 11 to petition Mary to exact extreme justice. In the past she had "extended her mercy, particularly and privately," but "familiarity had bred contempt" and rebellion had resulted; "through her leniency and gentleness much conspiracy and open rebellion was grown." It was now necessary for the mercy of the commonwealth that the "rotten and hurtful members" be "cut off and consumed." His meaning was clear. As the chronicler noted, "All the audience did gather there should shortly follow sharp and cruel execution."[29]

CHAPTER 46

GIBBETS AND HANGED MEN

∴

At present there is no other occupation than the cutting off of heads and inflicting exemplary punishment. Jane of Suffolk, who made herself Queen, and her husband have been executed; Courtenay is in the Tower; and this very day we expect the Lady Elizabeth to arrive here, who they say has lived loosely like her mother and is now with child. So when all these heads are off no one will be left in the realm able to resist the Queen.[1]

—RENARD TO PHILIP,
FEBRUARY 19, 1554

IN THE DAYS AND WEEKS FOLLOWING THE DEFEAT OF THE REBELLION a stream of rebels were arrested. Prisons overflowed and churches became jails as hundreds of suspected traitors were questioned and tried.[2] Gallows were erected at each of the city gates and at principal landmarks in Cheapside, Fleet Street, and Smithfield, on London Bridge, and at Tower Hill. The whitecoats who had gone over to the rebels were hanged at the doors of their houses in the city. As the executions continued, the smell of rotting corpses polluted the air. Renard wrote that "one sees nothing but gibbets and hanged men"— a warning to citizens of the cost of rebellion.[3]

Yet in the midst of this wave of retribution there was clemency too. As the London diarist Henry Machyn recorded, some of "the Kent men went to the court with halters about their necks and bound with cords," walking two by two through London to Westminster; the "poorer prisoners knelt down in the mire, and there the Queen's grace looked out over the gate and gave them all pardon and they cried out 'God save Queen Mary!' as they went."⁴ Mary's victory was secure, the defeat and humiliation of the rebels total. The public spectacle of reconciliation underscored the scale of her triumph.

FIVE DAYS AFTER Wyatt's surrender, Lady Jane Grey and her husband were put to death. Although neither Jane nor Guildford Dudley had taken part in Wyatt's rebellion, they were now too great a threat to live. Both had been found guilty of high treason and condemned in November the previous year, but then Mary had protested Jane's innocence and maintained that her conscience would not permit her to have Jane put to death.⁵ Now the involvement of Jane's father, the duke of Suffolk, who was also to be executed, sealed his daughter's fate.

At ten o'clock on Monday, February 12, Guildford Dudley was beheaded on Tower Hill. The seventeen-year-old Lady Jane watched as her husband departed from his prison in the Beauchamp Tower for the scaffold and then afterward as "his carcass, thrown into a cart and his head in a cloth," was brought back for burial in the chapel in the Tower precinct. It was, as the London chronicler described, "a sight to her no less than death."⁶ An hour later, Jane was collected by Sir John Brydges, lieutenant of the Tower, and, dressed in black, led out to the scaffold on Tower Green. She prayed as she went. Two gentlewomen accompanied her, both weeping as they approached the gallows.

At the block Jane addressed the crowd before her: "Good people, I am hither to die, and by a law I am condemned to the same." She confessed her guilt for her part in Northumberland's attempted coup but denied her involvement in Wyatt's rebellion, claiming to be "innocent before God, and the face of you, good Christian people, this day." After removing her headdress, gloves, and gown, she bent down, begging the executioner to "despatch me quickly," and asking him "Will you take [my head] before I lay me down?" The hangman answered, "No, madame." After tying a handkerchief around her eyes, she groped for the block. Panicking, she called out, "What shall I do? Where is it?" Taking pity on the young woman, one of the bystanders led her to it. She laid her head on the block and said, "Lord, into thy hands I commend my spirit." The ax fell; with one sweep her head was removed.[7]

AS THE EXECUTIONS continued, attention turned to Elizabeth, in whose name the rebels had acted. On January 26, the day after Wyatt had raised his standard at Rochester, Mary had written to her sister, requesting that she come to court:

> *Right dear and entirely beloved sister,*
>   *We greet you well. And where certain evil-disposed persons, minding more the satisfaction of their own malicious and seditious minds, than their duty of allegiance towards us, have of late foully spread divers lewd and untrue rumours . . . do travail to induce our good and loving subjects to an unnatural rebellion against God, Us and the Tranquillity of the realm, we, tending the surety of your person, which might chance to be in some peril, if any sudden tumult should arise where you now be, or about Donnington, whither as we understand, you are minded shortly to remove, do therefore think expedient you should put yourself in good readiness, with all convenient speed, to make your repair hither to us . . .*
>
>   *Your loving sister, Mary the Queen.*[8]

Elizabeth had excused herself from the queen's summons, citing ill health. Now, with the rebellion quashed, the government acted. On February 9, three councillors were sent to Elizabeth's residence at Ashridge in Hertfordshire, charged with bringing her to court. The two royal doctors who had been sent ahead to report on her condition concluded that she was fit to be moved, despite her protestations. Three days later she left Ashridge, bound for London.[9] On the same day, February 12, Edward Courtenay, the man the rebels had hoped to place on the throne with Elizabeth, was taken to the Tower as a prisoner.

After a slow journey to London, which took eleven rather than the five days planned due to Elizabeth's apparent illness, she arrived in the city in an open litter, dressed in white to proclaim her innocence. From Smithfield and Fleet Street she proceeded to Whitehall, passing the gallows and city gates decorated with severed heads and dismembered corpses, and followed by great crowds of people. A hundred horsemen in velvet coats rode in front of her; another hundred behind in scarlet cloth trimmed with velvet.[10] Renard wrote, "She had her litter opened to show herself to the people, and her pale face kept a proud, haughty expression in order to mask her vexation."[11]

Upon her arrival at Whitehall, Mary refused to see her. She was lodged in a remote and secure part of the palace, adjacent to the Privy Gardens, from which neither she nor her servants could go out without passing through the Guard. Renard made clear what he thought should happen to Elizabeth: "The Queen is advised to send her to the Tower, since she is accused by Wyatt, named in the letters of the French ambassador, suspected by her own councillors, and it is certain that the enterprise was undertaken in her favour . . . if now that the occasion offers, they do not punish her and Courtenay, the Queen will never be secure."[12]

Meanwhile, as more leaders of the rebellion were arrested and questioned, the evidence against Elizabeth mounted. It emerged that Sir James Croft had stopped at Ashridge on his way to raise the Marches and that he and Wyatt had advised Elizabeth to move to Donnington, her castle two miles north of Newbury. Her servant Sir William St. Loe, who had been sent with a letter to Wyatt, was subsequently found with two of the rebel leaders at Tonbridge. Equally incriminating was the fact that a copy of Elizabeth's letter excusing herself from the queen's summons to court had been found in the seized dispatches of the French ambassador, Noailles. Elizabeth had, at the very least, been in contact with the conspirators, though as yet there was no evidence that she had approved of their designs or known of their plan. In the Tower, Gardiner pressed Wyatt to confess concerning Elizabeth, but the rebel leader would disclose nothing. At his trial, Wyatt admitted only that he had sent her a letter advising her to get as far away from London as she could, to which she had replied, though not in writing.

It was the flimsiest of evidence, but for the Council it was enough. On Friday, March 16, Elizabeth was formally charged with involvement in Wyatt and Carew's conspiracies. The following day, she would be imprisoned as a suspected traitor.

❧

WHEN THE MARQUESS of Winchester and the earl of Sussex arrived
to take Elizabeth by barge to the Tower, she begged to be given more
time and the opportunity to write to Mary, a request the commissioners
granted.[13] Addressed "To the Queen," her letter sought to secure her
freedom and save her life:

> If any ever did try this old saying—that a King's word was more
> than another man's oath—I most humbly beseech your Majesty
> to verify it in me, and to remember your last promise and my
> last demand: that I be not condemned without answer and due
> proof: which it seems that now I am, for that without cause pro-
> vided I am by your Council from you commanded to go unto
> the Tower; a place more wonted for a false traitor, than a true
> subject. . . . I never practiced, counselled or consented to any
> thing that might be prejudicial to your person any way, or dan-
> gerous to the state by any mean. And therefore I humbly beseech
> your Majesty to let me answer afore your self, and not suffer me
> to trust to your councillors . . .
>
> Yet I pray God, as evil persuasion persuade not one sister
> against the other; and all for that have heard false report, and
> not hearken to the truth known. Therefore once again, with
> humbleness of my heart because I am not suffered to bow the
> knees of my body, I humbly crave to speak with your highness.

More than half of her second sheet of paper was left blank; she
scored it with diagonal lines so that no words could be added and
attributed to her, and then she added a final appeal:

> I humbly crave but only one word of answer from yourself, Your
> Highness's most faithful subject that hath been from the begin-
> ning and will be to my end, Elizabeth.[14]

By the time she had finished her plea, the tide had risen and it was
too late to depart. Her imprisonment would have to wait for the follow-

ing day. Mary raged at Sussex and Winchester for granting her permission to write: "They would never have dared to do such a thing in her father's lifetime," and she "only wished he might come to life again for a month."[15]

At nine the following morning, Palm Sunday, Elizabeth was conducted downstream to the Tower, the place where her mother had met her death. At first Elizabeth refused to land at Traitor's Gate, saying she was not a traitor but came "as true a woman to the Queen's majesty as any is now living, and thereon will I take my death."[16] She was given no choice and entered the Tower across the drawbridge, passing the scaffold on which Lady Jane Grey had been executed. She was taken to the royal palace within the Tower precinct, where the councillors left her, turning the keys in the door as they went.[17]

Days later, Elizabeth was formally examined by the Council. Questioned as to her contact with Sir James Croft and her proposed move to Donnington, Elizabeth stalled, saying "she did not well remember any such house," but then declared, "Indeed, I do now remember that I have such a place, but I never lay in it in all my life. And as for any that hath moved me thereunto, I do not remember." When Croft was brought before her, Elizabeth recovered her memory: "And as concerning my going unto Donnington Castle, I do remember that Mr Hoby and mine officers and you Sir James Croft, had such talk," but, she added defiantly, "what is that to the purpose my lords, but that I may go to mine houses at all times?"[18]

On April 3, Renard relayed to the emperor the queen's assurances that "fresh proof is coming up against her [Elizabeth] every day, and there are several witnesses to assert that she had gathered together stores and weapons in order to rise with the rest and fortify a house in the country [Donnington] whither she had been sending her supplies."[19] In her first Parliament, Mary had restored the ancient constitutional law by which overt or spoken acts of treason had to be proved before any English person could be convicted as a traitor. Mary could not convict Elizabeth on the evidence of intercepted letters because they were written in cipher and could be forgeries. She told Renard that she and her Council were laboring to discern the truth but insisted that the law must be maintained.

WYATT WENT TO the block on Tower Hill on April 11. Upon the scaffold, he addressed the crowd: "Whereas it is said and whistled abroad, that I should accuse my lady Elizabeth's grace and my lord Courteney; it is not so, good people . . . as I have declared no less to the Queens Council."[20] Having made his confession, he knelt down upon the straw and laid his head on the block. He then sat up again to tie the handkerchief around his eyes, raised his hands, and then returned to the block. At one stroke the hangman beheaded him. His corpse was taken to Newgate to be parboiled, after which it was cut into four pieces and each quarter displayed in a different part of the city.[21] His head, placed on top of the gibbet at St. James's, was stolen within a week.

The day after his execution, a group of councillors visited Elizabeth in the Tower.[22] Despite Wyatt's exoneration of her, pressure remained on the princess to admit her guilt. Mary still refused to proceed against her sister with insufficient evidence. Finally with Elizabeth maintaining her innocence, the decision was made to move her to Woodstock, a remote country house in Oxfordshire, "until such time as certain matters touching her case which be not yet cleared may be thoroughly tried and examined." Here she would be placed in the custody of Sir Henry Bedingfield, a Catholic gentleman of proven loyalty whose father had been steward to Katherine of Aragon during her last days at Kimbolton.[23] On May 19, Elizabeth left the Tower for Woodstock. As Mary stated in her instructions to Bedingfield, she was to be "safely looked unto for the safeguard of her person, having nevertheless regard to her. In such good and honourable sort as may be agreeable to our honour and her estate and degree."[24] It was an important caveat, one that Mary had not been afforded during her confinement in the infant Elizabeth's household at Hatfield.

Elizabeth would spend the next eleven months under house arrest. As Don Juan Hurtado de Mendoza, a Spanish noble, surmised to the bishop of Arras, "It was indispensable to throw the Lady Elizabeth into prison, and it is considered that she will have to be executed, as while she lives it will be very difficult to make the Prince's entry here safe, or accomplish anything of promise."[25]

CHAPTER 47

SOLE QUEEN

∴

On the word of a Queen I assure you, that if the marriage appear not before the court of Parliament, nobility and commons, for the singular benefit of the whole realm, then I will abstain—not only from this, but from any other.[1]

THIS WAS MARY'S PROMISE, MADE AT THE GUILDHALL AS WYATT threatened London. She would submit treaty to "the people" for ratification—a step her male predecessors had never taken. As Parliament prepared to meet in the days after the rebellion, such was the climate of fear and uncertainty that it was initially proposed that Parliament meet in Oxford. When it did meet, in London, Mary was not present.[2] In his opening address on April 5, Gardiner proceeded to make the case for the marriage treaty:

> whereas they [the conspirators] had said that his Highness wished to conquer the kingdom, in reality the kingdom was conquering Philip and his dominions . . . therefore trusted that they would not offer any opposition but rather render their humble thanks to the Queen for her affection and show their gratitude by deeds.[3]

In spite of their fears, both houses ratified the marriage treaty within ten days of Parliament's opening. Renard wrote a triumphant letter, mocking "the heretics and French who hoped there would be violent dissent."[4]

To secure English acceptance of the alliance, the emperor had conceded highly favorable terms. Although Philip was granted the right to enjoy the style and name of king of England, the treaty denied him regal power and limited his involvement to assisting the queen in the administration of her realm insofar as the "rights, laws, privileges and customs" of both kingdoms permitted.

Should Mary die before Philip, he would have no further claim to authority in England. The succession to the English crown was limited to Mary's right of inheritance, and only the children from their marriage might succeed them. Don Carlos, Philip's existing heir, did not have a claim. No foreign office holders could be introduced into English government, and England would not be involved in Habsburg wars, it being stated explicitly that England was not to be drawn into the wars between Emperor Charles V and Henry II, the king of France.

In the first draft of the marriage settlement, Philip had only to acknowledge that Mary was not bound to offer any more assistance in the Habsburg-Valois struggle than promised in two treaties signed by Henry VIII some ten years earlier. But at the last moment Gardiner inserted an additional clause stating that England "by occasion of this matrimony, shall not directly or indirectly be entangled with the war that now is betwixt Charles and the French King." Moreover, Philip shall "see the peace between the said realms of France and England observed, and shall give no cause of any breach."⁵

The treaty specifically sought to separate Mary as queen of England from Mary, Philip's spouse, so as to underline that her power and status would not be diminished by the marriage. Mary was to be "sole Queen." The act ratifying the treaty stipulated,

> that your Majesty as our only Queen, shall and may, solely use, have, and enjoy the Crown and Sovereignty of, and over your Realms, Dominions, and Subjects . . . in such sole and only estate, and in as large and ample manner and form . . . after the hitheration of the said marriage, and at all times during the same . . .

It was an attempt to address concerns about the status of a married queen regnant, given the traditional subjugation of women. As Renard reported on January 7, the pretext for summoning Parliament had been "furnished by two English lawyers who have been prompted to say that by English law, if his Highness marries the Queen, she loses her title to the crown and his Highness becomes King."[6] There were no precedents, and Wyatt's rebellion had been inspired by fears that Mary's marriage would lead to enslavement by the Spanish. But at the formal betrothal in March, Mary had once more pledged her commitment to the national interest:

> The Queen knelt down and called God to witness that she had not consented to marry out of carnal affection or desire, not for any motive except her kingdom's honour and prosperity and the repose and tranquillity of her subjects, and that her firm resolve was to keep the marriage and oath she had made to the crown.[7]

While the marriage treaty prescribed Mary's independent sovereignty, another act passed in the same Parliament, the Act Concerning Regal Power, stated that Mary held her regal power as fully and absolutely as her male predecessors had. According to an account written twenty-five years later by Sir William Fleetwood, recorder of London, this additional act was passed after a conspiracy that proposed that Mary "take upon the title of Conqueror" so that she might "at her pleasure reform the monasteries, advance her friends, suppress her enemies, establish religion, and do what she like."[8] Given the unprecedented nature of female rule, there was no existing statute, including Magna Carta, that limited the authority of a queen.

Fleetwood described how, having been presented with the proposal, Mary read it "over and over again, and the more she read and thought of it, the more she misliked it," believing it a breach of her coronation oath, by which she had promised "to keep to the people of England and others your realms and dominions the laws and liberties of this realm." She then "cast it into the fire," after which the chancellor "devised the said Act of Parliament."[9]

To prevent confusion among "malicious and ignorant persons," the bill for the act, drafted by Gardiner, declared that "the regal power of this realm is in the Queen's Majesty as fully and absolutely as ever it was in any of her most noble progenitors Kings of this realm." It was passed in the Commons and two days later in the Lords.

> Be it declared . . . that the Law of this Realm is and ever hath been and ought to be understood, that the Kingly or Regal office of the Realm . . . being invested either in male or female, are, and be, and ought to be, as fully, absolutely and entirely deemed, judged, accepted, invested and taken in the one as in the other.[10]

The act clarified the ambiguity of Mary's status as queen regnant. By throwing the proposal into the fire, Mary had declared her intent to be a parliamentary queen. Her sovereignty would be dependent on and prescribed by statute law. Thus Mary had chosen to follow the precedents of her male progenitors. The inauguration of female sovereignty could not have been placed in safer hands.

As Mary made her speech at Parliament's dissolution in May, she was interrupted five or six times by shouts of "God save the Queen!" as most of those present were "moved to tears by her eloquence and virtue."[11]

MARY NOW WROTE to Philip, informing him that Parliament had ratified the marriage articles and expressing her "entire confidence that his coming to England should be safe and agreeable" to him.[12]

Though Philip had pledged to be an obedient son and follow his father's will, the marriage held few personal attractions for him. Mary was eleven years his senior, and he referred to her as his *cara y muy amada tía* (dear and beloved aunt). Further, he disavowed the treaty, declaring that he was not bound by an agreement that had been reached without his knowledge. He would sign it so that the marriage could take place, "but by no means in order to bind himself or his heirs to observe the articles, especially any that might burden his conscience."[13]

As the prince prepared to leave La Coruña for England, Charles wrote to the duke of Alva, who was accompanying him, "For the love of God, see to it that my son behaves in the right manner; for otherwise I tell you I would rather never have taken the matter in hand at all."[14]

CHAPTER 48

GOOD NIGHT, MY LORDS ALL

∴

Wᴵᵀᴴ PARLIAMENT DISSOLVED AND THE MARRIAGE TREATY RATIFIED, preparations began in earnest for Philip's arrival and the royal wedding, which was to take place at Winchester Cathedral, the episcopal seat of Bishop Gardiner. The gallows scattered throughout the City of London, where the condemned rebels had hung, were taken down; the cross at Cheapside was repaired and a scaffold erected for the celebrations to welcome the prince.[1]

Mary had commissioned a suit to be made for Philip's entry into Winchester and for the wedding itself, together with hangings for the royal bed embroidered with the arms and devices of Spain and England. Some 350 Englishmen had been selected as Philip's household officers, among them individuals who had supported Mary in July 1553, such as John Huddleston. All had been assembled before the chamberlain of the royal household and asked to swear an oath of allegiance, and they, together with a hundred archers who were to join the guard Philip brought with him, now traveled to Southampton to await the prince's long-anticipated arrival.[2]

Finally, on June 16, Mary and her entire court set out from Richmond for Winchester and there took up residence in the Episcopal Palace of Bishop's Waltham, which had been specially prepared ahead of her arrival.

The decision to hold the wedding ceremony outside London had been driven by fears of disorder in the capital. Rumor and discontent were rife. Seditious prophecies were published in London to the effect that Philip's delay in embarking for England was caused by his reluctance to marry Mary and that the Spaniards would not let him come.[3]

As Renard reported on July 9, "the officers appointed for his Highness' service have been living at Southampton at great expense for a long time and are now beginning to leave that place, speaking strangely of his Highness."[4] Two aldermen in the City of London were ordered to keep watch every night and one or two constables until three or four in the morning for fear of "some disturbances among the citizens in detestation of the Spanish affair."[5] Pensions were distributed by the imperial ambassador to "render his Highness's coming secure," and the sum of 5,000 crowns was distributed among a number of gentlemen and officers who had served the queen in the last rebellion, "in order to keep them well disposed." In the hope that all would go smoothly, Simon Renard drew up guidelines for Philip, suggesting how he might ingratiate himself with the English people:

Notes for Prince Philip's Guidance in England

Item: when his Highness enters the kingdom, he will be well-advised to caress the nobility and be affable, show himself often to the people, prove that he wishes to take no share in the administration, but leave it all to the Council and urge them to be diligent in the exercise of justice, caress the nobles, talk with them on occasion, take them out to hunt with them. If he does so, there is no doubt whatever that they will not only love his Highness, but will adore him.

Item: it will be well to show a benign countenance to the people and lead them to look for kindness, justice and liberty.

Item: as his Highness knows no English it will be well to select an interpreter and have him among his attendants so that he may converse with the English. And let his Highness endeavour to learn a few words in order to be able to salute them. Then, as time goes on, he will be able to decide what he had better do in order to achieve his purposes.

Item: no soldiers from the ships must be allowed to land here, in order not to confirm the suspicion inculcated by the French, that his Highness wishes to conquer the realm by force.[6]

At three in the afternoon of Thursday, July 19, Philip finally landed at Southampton. A great throng of nobles and gentry met his ship, and the earl of Arundel presented him with the Order of the Garter, which was buckled just below his knee, and a mantle of blue velvet fringed with gold and pearl. The prince was rowed ashore the following day in a magnificent state barge covered with white and black cloth, furnished with fine carpets and a chair of brocade, and manned by twenty men dressed in the queen's livery of green and white.[7] An English household of 350, headed by the earl of Arundel, had been made ready for the prince, but Philip had brought his own, immediately causing tension between the English and the Spaniards.

In London the populace marked the Spanish prince's safe arrival with officially organized bonfires and feasting, as well as "ringing and playing." Two days later, processions, Te Deums, and more ringing of bells were ordered in every parish of London.[8] Philip sent the count of Egmont to Winchester to "inform the Queen of his arrival, visit her, tell her of his health and assure her of his affection." The next day Gardiner arrived with a large diamond as a gift from Mary. Philip reciprocated with a diamond of his own, though unfortunately it was noted to have been "considerably smaller." Mary also sent "a very richly wrought poignard, studded with gems, and two robes, one of them as rich and beautiful as could be imagined."[9] Mary issued a proclamation summoning all those who were to attend the wedding:

> Forasmuch as (God be thanked) the Prince of Spain is now safely arrived and come unto this the Queen's highness' realm of England, her grace's pleasure therefore is that all noblemen and gentlemen, ladies and others appointed by her Majesty to attend upon her grace against the time of her marriage, do with all convenient speed make their repair to her grace's city of Winchester, there to give their attendance upon her highness.[10]

At the Church of the Holy Rood in Southampton, which had been lavishly adorned for his visit with brocade, gold fabrics, and embroidered canopies, Philip heard Mass and gave thanks for his safe voyage. Later, at the house that had been prepared for him, he addressed the English councillors who had gathered there. He had come to live among them, he said, not as a foreigner but as a native Englishman, not for want of men or money but because God had called him to marry their virtuous sovereign. He thanked them for their expressions of faith and loyalty and promised that they would find him a grateful and loving prince. Then, turning to the Spanish nobles in his entourage, he expressed his hope that, as they remained in England, they would follow his example and conform to the customs of the country. As he finished speaking, he raised to his lips a flagon of English ale and drank farewell to the men who were gathered before him.[11]

Having spent the weekend resting in Southampton, Philip set out on the twelve-mile ride to Winchester, through pouring rain, escorted by a guard of a hundred men wearing his livery. About six in the evening, Philip entered Winchester, mounted on a white horse and wearing a rich coat of cloth of gold, a feather in his hat and dressed in a suit embroidered with gold, "the English and Spanish nobles, one with another, riding before him."[12] At the cathedral, amid a fanfare of trumpets and bell ringing, the bishop of Winchester, the lord chancellor, and five other bishops greeted him. After praying in front of the sacrament Philip was taken by torchlight to his lodging in the dean's house to prepare for his first meeting with the queen.

At about ten in the evening, Philip walked through the gardens to the Bishop's Palace, where he and Mary were to meet. Surrounded by three or four councillors and her ladies-in-waiting, Mary came out to the door of her chamber and "very lovingly, yea, and most joyfully received him." She was dressed in a gown of black velvet over an underskirt of frosted silver adorned with magnificent jewels. Hand in hand they sat down and for about half an hour remained in pleasant conversation. Philip spoke in Spanish, Mary replied in French. Philip then rose and kissed the other ladies present, and his attendants kissed the queen's hand. As he departed, he said, "Good night, my lords all," in English, as Mary had just taught him to do.[13]

At three the following afternoon, the prince made his first public visit to the queen. Accompanied by a number of English nobles, he walked on his own behind them, "in a cloak of black cloth embroidered with silver, and a pair of silver hose." Entering the courtyard of the Bishop's Palace to the sound of music, he passed into the Great Hall, where Mary received him in the presence of the people. Taking him by the hand, she led him into the Presence Chamber, and there they talked for a quarter of an hour under the cloth of estate, "to the great comfort and rejoicing of the beholders." Philip took his leave and went to Evensong at the cathedral, returning afterward to his lodging alone.

According to the Scotsman John Elder, who was present at court, Philip struck observers in England as the image of a true king:

> Of visage he is well favoured . . . with a broad forehead, and grey eyes, straight-nosed and manly countenance. From the forehead to the point of his chin, his face groweth small. His pace is princely, and gate [gait] so straight and upright, as he loseth no inch of his height; with a yellow head and yellow beard. And thus to conclude, he is so well proportioned as nature cannot work a more perfect pattern; and, as I have learned, of the age of 28 years; whose majesty I judge to be of a stout stomach, pregnant-witted and of most gentle nature.[14]

It was a marriage that promised much, though it remained to be seen whether Mary's hopes for both a political partnership and a personal union could be realized.

PART FOUR

A King's Wife

CHAPTER 49

WITH THIS RING I THEE WED

∴

PHILIP AND MARY WERE MARRIED ON JULY 25, 1554, THE FEAST OF Saint James, the patron saint of Spain. It was a marriage intended to recast England in Europe and breed a new line of Catholic princes. And it was the first wedding of a reigning English queen.

The ceremony was one of unparalleled pomp and extravagance. Winchester Cathedral was decorated resplendently with banners, standards, streamers, and tapestries, all emblazoned with Spanish regalia. A raised wooden platform, covered with carpets, reached from the main door of the church to the choir, at its center a dais in the shape of an octagon, the setting of the solemnization of the marriage.[1] The arrangements for the wedding were based on those of Mary's mother's marriage to Prince Arthur. The ceremony was to be traditional and performed in Latin by Bishop Gardiner, assisted by five other bishops, all attired in copes and miters.

At about eleven in the morning, Philip arrived at the cathedral, accompanied by many Spanish knights and wearing a doublet and hose of white satin, embroidered with jewels, and a mantle of cloth of gold—which Mary had sent him—ornamented with jewels and precious stones, together with the ribbon of the Order of the Garter that had been presented to him at Southampton.[2] Half an hour later Mary arrived, dressed in a gown of white satin and a mantle to match Philip's, which "blazed with jewels to an extent that dazzled those who gazed upon her." On her breast she wore a piece of jewelry called "La Peregrina," set with two diamonds, one the gift from Philip in June, the other from Charles V, which had previously been set in the ring given to the Portuguese princess Isabella, whom he had married after breaking off his betrothal to Mary in 1525. Mary's sword was borne before her—a sign that she was monarch—by the earl of Derby and the marquess of Winchester. The lord chamberlain, Sir John Gage, carried her train.

Once the full party had assembled, Don Juan Figueroa, regent of Naples, handed to Gardiner two pronouncements by which Charles V bestowed on his son the Kingdom of Naples and the Duchy of Milan. Gardiner at once declared to the assembly, "it was thought the Queen's Majesty should marry but with a prince; now it was manifested that she should marry with a King."[3] Then the banns were bidden in Latin and in English, with Gardiner declaring that if "any man knoweth of any lawful impediment between the two parties, that they should not go together according to the contract concluded between the both realms, then they should come forth, and they should be heard."

According to the official account recorded by the English heralds, Mary was given to Philip "in the name of the whole realm" by the marquess of Winchester and the earls of Derby, Bedford, and Pembroke.[4] The pair exchanged vows in Latin and English: "This gold and silver I thee give: with my body I thee worship; and withal my worldly Goods I thee endow."[5] Mary then pledged "from henceforth to be compliant and obedient . . . as much in mind as in body"—in direct contradiction to Gardiner's insistence that in the marriage contract Philip must undertake to marry as a subject.[6] And whereas Mary endowed Philip with all her "worldly goods," Philip merely endowed Mary with all his "moveable goods."[7] Her wedding ring "was a round hoop of gold without any stone, which was her desire, for she said she would be married as maidens were in the old time, and so she was."[8]

Philip and Mary then proceeded hand in hand under a rich canopy borne by six knights. At the choir, a psalm was sung while the king and queen knelt before the altar, a taper in front of each of them. They then retired to their canopied seats on the raised dais to listen to the Gospels, reemerging to kneel before the altar for Mass. The king of arms solemnly proclaimed Philip and Mary king and queen, declaring their titles and style:

Philip and Mary by the grace of God King and Queen of England, France, Naples, Jerusalem, and Ireland; Defenders of the Faith; Princes of Spain and Sicily; Archdukes of Austria; Dukes of Milan, Burgundy and Brabant; Counts of Habsburg, Flanders and Tyrol.[9]

Their joint style had been difficult to agree on. The English Council had strongly resisted Philip being named before the Queen, but he had insisted "that no law, human or divine, nor his Highness's prestige and good name, would allow him to be named second, especially as the treaties and acts of Parliament gave him the title of King of England."[10] England was now part of a much larger European empire.

AT THREE IN THE afternoon, to the blare of trumpets and cheers of the crowd, the royal couple walked hand in hand—the sword of state borne before the king by the earl of Pembroke—under a canopy back to the queen's palace for the wedding banquet.[11]

Philip and Mary took their places at a raised table at the head of four long tables where the Spanish and English nobility were seated. Mary was served on gold plates, Philip on silver to indicate his subordinate status. Musicians played at the end of the hall throughout the banquet. When the feast was over and the queen had drunk a cup of wine to the health and honor of the guests, the party moved to an adjoining hall for dancing and entertainment. There was "such triumphing, banqueting, singing, masking and dancing, as was never seen in England heretofore, by the report of all men."[12] The king then retired to his chamber, the queen to hers, where they dined in private.

The evening ended with the blessing of the marriage bed. As one of Philip's gentlemen wrote soon after, "the Bishop of Winchester blessed the bed, and they remained alone. What happened that night only they know. If they give us a son, our joy will be complete."[13]

CHAPTER 50

MUTUAL SATISFACTION

ON AUGUST 4, THE BISHOP OF ARRAS WROTE TO RENARD, EXPRESSING his "incredible content, that the marriage for which both had worked, for so long, was accomplished, to the mutual satisfaction of both parties" and that the king "was behaving in every way so well, that he had gained the approbation of all in England." He foresaw many difficulties ahead but hoped that with gentleness and benignity they might not prove too great.[1]

After ten days of honeymooning in Winchester, the royal couple began their journey back to London, stopping en route at Windsor on the third for Philip's installation as knight and cosovereign of the Order of the Garter.[2] The earl of Arundel once again deputized for Mary, investing Philip with the robe, while Mary placed the collar around his neck.

On the eleventh they moved to Richmond as final preparations were made for their formal entry into the capital.

AT TWO O'CLOCK on Saturday, August 18, Philip and Mary were met at Southwark by the lord mayor and aldermen and crossed into the city by London Bridge. Behind them followed the lords of the Council, foreign ambassadors, and the nobility of England and Spain, all on horseback, two by two in rank order. The lord mayor of London knelt down before them and gave the queen the mace, a symbol of power and authority in the city. The king and queen remounted their horses and, with two swords of state before them, rode into the city.

Some weeks before, Mary had issued a proclamation ordering all her subjects to extend "courtesy, friendly and gentle entertainment" to the Spaniards, "without either by outward deeds, taunting words, or unseemly countenance" giving any insult to the visitors. Londoners were in a benevolent mood, and there was little ill feeling displayed toward the new king. The city had been decorated with splendid pageants for the occasion. At London Bridge two vast figurines greeted the royal couple. The mythical giants Corineus Britannus and Gogamogog Albionus, warriors from Geoffrey of Monmouth's twelfth-century history of Britain, held between them a tablet on which were written verses lavishing praise on Philip and giving thanks for his safe arrival:

> O noble Prince sole hope of Caesar's side
> By God appointed all the world to guide
> Right heartily welcome art thou to our land
> The archer Britayne yeldeth thee her hand,
>
> And noble England openeth her bosom
> Of hearty affection for to bid thee welcome.
> But chiefly London doth her love vouchsafe,
> Rejoycing that her Philip is come safe.[3]

The king and queen rode on into Gracechurch Street, where Henry VIII was portrayed, a scepter in one hand and a book in the other, upon which was written *"Verbum Dei,"* "the Word of God." It was the image that had appeared on the title page of the Great Bible of 1539, the first authorized version in English, which had shown Henry distributing the English Bible to his subjects—anathema to Catholics, who believed that scripture in the vernacular undermined the sanctity of its meaning. Such a provocative image of Protestant triumphalism was hardly what might be expected in a pageant welcoming a Catholic king and queen. After Mary and Philip had passed, Gardiner threatened the painter, Richard Grafton, with imprisonment in the Fleet. Grafton responded that he thought he had done well, declaring, "If I had known the same had been against your lordship's pleasure, I would not have so have made him." Grafton was ordered to paint out the book and replace it with a pair of gloves.[4]

At the end of Gracechurch Street stood a triumphal arch adorned with statues and paintings, created by the merchants of the steelyard. On the left stood the figure of a woman, Hispania, supporting a castle; on the right stood Britannia with the arms of England. The pageant was decorated with pictures of battles on land and sea and the insignia of England and Spain. At the top of the arch was a mechanical image of King Philip on horseback and the inscription "In honour of worthy Philip the fortunate and most mighty Prince of Spain, most earnestly wished for."[5] At Cornhill, another pageant, surmounted with images of the royal couple, featured representations of four noble Philips from history: Philip, king of Macedonia, father of Alexander the Great; Philip, the Roman emperor; Philip the Bold; and Philip the Good of Burgundy. The third pageant, in Cheap, depicted Orpheus and the nine Muses. Near them men and children, dressed like wild beasts, lions, wolves, bears, and foxes, danced and leaped, this spectacle "pleasing their majesties very well."[6]

The royal couple moved on to the little conduit at the west end of Cheap for the fourth pageant. Described as "the most excellent pageant of all," it showed Philip and Mary's shared genealogy from Edward III of England. Under a great tree was an old man, signifying Edward III, lying on his side with a white long beard, a closed crown on his head, and scepter and ball in his hands. On top of the tree the queen was shown on the right and the king to the left, and underneath letters of gold read:

> *England, if thou delight in ancient men*
> *Whose glorious acts thy fame abroad did blaze*
> *Both Mary and Philip their offspring ought thou then*
> *With all thy heart to love and to embrace*
> *Which both descended of one ancient line*
> *It hath pleased God by marriage to combine.*[7]

Philip was presented not as the Spaniard of popular fears but as an Englishman. Mary's own Spanish lineage was also ignored, and she was depicted as being wholly English. Their marriage was cast as one of concord and reconciliation: being both descended from John of Gaunt, duke of Lancaster, their marriage had united the divided Lancastrian house. The pageant highlighted the fact that Katherine of

Aragon, Charles V, and Philip could be traced back to Edward III through John of Gaunt; while Roman Catholicism, which for twenty years had been reviled as foreign and traitorous, was represented as the true patriotic faith of England.

At St. Paul's a sumptuously dressed scholar presented the king and queen with a book, while at Fleet Street, Mary and Philip witnessed the final pageant. Set around a castle decorated with the "arms of all Christian realms," four characters—a king and a queen (Philip and Mary), Justice bearing a sword, and Equality holding a pair of balances—were each crowned by a figure that descended on a rope from the top of the pageant. An inscription below read:

> *When a man is gentle, just and true,*
> *With virtuous gifts fulfilled plenteously*
> *If Wisdom then him with her crown endure*
> *He govern shall the whole world prosperously.*
> *And sith we know thee Philip to be such,*
> *While thou shalt reign we think us happy much.*[8]

TWO WEEKS LATER, Philip wrote to his sister, the princess regent of Spain, telling her, "We have visited London, where I was received with universal signs of love and joy."[9] But despite the welcoming pageantry, anti-Spanish feeling was never far away.

On August 20, two days after the celebrations, the city authorities were ordered to take the pageants down for fear of vandalism.[10] At the time of the royal couple's entry into London, the Tower chronicler described how "there was so many Spaniards in London that a man should have met in the streets for one Englishman above four Spaniards, to the great discomfort of the English nation."[11] And Renard told the emperor, "They, the English, loudly proclaim that they are going to be enslaved, for the Queen is a Spanish woman at heart and thinks nothing of Englishmen, but only of Spaniards and bishops."[12] It was going to be difficult, he told Charles, to reconcile Spaniards with Englishmen. The language was an obstacle, the English hated foreigners, "and the slightest altercation might be enough to bring about a very dangerous situation."[13]

CHAPTER 51

THE HAPPIEST COUPLE
IN THE WORLD

．．
．．
．．

*He [the king] treats the Queen very kindly, and well knows how
to pass over the fact that she is no good from the point of view of
fleshy sensuality. He makes her so happy that the other day when
they were alone she almost talked love-talk to him, and he replied
in the same vein.*[1]

—RUY GÓMEZ DE SILVA, PRINCE OF
ÉBOLI, TO CHARLES'S SECRETARY,
FRANCISCO DE ERASO, AUGUST 12,
1554

IN A PRIVATE LETTER TO A FRIEND, RUY GÓMEZ DE SILVA, A MEMBER
of Philip's entourage, revealed a somewhat different view: "To speak
frankly with you, it would take God himself to drink this cup . . . and
the best one can say is that the King realises fully that the marriage was
made for no fleshly consideration, but in order to cure the disorders of
this country and to preserve the Low Countries."[2]

Philip had intended to stay in England for only a short time, though
Mary was probably unaware of this. On the eve of his arrival in
England, the French had defeated imperial forces at Marienburg, the
gateway to the Netherlands. Brussels had looked vulnerable to French
attack, and Philip had brought 4,000 troops to go on to the Netherlands.
Charles had instructed Philip to take only a few of his servants ashore
with him in England and, immediately after the marriage and having
spent just six or eight days with his bride, to sail straight to Flanders.[3]
But then the military situation improved, and the emperor decided to

delay his son's journey to Flanders: "You had better stay where you are and be with the Queen, my daughter, busying yourself with the Government of England, settling affairs there and making yourself familiar with the people, which it is most important you do for present and future considerations."[4] Mary was delighted that Philip was to remain in England, and in a letter to her father-in-law she declared:

I see a proof of your Majesty's watchful care for the realm's and my own interests, for which, and above all for having so far spared the person of the King, my husband, I most humbly thank you . . . always praying God so to inspire my subjects that they may realise the affection you bear this kingdom, and the honour and advantages you have conferred upon it by this marriage and alliance, which renders me happier than I can say, as I daily discover in my husband and your son, so many virtues and perfections that I constantly pray God to grant me grace to please him and behave in all things as befits one who is so deeply embounden to him.[5]

IN A LETTER to a friend in Salamanca, a Spanish courtier wrote of Philip's first months in England:

Their Majesties are the happiest couple in the world, and more in love than words can say. His Highness never leaves her, and when they are on the road he is ever by her side, helping her to mount and dismount. They sometimes dine together in public, and go to mass together on holidays.

But, he continued:

the Queen, however, is not at all beautiful: small, and rather flabby than fat, she is of white complexion and fair, and has no eyebrows. She is a perfect saint and dresses badly. All the women here wear petticoats of coloured cloth without admixture of silk, and above come coloured robes of damask, satin or velvet, very badly cut.

The dominant style at the English court and that favored by Mary was French. Her clothes were not to Spanish tastes, and, as the Spaniard added, neither were the English revelries:

> There are no distractions here except eating and drinking, the only variety they understand . . . there is plenty of beer here, and they drink more than would fill the Valladolid river. In the summer the ladies and gentlemen put sugar in their wine, with the result that there are great goings on in the palace.[6]

Philip's efforts to secure the goodwill of the English were being undermined by tensions between the Spanish household Philip had brought with him and the English entourage that had been prepared for his arrival. "The English hate the Spaniards worse than they hate the devil," wrote one of his household. "They rob us in town and on the road; and one ventures to stray two miles but they rob him; and a company of Englishmen have recently robbed and beaten over fifty Spaniards. The best of it is that the councillors know all about it and say not a word."[7]

Philip looked to resolve the issue by retaining the English in formal ceremonial positions, such as cupbearers, gentlemen waiters, and carvers, while Spaniards remained in his personal suite. But complaints and tensions continued. Philip would write to Francisco de Eraso, his father's secretary, of the embarrassment caused by the two households, "not so much on account of the expense as of the troubles it gave me." Of the English servants, Philip expressed major reservations: "They are accustomed to serving here in a very different manner from that observed at his Majesty's Court, and as you know I am not satisfied that they are good enough Catholics to be constantly about my person."[8]

By the beginning of September, Renard was reporting, "very few Englishmen are to be seen in his Highness's apartments."[9] Given the acrimony, a number of Spanish noblemen and gentlemen obtained permission to depart. As the Spanish correspondent put it, "we are all desiring to be off, with such longing that we think of Flanders as a paradise."[10]

On Sunday, November 25, Spanish courtiers staged a cane play—a *juego de cannas,* a joust in which canes replaced lances—before the queen and English noblemen at Whitehall. The king rode in red, everyone else in yellow, green, white, or blue, "with targets and canes in their hand, hurling rods one at another, and the trumpets in the same colours and drums made of kettles, and banners in the same colours."[11] It was a spectacular display of color and sporting prowess, but it did little to win over English hearts, as the Count Gian Tommaso Langosco da Stroppiana noted: "It left the spectators cold, except for the fine clothes of the players, and the English made fun of it."[12]

Months later, it emerged that the cane play had been the occasion of a treasonous conspiracy. A man named Edward Lewkner alleged that he had arranged with Sir Francis Verney and Captain Edward Turner to kill Philip and his Spanish attendants during the contest.[13] He claimed that more than three hundred people had been involved in the plot, which was to have been carried out in the third round of the tournament. But when only two rounds were staged, the plan could not be executed.[14]

DESPITE THE TREASONOUS plottings against him, Philip quickly began to appropriate the images of royalty. Substantial sums were spent on embroidered cloths of estate, badges, and heraldic devices decorated with the king's and queen's initials.[15] In September 1554, new coins were issued on which both Mary and Philip appeared in profile, "the double face."[16] The king's was pictured on the dominant left-hand side, the position hitherto reserved for the reigning monarch, with a single crown floating above them both. One pamphleteer complained that Philip was being turned into a "King of England indeed," his name appearing on proclamations and on charters and "on the coined money going abroad current."[17]

Before Mary's wedding, Stephen Gardiner had stipulated that English subjects be explicitly assured that after the marriage Philip would be "rather as a subject than otherwise; and that the Queen should rule all things as she doth now."[18] Yet two days after the wedding the Privy Council stipulated that "a note of all such matters of

Estate as should pass from hence should be made in Latin and Spanish from henceforth."

Mary also issued an instruction, written in her own hand, to the lord Privy Seal, "First to tell the King the whole state of the Realm with all things appertaining to the same, as much as you know to be true. Second to obey his commandment in all things" and to declare his opinion on any matter the king wished "as becometh a faithful counsellor to do."[19] The Spaniards' view of the marriage was quite different from that of the English. They believed that Philip would provide the male element lacking in Mary's monarchy: he would "make up for other matters which are impertinent to women."[20]

The focus of Philip's energies quickly became reconciliation with Rome. He petitioned the pope to augment Cardinal Pole's powers so that he might negotiate for a general settlement with regard to Church property.[21] Finally the pope was persuaded. "It would be far better," he agreed, "for all reasons human and divine, to abandon all the Church property [in England], rather than risk the shipwreck of this understanding."[22] Philip sent Renard to Flanders to reason with Pole, who agreed not to exercise any jurisdiction without the king and queen's consent.[23] On November 3, 1554, the Council consented to admitting Pole into the realm. Lord Paget and Sir Edward Hastings were sent to conduct him from the imperial court, and Parliament was summoned to repeal Pole's attainder and condemnation for treason.

England's imminent return to Roman Catholicism was a tremendous coup for the Habsburgs. As Renard wrote to the emperor:

> I thought it my duty to write at once to Your Majesty, well knowing that this long looked for miraculous event, so big with consequences of the greatest importance to Christendom, will give you great pleasure. . . . Your Majesty too well understands how great was the joy felt by the King [Philip] and all his court for it to be necessary that I should describe it. Indeed, he had good reason to render thanks to God that such fruit, fertile in the increase of authority for him, should already come of the match, encouraging us to hope that God means to incline the enemy's [France's] heart to the desire of lasting peace.[24]

A week later, the king and queen returned to Westminster Abbey for the opening of Parliament. According to Count Langosco da Stroppiana, the waiting crowds called out, "Oh how handsome the King is! . . . Oh! What a good husband he is! How honourably and lovingly he treats the Queen!"[25] At the abbey the king and queen knelt and kissed the cross. The new bishop of Lincoln, John White, preached an English sermon, which was then summarized in Latin. The text was from Jeremiah. It said that those who had separated from the Roman Church did not harbor thoughts of peace any more than those guilty of sedition or disobedience to the king and queen. In conclusion the bishop urged the "firm establishment of our true Catholic religion."[26]

CHAPTER 52

TO RECONCILE, NOT TO CONDEMN

∴

A year has passed since I began to knock at the door of this royal house, and none has opened to me. King, if you ask, as those are wont to do who hear a knock at the door: who is there? I will reply, it is I, who, rather than consent that this house should be closed to her who now possesses it with you, preferred banishment and twenty years of exile. And if I speak thus, is it not a sufficient claim to be permitted to return home and to approach you?[1]

—CARDINAL POLE TO PHILIP,
SEPTEMBER 1554

SINCE HIS APPOINTMENT AS PAPAL LEGATE ON AUGUST 5, 1553, Cardinal Pole had been petitioning Mary to allow him to return to England. He had traveled as far as Brussels but had been prevented from going any farther as the emperor wanted to secure Philip's marriage to Mary before England embarked on the path of Catholic restoration.

Pole, however, argued that nothing should stand in the way of the Church's immediate and unconditional return to Rome.[2] He believed the queen's marriage to Philip was "even more universally odious than the cause of the religion," and Mary feared his hostility to it.[3] As the months passed and there was no sign of his zealous advice being heeded, the cardinal's letters to Mary became more and more strident. "It is imprudent and sacrilegious to say that matters of religion must be cleverly handled, and left until the throne is safely established," he wrote; "what greater neglect can there be . . . than by setting aside the honour of God to attend to other things, leaving religion to the end?"[4]

In many ways Pole and Mary were kindred spirits. Both had suffered for their faith and lived through years of isolation in fear of death. Pole had been in exile for much of his life; both had lost their mothers to Henry VIII's cruelty. But England had changed in his twenty-year-long exile, since Henry's break with Rome and the execution of his elder brother, Henry, Lord Montague, and his mother, Margaret Pole. Years of antipapal propaganda had left many English people hostile to the idea of a return of papal authority. A generation had grown up knowing only the king as head of the Church. Meanwhile, Church lands had fallen into secular hands and their "possessioners" were not prepared to give them up. Finally, though, with the Spanish marriage concluded and a compromise reached, Parliament repealed Pole's attainder for treason and the cardinal could return to England.

On November 20, some fifteen months after his appointment as legate, Pole landed at Dover. Two days later, he journeyed to London, accompanied by an ever-increasing train of English noblemen and councillors. With Londoners lining the banks of the Thames, Pole took to the river at Gravesend, his large silver cross, an emblem of his legatine authority, prominent in the state barge. At noon he arrived at Whitehall, where he was met on a landing stage by Philip. With the sword of state borne before them, the king and cardinal proceeded to the Presence Chamber, where the queen awaited them. Pole had not seen Mary since she was a young princess. He knelt in front of the queen; she "received him with great signs of respect and affection; both shed tears."[5]

A week after his arrival in England, Pole appeared before both Houses of Parliament at Whitehall. Having expressed his gratitude for the admission into the realm of a man hitherto "exiled and banished," he outlined the cause of his coming. The pope had, he claimed, "a special respect for their realm above all other." While others nations had been converted gradually, "this island the first of all islands, received the light of Christ's religion."

It was a spurious appeal to English nationalism, a providential version of history, intended to make Roman Catholicism suitably English. England was, in Pole's view, the chosen Catholic nation. God "by providence hath given this realm prerogative of nobility above other," and Mary was deemed its savior. "When all light of true religion seemed utterly extinct, as the churches defaced and altars overthrown . . . in a few remained the confession of Christ's faith, namely in the breast of the Queen's excellency." When people conspired against her and "policies were devised to disinherit her, and armed power prepared to destroy her . . . she being a virgin, helpless, naked and unarmed, prevailed, and had the victory over tyrants." Mary was the Virgin Queen who had restored the national religion.

With carefully chosen words Pole assured Parliament that his commission was "not one of prejudice to any person":

> I come not to destroy but to build. I come to reconcile, not to condemn. I come not to compel, but to call again. I come not to call anything in question already done, but my commission is of grace and clemency to such as will receive it, for touching all matters that be past, that shall be as things cast into the sea of forgetfulness.[6]

Two days later, a delegation from Parliament presented themselves at Whitehall, where Gardiner made their supplication:

> We the lords spiritual and temporal, and the commons of this present Parliament assembled, representing the whole body of the realm of England and dominions of the same, do declare ourselves very sorry and repentant of the schism and disobedience committed in this realm and the dominions of the same, against the said See Apostolic . . . that we may, as children repentant, be received into the bosom and unity of Christ's church. So as this noble realm, with all the members thereof, may in unity and perfect obedience to the See Apostolic.[7]

At five in the afternoon of Saint Andrew's Day, November 30, Pole was conducted in full pontifical robes from Lambeth Palace to Westminster. There, with the Lords and Commons and the king and queen kneeling before him in their robes of estate, he formally absolved the country from its years of schism:

> We, by apostolic authority given unto us by the most holy lord Pope Julius III, his Vice-regent on earth, do absolve and deliver you, and every [one] of you, with the whole Realm and the Dominions thereof, from all Heresy and Schism, and from all and every judgement, Censures and pains, for that cause incurred; & also so we do restore you again unto the unity of our Mother the holy Church . . . in the name of the Father, of the son and of the Holy Ghost.[8]

According to John Elder, it "moved a great number of the audience with sorrowful sighs and weeping tears to change their cheer." England had returned to the Catholic fold. It was a moment of high ceremony and emotion.

That evening Mary gave a banquet for the king and his gentlemen, and after supper there were dancing and masques. The king had that day shown "liberality to the ladies of the court, who were dressed in the gowns he had given them."[9] The news of England's return to the fold quickly reached Rome, whereupon the pope ordered processions, "giving thanks to God with great joy for the conversion of England to his Church."[10]

THE SUNDAY AFTER the reconciliation with Rome—the first day of Advent—Mary, Philip, and Pole attended a High Mass sung by the bishop of London at St. Paul's Cathedral. The crowds "both in the church and in the streets, were enormous, and displayed great joy and piety, begging the cardinal for his blessing."[11]

After Mass, Gardiner preached at St. Paul's Cross, basing his sermon on the Book of Romans:

> Now also it is time that we awake out of our sleep, who have slept or rather dreamed these twenty years past. For as men intending to sleep do separate themselves from company and desire to be alone, even so we have separated ourselves from the

See of Rome, and have been alone, no realm in Christendom like us.

He continued:

During these twenty years we have been without a head. When King Henry was head perhaps there was something to be said for it, but what a head was Edward, to whom they had to give a protector! He was but a shadow. Nor could the Queen, being a woman, be head of the Church . . . now the hour is come . . . the realm is at peace . . . It is time for us also to awake.[12]

At the end "all those present, over fifteen thousand people, knelt down" to receive Pole's blessing, crying out "Amen, amen!" "A sight to be seen it was, and the silence was such that not a cough was heard."[13]

CHAPTER 53

THE QUEEN IS WITH CHILD

⋰⋱

U PON HIS ARRIVAL AT WHITEHALL ON NOVEMBER 24, CARDINAL Pole had addressed Mary with the opening words of the Ave Maria: "Hail, thou art highly favored, the Lord is with thee: blessed art thou among women," the words by which the Angel Gabriel had heralded the Virgin Mary's conception of Jesus. Pole's greeting was, it seems, equally prophetic. Shortly after he left, Mary sent a messenger after him. She had felt her child stir when Pole greeted her; she knew she was pregnant.[1]

It followed weeks of rumor and fevered speculation. Renard had written in his dispatch in mid-September, just two months after the wedding, that one of the queen's physicians had told him that the queen "is probably with child." The English ambassador in Brussels, Sir John Mason, reported weeks later, in response to the emperor's question "How goeth my daughter's belly forward?" that although he had heard nothing formally from the queen, others had told him "her garments wax very strait."[2]

With the pregnancy now seemingly confirmed, letters were sent from the Council to bishops ordering Te Deums to be sung and special prayers offered for this "good hope of certain succession" and to give thanks for her "quickening with child, and to pray."[3] The news was proclaimed across Europe. "The Queen is with child," announced Ruy Gómez; "may it please God to grant her the issue that is so solely needed to set affairs right here and make everything smooth . . . this pregnancy will put a stop to every difficulty."[4] Every aspect of Mary's appearance was scrutinized and reported on. Writing to the emperor in November, Renard told him, "There is no doubt that the Queen is with child, for her stomach clearly shows it and her dresses no longer fit her."⁵ And later the same month: the "lady is well with child. God be thanked! For she has felt the babe and presents all the usual signs on her breasts and elsewhere."⁶

In the days before Christmas, Mary wrote to her father-in-law:

> As for that child which I carry in my belly, I declare it to be alive and with great humility thank God for His great goodness shown to me, praying Him so to guide the fruit of my womb that it may contribute to His glory and honour, and give happiness to the King, my Lord and your son, to your Majesty, who were my second father in the lifetime of my own father, and are therefore doubly my father, and lastly that it may prove a blessing to the realm.⁷

Charles responded with enthusiastic expectation: "Be it man, or be it woman, welcome shall it be; for by that we shall be at the least come to some certainty to whom God shall appoint by succession the government of our estates."

It was a sentiment shared by many. As long as Mary remained childless, there was grave anxiety in the kingdom, as John Mason explained during his audience with the emperor: "It maketh all good men tremble to think the Queen's highness must die, with whom, dying without fruit, the realm were as good also to die."⁸ The future of the Catholic restoration would depend on the fruitfulness of the marriage.

MARY WAS EXPECTED to give birth on or before May 9. The chamber and nursery were made ready, the chief gentlewomen of the kingdom summoned to witness the birth, wet nurses and rockers put on standby, and the royal cradle "sumptuously and gorgeously trimmed" and a Latin verse and English translation inlaid upon it:

> *The child which thou to Mary, O Lord of might! hast send,*
> *To England's joy, in health preserve, keepe, and defend!*⁹

A series of letters announcing the baby's safe arrival was prepared and signed by Mary herself, ready to be sent to the pope, the emperor, the king of France, the doge of Venice, and the queen regent of Flanders. In most, the sex of the child and date of delivery were left blank to be filled in by clerks at the last minute, but the letter to the pope specifically informed "his Holiness" of the "happy delivery of a prince."[10]

Because of the dangers of childbirth, provision was made in the event of Mary's death for Philip to be made guardian of the realm during the minority of the expected child. He would still be confined within the limits of the marriage treaty and could not call Parliament, declare war, or arrange for a marriage of his heir without the consent of a council of eighteen peers.[11] The final bill of regency justified the need to avoid the "dolorous experience of the inconstant government during the time of the reign of the late King Edward the sixth." For this and other reasons, the king was to have charge of "the rule, order, education and government" of any children and the "rule, order and government (under such issue or issues)" of the realm during the minority of the heir.[12]

Finally, at the beginning of April, the king and queen moved to Hampton Court in advance of Mary's confinement. Mary preferred Windsor, but it was considered too far from London for her to be secure. At Hampton Court she would have the protection of her full guard and have closer access to the troops from the city and the arsenal at the Tower.

Two weeks later, Mary underwent the usual ceremonies in advance of "the lying-in" and withdrew to her chamber with her ladies and gentlewomen. On Saint George's Day, April 23, she showed herself at a window of the palace as she watched Philip lead the celebrations of the Garter, in which the king, Gardiner, the lord chancellor, knights and lords, and numerous clerks and priests, dressed in copes of cloth of gold, processed with three crosses, singing "Salve Festa Dies." As Mary looked out from her chamber she turned side-on to show off her great belly—"that a hundred did see her grace."[13]

While Mary prepared for the birth, Elizabeth was summoned to court from Woodstock.[14] She arrived in late April and repaired to the prince of Wales's lodging, which had been built for her brother,

Edward. It was more than two years since the sisters had seen each other, but after arriving at court Elizabeth was kept waiting three weeks before Mary agreed to see her. Then, at ten at night, Elizabeth received her summons. With guards bearing torches, she was escorted through the garden to the privy lodging and, accompanied by Susan Clarencius, Mary's favorite woman, was ushered into the queen's presence.

Elizabeth knelt while Mary spoke over her, chiding her for her refusal to acknowledge her offense in Wyatt's rebellion. "You will not confess your offence, but it stands stoutly in your truth. I pray God it may so fall out," she told her. "If it doth not," Elizabeth answered resolutely, "I request neither favour nor pardon at your Majesty's hands. . . . I humbly beseech your Majesty to have a good opinion of me, and to think me to be your true subject, not only from the beginning hitherto, but for ever, as long as life lasteth."[15]

As Mary and Elizabeth were finally reconciled, the country held its breath for the birth of its heir.

AT DAYBREAK ON Tuesday, April 30, bells rang out the news that Mary had safely delivered. Henry Machyn wrote in his diary, "the Queen's grace was delivered of a prince, and so there was great ringing through London and divers places, Te Deum laudamus sung."[16] Soon after midnight, "with little pain and no danger," she had given birth to a son.

The news was received with unadulterated joy. Shops were shut as people rushed to church. Bonfires were lit and tables of food and wine set up as spontaneous street parties erupted all over London.[17] "How fair, how beautiful and great a prince it was as the like had not been seen," as one preacher noted.[18] Reports quickly spread to courts across Europe. Thomas Gresham, the English ambassador to the Netherlands, reported how news had reached Antwerp that "the Queen was brought to bed of a young Prince on 30th April," and the city's great bell was rung in celebration. The English merchants fired their guns across the water, and the regent sent the English mariners 100 crowns with which to celebrate the news.[19] By the evening of May 2, the imperial court was "rejoicing out of measure" to hear of the prince's birth.

CHAPTER 54

HER MAJESTY'S BELLY

∴

T HE BELLS WERE SOON SILENCED AND THE BONFIRES EXTINGUISHED. The rumors were false. The queen had not gone into labor, and fresh calculations had to be made. As the Venetian ambassador, Giovanni Michieli, reported in late May:

> Everything is in suspense, and dependant on the result of this delivery, which, according to the opinion of the physicians, unless it takes place at this new phase of the moon two days hence, may be protracted beyond the full [moon] and [its] occultation, on the 4th or 5th of next month; her Majesty's belly having greatly declined, which is said yet more to indicate the approaching term.[1]

Days passed, but the labor pains did not begin. Speculation continued to fill letters and ambassadorial dispatches. Ruy Gómez observed on May 22 that he had seen the queen walking in her garden with such a light step that "it seems to me that there is no hope at all for this month."[2] Renard wrote, "Everything in this kingdom depends on the Queen's safe deliverance." If she did not bear a child, he foresaw "trouble on so great a scale that the pen can hardly set it down . . . the delay in the Queen's deliverance encourages the heretics to slander and put about false rumours; some say that she is not with child at all."[3] Philip had already expressed his doubts. Writing in April to his brother-in law Maximilian of Austria, he declared, "The Queen's pregnancy turns out not to have been as certain as we thought. Your highness and my sister manage better than the Queen and I do."[4]

The summer turned increasingly bleak; the weather was so bad "that the like is not remembered in the memory of man for the last fifty years."[5] Mary grew more and more reclusive, sitting in one place for hours at a time, wrestling with depression and anxiety, neither leaving her chamber nor giving audience to anyone.[6] To those who saw her she looked pale and ill, weeping and praying that her labor pains begin. Her prayer book survives, the pages worn and stained around a page bearing a prayer for the safe delivery of a woman with child.[7]

As the weeks passed, the mood became one of despair. Some said the queen was dead; seditious talk was everywhere. Every few days new libels against her were thrown into the streets, stirring up fears and encouraging rebellion. By June, the earl of Pembroke and a number of troops had to be brought in to keep order in London. Protestant pamphleteers alleged that the king kept company with whores and commoners' daughters while Mary was confined to her rooms. Rumors circulated that Mary had never been pregnant at all "but that a supposititious child is going to be presented as hers"; or that the fetus had been a pet monkey or a lapdog; or that the Queen had delivered "a mole or lump of flesh and was in great peril of death."[8] Posters were nailed to the palace door and abusive papers thrown into the queen's own chamber. Others said the queen had been deceived by a tympany or some other disease to believe herself to be pregnant but was not. Some thought that she had miscarried, others that she was bewitched.[9]

The French ambassador, Noailles, scoffed at the solemn prayers and anxious anticipation, believing the queen's pregnancy to be an elaborate farce. He had been informed by two of Mary's intimate female attendants, Susan Clarencius and one of the midwives, "that the Queen's state was by no means of the hopeful kind generally supposed, but rather some woeful malady, for several times a day she spent long hours sitting on her floor with her knees drawn up to her chin," a position that no pregnant woman could have assumed without considerable pain. The midwife, "one of the best midwives in the town," believed the queen, "though pale and peaked," was not pregnant. "The said midwife, more to comfort her with words than anything, tells her from day to day that she has miscalculated her pregnancy by two months, the royal physicians either too ignorant or fearful to tell the Queen" the truth and so would refer only to a "miscalculation" in the time of her delivery.[10]

In a letter to Eraso, Ruy Gómez wrote, "All this makes me wonder whether she is with child at all, greatly as I desire the thing to be happily over."[11] Philip shared Gómez's sentiments and grew restless. "From what I hear," Michieli wrote in a dispatch, "one single hour's delay in this delivery seems to him a thousand years."[12] He had been expected in Flanders since May, and on June 6 the emperor was still postponing the interment of Queen Joanna, Philip's grandmother, in the hope that his grandson would arrive at any time. Philip had made preparations to leave as soon as the child was born and Mary was out of danger. According to Michieli, the hope of childbirth "has so diminished that but little reliance can now be any longer placed on it"; he concluded that "the pregnancy will end in wind rather than anything else."

By the end of June, the doctors had given up trying to predict when the queen would be delivered. On the twenty-sixth, Michieli wrote, "There is no one, either of the physicians or the women, or others, all having been deceived, who at present dare any longer form any opinion about it, all persons resigning themselves to such hour and time as shall best please our Lord God."[13]

The delay was interpreted in different ways. In mid-June two gentlemen "of no ordinary repute" were imprisoned in the Tower, charged with "having spoken about this delivery licentiously, in a tone unbecoming their grade."[14] People closest to Mary believed that a miracle would come to pass "in this as in all her Majesty's other circumstances, which the more they were despaired of according to human reason and discourse, the better and more auspicious did their result then show itself." The queen's child would prove to the world once and for all that her affairs "were regulated excessively by Divine Providence."[15]

AT THE END of July, daily processions and prayers for the royal baby's delivery were halted. On August 3, with no public announcement and on the pretext that Hampton Court needed to be cleaned, the court moved to the far smaller residence of Oatlands, allowing for the

large retinue of gentlewomen, rockers, and nursery staff to be dismissed. As the Venetian ambassador wrote:

> Although no one dares to proclaim it . . . the fact is that the
> move has been made in order no longer to keep the people of
> England in suspense about this delivery, by the constant and
> public processions which were made, and by the Queen's
> remaining so many days in retirement . . . to the prejudice of her
> subjects; as not only did she transact no business, but would
> scarcely allow herself to be seen by any of her ladies who, in
> expectation of childbirth, especially the gentlewomen and the
> chief female nobility [who] had flocked to court from all parts of
> the kingdom in such very great number, all living at the cost of
> her Majesty.[16]

There had been no baby. Like her mother forty years before, Mary
had been deluded into believing that she was pregnant. Wise after the
event, Michieli described how "from her youth" she had suffered from
the "retention of menstrual fluids" and the "strangulation of her
womb." Her body swelled, and her breasts enlarged and sent out milk.
"It was this which had led to the empty rumour of her pregnancy."[17]

THE OUTCOME OF the pregnancy had been of central importance to
the peace negotiations between the French king and emperor, held
under English auspices at La Marque in May. The latest round of hostilities, which had erupted in 1551, had reached a stalemate. The birth of
an heir to the English throne would have given the emperor immense
benefit, but if the queen and child died, the advantage would be with
the French.

For the English, a great deal was at stake: the revival of England's
prestige in continental politics, an improvement of relations with
France, and, of greatest importance, the prevention of a new war in
which Spain might try to involve England. But as the negotiations
continued, it became clear that neither the Habsburgs nor the Valois
were willing to give much ground. As the talks reached an impasse,
news came at the beginning of June of Mary's failed pregnancy and of

the election of Giovanni Pietro Carafa, a seventy-nine-year-old Neapolitan and great enemy of the Habsburgs, as pope. The conference came to an abrupt end: the French had lost their fear.

Now, with no immediate prospect of an heir, Philip prepared to depart England for the Low Countries. Nervous of informing Mary of his intentions, he rehearsed how he would tell her in a draft letter, sent probably to Ruy Gómez: "Let me know what line I am to take with the Queen about leaving her and about religion. I see I must say something, but God help me!"[18] Philip decided to leave most of his household in the hope of convincing the queen that he would return quickly. Yet, as the Venetian ambassador reported, "it is said more than ever, that he will go to Spain, and remove thence his household and all the others by degrees."[19]

Philip would be leaving England with the Catholic restoration achieved and the enforcement of Catholic obedience under way. Six months before, the medieval treason laws, repealed by Edward VI, had been restored. The secular authorities were empowered once more to deal ruthlessly with religious opponents: seditious words and activities would be punished. With the rising threat of disorder and rebellion, the restoration of Catholicism was to take on a ferocious edge: heretics would be burned alive.

CHAPTER 55

BLOOD AND FIRE

∴

ON MONDAY, FEBRUARY 4, 1555, JOHN ROGERS, CANON OF ST. PAUL'S, was led out to Smithfield, condemned as a heretic. Great crowds lined the streets to watch the procession, among them his wife and eleven children. As he stood at the stake, he was offered a pardon on condition that he recanted, but he refused. He exhorted the people to stand firm in the faith that he had taught them. When the fire took hold of his body, he "washed his hands in the flame as he was in burning."[1] As Renard related, "Some of the onlookers wept; others prayed God to give him strength, perseverance and patience to bear the pain and not to recant; others gathered the ashes and bones and wrapped them up to preserve them."[2]

Rogers's death was followed just days later by those of two country parsons—Laurence Saunders, the rector of All Hallows in Coventry, and Dr. Rowland Taylor, the rector of Hadleigh, Suffolk—and by the former bishop of Worcester and Gloucester, John Hooper. Each was burned in the district in which he had first officiated.

Hooper, like the other condemned martyrs, had denied papal supremacy over the Church and the Real Presence of Christ in the Eucharist. He was imprisoned in the Fleet on September 1, 1553, and remained there for more than seventeen months. At the end of January 1555, he was brought before Stephen Gardiner and a number of other bishops and urged to give up his "evil and corrupt doctrine" and to conform to the Catholic Church.[3] If he recanted, he would have the queen's mercy. He refused, and on February 9 he was burned. Standing on a high stool and looking over the crowd of several thousand that had gathered to watch him, he prayed.

An eyewitness described how "in every corner there was nothing to be seen but weeping and sorrowful people."[4] Faggots were laid around the stool and reeds placed in and between Hooper's hands. Then the fire was lit. The wind at first blew the flames from him and, having burned his legs, the fires were almost extinguished. More faggots and reeds were brought, and finally the two bladders of gunpowder tied between his legs ignited. In the end he could move nothing but his arms; then one fell off and the other, with "fat, water and blood dropping out at his fingers' ends," stuck to what was left of his chest. It had taken forty-five minutes of excruciating agony to kill him.[5] It was a horrific death and a sight that would be repeated nearly three hundred times during Mary's reign.

A WEEK AFTER Hooper's death, six other men—William Pygot, a butcher from Braintree; Stephen Knight, a barber at Malden; Thomas Haukes, a gentleman in Lord Oxford's household; William Hunter, a nineteen-year-old apprentice; Thomas Tomkins, a weaver from Shoreditch; and John Laurence, a priest—were denounced to Bishop Bonner as Protestant heretics. Having been defrocked, Laurence was brought to Colchester on March 29. He had been shackled in prison with such heavy irons and so deprived of food that he was too weak to walk to the stake and had to be carried there and burned sitting on a chair. His young children went before the fire and cried out, "Lord, strengthen thy servant and keep thy promise." Laurence and the other five men had been offered the chance to recant, but all remained defiant. As Thomas Haukes declared, "No, my Lord, that will I not; for if I had an hundred bodies I would suffer them all to be torn in pieces rather than recant."[6] He was condemned on February 9 and burned four months later.

At the request of his friends, who feared the extent of his pain in the fire, Haukes agreed that, if it were tolerable, he would lift his hand above his head before he died. Having been strapped to the stake and engulfed by the flames, he raised his hands and clapped them together to the cries and rejoicing of the crowd.[7]

IN EARLY 1555, the Privy Council sent a writ to Sir Nicholas Hare, master of the Rolls, and other justices of the peace in the county of

Middlesex for the execution of William Flower, signifying to them that "For as much as the said Flower's offence was so enormous and heinous, there further pleased for the most terrible example he should before he were executed have his right hand stricken off."[8]

William Flower had been condemned for striking a priest with a wood knife in St. Margaret's Church, Westminster. He was burned on April 24, 1555, as the Council's letter had instructed. Most of the burnings in the summer were in London and Essex, in the diocese of Edmund Bonner, bishop of London, who soon became synonymous with the persecution. Orders were sent to find anyone guilty of heresy and report them to the authorities. Towns and villages were searched to find those who held heretical opinions and refused to observe the Catholic faith. Many of the victims were agricultural laborers and artisans denounced by their neighbors or their families, the victims of private grievances or local disputes.

Margaret Polley, a woman living in Pembury near Tonbridge, was the first woman to be burned in Mary's reign. She had maintained that there was no reference to the Roman Catholic Church in the Bible and denied the Real Presence in the Mass. She was burned on July 18, 1555, along with two other martyrs in a gravel pit just outside Dartford in Kent. The local farmers brought cartloads of cherries to sell to the spectators.[9] Other women followed. Alice Benden of Staplehurst in Kent was reported to the authorities by her own husband and disowned by her father. She had refused to attend church as, she said, too much idolatry was practiced there. For nine weeks she was incarcerated in the bishop's prison, living only on bread and water and with no change of clothes. In John Foxe's description, she became "a most piteous and loathsome creature to behold." When offered the chance of freedom if she reformed, she declared, "I am thoroughly persuaded by the extremity that you have already showed me, that you are not of God, neither can your doings be Godly." She remained imprisoned and was burned with six others in Canterbury in June 1557.[10]

As the months went on, the persecution spread beyond Bonner's diocese to Wales, East Anglia, and the North. In the diocese of Chester, George Marsh, a young widowed farmer from Cumberland, had been ordained as a priest during the reign of Edward VI. After

Mary's accession he returned from London to Lancashire, denounced the Mass and papal supremacy, and was subsequently arrested. He was condemned as a heretic and sentenced to be burned at Spittle Broughton, just outside the north gate of Chester, on April 24, 1555. Offered a pardon if he recanted, he refused, saying he loved life and wanted to live but not at the cost of betraying Christ. Having walked to the site of his execution in shackles, a chain was fastened around his waist. On his head was placed a jar filled with tar and pitch so that when the flames reached it the contents would pour down. It was a gusty day and a gradual death, as very slowly the flames engulfed his body."

On the island of Guernsey, a woman named Katherine Cowchen lived with her two daughters, Perotine Massey and Guillemine Gilbert. Perotine had informed the authorities that a local woman, Vincent Gosset, had stolen a gold goblet. In revenge Gosset denounced Cowchen and her two daughters as heretics. All three were convicted of heresy and sentenced to death by burning. Perotine had not told the authorities she was pregnant. When the faggots were lit, the fire caused her to give birth to her baby son, who fell onto the burning faggots. One of the spectators rushed forward to save the baby and pulled him out of the fire, but the local sheriff ordered that the baby be thrown back. He was burned with his mother, grandmother, and aunt."

NEITHER MARY NOR Pole had expected to burn so many; they wanted the heretics to be reconciled rather than die and for the burnings to be carried out judiciously and without vindictiveness. Mary ordered that a councillor be present to supervise each burning in London and that during each execution "some good and pious sermons be preached." Writing in December 1554, she had declared:

Touching the punishment of heretics, I believe it would be well to inflict punishment at this beginning, without much cruelty and passion, but without however omitting to do such justice on those who choose by their false doctrines to deceive simple persons, that the people may clearly comprehend that they have not

been condemned without just cause, whereby others will be
brought to know the truth, and will beware of letting themselves
be induced to relapse into such new and false opinions.[13]

However, willful disobedience to the Catholic Church—heresy—was
the worst of sins and needed to be extirpated, lest it "infect" more.

But rather than extinguishing Protestant sentiment, as Mary
intended, the burnings served only to define more clearly the
Protestants as a dissident group. Moreover, the courage of the martyrs
stirred the admiration of many of those who saw them die. Such was
the "murmuring about the cruel enforcement of the recent acts of
Parliament on heresy which had now begun, as shown publicly when
Rogers was burnt," reported Renard to Philip after the first London
burnings, "I do not think it well that your Majesty should allow further
executions to take place unless the reasons are overwhelmingly strong
and the offences committed have been so scandalous as to render the
course justifiable in the eyes of the people."[14] Four months later,
Michieli made similar observations:

> Two days ago, to the displeasure as usual of the population here,
> two Londoners were burnt alive, one of them having been a
> public lecturer in Scripture, a person sixty years of age, who was
> held in great esteem. In a few days the like will be done to four
> or five more; and thus from time to time to many others who are
> in prison for this cause and will not recant, although such sever-
> ity is odious to many people.[15]

Increasingly, Protestantism was associated with resistance to
Spanish domination and the defense of English liberty, with Philip
being held responsible by many for the burnings. However, just days
after John Rogers's execution, Alfonso de Castro, Philip's confessor,
preached a sermon at court with the king's sanction, attacking the
burnings and "saying plainly that they learned it not in scripture, to
burn any for conscience sake; but the contrary, that they should live
and be converted."[16] Renard advised Philip that haste in religious matters should be avoided:

Religion is not yet firmly established and . . . the heretics are on the watch for every possible opportunity to revive error and compromise the good beginning that has been made. They use as an argument the cruel punishments which they assert are being applied, with recourse to fire rather than doctrine and good examples, to lead the country back [to Catholicism].[17]

Although Philip did not play the direct role many attributed to him, he did nothing to forestall the persecution, and the burnings continued. But for Mary, to halt the process would have been to condone heresy, and this she could never do. It was an affront to her conscience that had been forged in the fires of persecution in the years before she had become queen. As the Venetian ambassador, Giovanni Soranzo, observed, during her brother's reign Mary had not conformed to the new religious service, "her belief in that into which she was born being so strong that had the opportunity offered, she would have displayed it at the stake."[18]

CHAPTER 56

EXTRAORDINARILY IN LOVE

∴

*My lord and good father. I have learnt by what the King, my
Lord and good husband, has told me and also by the letter
which you were pleased to send me that for a long time past
the state of your affairs has demanded that your Majesty and
he should meet in order to be able to confer together and
reach the appropriate decisions. However, you have been
pleased to put off the moment of separating him from me until
now, for which I humbly thank your Majesty. I assure you,
Sire, that there is nothing in this world that I set so much
store by as the King's presence. But as I have more concern
for your Majesties' welfare than my own desires, I submit to
what regard you as necessary. I firmly hope that the King's
absence will be brief, for I assure your Majesty, that quite
apart from my own feelings, his presence in this kingdom has
done much good and is of great importance for the good governance of this country. For the rest, I am content with whatever may be your Majesty's pleasure.*[1]

—MARY TO CHARLES V,
JULY—AUGUST 1555

ON AUGUST 27, MARY AND PHILIP RODE FROM HAMPTON COURT
through London to Greenwich, accompanied by the lord mayor and
aldermen, the English and Spanish nobility, and Cardinal Pole. Mary
had planned to travel by barge and Philip to ride through the city, but
at the last moment she chose to give Londoners the "satisfaction of seeing her likewise in his company."

The streets thronged with people, joyful not only to see the king and queen together but to be reassured, after months of rumors during her supposed pregnancy, that their queen was not dead. As Michieli wrote, "when they knew of her appearance, they all ran from one place to another, as to an unexpected sight." It was "as if they were crazy, to ascertain thoroughly that it was her, and on recognising and seeing her in better plight than ever, they by shouts and salutations, and every other demonstration, then gave greater signs of joy."[2] Two days later, Philip departed by river to commence his journey to Dover and then to Flanders. Mary watched at a window from the palace at Greenwich as the barge prepared to leave, and Philip waved his hat in her direction, "demonstrating great affection."[3] It was, for Mary, a sorrowful parting:

> The Queen . . . chose to come with him through all the chambers and galleries to the head of the stairs, constraining herself the whole way to avoid, in sight of such a crowd, any demonstration unbecoming her gravity, though she could not but be moved when the Spanish noblemen kissed her hand, and yet more, when she saw the ladies in tears take leave of the King, who, according to the custom of the country, kissed them one by one. On returning, however, to her apartments, placing herself at a window which looks on the river, not supposing herself any longer seen or observed by anyone, it was perceived that she gave free vent to her grief by a flood of tears, nor did she once quit the window until she had not only seen the King embark and depart, but remained looking after him as long as he was in sight.[4]

Philip and his retinue stayed at Canterbury for several days, awaiting good weather and the arrival of Flemish ships at Dover. Men were out on the road nearly every hour, carrying letters between the king and queen, and messengers waited about the courtyard of Greenwich Palace night and day, "booted and spurred ready for a start." As Michieli reported, "the Queen not content with having sent two of her chief chamberlains in the King's company for the purpose of being acquainted with all that takes place, writes to him daily in her own hand, and despatches courtiers, demonstrating in every way her great desire."⁵ But Philip wrote less and less. When Michieli had an audience with the queen on September 13, she told him "very passionately with tears in her eyes, that for a week she had had no letters from him [Philip]."⁶ Meanwhile, Michieli's informant described how Mary mourned as if grief-stricken, "as may be imagined with regard to a person extraordinarily in love."

> The Queen remains disconsolate, though she conceals it as much as she can, and from what I hear mourns the more when alone and supposing herself invisible to any of her attendants. During this absence Cardinal Pole will reside with her, lodgings having been assigned to him in the palace, that he may comfort and keep her company, Her Majesty delighting greatly in the sight and presence of him.⁷

In letters to Philip, Pole recounted how Mary spent her day, passing "the forenoon in prayer after the manner of Mary [Magdalene], and in the afternoon admirably personates Martha, by transacting business."⁸

Two weeks after the king's departure, Simon Renard left England. With Philip's arrival, his confidential relationship with the queen had ended. He had asked to be recalled, but Charles had refused, replying that he must stay in England to give Philip the benefit of his considerable knowledge of "the condition of affairs" derived from his long residence there.⁹ By March 1555, Renard was given leave to depart. Mary said of him in a letter to Charles V, "He was here with me through very dangerous times and that he showed himself during the marriage negotiations to be a most indispensable minister, inspired by the greatest desire to serve us and the greatest zeal for my affairs."¹⁰ She presented him with more than 1,200 ounces of plate as a token of gratitude.¹¹

Having arrived at court for the queen's confinement in late spring, Elizabeth remained with Mary until the autumn. By September, Noailles observed, she was "more in favour than she used to be, going every day to mass with the Queen and often in her company."¹² In mid-October, she obtained leave to withdraw and left the court for Hatfield. At the same time many of Philip's household servants, soldiers, and pages also began to withdraw, "with a mind," Michieli noted, "not to revisit this country for a very long while."[13]

By December, all those who remained were instructed to join the king in the Low Countries. Federico Badoer, the Venetian ambassador to the emperor, reported:

> The King's confessor [Alfonso de Castro] has arrived here, and repeated a variety of foul language uttered by the English, indicating their ill-will towards his Majesty and the Spanish nation [and says] that on seeing him and the rest of the attendants depart, they made great rejoicing well-nigh universally; and he goes saying that the Queen's wish again to see the King is very great, nay boundless.[14]

Philip sought to stay in touch with English affairs through a body of advisers—a Council of State—that he established on his departure. The councillors were to reside at court, consider "all causes of state and financial causes and other causes of great moment," and write to Philip three times a week.[15] The reports, in Latin, were written by First Secretary Sir William Petre and then returned by Philip's secretary, annotated with comments in the margin or at the foot of the page. "It seems well done"; "the King is most grateful to be told"; "the King explains his wishes in letters to the councillors": such were typical of Philip's comments on matters ranging from prospective legislation and the nomination or recall of ambassadors to the condition of the shires and the defense of the realm.[16] Important statutes and proclamations continued to be sent to the king for his signature, but as he turned his attention to the Netherlands, his correspondence became less frequent.

In October 1555, Charles resigned the lordship of the Netherlands to Philip and in January 1556 the crowns of Aragon and Castile. He sent a message with one of his gentlemen to Mary "with congratulations on her being able for the future to style herself the Queen of many and great crowns, and on her being no less their mistress than of her own crown of England."[17] Philip now desired power in England in his own right, not simply as a regent for the heir. He began to put pressure on Mary that he be crowned and even suggested this might be a condition of his return to England.[18] On October 12, Badoer wrote that "the King of England had informed his wife that he was most anxious to gratify her wish for his return, but that he could not do so without being given an honourable share in the government of the realm."[19]

Yet Mary hesitated to propose his coronation. Parliament was full of opposition, and, as she relayed to Badoer, "she knew it to be impossible to form either of these important resolutions without greatly endangering her crown, but that she hoped in the course of a short time to comfort the King with what he seems to desire."[20] At the end of December, Mary wrote to Philip, "apologising for her non-adoption of any of the resolutions desired by him in the matter of the coronation, or with regard to waging war on the Most Christian King [of France]."[21] Rumors were circulating of Philip's lascivious antics abroad, and Mary began to lose hope of her husband's imminent return.[22] As Noailles recounted in a letter of December 30, Mary "told her ladies, that she had done all possible to induce her husband to return, and as she found he would not, she meant to withdraw utterly from men, and live quietly, as she had done the chief part of her life before she married."[23]

COMMITTED TO THE FLAMES

O N THE MORNING OF MARCH 21, 1556, THOMAS CRANMER, THE
sixty-six-year-old former archbishop of Canterbury, was burned alive
in the town ditch in Oxford. Thrusting his hand into the flames, he
spoke the words "For as much be as my hand offended, writing contrary to my heart, my hand shall first be punished therefor."[1]

Cranmer was the highest profile of the Marian martyrs and one
Mary had always been determined to condemn as a heretic. It was he
who had encouraged her father's break with Rome; he who had, as
archbishop of Canterbury, declared Katherine of Aragon's marriage
invalid; and he who had performed the wedding of Henry VIII and
Anne Boleyn. Upon Mary's accession he had been condemned with
Lady Jane Grey and three of Northumberland's sons for high treason
for his support of Jane's accession, but his sentence had not been carried out.

Mary bore Cranmer a deep and personal grudge, and even though
Church law said that as a repentant heretic he should be pardoned, she
was determined that he burn. She wanted his death to be for heresy,
not for secular offenses. Given his status as archbishop of Canterbury,
she had had to wait for the restoration of papal jurisdiction. For two
and a half years he had languished in prison, awaiting his inevitable
fate.

IN MARCH 1554, Cranmer, together with Hugh Latimer, the former
bishop of Worcester, and Nicholas Ridley, the former bishop of
London, were moved from the Tower of London to Oxford and placed

in the Bocardo, the town prison. Several weeks later, a disputation on the Eucharist was held at St. Mary's Church during which each of the Protestant leaders made their case to an audience of nearly a thousand Catholics. It was never intended to be a fair hearing; the prisoners were to be delivered to the commissioners "so that their erroneous opinions being by the word of God justly and truly convinced, the residue of our subjects, may be thereby the better established in the true Catholic faith."[2] After four days of debate, the Protestants were told they had been defeated. They were declared heretics, excommunicated, and returned to their prison cells. For the next seventeen months, Cranmer remained almost completely isolated in the Bocardo.

On September 12, 1555, Cranmer's trial for heresy began at St. Mary's Church. He faced fifteen charges: six dealing with his matrimonial affairs, six others with his repudiation of papal authority, and three with heretical doctrines. He refused to recant and to acknowledge papal supremacy and the Real Presence. The trial ended, the case had to be referred to Rome, and Cranmer was sent back to the Bocardo. Three weeks later, Ridley and Latimer faced their trial. Both refused to recant; both were condemned to death. On October 16, they were taken to a stake sunk into a ditch outside the northern wall of the city near Balliol College. Cranmer was brought out of his cell to watch. For three hours Dr. Richard Smith, an Oxford theologian, preached as Ridley and Latimer waited for their deaths. Finally they were fastened to the stake and the faggots were lit. "Be of good comfort mister Ridley, and play the man," Latimer called out, "we shall this day light such a candle by God's grace in England, as (I trust) shall never be put out."[3] Latimer was quickly engulfed by the flames.

Ridley's death was much slower. The faggots had been stacked so thickly that the fire could not burn through them. His legs burned, but the flames did not rise above his body to the gunpowder around his neck. "Let the fire come unto me, I cannot burn!" he cried.[4] Faggot after faggot was thrown around Ridley's head and further fuel added to the fire. Finally the gunpowder was ignited and he died.[5]

ON DECEMBER 4, Cranmer's fate was decided in Rome. He was deprived of his archbishopric "and of all ecclesiastical dignities," and permission was given for his execution. On January 27, the Venetian ambassador, Giovanni Michieli, reported that "the sentence against the late Archbishop of Canterbury will soon be executed, he remaining more obstinate than ever in his heresies."[6] A few days later, under pressure of interrogation, Cranmer admitted to every fact brought before him and signed his first submission. He stated that he would accept the supremacy of the pope because the king and queen had ordered him to do so and he would always obey his sovereigns.[7] Within days he signed a second recantation conceding more:

> I, Thomas Cranmer, doctor in divinity, do submit myself to the catholic church of Christ, and to the Pope, supreme head of the same church, and unto the King and Queen's majesties, and unto all their laws and ordinances.[8]

Mary must have been informed of his recantation but chose to ignore it; she was determined to be rid of the man who had caused her and her mother so much suffering.

On February 14, Cranmer was publicly degraded from holy orders in the church of Christ Church College. It was a ritual humiliation conducted by his old enemy Edmund Bonner, the bishop of London. After his crimes had been read out, Cranmer was forced to put on the vestments of an archbishop and then of a priest, after which each was stripped from him. His head was shaved to remove his tonsure, and his fingers were scraped to remove the holy oil that had ordained him. Then, dressed in a townsman's cloak and cap, Cranmer was handed over to the secular authorities, who returned him to the Bocardo. He made two more recantations, but to little effect. On the twenty-fourth a writ was issued to the mayor of Oxford ordering that "in a public and open place" Cranmer be "for the aforesaid cause committed to the flames in the presence of people; and have that Thomas Cranmer actually consumed by that same fire, for a manifest example to other Christians of the detestation in which such crimes are held."[9]

In his fifth and sixth recantations, Cranmer condemned himself in the most abject terms; he was "a blasphemer, persecutor and insulter . . . who surpassed Saul in wickedness and crime"; he was "unworthy of all kindness and goodness but rather deserving of . . . divine and eternal punishment." He continued that he had been "the cause and originator" of Henry's divorce, "which fault was in truth the seedbed of all the woes and disasters of this realm," and was therefore guilty "of the murder of so many upright men . . . the schism which split the whole kingdom . . . the slaughter of so many minds and bodies such that my reason can hardly grasp." He was, he maintained, "the most wicked all the earth has ever born."[10]

THE MORNING OF Saturday, March 21, 1556, was wet and dull. Given the weather, the sermon, normally delivered before the burning at the stake, was preached in St. Mary's Church.

Cranmer was expected to deliver his seventh recantation, retracting his rejection of the Real Presence in the Eucharist. Dr. Henry Cole, provost of Eton, first preached the sermon explaining the reasons for Cranmer's execution. Then, standing on a raised platform in a packed church, Cranmer began:

> And now I come to the great thing, that so much troubleth my conscience more than any thing that ever I did or said in my whole life, and that is the setting abroad of a writing contrary to the truth: which now here I renounce and refuse as things written with my hand, contrary to the truth which I thought in my heart, and written for fear of death, and to save my life if it might be. . . . And for as much be as my hand offended, writing contrary to my heart, my hand shall first be punished therefor: for may I come to the fire, it shall be first burnt. . . . As for the Pope, I refuse him as Christ's enemy and Antichrist, with all his false doctrine.[11]

The church descended into noise and protest. Cranmer was pulled from the stage and dragged through the streets to the place of execution, where Ridley and Latimer had suffered, and fastened to the stake with an iron chain. He held his hand in the flames, crying out, "Unworthy right hand!"[12] that which had signed the recantations. The sixty-six-year-old was soon dead. What had been intended to be a great coup—the public recantation of the architect of the English reformation—had been ruined.

The government immediately set about limiting the damage. The following day, Passion Sunday, Dr. Cole preached a denunciation of Cranmer in the church where he had spoken the day before. Within days John Cawood printed *All the Submissions and Recantations of Thomas Cranmer*, which ended with Cranmer's final expected recantation, rather than the one he had actually delivered. As the Venetian ambassador observed:

On Saturday last, 21 March, Cranmer, late Archbishop of Canterbury was burnt, having fully verified the opinion formed of him by the Queen, that he had feigned recantations thinking to save his life, and not that he had received any good inspiration, so she considered him unworthy of pardon.[13]

CHAPTER 58

A GREAT AND RARE EXAMPLE
OF GOODNESS

.·.

AT THREE ON THE AFTERNOON OF MAUNDY THURSDAY, APRIL 3, 1556, Mary, accompanied by Cardinal Pole, her Council, and her chaplains, entered the Great Hall at Greenwich Palace. Gathered at the entrance were Mary's chief ladies and gentlewomen in long linen aprons and towels around their necks. Each carried a silver ewer full of water and bunches of flowers. Mary wore a gown of purple velvet, its sleeves touching the ground. On either side of the hall were forty-one poor women, one for every year of the queen's life, seated on benches, their feet on stools. The women's right feet had been washed in preparation for the ceremony, first by a servant, then by the under almoner, and then by the grand almoner, the bishop of Chichester.

Kneeling before the first of the poor women, Mary took the woman's right foot in her hand, washed it and dried it, and, having signed it with the cross, kissed the foot with "reverence and solemnity." To each of the women she did the same, moving one by one along each side of the hall, always on her knees, accompanied by one of the noblewomen attending her with basin and towel.

Rising to her feet, Mary went again to each of the poor women, this time with a large wooden platter filled with pieces of salted fish and two large loaves of bread. Having distributed the alms she returned with a wooden bowl filled with either wine or hippocras and then gave each of the women a piece of rich cloth and a leather purse containing forty-one pennies. Finally she presented to the women the apron and towel that each of the noblewomen had worn. She then left the hall to remove her purple gown. Half an hour later she returned, preceded by a servant carrying the gown. As the choristers sang, she went around the room, twice examining the women one by one; returning for the third time, she gave the gown to the woman she had deemed the poorest and oldest of them.

THE FOLLOWING DAY, Good Friday, the queen came down from her oratory for the Adoration of the Cross. Kneeling at a short distance from the cross, she moved toward it on her knees as she prayed and kissed it "with such devotion as greatly to edify all those who were present." Then, reciting prayers and psalms, Mary began the ceremony of the benediction of the cramp rings and the touching for the "king's evil," a healing ritual for sufferers of scrofula. An enclosure had been formed to the right of the high altar with four benches placed in a square. Mary stood in the center and knelt down before two large, covered basins, each filled with gold and silver rings. One basin contained Mary's own rings, the other those of private individuals, each labeled with its owner's name.

After the basins were uncovered, Mary began reciting prayers and psalms, and then, taking the rings in her hand, she passed them from one hand to the other. She then withdrew to an altar in a private gallery. There she knelt, made her confession to and received absolution from Cardinal Pole, and then proceeded to bless the four scrofulous women who had gathered before her. The first sufferer was brought before her, and, still on her knees, Mary pressed her hands in the form of a cross on one of the woman's sores "with such compassion and devotion as to be a marvel." When all four sufferers had received the royal touch, Mary made the sign of the cross with a gold coin and placed it on a ribbon around their necks. After washing her hands, Mary returned to her oratory. As Marc Antonio Faitta, the secretary to Pole, concluded,

> Having been present myself in person at all these ceremonies, her Majesty struck me as affording a great and rare example of goodness, performing all those acts with such humility and love for religion, offering up her prayers to God with so great devotion and affection, and enduring for so long a while and so

patiently much fatigue; and seeing thus, that the more her Majesty advances in the rule of this kingdom, so does she daily afford fresh and greater opportunities for commending her extreme piety, I dare assert that there was never a Queen in Christendom of greater goodness than this one.'

By exercising her "healing power," Mary had demonstrated once again that a female monarch could conduct the ceremonies previously prescribed only to a "divinely appointed" king.

CHAPTER 59

STOUT AND DEVILISH HEARTS

∴

For many consecutive days a comet has been visible, as it still is, and with this opportunity a gang of rogues, some twelve in number . . . went about the city saying we should soon see the day of judgment, when everything would be burnt and consumed. These knaves, with a number of others, availing themselves of this device, agreed to set fire to several parts of the city, to facilitate their project of murder and robbery.[1]

—GIOVANNI MICHIELI,
MARCH 17, 1556

ON MARCH 5, 1556, A BLAZING COMET APPEARED IN THE SKY OVER London. Night after night for a week it shone, and Londoners looked up at it with "great wonder and astonishment."[2] These were fearful and uncertain times; "the stout and devilish hearts of the people of England" were once again ready "to work treason and make insurrections."[3] Yet what was initially thought to be civil unrest in London would reveal itself to be much more: a plot to overthrow Mary.

Born of political disaffection and Protestant intrigue, the conspiracy sought to exploit the popular discontent that had been growing since the previous summer. "The greatest rain and floods that ever was seen in England . . . [in which] both men and cattle drowned" had led to poor harvests and famine across England.[4] Mary's pregnancy had been unsuccessful, the peace conference at La Marque had failed, and the religious persecution continued with the burnings of Bishops Ridley, Latimer, and Cranmer. Renard warned that "unless steps are taken to remedy this state of affairs, it is impossible that trouble will not ensue . . . all the executions have hardened many hearts, for it has been seen how constant, or rather stubborn, these heretics prove at the stake." He had, the ambassador concluded, "never seen the people in such an ugly mood as they are at present."⁵ Rumors of sedition and incipient rebellion became commonplace amid growing fears that Philip was to be crowned. When Parliament met in October 1555, rumors circulated that the demand of a subsidy was for the king's coronation.⁶

A few days into the parliamentary session, the Privy Council, fearing insurrection, closed all houses of public dancing and gambling in London on the grounds that they provided opportunities for seditious assemblies.⁷ At the same time, three Suffolk men were imprisoned in the Tower, one of them having declared on the day Parliament opened that "to free the kingdom from oppression it would be well to kill the Queen."⁸ Seditious pamphlets, written by English exiles and filled with accounts of Habsburg tyranny in Naples and Milan, circulated on the streets of London.⁹ By the end of October, the queen had abandoned all hope of persuading Parliament to consider Philip's coronation. She remained determined, however, to pass bills allowing crown lands and revenues to be returned to the Church and for the estates of Protestant exiles who had fled abroad to be confiscated.

The death on the night of November 12 of the lord chancellor, Stephen Gardiner, made Mary's task even more difficult. His health had been failing since the spring, and he had struggled to speak at the opening of Parliament. Without her primary supporter, Mary was left to face the Commons alone. Her determination to restore the crown lands was matched by the Commons' reluctance to let them go for fear that they would have to give up their own gains.¹⁰ Though Mary succeeded in passing this bill, the other great measure, the exiles bill, was defeated after Sir Anthony Kingston, a member of the Commons, locked the doors of the chamber, forcing a division. Three days later, Parliament was dissolved and Kingston was imprisoned in the Tower.

By the new year, discontentment had deepened. In January, as the pace of religious persecution quickened, the Council decreed that the queen's pardon should no longer be offered to heretics at the stake because of the contempt with which the offer was habitually treated. Moreover, it ordered that those in the crowds at the burnings who were understood to be "comforting, aiding or praising the offenders, or otherwise use themselves to the ill example of others" would be imprisoned." On January 27, seven people—five men and two women—were burned at Smithfield and a few days later five more at Canterbury. In February, the Treaty of Vaucelles, by which hostilities between France and Spain were to be suspended for five years, left England marginalized, as it had been excluded from the negotiations. Philip, in his first act as king of Spain, was blamed for the blow to national prestige. As the comet appeared in the sky in March, Philip's astrologers advised that a major rising was to be expected in England." It was in these circumstances that the plot to depose Mary, hatched on both sides of the Channel, began to take shape.

LED BY SIR HENRY DUDLEY, a cousin of the late duke of Northumberland, and with the complicity of the French ambassador, Antoine de Noailles, the conspiracy sought to break the Spanish alliance and replace Mary with Elizabeth." After setting fire to several areas of the city to disguise their purpose, the plotters—among whom were Sir Anthony Kingston, released from the Tower after two weeks' imprisonment, and Christopher Ashton, Dudley's father-in-law—planned to rob the Exchequer of £50,000 in silver bullion and flee to the Isle of Wight in two of the queen's ships, already commandeered. There they would raise forces and effect a national rebellion while Dudley sailed from France with a number of other exiles. But before the plan could be executed, Thomas White, an Exchequer official, leaked the plot to Cardinal Pole." At first the Council waited, giving the conspirators time to begin executing the plot, while secretly moving bullion out of the Exchequer. Finally, on March 18, the government acted. The chief conspirators were arrested and sent to the Tower." The Venetian ambassador reported on the twenty-fourth:

> The suspicion about the conspirators who purposed setting fire to several quarters of the city for the sake of plunder, had a different root and origin to what was reported, a plot having been lately discovered of such a nature that, had it been carried into effect as arranged, it would doubtless . . . considering the

ill-will of the majority of the population here on account of the
religion . . . have placed the Queen and the whole kingdom in
great trouble, as it was of greater circuit and extent than had
been at first supposed.[16]

Lengthy inquiries followed throughout March and April as the web
of conspiracy became ever wider, revealing links to Exchequer officials, fugitives in France, and gentry and officials across the country,
including Sir Anthony Kingston, Sir William Courtenay, Sir John
Pollard, and Richard Uvedale, captain of the Isle of Wight. On April
4, Dudley and most of his fellow conspirators were declared traitors,
although by remaining in France Dudley escaped arrest. Two weeks
later, the rebel John Throgmorton and Uvedale were hanged and quartered at Tyburn. Kingston died on his way to London. Eventually ten
men were executed.

The plot had thrown the popular discontent and the willingness of
France to intervene against Mary into sharp relief. All the plotters were
heretics; many of them were associates of Sir Thomas Wyatt, who had
been released from the Tower six months before. Their common cause,
as with Wyatt's rebellion two years before, was the unpopularity of the
Spanish marriage, added to which was the new fear that Philip might
be crowned king of England.

The conspiracy left Mary in a state of profound distress. The queen
"rages against her subjects," wrote Noailles. "She is utterly confounded
by the faithlessness of those whom she most trusted, seeing that the
greater part of these miserable creatures [Dudley's conspirators] are kith
and kin or favoured servants of the greatest men in the kingdom, even
Lords of the Council."[17] Such was Mary's fright that she would not allow
Cardinal Pole to leave her for the ceremony of his consecration to the
archbishopric of Canterbury, due to take place in his cathedral on March
25. He was instead consecrated in the Friars' Church at Greenwich.[18] By
the summer there was reported to be something of a "siege mentality" at
court. Mary no longer appeared in public, living instead in a state of
seclusion, the palace full of armed men and the queen so afraid that she
dared not sleep more than three hours a night.[19] "All the nobility and
gentry of the country have been desired to keep on the watch and ready
to present themselves on the first summons."[20]

In the midst of such uncertainty, Mary grew ever more anxious for Philip's return, as Michieli related:

For many months, the Queen has passed from one sorrow to another, your Serenity can imagine what a life she leads, comforting herself as usual with the presence of Cardinal Pole, to whose assiduous toil and diligence, having entrusted the whole government of the kingdom, she is intent on enduring her trouble as patiently as she can. [21]

Two months later, he wrote:

The Queen's face has lost flesh greatly since I was last with her, the extreme need she has of the consort's presence harassing her . . . she having also within the last few days lost her sleep. [22]

In the middle of March, on the queen's instructions, the English ambassador, Sir John Mason, asked Philip "to say frankly in how many days he purposed returning" to the kingdom. Mason gently suggested that the king would "comfort the Queen, as also the peers of the realm, by his presence, saying that there was no reason yet to despair of his having heirs."[23] In April, Mary changed tack, sending Lord Paget as her envoy. As Badoer wrote, "I understand that the chief object of his discourse was to inspire the King with that hope, on his return to England, of being crowned, which has never yet been given him by the Queen his consort."[24] In a letter to the emperor on July 15, Mary made clear her despair and disillusionment:

It would be pleasanter for me to thank your Majesty for sending me back the King, my lord and good husband, than to dispatch me an emissary to Flanders . . . However, as your Majesty has been pleased to break your promise in this connection, a promise you made to me regarding the return of the King, my husband, I must perforce be satisfied, although to my unspeakable regret. [25]

Mary now spent her time in "tears, regrets and writing letters to bring back her husband," oscillating between a sense of anger and abandonment.[26] Increasingly she became frustrated with Philip and was reported to be "scratching portraits of her husband which she keeps in her room."[27] Finally, she wrote to the emperor once more, pleading that he hasten his son's return and arguing that it was for the safety of the realm:

> My Lord and good father, I wish to beg your Majesty's pardon for my boldness in writing to you at this time, and humbly to implore you, as you have always been pleased to act as a true father to me and my kingdom, to consider the miserable plight into which this country has now fallen. . . . Unless he [Philip] comes to remedy matters, not I only but also wiser persons than I, fear that great danger will ensue for lack of a firm hand, and indeed we see it before our eyes.[28]

CHAPTER 60

OBEDIENT SUBJECT AND
HUMBLE SISTER

∴

O N MAY 26, MORE THAN TWO MONTHS AFTER THE COLLAPSE OF Dudley's conspiracy, two of Mary's most trusted servants, Sir Henry Jerningham and John Norris, were sent to Elizabeth at Hatfield with a posse of troops. An armed guard was put around her house, and her lady mistress, Katherine Ashley, her Italian teacher, Giovanni Battista Castiglione, and three other women of her household were arrested and taken to London. A search of Ashley's chambers at Somerset House found incriminating anti-Catholic and anti-Spanish literature. According to the Venetian ambassador, all confessed to knowing of Dudley's plot. Mary's courier Francesco Piamontese was sent to Philip in Brussels to seek his counsel with regard to Elizabeth.[1]

The advice Mary received was heavily influenced by Habsburg interests. Although there was evidence that Elizabeth had been involved in treasonous activity, any action against her would threaten her succession. In default of Elizabeth as heir, the English throne would go to Mary, queen of Scots, who was betrothed to the dauphin of France. If Philip were to triumph in the Habsburg-Valois struggle, this was something he had to prevent. Once again, English dynastic interests were to be subsumed to Habsburg strategic ones. Piamontese returned to London with an unequivocal message from the king: no further inquiries should be made into Elizabeth's guilt, nor any suggestion made that her servants had been implicated in the plot with her authority.

Hastings and Englefield were sent to Elizabeth to inform her of her servants' confessions but also to "console and comfort her on behalf of her Majesty" and to assure her that Mary trusted in her innocence.[2] The armed guard was stood down, and Elizabeth was presented with a diamond ring, a symbol of purity, as a gesture of the queen's goodwill.[3] But, unable to feign total trust in her sister's fidelity, Mary ordered that she be placed in the guardianship of Sir Thomas Pope, a loyal privy councillor and steadfast Catholic, who was put in charge of her household. As the Venetian ambassador related, Elizabeth was "in ward and custody," but in "decorous and honourable form," as Philip had decreed.[4]

IN JULY, ANOTHER conspiracy came to light, this time involving a young schoolmaster. Impersonating Edward Courtenay, the man issued a bogus proclamation at Yaxley in Suffolk, declaring that Mary was dead and that he, Courtenay, was king and "ye Lady Elizabeth" was queen.[5] In the event, the rebellion never got off the ground and the pretender was executed. Once again Elizabeth had been invoked at the heart of a conspiracy seeking to depose Mary, yet this time, in line with Philip's instructions, the assumption was made that Elizabeth was innocent. At the end of the month, the Council wrote to Sir Thomas Pope, informing him of the wicked behavior of the conspirators "and how for that intent they had abused her grace's name" by proclaiming Elizabeth the queen.[6]

Elizabeth responded with extravagant declarations of loyalty. Writing to Mary on August 2, she contrasted "the old love of pagans to their prince" to "the rebellious hearts and devilish intents of Christians in name, but Jews in deed, towards their anointed King." She invoked Saint Paul to confirm that rebels were indeed devilish, and continued:

> Among earthly things, I chiefly wish this one: that there were as good surgeons for making anatomies of hearts that might show my thoughts to your Majesty as there are expert physicians of the bodies, able to express the inward griefs of their maladies to their patient. For then I doubt not but know well that whatsoever other should suggest by malice, yet your Majesty should be sure by knowledge, so that the more such misty clouds obfuscate the clear light of my truth, the more my tried thoughts

should glister to the dimming of the hidden malice . . . And like as I have been your faithful subject from the beginning of your reign, so shall no wicked persons cause me to change to the end of my life. And thus I commit your majesty to God's tuition, whom I beseech long time to preserve . . . your majesty's obedient subject and humble sister, Elizabeth.[7]

During the autumn of 1556, relations between the two sisters seemed to continue to improve. Elizabeth was freed from Sir Thomas Pope's supervision and invited to spend Christmas at court. She left Hatfield escorted by two hundred liveried gentlemen on horseback and on November 28, amid cheering crowds, entered the City of London, proceeding to her residence at Somerset House. Three days later, she was received by the queen with honor and amicability. But then suddenly, without any warning, all changed: the invitation for Christmas was withdrawn, and on December 3, Elizabeth retraced her steps back through the city to Hatfield. She was no longer welcome at court.[8]

PHILIP'S SUPPORT OF Elizabeth had come at a price. With slight prospect of an heir to the English throne born of Mary, he had looked to secure a marriage for Elizabeth that would preserve his interest in England and the Catholic restoration. The intended bridegroom was Emmanuel Philibert, prince of Piedmont and titular duke of Savoy.

The twenty-eight-year-old duke was Philip's cousin, a loyalist imperialist and committed Catholic who was determined to rid his duchy of the French force that had occupied it since 1536. He had come to England in December 1554 as the recognized candidate for Elizabeth's hand. But Elizabeth had proved unamenable: she did not want to commit to Habsburg interests and the Catholic cause. By the winter of 1556, the idea had been revived and Philip pressured Mary to force Elizabeth to submit to his will. Mary threatened Elizabeth with a parliamentary declaration of her bastardy and an acknowledgment of Mary, queen of Scots, as her heir if she would not comply.[9] Elizabeth remained resistant, and Mary sent her sister from court.

A letter written in French in Mary's own hand at the beginning of 1557 reveals the tension between Mary and Philip over Elizabeth. He had sought to persuade Mary by arguing that she was bound by her faith and conscience to bring about Elizabeth's marriage to Philibert. But, as Mary explained in the first draft of her letter, her conscientious scruple against Elizabeth's marrying went back to her sister's birth in 1533. She then crossed out the passage and replaced it with the more benign statement that she did not understand his argument. In response to Mary's assertion that the marriage could not be carried out before parliamentary consent, Philip argued that if Parliament refused, he "would impute the blame to me." Mary begged him not to do that, saying that otherwise "I shall become jealous and uneasy about you, which will be worse to me than death," adding, "for I have already begun to taste [of such jealousy and uneasiness] too much to my great regret."

Mary was a submissive wife yet also a shrewd politician: it would not be possible, she declared, for the marriage to be carried out in his absence. He would need to come to England; then they could pray together to God, "who has the direction of the hearts of kings in his hand."[10]

CHAPTER 61

A WARMED OVER HONEYMOON

AT FIVE IN THE AFTERNOON OF MARCH 20, 1557, PHILIP FINALLY returned to England. A thirty-two-gun salute greeted him at Greenwich Palace amid shouts of "God save the King and Queen."¹ The following day, the bells of London rang out in celebration. A series of entertainments—banquets, dances, and masques of welcome—culminated on the twenty-third in a grand civic festival as Philip, Mary, and the nobles and ladies of the realm rode through London. It was, as one diplomat described it, "a warmed over honeymoon."²

Yet despite the festivities, there was little disguising the true purpose of Philip's visit. The king had returned for money and an English declaration of war against France, a prospect very few Englishmen were happy with.

MONTHS EARLIER, the Habsburg-Valois conflict had reignited. In September 1556, the duke of Alva, Philip's viceroy in Naples, had launched an invasion of the papal states some thirty years after the armies of Charles V had destroyed Rome. Denouncing Charles V as a "heretic, schismatic and tyrant" whose aim had been to oppress the Holy See and Philip as the "son of iniquity," the eighty-year-old Italian Pope Paul IV persuaded the French to join him in an attempt to drive Habsburg forces out of Italy.

Philip's attention immediately turned to England. He sought to relieve the pressure in Italy by striking at the Franco-Flemish frontier. He was effectively bankrupt and desperately needed money and men and an English declaration to defend the Low Countries.³ Philip's

envoy, Figueroa, presented his demands at a series of meetings with
the Privy Council held in the queen's chambers at St. James's in
mid-November.[4] Though the Council approved sending money and
naval support, it was not prepared to commit troops or renew the
Anglo-Flemish treaties for fear of provoking war with France.

On the night of January 5–6, the French launched a surprise attack
on the town of Douai on the Flemish frontier. The Treaty of Vaucelles
was broken, and on the thirty-first war was formally declared between
France and Spain.[5] Although there was no direct threat to England,
Mary had already begun to prepare the country for war. In January,
sheriffs of several eastern and midland counties were summoned to
report on how many troops could be mustered; royal pensioners were
equipped with new standards bearing the arms of Philip and Mary
"with a great eagle above"; ships were ordered to be refitted, and further reinforcements were sent to Calais.[6] The English navy had been
greatly expanded during the previous eighteen months, and two large
new ships, the *Philip and Mary* and a new *Mary Rose*, were ready by the
beginning of 1557.[7] The Council grudgingly approved the raising of
6,000 foot and 600 horse, which they were bound by treaty to send to
Philip if the Netherlands were attacked.

On January 20, a muster of royal pensioners at Greenwich Park
took place in front of the queen. With trumpets blowing and standards
unfurled, the men at arms rode past her three abreast. Their standards,
combining Philip and Mary's arms, symbolized the union of the two
powers against the common enemy. On one side, the Castilian colors
of red and yellow surrounded the white hart of England; on the other
was the black eagle of the Habsburgs with gilded legs.[8] After the muster a tumbler performed many feats "that her grace did like." She "did
thank them all for their pains" and went back into the palace much
heartened.[9]

Henry II of France had sent clear instructions to Noailles: the principal thing he desired was to be kept on "friendly terms with the Queen
of England . . . so that in that direction, if possible, nothing should
happen to thwart me, and so that during these wars I may not have
them [the English] for open and declared enemies."[10] Within days,
Mary was informed of Philip's imminent departure for England and
that the French, by breaking the truce, had left him no choice but to

raise land and sea forces to prevent the pope and the French from waging war in the Kingdom of Naples.[11] Mary begged Philip "not to be
afraid to come [back]," assuring him that his presence would "enable
him to obtain what he wants."[12]

WHEN PHILIP RETURNED to England in late March 1557, both he
and the queen petitioned the Council for a declaration of war. On April
1, Mary summoned the councillors to her and, in Philip's presence,
made a speech outlining the reasons for war, with Mary now choosing
to play up her wifely obligations:

> She expounded to them the obedience which she owed her hus-
> band and the power which he had over her as much by divine as
> by human law, citing to them many examples from the Old and
> New Testament, and begged them to consider the greatness and
> prosperity of the kingdom of France, which was already menac-
> ing the whole world. So that if they did not decide to aid her
> husband, who was beginning to be the weaker party (because of
> the recent misfortunes of the Emperor his father), they might be
> sure that the King of France, having driven the King her hus-
> band from Italy, as he was about to do through lack of help,
> would soon afterward turn to them and drive them out of their
> own house.[13]

The councillors asked for time to deliberate and returned two days
later to deliver their verdict: it "ought not and could not declare war."[14]
They would approve financial and naval support to Philip but would
not promise troops or declare openly against France.[15] The realm, they
maintained, was in no condition to wage war: food was scarce, the cof-
fers were empty and the people discontented. It would be disastrous to
cut off England's trade with France because neither Spain nor Flanders
could supply all that was needed. Finally, they stated that the marriage
treaty expressly forbade Philip to draw England into his struggle with
France.[16]

Mary was furious. She ordered the councillors to meet again and
draft a reply that would "satisfy her and her husband."[17] The Council

remained defiant, and the stalemate continued. Yet Mary was determined to fulfill Philip's demands.[18] As Noailles reported, Mary would force "not only men, but also the elements themselves, to consent to her will."[19] On April 13, before the court removed to Greenwich for Easter, Mary summoned the councillors privately to her room and threatened each of them, "some with death, others with the loss of their goods and estates, if they did not consent to the will of her husband."[20] They now offered money and troops, but Philip refused to be satisfied with anything less than an open declaration of war.

CHAPTER 62

A PUBLIC ENEMY TO OURSELVES

∴

ON APRIL 23, 1557, SIR THOMAS STAFFORD, AN ENGLISH PROT-
estant exile, landed on the Yorkshire coast at Scarborough with two
French ships and a force of up to a hundred English and French rebels
and seized Scarborough Castle.[1] His aim was to depose Mary, an
"unrightful and unworthy Queen" who had "forfeited the right by her
marriage with a Spaniard."[2]

Styling himself "protector of the realm," he came, he said, to deliver
his countrymen of the tyranny of strangers and warned of an influx of
Spaniards who would enslave the people. He would "defeat the most
devilish device of Mary," who "most justly deserved to be deprived
from the Crown, because she being naturally born half Spanish and
half English, beareth not herself indifferently towards both nations, but
showing herself a whole Spaniard, and no English Woman, in loving
Spaniards, and hating Englishmen." For the defense of the country, he
promised that the crown would revert "to the true English blood of our
own natural Country."[3]

The government reacted quickly. Within five days, the earl of
Westmoreland had retaken the castle, and on April 30 a proclamation
was issued in London announcing Stafford's capture. He was tried,
condemned, and executed for treason at Tyburn a month later.

The rebellion provided the catalyst for the declaration of war with
France. Writing to Emmanuel Philibert, duke of Savoy, from London
on April 28, the Spanish commander, Don Bernardino de Mendoza,
declared, "As for the breach of the truce, the French have spared us the
trouble."[4] And in London, on June 7, 1557, the queen's heralds formally
proclaimed war with France:

Although we, the Queen, when we first came to the throne, understood that the Duke of Northumberland's abominable treason had been abetted by Henry, the French King, and that since then his ministers had secretly favoured Wyatt's rebellion . . . we attributed these doings to the French King's ministers rather than to his own will, hoping thus patiently to induce him to adopt a truly friendly attitude towards us . . . the other day he sent Stafford with ships and supplies to seize our castle of Scarborough . . . for the above reasons, and because he has sent an army to invade Flanders which we are under obligation to defend, we have seen fit to proclaim to our subjects that they are to consider the King of France as a public enemy to ourselves and our nation, rather than to suffer him to continue to deceive us under colour of friendship.[5]

When the English herald conveyed England's declaration of war to Henry II, he made clear who he believed was the real instigator of the conflict between England and France: "The Queen . . . did what she has done against me under compulsion, her husband having given her to understand that unless she declared herself he would depart that kingdom, and never return hither to see her . . . she was forced to do what she has done." He declared that as the herald had come in the name of a woman it was unnecessary for him to listen any further, "as he would done had he come in the name of a man." Laughing, he asked his ambassadors to "consider how I stand when a woman sends [a declaration] to defy me to war, but I doubt not that God will assist me."[6]

WITHIN WEEKS OF England's entry into the war, Philip left England. Mary accompanied him to Dover, from which he set sail, and at three in the morning of July 6, the king and queen parted company at the quayside. They would never see each other again.

Several days later, an English force of more than 1,000 led by the earl of Pembroke followed the king across the Channel. Many of the officers were former rebels and plotters, including Sir Peter Carew, Lord Robert Dudley, the son of the duke of Northumberland, Sir

James Croft, and Sir Nicholas Throckmorton. War provided opportunities for service and honor and allowed those involved with sedition and rebellion to make their peace with the government. Initially the English army had some success. On August 10, a French force advancing to raise the siege at Saint-Quentin was heavily routed. Although the English missed the battle, men under the earl of Pembroke took part in the capture of the city some weeks later. "Both sides fought most choicely," wrote one Spanish officer, "and the English best of all."[7] The news was greeted in England with widespread celebrations.[8] It looked to have been a successful end to the campaigning season, but the French were intent on quick revenge and believed that the winter would be the best time to attack the garrison at Calais, the last English territory in France, as the marshes would be frozen.

ON NEW YEAR'S DAY 1558, 27,000 French troops attacked Calais. On the third, Thomas, Lord Wentworth, now lord deputy of Calais, described the dire situation in a letter to Philip:

> Sire: I have received your Majesty's letter informing me that the French are moving against Calais. Indeed they have been camping before this town for three days. They have set their batteries in position, and have stormed the castle at the entrance to the port, and also the other castle on the road leading to France. Thus they have occupied all our territory, and nothing remains for them to do except to take this town. If it is lost, your Majesty knows what great facility it would give them to invade your territories of Flanders.[9]

By the seventh, the French had entered the castle and Wentworth surrendered. The diarist Henry Machyn recorded the loss:

> The x day of January, heavy news came to England, and to London, that the Fre[nch had won] Calais, the which was the heaviest tidings to London and to England that ever was heard of, for like a traitor it was sold and d[elivered unto] them the [blank] day of January.[10]

The garrison was ill prepared and undermanned. French forces led by Francis, duke of Guise, had been able to take it by surprise by launching their attack in midwinter.[11] The garrisons of Guisnes and Hammes held out until January 21, when forces under William, Lord Grey, short of ammunition and food, also surrendered. Just a few months after the victory at Saint-Quentin, the French had inflicted a catastrophic defeat on the English.

The recriminations began almost immediately. Lord Wentworth, it was claimed, was a heretic and had intrigued with others within and outside of Calais. Many Englishmen believed that Philip had done less than he could to assist the garrison, while the Spanish argued that the fortress had been lost through English incompetence. As the last remnant of the English claim to the continental monarchy, Calais had a highly symbolic value, arguably outweighing its economic and military importance. Calais had been captured by Edward III in 1347 and was the sole remnant of the Anglo-French empire that had endured from the Normans to the Wars of the Roses.

But neither the Council nor Parliament was prepared to sanction the granting of funds to send forces to recover Calais. "We feel compelled to urge you," Philip wrote to the Privy Council, "to be swayed by no private interests or passions, but only by your care for the welfare of the kingdom, lest its reputation for power and greatness, earned the world over in former times, be lost now through your own neglect and indifference."[12] Yet it was less English pride than Habsburg strategic interests that dictated Philip's concerns. As he wrote to Pole of the loss of Calais, "that sorrow was indeed unspeakable, for reasons which you may well imagine and because the event was an extremely grave one for these states."[13]

CHAPTER 63

THE GRIEF OF THE
MOST SERENE QUEEN

∴

A war between your Highness [the Pope] and King Philip must produce the gravest danger and harm to the whole Christian Commonwealth . . . only Satan, could have sown the seeds of this dissension.[1]

—CARDINAL POLE TO POPE PAUL IV

BY DECLARING WAR ON FRANCE, IT WAS ALMOST INEVITABLE THAT England would be drawn into conflict with Henry II's ally, Pope Paul IV. For several months Cardinal Pole had sought to prevent military action and bring about a peaceful settlement, but to no avail. Writing to the pope, he explained:

If to all good men this war between your Holiness and King Philip is most painful, by reason of the very many and grievous perils and damages with which it seems to threaten not one realm alone, but the entire Christian commonwealth, to me of necessity it is the more bitter, the more I find myself bound by all the ties of devotion and reverence to your Holiness, and by those of love to the King.[2]

Meanwhile, the pope was aggrieved that Mary had not shown any regret over the war against the papacy, nor had she exerted herself to prevent it. As Cardinal Giovanni Morone, the vice protector of England, reported, he had "been told on good authority" that she had aided Philip with money, which had "greatly exasperated" the pope, who was refusing to dispatch English business.[3]

On April 9, 1557, as the Privy Council was debating whether to declare war on France, Pope Paul IV had withdrawn his nuncios and legates from Philip's dominions. Pole was specifically mentioned and deprived of his legatine power, and the See of Canterbury was deprived of its legatine status.[4] Mary was horrified. "The grief of the most serene Queen," Pole wrote in his first anguished protest to Rome, "may be more easily estimated by the Pope, he having had experience of her extreme piety in bringing back this kingdom to obedience to the Church than he, Pole, can write it."[5] In letters to the pope, Mary and the Council stressed how much damage would be done to the realm by the withdrawal of the legate at such a critical stage in the process of Catholic restoration and likened the realm to a convalescing invalid who faced the withdrawal of his physician.[6] Given Mary's faith and fidelity to the Holy See, petitions to Rome would, it was believed, succeed in revoking the decree as far as it related to Pole.

On June 12, the Venetian ambassador in Rome, Bernardo Navagero, reported that the Roman Inquisition was investigating Pole as a suspected Lutheran.[7] The new pope held deep suspicions about Pole's religious opinions. In the 1530s, Pole had belonged to a group, the Spirituali, who had hoped for reconciliation with the Lutherans and sought an accommodation with them on the issue of salvation by faith alone. But by the 1550s, Pope Paul IV saw such doctrinal compromises as heresy. On June 14, 1557, Pole was formally recalled to Rome.[8] In acknowledgment of Mary's obedience to Rome and his concern for the restoration of the English Church, Paul IV announced that he would relax his general policy toward England and appoint a new papal legate, the eighty-year-old Franciscan friar William Peto, formerly the confessor of Katherine of Aragon.[9]

Mary learned the news as she was accompanying Philip to Dover on the eve of his departure.[10] She was outraged. When the papal nuncio bearing the official briefs reached Calais in July, he was refused admission into the realm. Mary would ensure that she never received the official notification of Pole's recall or Peto's appointment. Pole wanted to go to Rome to clear his name, but Sir Edward Carne, Mary's ambassador in Rome, warned him that he would be imprisoned by the

Inquisition." Mary had no intention of letting him go and expressed her amazement that a man who had performed such distinguished services for the Church and whose presence was so essential to the task in hand should be withdrawn. She was confident that the pope would realize that she knew best about affairs in her kingdom and would grant her request, praying that he restore the legation of Cardinal Pole and beseeching him to "pardon her if she professed to know the men who are good for the government of her kingdom better than His Holiness."¹² If any disturbance should take place in England, she protested, it would be for that reason. At the same time, Peto declined the legateship on the grounds of age and infirmity.

By mid-August there was a deadlock. The pope had no intention of giving way and restoring Pole's legation, even though no charges had been leveled against him, while Mary refused to send Pole to Rome in exchange for Peto. Instead, she dispatched fresh instructions to Carne as to how to react if actual charges of heresy were made against Pole. If Pole were found guilty of heresy, Carne was to declare that Mary would be his "greatest enemy," but unless or until proof of such a crime could be found, she would take him for a good and Catholic man. Moreover, Mary argued, as an Englishman and archbishop of Canterbury, Pole must be tried in England, as Cranmer had been two years before. If the pope refused the request, Carne was instructed to leave Rome, but only after informing all the cardinals that "the Queen and Council and the whole kingdom of England, will never swerve from their devotion, reverence and obedience to the See Apostolic and to his Holiness' successors, although for a certain period they were compelled not to obey Pope Paul IV."¹³ Charges were not made and diplomatic relations were not broken off, though rumors circulated around the curia that England was about to go into schism once more.

The conclusion of peace between Philip and the pope on September 12, 1557, was greeted with great jubilation in London.¹⁴ By one of the articles of the Treaty of Cave between the pope and the Habsburgs, it was agreed that Pole's legation would be restored, though this never happened. Pole's position remained unchanged, and he continued, unsuccessfully, to petition the pope for vindication. He talked of the "sword of grief" with which the pope had pierced his soul.¹⁵ The man who had absolved England from heresy three and a half years earlier

was now a fugitive heretic. Pole could not accept that Paul IV, his former friend, had turned against him. He wrote to the pope, begging him
to say he had only been testing Pole's loyalty "as Christ is wont to place
his dearest children in purgatory to try them."[16]

Just four years before, Mary had described herself as the Holy See's
"most obedient and affectionate" daughter; his Holiness had no more
loving daughter than herself. Now, as the last months of her life drew
near, her relations with the pope became significantly strained.[17] It was
a great irony that upon Mary's death, the pope would initially express
gratification upon the accession of Elizabeth as an improvement on her
sister.[18]

CHAPTER 64

READINESS FOR CHANGE

∵ ∵

IN 1557, GIOVANNI MICHIELI, THE VENETIAN AMBASSADOR, LEFT England. In his final report, the *relazione*, he gave a detailed account of the character and concerns of the then-forty-one-year-old queen.

Above all, he praised Mary's devotion and piety. "Besides her noble descent," he wrote, she was "a very great and rare example of virtue and magnanimity, a real portrait of patience and humility, and of the true fear of God." Indeed, few women in the world were known to be more "assiduous at their prayers than she is," always keeping to the canonical hours and observing Communions and fast days. She had lived a life "little short of martyrdom, by reason of the persecution she endured."

In her youth, he reflected, Mary "was considered not merely tolerably handsome, but of beauty exceeding mediocrity." However, the queen's aspect was now "very grave," with "wrinkles, caused more by anxieties than by age, which make her appear some years older." Though "like other women," she could be "sudden and passionate, and close and miserly," she maintained a "wonderful grandeur and dignity."

Despite being "valiant" and "brave," Mary was prone to "deep melancholy"—a product, Michieli surmised, of "monstrous retention" and "suffocation of the matrix [womb]," a disease thought to be caused by the retention of menstrual fluids and a condition from which she had suffered for many years. But "the remedy of tears and weeping, to which from childhood she has been accustomed, and still often used by her" was no longer sufficient and now she required to be "blooded either from the foot or elsewhere, which keeps her always pale and emaciated."

Principal among Mary's distresses were those that arose from her love for Philip and her resentment of her sister, Elizabeth. Philip's constant traveling left Mary bereft, "not only of that company, for the sake of which (besides the hope of lineage) marriages are formed," but the separation "which to any person who loves another heartily, would be irksome and grievous" is felt particularly by a woman so "naturally tender." Her "fear and violent love" for Philip left her constantly in a state of anxiety. If to this were added jealousy, the ambassador continued, "she would be truly miserable," as to be parted from the king was one of the "anxieties that especially distresses her."

Added to this was her "evil disposition," as Michieli described it, "towards her sister Elizabeth"; although the queen pretended otherwise, "it cannot be denied the scorn and ill will she bears her." When faced with Elizabeth, "it was as if she were in the presence of the affronts and ignominious treatment to which she was subjected to on account of her mother," Anne Boleyn. Worse still, Mary saw "the eyes and hearts" of the nation already fixed on Elizabeth as her successor, given Mary's lack of an heir. Much to Mary's dismay, she perceived that no one believed "in the possibility of her having progeny," so that "day by day" she saw her authority and the respect induced by it diminish. Besides this, "the Queen's hatred is increased by knowing her to be averse to the present religion . . . for although externally she showed, and by living Catholically shows, that she has recanted, she is nevertheless supposed to dissemble and to hold to it more than ever internally."

Mary had, the Venetian reflected, become a queen of regrets. She had been "greatly grieved" by many insurrections, conspiracies, and plots that continually formed against her at home and abroad, and she mourned the decline of the "affection" universally evinced toward her at the beginning of her reign, which had been "so extraordinary that never was greater shown in that kingdom towards any sovereign." The country was, Michieli said, "showing a greater inclination and readiness for change" than ever before. The "fruitlessness" of Mary's marriage was a source of profound regret, and the lack of an heir threatened the restoration of Catholicism and the obedience of the English Church to Rome, which was now sustained by her "authority and presence." But, Michieli added, "nor is it to be told how much hurt that vain pregnancy did her."

If the queen predeceased Philip, he would be deprived of the kingdom; but more important was the fear that the king's "enemies" would
seek to occupy England "or cause the realm to fall into their hands."
Michieli ended his *relazione* with a list of possible claimants for the
English throne: first, Elizabeth, whose right was based on the will of
Henry VIII and the Act of Succession; then Mary, queen of Scots, who
claimed an absolute hereditary right; and the two sisters of the late
Lady Jane Grey, who claimed precedence over Elizabeth on account of
the will of Edward VI. Yet, as Michieli concluded, even if Mary were
to be "undeceived," which "as yet she is not," about the possibility of
having children, she wished to avoid naming a successor and "will
rather leave it to time to act, referring the matter after her death to
those whom it concerns either by right or by force."[1]

CHAPTER 65

THINKING MYSELF TO
BE WITH CHILD

∴

WITHIN SIX MONTHS OF MICHIELI'S *RELAZIONE*, MARY AGAIN believed she was pregnant. This time she waited until her sixth month and then in January 1558 sent word to Philip.[1] "The news of the Queen, my beloved wife," Philip wrote to Pole, "has given me greater joy than I can express to you, as it is the one thing in the world I have most desired and which is of the greatest importance for the cause of religion and the care and welfare of our realm." It has "gone far to lighten the sorrow I have felt for the loss of Calais."[2]

Weeks later, Don Gómez Suárez de Figueroa, count of Feria, was sent to England. He was to express Philip's delight at the news of his wife's impending labor but also to try to discover if it might be true. Many believed it was not, and this time no preparations were made for her confinement. Upon arriving in England, Feria quickly came to the conclusion that Mary was only "making herself believe that she is with child, although she does not own up to it."[3]

Yet Mary remained convinced, and on March 30, as she approached what she believed to be the ninth month of her pregnancy, she made her will:

> Thinking myself to be with child in lawful marriage between my said dearly beloved husband and lord, although I be at this present (thanks be unto Almighty God) otherwise in good health, yet foreseeing the great danger which by God's ordinance remain to all women in their travail of children, have thought good, both for the discharge of my conscience and con-

tinuance of good order within my realms and dominions, to declare my last will and testament.

In the event of her death, the crown would be left to "the heirs, issue and fruit" of her body, while Philip, her "most dear and entirely beloved husband," would be appointed guardian and regent for the prince or princess.

BY MAY, MARY'S HEALTH had deteriorated: she suffered from intermittent fevers, insomnia, headaches, and loss of vision. It was clear that there was no pregnancy. Writing to Philip, Feria described how "she sleeps badly, is weak and suffers from melancholy; and her indisposition results in business being handled more slowly than need be."[4]

Over the summer Mary grew progressively weaker. In August, she caught influenza, then endemic in the country, and was moved from Hampton Court to St. James's Palace. Forced to acknowledge the seriousness of her condition, she added a codicil to her will: "feeling myself presently sick and weak in body," she admitted that it was unlikely she was with child. "Forasmuch as God hath hitherto sent me no fruit nor heir of my body, it is only in his most divine providence whether I shall have any or no." If God did not grant her an heir, she would be "succeeded by my next heir and successor by the Laws and Statutes of this realm."[5] She stopped short of acknowledging Elizabeth by name but exhorted Philip to protect and care for England "as a father in his care, as a brother in his love and favour . . . and a most assured and undoubted friend to her country and subjects."

On October 29, Antonio Surian, the Venetian ambassador, who was with Philip, wrote to the doge and Senate:

A few days ago, his Majesty received news from England that the Queen was grievously ill, and her life in danger, which intelligence, most especially at the present moment being of very great importance, so disquieted his Majesty, and all these lords, that it was immediately determined to send the Count de Feria to visit the Queen, in the name of her consort but as when the count was about to depart, fresh advice arrived that her

Majesty's health had improved his departure was delayed . . . the
matter to be treated by him is the marriage of Milady Elizabeth,
to keep that kingdom in any event in the hands of his Majesty's
confidence.[6]

By the terms of the marriage treaty, Philip's prerogatives in England
would cease with Mary's death. In April, the marriage between Mary,
queen of Scots, and the French dauphin, the future Francis II, had
finally taken place. If Mary Stuart's claim to the English throne could be
secured, France's position would be strengthened immeasurably and tip
the balance in the Habsburg-Valois struggle. Even if Elizabeth succeeded, Philip feared that her Protestant sympathies would lead to a
diplomatic realignment that would leave Spain isolated.

Feria was instructed to visit Elizabeth on the king's behalf, present
his compliments, express Philip's hope that the amity would continue
between Spain and the Tudor dominions, and ingratiate himself with
the men around her. Elizabeth responded favorably, declaring that she
would always be grateful to Philip because "when she was in prison
[the king] had shown her favour and helped to obtain her release," but
dismissed the suggestion that she might marry the duke of Savoy.[7]
Meanwhile, Feria was "to try and dispose the Queen to consent to
Lady Elizabeth being married as her sister, and with the hope of succeeding to the crown."[8]

The first few days of November saw some alleviation in the queen's
condition, and as Parliament met, the Council petitioned her to make
"certain declarations in favour of the Lady Elizabeth concerning the
succession." On November 6, Mary bowed to the inevitable: she "consented" and accepted Elizabeth as her heir. It was what she had fought
to avoid most of her life, but now, realizing that death was near, she had
no choice. Sir Thomas Cornwallis, the comptroller of the royal household, and John Boxall, secretary to the Privy Council, were sent to
Hatfield to give Elizabeth the news. Mary asked that Elizabeth pay her
debts and keep the Catholic religion as it had been established.[9] She
knew it was a futile plea.

While Mary lay dying, the court began to move to Hatfield, as
"many personages of the kingdom flocked to the house of 'milady'
Elizabeth, the crowd constantly increasing with great frequency."[10]

CHAPTER 66

REASONABLE REGRET
FOR HER DEATH

∴

JUST BEFORE MIDNIGHT ON WEDNESDAY, NOVEMBER 16, 1557, MARY received the last rites in her chamber at St. James's Palace. A few hours later, between five and six in the morning, she died. She was forty-two.

During her last few days, the celebration of Mass had been at the center of her conscious existence, and as dawn broke on Thursday morning, she had lifted her eyes at the Elevation of the Host for the final time. According to one later account, she had "comforted those of them that grieved about her, she told them what good dreams she had, seeing many little children, like Angels playing before her, singing pleasing notes."¹ Hours later, the lord chancellor, Nicholas Heath, announced to Parliament that Mary was dead. Any sorrow that might have been felt was quickly overshadowed by rejoicing for the accession of a new queen.

At Whitehall, Elizabeth was formally proclaimed as heralds rode out to the cross at Cheapside to make the announcement before the lord mayor and aldermen of the city.² By midafternoon, "all the churches in London did ring, and at night did make bonfires and set tables in the street, and did eat and drink and made merry for the new Queen Elizabeth, Queen Mary['s] sister."³ Just six hours after Mary's death, Elizabeth was proclaimed queen.

Across the river at Lambeth Palace, Cardinal Pole also lay dying. The news of the queen's passing appeared to hurry his own demise. For nearly a quarter of an hour he remained silent, absorbing what he had just heard; "though his spirit was great, the blow nevertheless having entered his flesh, brought on the paroxysm earlier, and with more intense cold." Turning to Ludovico Priuli and Thomas Goldwell, bishop of St. Asaph, two of his closest attendants, he remarked on the symmetry, the "great conformity," as he described it, of their lives. She, like himself, "had been harassed during many years for one and the same cause, and afterwards, when it pleased God to raise her to the throne, he had greatly participated in all her other troubles entailed by that elevation."[4] Just twelve hours after Mary's passing, he too died, unreconciled with and condemned by the pope.

A messenger was sent to Philip with news of his wife's death. Just weeks before, both his father, the Emperor Charles V, and his aunt Margaret of Flanders, the regent of the Netherlands, had also died. "You may imagine what a state I am in," he wrote to his sister in Spain; "it seems to me that everything is being taken from me at once." Of Mary he added, "May God have received her in His glory! I felt a reasonable regret for her death. I shall miss her, even on this account."[5] Mary remained second to Habsburg strategic interests; Philip's comments were made in the middle of a paragraph detailing progress in the peace negotiations at Cercamp. He instructed Feria to secure the jewels that Mary had bequeathed him in her will and to represent him with suitable dignity at her obsequies.

WITHIN HOURS of Mary's death, the preparation of her body began. Her heart and bowels were removed, her belly opened and filled with preservative herbs and spices. She was placed in a lead coffin and then a wooden chest. For the next three weeks, her corpse lay in state in the Privy Chamber of St. James's Palace, which had been hung with black cloth and adorned with the royal arms. The coffin stood upon trestles, covered with a pall of rich cloth of gold. Every day her gentlewomen prayed about the coffin and heard Masses, and through the night her hearse was illuminated with burning candles.

In life Mary had received visitors in her Privy Chamber under the cloth of estate; now, in death, mourners looked upon her body and paid their respects. Though dead, Mary would remain in possession of sovereignty until her burial some weeks later. As was customary during the weeks of transition, a lifelike, life-size wooden effigy dressed in the coronation robes and bearing the orb and scepter acted in place of the dead monarch. A fifteenth-century guide, "What Shall Be Done on the Demise of a King Anointed," gave instructions to "make an image like him clothed in a surcoat, with a mantel of estate, the laces goodly lying on his belly, his sceptre in his hand, and a crown on his head, and so carry him in a chair open, with lights and banners, accompanied with lords and estates as the council can best devise."[6] Around it the routines of court life continued. As Feria noted, "the house is served exactly as it was before." Food was placed on the royal table; gentleman ushers officiated with their white wands; guards stood at doors of the chamber within which sat the five-foot-five wooden figure.[7]

The marquess of Winchester, the most senior of Mary's surviving councillors, was put in charge of the funeral arrangements. The ceremony, conducted according to "King Henry VIII's funeral book," was to be traditional, Catholic, and expensive.[8] Preparations continued for nearly a month as the dead queen remained in state at St. James's. Finally, on December 10, with the arrangements made and mourning clothes and funeral accoutrements prepared, a solemn procession of black-robed heralds, lords, ladies, and household officers entered the privy apartments. Mary's coffin was held aloft and carried to the Chapel Royal, where the high altar had been trimmed with purple velvet. At three in the afternoon lords and ladies assembled in the Presence Chamber and Great Chamber along with the officers of the household. The bishops went into the Presence Chamber, censed the coffin, and said prayers. The coffin, borne under a canopy of purple velvet, was then taken up by eight gentlemen and in ordered procession made its way to the chapel.

Three days later, the funeral cortege made its final journey to Westminster Abbey. Banners of the English royal arms led the king and queen's household officers, who, dressed in black, marched two by two in rank order. Behind them five heralds bore the masculine regalia of sovereignty—the banner of English royal arms embroidered with gold, the royal helmet, the royal shield, the royal sword, and the coat of armor, as if a king were being buried. A wheeled chariot bearing Mary's coffin followed, accompanied by the painted effigy "adorned with crimson velvet and her crown on her head, her sceptre in her hand and many goodly rings on her fingers."[9] At each corner of the funeral chariot a herald on horseback bore a banner of the four English royal saints. After the chariot followed the chief mourner, Margaret Douglas, countess of Lennox, and Mary's ladies-in-waiting, all in black robes, attending her in death as they had in life.[10]

The procession halted at the great door of the abbey, where it was met by four bishops and an abbot, who censed the coffin before it and the effigy were taken inside. There Mary's body laid overnight in the hearse that had been specially built to receive it, watched over by a hundred gentlemen in mourning clothes and the queen's guard, each holding burning torches.[11]

The next morning, the funeral Mass was sung and John White, bishop of Winchester, preached the funeral sermon.[12] He had been present at Mary's death and related how "if angels were mortal, I would rather liken this her departure to the death of an angel, than of a mortal creature." He then delivered an oration, praising Mary's virtues:

> She was a King's daughter, she was a King's sister, she was a King's wife. She was a Queen, and by the same title a King also. . . . What she suffered in each of these degrees before and since she came to the crown I will not chronicle; only this I say, howsoever it pleased God to will her patience to be exercised in the world, she had in all estates the fear of God in her heart . . . she had the Love, Commendation and Admiration of all the World. In this church she married herself to the realm, and in token of faith and fidelity, did put a ring with a diamond on her finger, which I understand she never took off after, during her life . . . she was never unmindful or uncareful of her promise to the realm.

He continued:

> She used singular mercy towards offenders. She used much pity and compassion towards the poor and oppressed. She used clemency amongst her nobles. . . . She restored more noble houses decayed than ever did prince of this realm, or I did pray God ever shall have the like occasion to do hereafter.

The bishop said little about Mary's religious policies but defended her sincere faith. "I verily believe, the poorest creature in all this city feared not God more than she did."[13]

It was a powerful speech based on two verses from Ecclesiastes: "I praised the dead which are already dead more than the living, which are yet alive" and "for a living dog is better than a dead lion." He sought to disguise his words with apparently harmless analogies, but his meaning was clear: a dead Mary was better than a living Elizabeth. After this encomium, the best that White could say of Elizabeth was that she was royal like Mary and held the realm "by the like title and right." He concluded by "wishing her a prosperous reign in peace and tranquillity"—"if it be God's will."[14] The next day the bishop was informed that "for such offences as he committed in his sermon at the funeral of the late Queen," he was to be confined to his house at Elizabeth's pleasure.[15]

At the offertory of the Mass that followed, the regalia was offered at the altar, one by one, and the queen's coat of armor, sword, shield, and banner of arms returned symbolically to God. The effigy and other tokens of royalty were removed from the coffin, which was carried to the chapel of Mary's grandfather Henry VII. A vault had been opened in the north aisle of Henry VII's chapel into which the coffin was lowered. After earth had been cast on top, Mary's household officers broke their white staffs of office and threw them into the grave. The heralds cried, "The queen is dead, long live the queen!" and people tore down the banners and cloth hangings for souvenirs. With trumpets blowing, the mourners and peers, officiating clergy, and Mary's officers all departed to dine at the abbot of Westminster's lodging, the last act of the regime.[16]

VERITAS TEMPORIS FILIA

... Witness [alas!] may Marie be, late Queen of rare renown
Whose body dead, her virtues live, and doth her fame resowne....

She never closed her ear to hear the righteous man distress
Nor never spared her hand to help, when wrong or power oppress

Make for your mirror [Princes all] Marie, our mistress late. . . .
Farewell, O Queen! O pearl most pure! that God or nature gave,
The earth, the heavens, the sprites, the saints cry honor to thy grave.

Marie now dead, Elizabeth lives, our just & lawful Queen,
In whom her sister's virtues rare, abundantly are seen.
Obey our Queen, as we are bound, pray God her to preserve,
And send her grace life long and fruit, and subjects true to serve.

—"Epitaph upon the Death of
Quene Marie, Deceased"
[ca. 1558][1]

THE FORGING AND RECASTING OF MARY'S REPUTATION BEGAN
immediately upon her death. One Richard Lante was imprisoned for
printing this elegy without license, and the verses were swiftly reissued
with a final stanza in praise of Elizabeth.[2] Mary had requested that her
executors "cause to be made some honourable tombs or decent memory" of her and her mother, but this, her dying wish, was ignored.
Instead the anniversary of Mary's death came to be remembered solely
as "Elizabeth's Accession Day," an annual day of celebration and
thanksgiving. Official prayers hailed the new queen, who had deliv-

ered the English people "from the danger of war and oppression, restoring peace and true religion, with liberty both of bodies and minds."[3]

Mary quickly became a figure of opprobrium, as Protestants returning from exile sought to ingratiate themselves with the new regime. In *The First Blast of the Trumpet against the Monstrous Regiment of Women*, written on the eve of Mary's death, John Knox condemned her as a "horrible monster Jezebel" and described how during her reign Englishmen had been "compelled to bow their necks under the yoke of Satan, and of his proud ministers, pestilent papists and proud Spaniards."[4] Knox argued that women were incapable of effective rule as they were by nature "weak, frail, impatient, feeble and foolish: and experience hath declared them to be inconstant, variable, cruel and lacking the spirit of counsel and regiment."[5] Female rule was "the subversion of good order, of all equity and justice." Yet Knox quickly had to refine his views to accommodate the accession of a Protestant queen.[6]

In his *Actes and Monuments of These Latter and Perillous Dayes*, John Foxe, the most infamous returning exile, celebrated the passing of Mary's reign. "We shall never find any reign of any Prince in this land or any other," he wrote, "which ever shows in it (for the proportion of time) so many great arguments of God's wrath and displeasure." His detailed account of the lives of the Protestant martyrs graphically portrayed "the horrible and bloody time of Queen Mary."[7]

Coinciding with the rise of the Accession Day festivities was the promulgation of an order that a copy of Foxe's *Actes and Monuments* be installed in every "cathedral church."[8] By 1600, Catholicism was firmly understood to be an "un-English" creed and Protestantism an entrenched part of England's national identity.

Foxe's account would shape the popular narrative of Mary's reign for the next four hundred and fifty years. Generations of schoolchildren would grow up knowing the first queen of England only as "Bloody Mary," a Catholic tyrant who sent nearly three hundred Protestants to their deaths, a point made satirically in W. C. Sellar and R. J. Yeatman's 1930s parody *1066 and All That*.[9] Mary's presence in a recent survey of the most evil men and women in history is testament to Foxe's enduring legacy.[10]

But there is, of course, a different Mary: a woman marked by suffering, devout in her faith and exceptional in her courage. From a childhood in which she was adored and feted and then violently rejected, a fighter was born. Her resolve almost cost her her life as her father, and then her brother, sought to subjugate her to their wills. Yet Mary maintained her faith and self-belief. Despite repeated attempts to deprive her of her life and right to the throne, the warrior princess turned victor and became the warrior queen.

The boldness and scale of her achievement are often overlooked. The campaign that Mary led in the summer of 1553 would prove to be the only successful revolt against central government in sixteenth-century England. She, like her grandfather Henry VII and grandmother Isabella of Castile, had to fight for her throne. In the moment of crisis she proved decisive, courageous, and "Herculean"—and won the support of the English people as the legitimate Tudor heir.

Mary was a conscientious, hardworking queen who was determined to be closely involved in government business and policy making. She would rise "at daybreak when, after saying her prayers and hearing mass in private," she would "transact business incessantly until after midnight."[11] As rebels threatened the capital in January 1554 and she was urged to flee, Mary stood firm and successfully rallied Londoners to her defense. She was also a woman who lived by her conscience and was prepared to die for her faith. And she expected the same of others.

Her religious defiance was matched by a personal infatuation with Philip, her Spanish husband. Her love for him and dependence on her "true father," the emperor Charles V, was unwavering. Her determination to honor her husband's will led England into an unpopular war with France and the loss of Calais. There was no fruit of the union, and so at her premature death there was no Catholic heir. Her own phantom pregnancies, together with epidemics and harvest failures across the country, left her undermined and unpopular. Her life, always one of tragic contrast, ended in personal tragedy as Philip abandoned her, never to return, even as his queen lay dying.

In many ways Mary failed as a woman but triumphed as a queen. She ruled with the full measure of royal majesty and achieved much of what she set out to do. She won her rightful throne, married her Spanish prince, and restored the country to Roman Catholicism. The

Spanish marriage was a match with the most powerful ruling house in
Europe, and the highly favorable marriage treaty ultimately won the
support of the English government. She had defeated rebels and preserved the Tudor monarchy. Her Catholicism was not simply conservative but influenced by her humanist education and showed many signs
of broad acceptance before she died. She was an intelligent, politically
adept, and resolute monarch who proved to be very much her own
woman. Thanks to Mary, John Aylmer, in exile in Switzerland, could
confidently assert that "it is not in England so dangerous a matter to
have a woman ruler, as men take it to be."[12] By securing the throne following Edward's attempts to bar both his sisters, she ensured that the
crown continued along the legal line of Tudor succession. Mary laid
down other important precedents that would benefit her sister. Upon
her accession as the first queen regnant of England, she redefined royal
ritual and law, thereby establishing that a female ruler, married or
unmarried, would enjoy identical power and authority to male monarchs. Mary was the Tudor trailblazer, a political pioneer whose reign
redefined the English monarchy.

Upon her accession Mary adopted the motto *Veritas Temporis
Filia*—Truth is the Daughter of Time—in celebration of her establishment as England's Catholic heir and the return of the "true faith." In
1558, her younger sister wrested the motto from the dead queen, for the
Protestant truth. It was not the only thing Elizabeth took from her predecessor. After Mary's death, the coronation robes of England's first
queen were hastily refurbished—with a new bodice and sleeves—to fit
its second.[13]

In certain things she is singular and without an equal; for not only is she brave and valiant, unlike other timid and spiritless women, but so courageous and resolute, that neither in adversity nor peril did she ever display or commit any act of cowardice or pusillanimity, maintaining always, on the contrary, a wonderful grandeur and dignity . . . it cannot be denied that she shows herself to have been born of a truly royal lineage.

—THE VENETIAN AMBASSADOR
GIOVANNI MICHIELI

ACKNOWLEDGMENTS

∴

THIS WAS THE BOOK I ALWAYS WANTED TO WRITE. FROM THE earliest days of my doctoral research I was driven by a desire to tell Mary's remarkable story, to push her to center stage as England's first queen and bring her out from the shadow of her younger sister, Elizabeth. I hope I have gone some way to achieving this.

In writing this book I have incurred many debts to scholars, writers, librarians, and friends. The staff of Cambridge University Library has been endlessly efficient, helpful, and friendly, as have those of the British Library and the National Archives. I must also thank Henry Bedingfeld for allowing me to view his family records at Oxburgh Hall. Various colleagues have provided help, inspiration, and guidance during the course of my research, including my former tutor David Starkey, Judith Richards, Jeri Mcintosh, Diarmaid MacCulloch, David Loades, Nicola Stacey, Stephen Alford, Richard Rex, Mia Rodriguez-Salgado, and Ian Archer. I should also like to thank the master and fellows of Corpus Christi for providing a supportive research environment and my colleagues in the Department of History at Royal Holloway, University of London. Teaching often aids research, and various students have, over the past few years, asked important questions, resulting in interesting discussions.

My agent, Catherine Clarke, has provided great encouragement, guidance, and support throughout. Susanna Porter, my editor at Random House, has always remained enthusiastic about the book, as has Jillian Quint. For assistance in the editing of the text, I owe great thanks to Lynn Anderson, who has been immensely efficient and incisive, and to all at Random House.

This book has been long in the making and would simply not have started or finished without the support of friends and family. Its completion is very much a shared achievement. To some I must offer specific thanks: to Kate Downes for her enthusiasm and invaluable support for me and the book; to Miri Rubin and Gareth Stedman Jones for their generous encouragement and inspiring discussion; to Alice Hunt for endless "Mary" chats and great friendship; to Judy Forshaw and Richard Swift for wine, dinners, and continued interest in the book. Sandra and David Swarbrick and Paul and Jenny Baker have provided constant love and support, and they, together with Chez Hall, James McConnachie, Alexander Regier, Jonathan Hall, Naomi Yandell, Pedro Ramos-Pinto, and all at Herbert Street, have provided great friendship. Alistair Willoughby and Andrew Burns have been generous readers of the manuscript, as has Rebecca Stott, who has been a valuable library comrade and friend during the final stages of writing. I owe particular thanks to Victoria Gregory, Rosie Peppin Vaughan, Jo Maybin, and Rebecca Edwards Newman, upon whom I have depended enormously. Isobel Maddison and her husband, Peter, have shown immense loyalty and patience, have supported me through difficult times, and have been crucial to the book's completion.

My thanks go to Amy and Emily Whitelock, Martin Inglis, and Eric Nason for their support and encouragement. It is with much sadness and regret that my grandfather Kenneth Whitelock, who bought me so many history books as a child, is not alive to read mine. Finally I would like to thank my parents, Paul and Celia Whitelock, for their love and concern. Having taken me on endless trips to castles and stately homes as I was growing up, it is doubtless they who inspired my initial desire to ponder the past.

NOTES

Abbreviations

Aff.Etr.	Archives du Ministère des Affaires Étrangères, Paris, France (Correspondance politique, Angleterre)
APC	*Acts of the Privy Council*, ed. J. R. Dasent et al., 46 vols. (London, 1890–1914)
AR	*The Antiquarian Repertory*, ed. F. Grose, 4 vols. (London, 1807–09)
BL	British Library
Cal. Pole	*The Correspondence of Reginald Pole*, ed. T. F. Mayer, 4 vols. (Aldershot, 2002)
CPR	*Calendar of Patent Rolls*
CS	Camden Society
CSPD	*Calendar of State Papers Domestic*
CSPF	*Calendar of State Papers Foreign*
CSPS	*Calendar of State Papers Spanish*
CSPV	*Calendar of State Papers Venetian*
DNB	*Dictionary of National Biography*
EETS	Early English Text Society
EHR	*The English Historical Review*
Foedera	*Foedera, Conventions, Litterae* . . . , eds. T. Rymer and R. Sanderson, 20 vols. (London, 1704–35)
HJ	*The Historical Journal*
HMC	Historical Manuscripts Commission
LP	*Letters and Papers, Foreign and Domestic, of the Reign of Henry VIII*, 1509–47, eds. J. S. Brewer et al., 21 vols. and addenda (London, 1862–1932)
NA	National Archives
PPC	*Proceedings and Ordinances of the Privy Council of England, 1386–1542*, ed. N. H. Nicolas, 7 vols. (London, 1834–37)
PPE	*The Privy Purse Expenses of the Princess Mary*, ed. F. Madden (London, 1831)
Statutes	*Statutes of the Realm*, eds. A. Luders et al., 11 vols. (London, 1810–28)
St.P.	*State Papers of King Henry the Eighth*, 11 vols. (London, 1830–52)
TNA SP	The National Archives, State Papers

AUTHOR'S NOTE

1. Beatrice White, *Mary Tudor* (London, 1935), p. vii.
2. A. F. Pollard, *The History of England from the Accession of Edward VI to the Death of*

Elizabeth (1547–1603) (London, 1910; reprinted New York, 1969), p. 172; D. Loades, *Mary Tudor: A Life* (Oxford, 1989), p. 8.

3.   G. R. Elton, *Reform and Reformation: England, 1509–1558* (London, 1977), p. 376.

INTRODUCTION: RESURRECTION

1.   James also brought the coffin of his mother, Mary, queen of Scots, from Peterborough and placed it next to that of Margaret Beaufort, mother of Henry VII, to emphasize his lineage.

2.   Marjorie Chibnall, *The Empress Matilda: Queen Consort, Queen Mother and Lady of the English* (Oxford, 1991), p. 102.

CHAPTER I. PRINCESS OF ENGLAND

1.   BL, Harley 3504, fols. 232r–233v.

2.   *AR* I, pp. 305–306.

3.   "The Sarum Rite," in E. C. Whitaker, *Documents of the Baptismal Liturgy*, ed. Maxwell E. Johnson, 3rd ed. (London, 2003), pp. 284–307.

4.   BL, Harley 3504, fol. 232.

5.   NA, PRO, OBS 1419; *CSPS* II, 23, p. 24.

6.   *CSPS*, supplement to vols. I and II, p. 34.

7.   *LP* I, i, 394, p. 184.

8.   *CSPS*, supp. to vols. I and II, pp. 34–35, 42–44.

9.   Ibid., p. 42.

10. Ibid., p. 43.

11. *CSPS* II, p. 38.

12. Ibid., p. 38.

13. *AR* I, pp. 304–305, 333, 336; BL, Harley 3504, fols. 272r–273r.

14. *AR* I, p. 305.

15. Sebastian Giustiniani, *Four Years at the Court of Henry VIII*, ed. and trans. R. Brown, 2 vols. (London, 1854), I, p. 181.

16. Ibid., p. 182; "token of hope" is David Loades's phrase; see *Mary Tudor: A Life* (Oxford, 1989), p. 9.

CHAPTER 2. A TRUE FRIENDSHIP AND ALLIANCE

1.   Giustiniani, *Four Years*, I, p. 181.

2.   E. Hall, *The Union of the Two Noble and Illustre Famelies of York and Lancaster* [hereafter Hall, *Chronicle*], ed. H. Ellis (London, 1809), p. 584.

3.   A. F. Pollard, *The Reign of Henry VII from Contemporary Sources* (London, 1913), III, pp. 2–5.

4.   James Gairdner, ed., "Journals of Roger Machado," in *Historia Regis Henrici Septimi* (London, 1858; 1966 reprint), pp. 170–75.

5.   G. Kipling, ed., *The Receyt of the Ladie Kateryne* (Oxford, 1990), p. 4.

6.   *CSPS* I, 305, p. 262.

7.   Kipling, *The Receyt of the Ladie Kateryne*, pp. 39–51.

8.   BL, Egerton 616, fol. 17; trans. in M. A. E. Wood, ed., *Letters of Royal and Illustrious Ladies of Great Britain*, 3 vols. (London, 1846), I, pp. 138–40.

9.   S. and H. M. Allen, eds., *Opus Epistolarum Des. Erasmi Roterodami* (Oxford, 1906), I, no. 214.

10. *CSPS* II, 17, p. 19.

11. *LP* I, i, 1475, p. 675.

12. *LP* I, ii, 2299, p. 1027.

13. *LP* I, ii, 2268, p. 4451; BL, Cotton Vespasian F III, fol. 15, printed in H. Ellis, ed., *Original Letters, Illustrative of English History . . . from Autographs in the British Museum and . . . Other Collections*, 11 vols. (1824–46), 1st series, I, p. 88.

CHAPTER 3. ARE YOU THE DAUPHIN OF FRANCE?

1. *AR* I, p. 306; *PPE*, p. xxi.
2. *CSPV* II, 1287, p. 558.
3. *Foedera*, XIII, p. 624.
4. Ibid., p. 632; *LP* II, ii, 4480, p. 1376.
5. Giustiniani, *Four Years*, II, p. 226.
6. *CSPV* II, 1085, p. 463.
7. Giustiniani, *Four Years*, II, p. 226.
8. *LP* II, ii, 4480, p. 1376.
9. *CSPV* II, 1088, p. 465.
10. *LP* II, ii, 4468, p. 1372.
11. Giustiniani, *Four Years*, II, p. 240; *CSPV* II, 1103, p. 474.
12. Ibid.

CHAPTER 4. A VERY FINE YOUNG COUSIN INDEED

1. *LP* III, i, 689, p. 230.
2. *LP* III, i, 869, pp. 303–306; 870, pp. 307–14; *CSPV* III, 67, pp. 47–50; 68, pp. 50–55; 69.
3. *LP* VIII, 263, p. 101.
4. BL, Cotton Caligula D VII, fol. 238v.
5. BL, Cotton Vespasian F XIII, fol. 129; *LP* III, i, 873.
6. *CSPV* II, 1298, p. 596.
7. *LP* III, i, 118, p. 37.
8. *LP* VIII, 263, p. 101.
9. *LP* III, i, 896, p. 323.
10. *LP* III, ii, 2333, pp. 987–91.
11. *LP* III, ii, 1443, p. 587.
12. *LP* III, i, 1150, p. 424.
13. *CSPS* II, 355, pp. 365–71.
14. *CSPS*, further supplement, p. 74.
15. Ibid., p. 71; D. Starkey, *Henry VIII: A European Court in England* (London, 1991), p. 91.
16. *CSPS*, further supplement, p. 74.
17. Hall, *Chronicle*, p. 635; *CSPS* II, 423, p. 430.
18. *CSPS* II, 441, p. 448.
19. R. Withington, *English Pageantry: An Historical Outline*, 2 vols. (Cambridge, 1918), I, p. 97; Hall, *Chronicle*, pp. 635–41; *LP* III, ii, 2233, pp. 987–89; *CSPS* II, 43, pp. 443–45.
20. *LP* III, ii, 2322, p. 983; 2333, p. 987; *CSPS* II, 427, pp. 434–37; 430, pp. 438–40.
21. *PPE*, p. xxxii.

CHAPTER 5. THE INSTITUTION OF A CHRISTIAN WOMAN

1. BL, Cotton Vespasian C III, fol. 177; *LP* IV, i, 184, p. 662.
2. J. L. Vives, *De Institutione Feminae Christianae*, eds. C. Fantazzi and C. Matheeussen, 2 vols. (Leiden, 1996), I, pp. 3, 11.
3. Ibid., p. 51.
4. J. L. Vives, "De Ratione Studii Puerilis, Epistola I," in *Opera Omnia*, ed. G. Majamsius, 8 vols. (Valencia, 1782), IV, p. 256. For a translation, see J. L.Vives, "Plan

of Studies for Girls," in *Vives and the Renascence Education of Women*, ed. F. Watson (London, 1912), pp. 137–50.

5. Watson, ed., *Vives and the Renascence Education of Women*, p. 147.

6. Printed and translated in J. W. O'Malley and L. A. Perraud, eds., *Collected Works of Erasmus: Spiritualia and Pastoralia* (London, 1998), p. 214.

7. BL, Royal 17 C XVI, fol. 2. In his "lady's book of hours" there is a copy of "The Prayer of St Thomas of Aquine," translated by Mary in 1527, when she was twelve.

8. *PPE*, p. xxiii.

9. See, e.g., *PPE*, p. 30.

CHAPTER 6. GREAT SIGNS AND TOKENS OF LOVE

1. *CSPS*, further supplement, p. 325.

2. *LP* IV, 600, pp. 266–68.

3. *St.P.* IV, p. 200; *LP* IV, i, 767, p. 337.

4. *LP* IV, i, 882, p. 388; *CSPS* III, i, 103, pp. 174–79.

5. *CSPS* III, i, 33, p. 82.

6. *CSPS* III, i, 60, p. 108.

7. G. Mattingly, *Catherine of Aragon* (London, 1942), p. 168.

8. BL, Cotton Vespasian C III, fol. 50.

9. Ibid., fol. 162.

10. *CSPS* III, i, 103, p. 175.

11. *St.P.* I, p. 160; *LP* IV, i, 1378, pp. 612–13.

12. *LP* IV, i, 1379, p. 616; 1380, p. 617.

13. *CSPS* III, i, pp. 1018–19.

CHAPTER 7. PRINCESS OF WALES

1. *LP* IV, i, 1484, p. 667.

2. *CSPV* II, 479, p. 188.

3. *CSPV* III, 1053, p. 455.

4. Hall, *Chronicle*, p. 703.

5. See P. Williams, *The Council in the Marches of Wales under Elizabeth I* (Cardiff, 1958), pp. 3–43, and F. Heyburn, "Arthur, Prince of Wales and His Training for Kingship," *Historian* 55 (1997), pp. 4–9.

6. BL, Cotton Vespasian F XIII, fol. 72, printed in Ellis, *Original Letters*, 1st series, II, pp. 19–20.

7. *LP* IV, i, 1691, pp. 752–53; 1577, pp. 707–11.

8. BL, Harley 6807, fols. 3r–6r (noted as John Fetherstone).

9. BL, Cotton Vitellius C I, fol. 8v.

10. BL, Cotton Vespasian F XIII, fol. 72, printed in Ellis, *Original Letters*, 1st series, II, pp. 19–20.

11. BL, Cotton Vitellius C I, fol. 9r.

12. BL, Cotton Vespasian F XIII, fol. 240r.

13. G. Duwes, *An Introductory for to Learn to Read, to Pronounce, and to Speak French* (1532?), ed. R. C. Alston, facsimile (Menston, 1972), sig. B62.

CHAPTER 8. PEARL OF THE WORLD

1. *LP* IV, i, 2079, p. 934.

2. *CSPV* III, 902, p. 395.

3. BL, Cotton Caligula D IX, fol. 272.

4. *CSPV* III, 1406, p. 607.
5. BL, Cotton Caligula D IX, fol. 272.
6. *LP* IV, ii, 2840, pp. 1, 271.
7. *LP* IV, ii, 3105, p. 1412.
8. *CSPV* IV, i, 105, p. 58.
9. *LP* IV, ii, 2981, p. 1337; *PPE*, p. xlviii.
10. The commission for this treaty is in *Foedera*, XIV, p. 195, dated April 23, 1527.
11. *CSPV* IV, i, 107, p. 61.
12. J. Lingard, *The History of England . . .* , 10 vols. (London, 1854), IV, p. 237, n3.

CHAPTER 9. THIS SHEER CALAMITY

1. G. Cavendish, *The Life and Death of Cardinal Wolsey by George Cavendish*, ed. R. S. Sylvester (London, 1959), p. 83; *LP* IV, 4942, p. 2145.
2. G. Ascoli, *La Grande-Bretagne devant l'Opinion Française depuis le Guerre de Cents Ans jusqu'à la Fin du XVIe Siècle* (Paris, 1927), p. 234.
3. H. Savage, ed., *The Love Letters of Henry VIII* (London, 1949), pp. 32–34.
4. *CSPS* III, ii, pp. 193–94.
5. *LP* IV, ii, 3140, p. 1429.
6. Ibid.
7. *LP* IV, ii, 3147.
8. *CSPS* III, ii, 113, p. 276.
9. *St.P.* I, pp. 194–95.
10. Ibid.
11. *CSPS* III, ii, 131, p. 301.
12. Ibid.
13. Wood, ed., *Letters of Royal and Illustrious Ladies*, II, pp. 201–203.
14. *CSPS* III, ii, p. 443.
15. *LP* IV, 4736, p. 2055.
16. *LP* IV, ii, 4875, p. 2109.
17. Ibid.
18. Wood, ed., *Letters of Royal and Illustrious Ladies*, II, pp. 32–33; T. Hearne, *Sylloge Epistolarum* (London, 1716), pp. 122–23.
19. *LP* IV, ii, 5016, p. 2177.
20. *CSPS* III, ii, 600, p. 861.
21. Cavendish, *Wolsey*, pp. 78–91.
22. *LP* IV, iii, 5694, p. 2520; *CSPV* IV, 482, pp. 219–20.
23. *LP* IV, iii, 5702, p. 2526; *CSPV* IV, 482, pp. 219–20.
24. *LP* IV, iii, 5702, p. 2526.
25. Ibid.; *CSPV* IV, i, 482, p. 259.
26. *LP* IV, iii, 5791, p. 2589.

CHAPTER 10. THE KING'S GREAT MATTER

1. *CSPS* IV, i, 83, p. 133.
2. G. Burnet, *The History of the Reformation*, ed. N. Pocock, 7 vols. (Oxford, 1865), IV, p. 35.
3. *CSPS* IV, i, 132, pp. 189–90.
4. *LP* IV, iii, 6667, p. 3004.
5. Hall, *Chronicle*, p. 780.
6. P. Friedmann, *Anne Boleyn: A Chapter of English History, 1527–1536*, 2 vols. (London, 1884), I, p. 130.

7. *CSPS* IV, ii, 584, p. 3.
8. *CSPS* IV, ii, 681, p. 112.
9. *CSPS* IV, i, 373, p. 633.
10. *CSPS* IV, ii, 1003, p. 527.
11. *LP* V, 308, p. 145; *CSPS*, IV, ii, 753, p. 199.
12. *LP* V, 216, p. 101.
13. *LP* V, 308, p. 145.
14. *LP* V, 238, pp. 110–111.
15. *LP* V, 238, p. 110.
16. *CSPS* IV, ii, 739, pp. 171–76.
17. *CSPS* IV, ii, 765, p. 212.
18. *CSPS* IV, ii, 775, p. 222.
19. Ibid., pp. 223–24.
20. *LP* V, 375; *CSPS* IV, ii, 778, p. 228.
21. *CSPS* IV, ii, 778, p. 228.
22. *LP* V, 187, p. 89.
23. *LP* V, 216, p. 100.
24. *CSPV* IV, i, 82, pp. 287–88.

CHAPTER 11. THE SCANDAL OF CHRISTENDOM

1. *LP* V, 696, pp. 335–36.
2. *LP* V, 1377, p. 591.
3. *LP* V, 1117, p. 501.
4. Hall, *Chronicle*, XXX, pp. 790–94.
5. *LP* V, 1484, pp. 623–24; 1485, pp. 624–26.
6. *LP* VI, 230, pp. 103–04; 614, pp. 282–83.
7. *CSPS* IV, ii, pp. 510–11.
8. *CSPS* IV, ii, pp. 597–559.
9. Ellis, ed., *Original Letters*, 3rd series, II, p. 276.
10. 24 Hen. VIII c.12; *Statutes*, III, pp. 427–29.
11. *LP* VI, 584, pp. 264–66; *CSPV* IV, 912, pp. 418–19.
12. *CSPS* IV, ii, 1073, p. 678.
13. *LP* VI, 759, p. 339; 760, p. 340.
14. *CSPS* IV, ii, 1062, pp. 646–67.
15. Ibid.
16. *LP* VI, 351, p. 168.
17. *LP* V, 513, p. 239.
18. *LP* V, 478, pp. 226–27.
19. *LP* VI, 720, p. 150.
20. *CSPS* IV, ii, 1058, p. 630.
21. *CSPS* IV, ii, p. 649.
22. *LP* VI, 568, pp. 252–54.

CHAPTER 12. THE LADY MARY

1. *LP* VI, 1112, p. 465.
2. *LP* VI, 1111, p. 464; Hall, *Chronicle*, pp. 805–806.
3. *CSPS* IV, ii, 1127, p. 795; *LP* VI, 1139.
4. BL, Harley 416, fol. 22; *LP* VI, 1207, p. 500.
5. TNA SP 1/79, pp. 121–22; *LP* VI, 1186, pp. 491–92.

6. *LP* VI, 1249, p. 510.
7. *LP* VI, 1528, p. 617.
8. Ibid.
9. Ibid., pp. 617–18.
10. *CSPS* IV, ii, 1161, p. 882.
11. TNA SP E 101/421/14; *LP* VII, 372.
12. *LP* VI, 1392.
13. *CSPS* IV, ii, 1144, p. 839; J. Foxe, *Actes and Monuments of These Latter and Perillous Dayes* . . . (London, 1583), book 9, p. 1396.
14. *LP* VI, 1558, p. 629.
15. Ibid.
16. *LP* VII, 14, p. 8.
17. *LP* VII, 171, p. 69; 530, p. 214.
18. *LP* VII, 214, p. 84.
19. *LP* X, 1134, p. 476.

CHAPTER 13. SPANISH BLOOD

1. BL, Arundel 151, fol. 195; *LP* VI, 1126.
2. *LP* VII, 83, p. 33.
3. BL, Cotton Otho C X, fol. 176 (much burned), printed in A. Crawford, ed., *Letters of the Queens of England 1100–1547* (Stroud, 1994), pp. 178–79.
4. *LP* VII, 162, p. 66.
5. *LP* VII, 232, p. 94.
6. *LP* VII, 83, p. 32.
7. *LP* VII, 171, p. 68.
8. *LP* VII, 83, p. 32.
9. *LP* VII, 296, p. 127; H. Clifford, *The Life of Jane Dormer, Duchess of Feria*, ed. J. Stevenson (London, 1887), pp. 81–82.
10. *LP* VII, 871, p. 323.

CHAPTER 14. HIGH TRAITORS

1. H. A. Kelly, *The Matrimonial Trials of Henry VIII* (Stanford, Calif., 1976), p. 169.
2. 25 Hen. VIII c. 21, 22; *Statutes*, III, pp. 471–74.
3. LS Her. VIII c. 12; *Statutes*, III, p. 450; J. A. Froude, *History of England from the Fall of Wolsey to the Defeat of the Spanish Armada*, 12 vols. (London, 1856) II, p. 171.
4. A. Neame, *The Holy Maid of Kent: The Life of Elizabeth Barton, 1506–1534* (London, 1971), p. 338.
5. M. St. C. Byrne, ed., *The Lisle Letters*, 6 vols. (Chicago and London, 1981), II, p. 130.
6. Neame, *Holy Maid of Kent*, p. 338.
7. BL, Cotton Titus B I, fol. 415.
8. BL, Cotton Otho C X, fol. 169v.
9. BL, Cotton Otho C X, fol. 202.
10. *LP* VII, 662, p. 254.
11. Ibid.
12. BL, Cotton Nero B VI, fol. 89r.
13. BL, Cotton Otho C X, fol. 254 (damaged by fire); *LP* VII, 1036, pp. 403–405.
14. *LP* VII, 1036, pp. 403–405.
15. *LP* VII, 214, p. 84.
16. *LP* VII, 530, p. 214.

CHAPTER 15. WORSE THAN A LION

1.   *LP* VIII, 189, p. 71.
2.   *LP* VII, 1193, p. 463.
3.   *LP* VIII, 200; *CSPS* V, i, p. 134.
4.   *LP* VIII, 263, p. 101.
5.   *LP* VIII, 429, p. 167.
6.   BL, Cotton Otho C X, fol. 176 (much burned), printed in Hearne, *Sylloge Epistolarum*, pp. 107–108.
7.   *LP* VIII, 429, p. 167.
8.   Ibid., p. 165.
9.   *LP* VIII, 948, p. 370.
10.   *LP* VIII, 1, p. 2.
11.   27 Hen. VIII c. 13, *Statutes*, III, p. 508.
12.   Quote from eyewitness William Rastell in N. Harpsfield, *The Life and Death of Sir Thomas More* . . . , ed. R. W. Chambers and E. V. Hitchcock (London, 1932), App. I, p. 245.
13.   C. Wriothesley, *A Chronicle . . . by Charles Wriothesley, Windsor Herald*, ed. W. D. Hamilton, 2 vols. (London, 1875–77) [hereafter *Wriothesley's Chronicle*], I, p. 29.
14.   *LP* VIII, 726, p. 272.
15.   *LP* VIII, 1105, p. 432.
16.   *CSPS* V, i, 148, p. 435; 210, p. 548.
17.   *CSPS* V, i, 218, pp. 559–60.
18.   *LP* VIII, 666, p. 253.
19.   *LP* VIII, 556, p. 210.
20.   *LP* IX, 776.
21.   *LP* IX, 873, p. 293.
22.   *LP* IX, 862, p. 290.

CHAPTER 16. SUSPICION OF POISON

1.   Crawford, *Letters of the Queens of England*, pp. 179–80.
2.   Hearne, *Sylloge Epistolarum*, pp. 107–108.
3.   *LP* X, 59, pp. 20–21.
4.   Ibid., p. 21.
5.   Ibid.
6.   *LP* X, 141, pp. 49–50.
7.   *St.P.* I, p. 452; *LP* X, 37, p. 14; 41, p. 16; 141, p. 51.
8.   *LP* XI, p. 51.
9.   *LP* X, 59, p. 22.
10.   *LP* X, 141, pp. 51–52.
11.   Ibid., p. 51.
12.   *LP* X, 54, p. 19.
13.   *LP* X, 141, pp. 47–48.
14.   *LP* X, 373, p. 148.
15.   *LP* X, 141, p. 52.
16.   *CSPV* II, 16, p. 33.
17.   *LP* X, 59, p. 22.
18.   *LP* X, 199, p. 69.
19.   *LP* XI, 141, p. 48; 199, p. 69.
20.   *LP* X, 307, pp. 117–18.

21. *LP* X, 307, p. 117.
22. *LP* X, 307, p. 116.
23. *CSPS* V, ii, pp. 12–13; *LP* X, 199, p. 69.
24. *LP* X, 307, pp. 116–17.

CHAPTER 17. THE RUIN OF THE CONCUBINE

1   *LP* X, 284, pp. 104–106.
2. *LP* X, 39, pp. 14–15.
3. *LP* X, 282, pp. 102–103.
4. *LP* X, 199, p. 70.
5. *LP* X, 282, p. 103.
6. *LP* X, 199, p. 70; *LP* X, 351, p. 134.
7. *LP* X, 282, p. 103.
8. *LP* VII, 1257, p. 485.
9. *LP* X, 752, p. 315.
10. *LP* X, 601, p. 245; *CSPS* V, ii, p. 84.
11. *LP* X, 601, p. 245.
12. Ibid.
13. Ibid., p. 243.
14. T. Amyot, "Transcript of an Original Manuscript, Containing a Memorial from George Constantyne to Thomas Lord Cromwell," *Archaeologia* 23 (1831), p. 64.
15. *LP* X, 908, p. 377.
16. Ibid.
17. Ibid., p. 378.
18. Ibid.; *Wriothesley's Chronicle*, I, p. 38.
19. *LP* X, 911, p. 382.
20. L. Wiesener, *La Jeunesse d'Elisabeth d'Angleterre* (Paris, 1878), p. 7.
21. *CSPS* V, ii, p. 574.
22. *LP* X, 908, p. 377.
23. *Wriothesley's Chronicle*, I, p. 43.
24. *LP* X, 901, p. 373.
25. *Wriothesley's Chronicle*, I, pp. 43–44.
26. *LP* X, 908, p. 377.
27. *St.P.* VII, p. 684; *LP* X, 726, p. 306.
28. *LP* X, 699, pp. 287–95.
29. *LP* X, 726, pp. 306–308.

CHAPTER 18. MOST HUMBLE AND OBEDIENT DAUGHTER

1. Hearne, *Sylloge Epistolarum*, p. 140. Only a fragment of this letter survives after the Cotton Library fire of 1731. BL, Cotton Otho C X, fol. 283r; *LP* X, p. 968.
2. BL, Cotton Otho C X, fol. 267v; Hearne, *Sylloge Epistolarum*, p. 147.
3. Hearne, *Sylloge Epistolarum*, p. 146; BL, Cotton Otho C X, fol. 268r (badly burned).
4. BL, Cotton Otho C X, fol. 287r for June 8; Hearne, *Sylloge Epistolarum*, p. 149.
5. BL, Cotton Otho C X, fol. 269v; Hearne, *Sylloge Epistolarum*, pp. 125–26.
6. Hearne, *Sylloge Epistolarum*, pp. 124–25; BL, Cotton Otho C X, fol. 269v (badly burned).
7. BL, Cotton Otho C X, fol. 263b, printed in Wood, *Letters of Royal and Illustrious Ladies*, II, pp. 250–52.
8. Hearne, *Sylloge Epistolarum*, p. 127.
9. *LP* XI, 7, pp. 7–8.

10. *CSPS* V, ii, 70, p. 184.
11. Hearne, *Sylloge Epistolarum*, pp. 137–38.
12. *CSPS* V, ii, 70, pp. 183–84.
13. Ibid.
14. *LP* X, 1134, pp. 475–76.
15. *CSPS* VI, i, 43, pp. 81–85; 47, p. 106.
16. R. Morice, "Anecdotes and Character of Archbishop Cranmer," in J. G. Nichols ed., *Narratives of the Days of the Reformation, Chiefly from the Manuscripts of John Foxe the Martyrologist*, 67, CS 77 (London, 1859), p. 259.
17. *LP* X, 1137; Hearne, *Sylloge Epistolarum*, pp. 142–43.
18. *CSPS* V, ii, p. 183; Hearne, *Sylloge Epistolarum*, p. 142; *LP* X, 1137, p. 478.

CHAPTER 19. INCREDIBLE REJOICING

1. Hearne, *Sylloge Epistolarum*, pp. 128–29; Wood, *Letters of Royal and Illustrious Ladies*, II, pp. 258–59.
2. *LP* XI, 7, pp. 7–8.
3. Ibid.
4. *CSPV* V, ii, 71, p. 195; *LP* XI, 40, p. 24.
5. *CSPS* V, ii, 71, p. 195.
6. *CSPS* V, ii, p. 199.
7. *LP* XI, 576, p. 229; 597, pp. 241–42.
8. *CSPS* V, ii, 85, p. 220.
9. *LP* XI, 148, p. 65.
10. *LP* XI, 7, p. 8; *CSPS* V, ii, 94, pp. 237–38.
11. *LP* XI, 7, p. 8.
12. *LP* X, 219, p. 96.
13. 28 Hen. VIII, c. 7, *Statutes*, III, pp. 655–62; *LP* XI, 40, p. 24.
14. *LP* XI, 221, p. 97.
15. *CSPS* V, ii, 94, p. 238.
16. *LP* XI, 1246, p. 507.
17. *LP* XII, i, 901, p. 406.
18. *LP* X, 1353; *LP* XII, i, pp. 367, 368, 779.
19. *Reginaldi Poli ad Henricum Octavum Britanniae regem, pro ecclesiasticae unitas defensione* (Strasbourg, 1555), fol. lxxxxiv, cited in T. Mayer, *Reginald Pole, Prince and Prophet* (Cambridge, 2000), p. 21.
20. *LP* XII, i, 1032, p. 471.
21. *Wriothesley's Chronicle*, I, pp. 59–60.
22. Byrne, *Lisle Letters*, III, pp. 576–77.
23. BL, Cotton Titus B, fol. 481; see also *LP* XII, 815, p. 361.

CHAPTER 20. DELIVERANCE OF A GOODLY PRINCE

1. BL, Cotton Nero C X, fol. 1; J. G. Nichols, *The Literary Remains of King Edward VI*, 2 vols. (London, 1857), p. xxiii; Crawford, *Letters of the Queens of England*, p. 199.
2. *Wriothesley's Chronicle*, I, p. 66; BL, Add 6113, fol. 81.
3. *LP* XII, ii, 890, p. 310.
4. *Wriothesley's Chronicle*, I, p. 64.
5. Simon Thurley, "Henry VIII and the Building of Hampton Court: A Reconstruction of the Tudor Palace," *Architectural History*, 1988, pp. 29–37.
6. *Wriothesley's Chronicle*, I, p. 66.
7. *LP* XII, ii, 911, p. 318.

8. *LP* XII, ii, 923, p. 325.
9. *Wriothesley's Chronicle*, I, p. 68; *LP* XII, ii, 911, pp. 318–20.
10. *LP* XII, ii, 970, p. 339.
11. Hall, *Chronicle*, p. 825.
12. *LP* XII, ii, 972, p. 339.
13. *LP* XII, ii, 1060, pp. 372–74.
14. Foxe, *Actes and Monuments*, book 8, p. 1087.
15. BL, Cotton Titus B I, fol. 121; *LP* XII, ii, p. 1075.
16. *LP* XIII, i, 1011, p. 373.
17. *PPE*, pp. 61, 67, 69.
18. Clifford, *Life of Jane Dormer*, pp. 61–62.
19. Byrne, *Lisle Letters*, V, p. 305.

CHAPTER 21. THE MOST UNHAPPY LADY IN CHRISTENDOM

1. *LP* XII, ii, 1004, pp. 348–49.
2. *LP* XIII, ii, 77, pp. 28–29.
3. Hearne, *Sylloge Epistolarum*, p. 141.
4. Ibid., p. 139; *LP* XIII, i, 1082, pp. 395–96.
5. *CSPS* VI, i, pp. 25–26.
6. Ibid., p. 26.
7. *LP* XII, i, 1141, p. 526.
8. *LP* XIV, i, 980, pp. 451–52.
9. TNA SP C 65/147, m. 22.
10. *Wriothesley's Chronicle*, I, p. 92.
11. *LP* XIV, i, 372, p. 143.
12. *LP* XIII, ii, 1148, p. 477; *LP* XIV, 377, p. 143; *LP* XV, 134, pp. 42–43.
13. *LP* XIII, 1148, p. 477.
14. *CSPS* V, ii, 61, p. 151.
15. *LP* XIV, i, 103, p. 41.
16. Ibid.
17. Hearne, *Sylloge Epistolarum*, pp. 149–51.
18. *LP* XIV, ii, 744, p. 275.
19. *LP* XIV, ii, 733, pp. 269–71.
20. *LP* XIV, ii, 52, p. 15.
21. *LP* XIV, i, 603, pp. 235–38.
22. *LP* XVI, 117, p. 59; 160, pp. 73–74; 175, pp. 80–81; 270, p. 115.
23. *LP* XVI, 270, p. 115.
24. *LP* XVII, 182, p. 83.
25. *LP* XVII, 371, p. 221.

CHAPTER 22. FOR FEAR OF MAKING A RUFFLE IN THE WORLD

1. *LP* XIV, ii, 754, p. 283.
2. *Wriothesley's Chronicle*, I, pp. 109–110.
3. Burnet, *History of the Reformation*, IV, pp. 425–26; *LP* XV, 823, p. 389.
4. *LP* XV, 823, p. 391; Burnet, *History of the Reformation*, IV, pp. 425–26; J. Strype, *Ecclesiastical Memorials; Relating Chiefly to Religion, and the Reformation of It, and the Emergencies of the Church of England, under King Henry VIII, King Edward VI, and Queen Mary the First* . . . , 3 vols. (London, 1721), I, p. 360.
5. Burnet, *History of the Reformation*, IV, p. 426; *LP* XV, 823, p. 389.
6. *LP* XV, 823, p. 391; Burnet, *History of the Reformation*, IV, pp. 425–26.

7.   Burnet, *History of the Reformation*, IV, p. 427.
8.   Ibid., p. 430.
9.   Strype, *Ecclesiastical Memorials*, I, p. 360.
10. *LP* XVI, XII, pp. 4–5; J. Kaulek, ed., *Correspondance Politique de MM. de Castillon et de Marillac* (Paris, 1885), p. 218.
11. *LP* XV, 766, p. 363; Kaulek, ed., *Correspondance Politique*, pp. 189–90.
12. *LP* XV, 804, p. 377.
13. *LP* XV, 823, pp. 389–91.
14. BL, Cotton Otho C X, fol. 242; *LP* XV, 824, pp. 391–94.
15. Hall, *Chronicle*, p. 839.
16. *LP* XV, 908, pp. 450–51; 930, pp. 454–60.
17. *LP* XV, 908, pp. 450–51; 925, pp. 456–58; 930; pp. 456–60.
18. See Foxe, *Actes and Monuments*, book 8, p. 1199.
19. Ibid., p. 1201.

CHAPTER 23. MORE A FRIEND THAN A STEPMOTHER

1.   *LP* XVI, 578, pp. 269–73; *Wriothesley's Chronicle*, I, pp. 121–22.
2.   *LP* XVI, 223, p. 100.
3.   *LP* XVI, 449, p. 222; *CSPS* VI, i, 149, pp. 305–306.
4.   *LP* XVI, 314, p. 149.
5.   *CSPS* VI, i, 161, p. 324; *LP* XVI, 835, p. 401.
6.   *CSPS* VI, i, 166, pp. 331–32; *LP* XVI, 897, p. 436.
7.   BL, Cotton Otho C X, fol. 250, printed in N. H. Nicolas, ed., *PPC*, p. 352.
8.   HMC, *Bath Papers*, 5 vols. (London, 1904–1980), II, pp. 8–9.
9.   *LP* XVII, 124, p. 50.
10. *CSPS* VI, i, 232, p. 472; *LP* XVII, 124, p. 50.
11. *CSPS* VI, i, 211, pp. 410–11; *LP* XVI, 1403, p. 653.
12. *LP* XVII, App. B, no. 13, p. 723.
13. *CSPS* VI, ii, pp. 223–24.
14. *LP* XVII, 251, pp. 124, 140.
15. *LP* XVII, 260, p. 140.
16. *LP* XVII, 1212, p. 669.
17. *CSPS* VI, ii, 87, p. 190; 94, p. 223.
18. *LP* XVIII, i, 894, p. 490.
19. *LP* XVIII, i, 873, p. 483.
20. *LP* XIX, i, 118, p. 64; 296, p. 189.
21. Wood, *Letters of Royal and Illustrious Ladies*, III, pp. 181–82.
22. Nicholas Udall, ed., *The First Tome or Volume of the Paraphrases of Erasmus upon the Newe Testamente* (London, 1548), vol. III, fol. ii.
23. F. Madden, ed., "Narrative of the Visit of the Duke of Najera to England in the Year 1543–4; Written by his Secretary, Pedro de Gente," *Archaeologia* 23 (1831), p. 353; *LP* XIX, i, pp. 7, 9.
24. J. O. Halliwell-Phillipps, ed., *Letters of the Kings of England, Now First Collected from the Originals*, 2 vols. (London, 1846), II, pp. 8–9.
25. BL, Harley 5087, no. 6, trans. Halliwell-Phillipps, *Letters of the Kings of England*, II, pp. 7–8.

CHAPTER 24. THE FAMILY OF HENRY VIII

1.   35 Hen. VIII c. 1; *Statutes*, III, p. 955.
2.   28 Hen. VIII c. 7; *Statutes*, III, pp. 655–62.

3. 35 Hen.VIII c. 1; *Statutes*, III, pp. 955–58.
4. *LP* XIX, i, 780, p. 477.
5. *LP* XVII, 124, p. 50.
6. *LP* XVIII, i, 804, pp. 454–55.
7. *LP* XIX, ii, 424, pp. 238–42.
8. TNA SP 1/190, fol. 156, printed in Crawford, ed., *Letters of the Queens of England*, pp. 216–17.
9. *LP* XIX, ii, 35, p. 16.
10. *LP* XX, i, 1263, p. 627.
11. *LP* XX, ii, 89, p. 43.
12. *LP* XX, ii, 788, pp. 376–77.
13. *LP* XX, ii, 639, p. 295.
14. *CSPS* XIII, 51, p. 109.
15. *LP* XXI, i, 1215, pp. 603, 1309.

CHAPTER 25. DEPARTED THIS LIFE

1. *CSPS* VIII, 204, p. 318.
2. Foxe, *Actes and Monuments*, book 8, p. 1242.
3. Ibid.
4. Ibid., p. 1243.
5. Ibid.
6. Ibid.
7. *LP* XXI, i, 605, p. 307.
8. *LP* XXI, ii, 769, p. 403.
9. *LP* XXI, ii, 555, pp. 283–89.
10. Lord Herbert of Cherbury, *The Life and Raigne of King Henry the Eighth* (London, 1649), p. 567.
11. TNA SP E 23/4/1, fol. iv.
12. *LP* XXI, ii, p. 360.
13. See Foxe, *Actes and Monuments*, book 8, p. 1290.
14. Strype, *Ecclesiastical Memorials*, II, pp. 10–11; part ii, pp. 3–4.
15. *CSPS* IX, p. 6.
16. *CSPS* IX, p. 101.
17. BL, Add 71009, fol. 45r.
18. W. K. Jordan, ed., *The Chronicle and Political Papers of King Edward VI* (London, 1966), p. 4.

CHAPTER 26. THE KING IS DEAD, LONG LIVE THE KING

1. P. L. Hughes and J. F. Larkin, eds., *Tudor Royal Proclamations*, 3 vols. (New Haven and London, 1964–1969), I, p. 381.
2. Society of Antiquaries, MS 123, fol. 1r.
3. *APC* II, pp. 7–8; College of Arms, MS I 7, fol. 29; Nichols, ed., *Literary Remains*, I, p. lxxxvii.
4. *APC* II, pp. 7–8; College of Arms, MS I 7, fol. 29, printed in Nichols, ed., *Literary Remains*, I, p. lxxxvii.
5. BL, Harley 5087, no. 35, printed in Nichols, ed., *Literary Remains*, I, pp. 39–40.
6. Strype, *Ecclesiastical Memorials*, II, ii, p. 9.
7. Martin A. Hume, ed., *Chronicle of King Henry VIII of England . . . Written in Spanish by an Unknown Hand* (London, 1889), p. 154.
8. A. Strickland, *Lives of the Queens of England*, 6 vols. (London, 1854), II, p. 443.

9. Strype transcribes a manuscript account of Henry VIII's funeral ceremonies in his *Ecclesiastical Memorials*, II, ii, pp. 3–18. Also see J. Loach, "The Function of Ceremonial in the Reign of Henry VIII," *Past and Present* 142 (1994), pp. 56–66.
10. Jordan, ed., *Chronicle of Edward VI*, p. 5.
11. College of Arms, MS I 7, in Nichols, ed., *Literary Remains*, I, p. cclxxx.
12. *CSPS* IX, p. 47.
13. R. Holinshed, *The Firste (–Laste) Volume of the Chronicles of England, Scotland and Irelande* (London, 1577), p. 614.
14. College of Arms, MS I 7, fol. 32, in Nichols, ed., *Literary Remains*, I, p. ccxci.
15. Nichols, ed., *Literary Remains*, I, p. ccxc.
16. *CSPS* IX, p. 47.
17. College of Arms, MS I 7, fol. 32, in Nichols, ed., *Literary Remains*, I, p. ccxci.
18. For the text of the *Liber Regalis*, see L. G. Wickham Legg, *English Coronation Records* (London, 1901), pp. 81–130.
19. Wickham Legg, *English Coronation Records*, p. 230.
20. J. E. Cox, ed., *Miscellaneous Writings and Letters of Thomas Cranmer* (London, 1846), pp. 126–27.
21. Hughes and Larkin, eds., *Tudor Royal Proclamations*, I, no. 275, p. 381.
22. Cox, *Writings of Thomas Cranmer*, II, p. 1267.
23. College of Arms, account in Nichols, ed., *Literary Remains*, I, p. ccxcv.
24. Jordan, ed., *Chronicle of Edward VI*, p. 5.

CHAPTER 27. FANTASY AND NEW FANGLENESS

1. *CSPS* IX, p. 38.
2. Ibid., p. 15.
3. Ibid., p. 495.
4. *CPR Edward VI*, II, pp. 20–23.
5. Bodleian Library, Tanner MS 90, fols. 157–168.
6. BL, Lansdowne 1236, fol. 26, in Ellis, *Original Letters*, 1st series, II, pp. 149–50.
7. Chapuys, dispatch to Antoine Perrenot, the emperor's minister, May 18, 1536. Referring to Jane Seymour, he wrote, "She is the sister of a certain Edward Seymour, who had been in the service of his Majesty [Charles V]." *LP* X, 901, p. 374. Edward Seymour had entered the emperor's service in early 1521 on the recommendation of Henry and Wolsey; see *LP* III, i, 1201, p. 452.
8. P. E. Tytler, ed., *England under the Reigns of Edward VI and Mary*, I, pp. 51–52, 60–61.
9. BL, Cotton Otho C X, printed in Strype, *Ecclesiastical Memorials*, II, pp. 58–59.
10. See E. Cardwell, *Documentary Annals of the Reformed Church of England, etc.*, 2 vols. (Oxford, 1844), I, pp. 4–31.
11. *CSPS* IX, p. 101.
12. Ibid., p. 298.
13. Strype, *Ecclesiastical Memorials*, II, pp. 59–60.
14. Ibid.
15. E. Rhys, ed., *The First and Second Prayer Books of Edward VI* (1910), p. 225.
16. *CSPS* IX, p. 351.
17. Ibid., pp. 360–61.
18. Ibid., p. 330.
19. Ibid., pp. 374–75.
20. Ibid., pp. 385–86.
21. Ibid., pp. 381–82.
22. Ibid.

CHAPTER 28. ADVICE TO BE CONFORMABLE

1. *APC* II, pp. 291–92.
2. Foxe, *Actes and Monuments*, book 9, p. 1332.
3. Ibid., p. 1333.
4. This remembrance was undoubtedly drawn up as a very definite response to Mary's letter of defiance dated June 22. Foxe, *Actes and Monuments*, book 9, pp. 1332–33.
5. Foxe, *Actes and Monuments*, book 9, pp. 1332–33.
6. *CSPS* IX, pp. 406–407.
7. Ibid., pp. 360–61.
8. Ibid., p. 394.
9. Ibid.
10. Ibid., p. 419.
11. John Hooker, *The Description of the Citie of Excester* (Devon and Cornwall Record Society, 1919), p. 61.
12. The articles are printed in A. J. Fletcher and D. MacCulloch, eds., *Tudor Rebellions* (Harlow, 2004), pp. 139–41.
13. TNA SP 10/8/30 (*CSPD Edw VI*, 327, p. 126).
14. "*De Mario vel Marianis me valde ang it, immo prope exanimat,*" in Tytler, *England under the Reigns of Edward VI and Mary*, I, p. 188.
15. Burnet, *History of the Reformation*, VI, pp. 283–84.
16. *CSPS* IX, p. 407.
17. Ibid., pp. 406–408.
18. TNA SP 10/8 no. 51 (*CSPD Edw VI*, 348, pp. 132–33), printed in Wood, *Letters of Royal and Illustrious Ladies*, III, pp. 213–14.

CHAPTER 29. THE MOST UNSTABLE MAN IN ENGLAND

1. *CSPS* IX, p. 453.
2. Hughes and Larkin, eds., *Tudor Royal Proclamations*, I, 351, p. 483.
3. R. Grafton, *A Chronicle at Large and Meere History of the Affayres of Englande . . .* , II, p. 522.
4. *CSPS* IX, p. 449.
5. *CSPS* X, pp. 5–6.
6. *CSPS* IX, p. 446.
7. Hughes and Larkin, eds., *Tudor Royal Proclamations*, I, p. 352.
8. *CSPS* X, p. 6.
9. Ibid., pp. 5–6.
10. TNA SP 10/9 no. 57 (*CSPD Edw VI*, 428, p. 158).
11. *CSPS* X, p. 5.
12. Ibid.
13. Ibid., pp. 56–57.
14. *CSPS* IX, p. 489.

CHAPTER 30. WHAT SAY YOU, MR AMBASSADOR?

1. *CSPS* X, p. 82.
2. Ibid., pp. 127–28.
3. *CSPS* IX, p. 450.
4. Ibid., pp. 449–51.

5. *CSPS* X, p. 117.
6. Ibid., pp. 94–96.
7. Ibid., pp. 124–35.

CHAPTER 31. AN UNNATURAL EXAMPLE

1. See *CSPS* X, p. 140.
2. Tytler, *England under the reigns of Edward VI and Mary*, I, p. 347.
3. Foxe, *Actes and Monuments*, book 9, pp. 1335–37.
4. *CSPS* X, pp. 172–73.
5. Foxe, *Actes and Monuments*, book 9, p. 1583.
6. *CSPS* X, pp. 205–209.
7. *CSPS* X, pp. 209–12; Foxe, *Actes and Monuments*, book 9, pp. 1333–34.
8. *CSPS* X, pp. 212–13; Foxe, *Actes and Monuments*, book 9, p. 1334.
9. *CSPS* X, p. 219.
10. *APC* III, p. 215.

CHAPTER 32. NAUGHTY OPINION

1. J. G. Nichols, ed., "The Diary of Henry Machyn, Citizen and Merchant Taylor of London . . . ," (London, 1848), p. 5.
2. *CSPS* X, p. 264.
3. Jordan, ed., *Chronicle of Edward VI*, p. 55.
4. *CSPS* X, pp. 258–60.
5. *APC* III, p. 239.
6. J. G. Nichols, ed., "Chronicle of the Grey Friars of London," CS, old series, 53 (London, 1852), p. 69; *APC* III, p. 239.
7. *APC* III, p. 239.
8. Ibid., p. 267.
9. Foxe, *Actes and Monuments*, book 9, p. 1337.
10. Ibid.; see also Jordan, ed., *Chronicle of Edward VI*, p. 67.
11. Jordan, ed., *Chronicle of Edward VI*, p. 56.
12. *CSPF Edward VI*, p. 75.
13. Jordan, ed., *Chronicle of Edward VI*, p. 56; BL, Harley 353, fols. 130–136v, printed in Nichols, ed., *Literary Remains*, I, pp. ccxxiv–ccxxxiv.
14. *CSPF Edward VI*, 393, pp. 137–38; *CSPS* X, pp. 310–17.

CHAPTER 33. MATTERS TOUCHING MY SOUL

1. Jordan, ed., *Chronicle of Edward VI*, p. 76.
2. Ibid., p. 333.
3. Ibid., pp. 338–39.
4. Ibid., pp. 333–34, 336–41.
5. Ibid., p. 343.
6. Ibid., p. 349.
7. Ibid., p. 348.
8. Jordan, ed., *Chronicle of Edward VI*, p. 78.
9. T. D. MacCulloch, ed., "The *Vita Mariae Angliae Reginae* of Robert Wingfield of Brantham," *Camden Miscellany* 28; CS, 4th series, 29 (London, 1984), p. 247.
10. *CSPV* X, p. 391.
11. Nichols, ed., "The Diary of Henry Machyn," p. 20.

CHAPTER 34. MY DEVICE FOR THE SUCCESSION

1. 5 Edw. VI c.1; *Statutes*, IV, I, pp. 130–31.
2. *CSPS* XI, pp. 8–9.
3. Inner Temple Library, Petyt MS 538, vol. 46, fol. 9, printed in Nichols, ed., *Literary Remains*, I, p. cxc.
4. Cited in S. T. Bindoff, "A Kingdom at Stake, 1553," *History Today* 3 (1953), p. 647.
5. *CSPS* XI, p. 46.
6. Nichols, ed., *Literary Remains*, pp. 571–72.
7. Inner Temple Library, Petyt MS 538, vol. 47, fol. 317.
8. *CSPS* XI, p. 57.
9. MacCulloch, ed., "The *Vita Mariae*," pp. 247–48.
10. BL, Royal 18 C XXIV, fol. 3/3v.
11. *CSPS* XI, p. 70.
12. A. Vertot, *Ambassades de Messieurs de Noailles en Angleterre*, 5 vols. (Leyden, 1763), II, pp. 35–38.
13. *CSPS* XI, p. 65.
14. Vertot, *Ambassades*, II, pp. 50–53.
15. E. Lodge, ed., *Illustrations of British History, Biography, and Manners, in the Reigns of Henry VIII, Edward VI, Mary, Elizabeth and James I, Exhibited in a Series of Original Papers . . . ,*" 3 vols. (London, 1838 ed.), I, pp. 226–27.
16. J. Burtt, ed., "Letters Illustrating the Reign of Queen Jane," *The Archeological Journal*, XXX (1873), p. 276.

CHAPTER 35. FRIENDS IN THE BRIARS

1. J. G. Nichols, ed., "The Chronicle of Queen Jane and Two Years of Queen Mary," (hereafter *CQJQM*), (London, 1850), p. 3.
2. *CSPS* XI, p. 80.
3. See A. Plowden, *Lady Jane Grey: Nine Days Queen* (Stroud, 2003), p. 84.
4. "Epistle of Poor Pratte to Gilbert Potter," in *CQJQM*, pp. 115–21.
5. *CSPS* XI, pp. 76, 79.
6. Ibid., p. 73.
7. *CSPS* XI, p. 74.
8. *CSPS* XI, pp. 73–74.
9. Suffolk Record Office, Eye Borough Records, Ipswich MS EE 2/E/3, fol. 26v; Foxe, *Actes and Monuments*, book 10, p. 1406.
10. Suffolk Record Office, Eye Borough Records, Ipswich MS EE 2/E/3, fol. 27r; Foxe, *Actes and Monuments*, book 10, pp. 1406–07.
11. BL, Lansdowne 3, fols. 48v–49.
12. *CQJQM*, p. 5.
13. Ibid., pp. 6–7.
14. *CSPS* XI, p. 88.
15. *CQJQM*, p. 8.
16. F. Madden, ed., "The Petition of Richard Troughton," *Archaeologia* 23 (1831), p. 25.

CHAPTER 36. TRUE OWNER OF THE CROWN

1. MacCulloch, ed., "The *Vitae Mariae*," p. 252.
2. *CSPS* XI, pp. 106–107.
3. Ibid., p. 79.

4. Hughes and Larkin, eds., *Tudor Royal Proclamations*, II, p. 3.
5. Oxburgh Hall, Bedingfeld Papers.
6. C. V. Malfatti, ed. and trans., *The Accession, Coronation and Marriage of Mary Tudor as Related in Four Manuscripts of the Escorial* (Barcelona, 1956), pp. 14–15.
7. *APC* IV, p. 296.
8. Malfatti, ed., *Mary Tudor*, pp. 16–17.
9. Ibid.
10. Hughes and Larkin, eds., *Tudor Royal Proclamations*, II, p. 3.
11. *Wriothesley's Chronicle*, II, pp. 88–89.
12. Nichols, ed., "The Diary of Henry Machyn," p. 37; Malfatti, ed., *Mary Tudor*, p. 20.
13. *CSPS* XI, p. 115.
14. Ibid., p. 108.
15. J. Stow, *The Annales of England* (London, 1592), p. 1035; *Wriothesley's Chronicle*, II, pp. 88–90; *CQJQM*, pp. 9–12; Nichols, ed., "The Diary of Henry Machyn," p. 37.

CHAPTER 37. MARYE THE QUENE

1. *CSPS* XI, pp. 259–60.
2. *CSPV* V, 934, p. 532.
3. Ibid., 934, p. 533.
4. MacCulloch, ed., "The *Vitae Mariae*," p. 252.
5. BL, Add 5841, fol. 272.
6. J. Loach, *Parliament and the Crown in the Reign of Mary I* (Oxford, 1986), p. 1.
7. *CSPS* XI, pp. 109–110.
8. Vertot, *Ambassades*, II, pp. 82–100.
9. Aff. Etr. IX, fols. 50, 53, quoted in E. H. Harbison, *Rival Ambassadors at the Court of Mary I* (Princeton, 1940), p. 54.
10. Aff. Etr. IX, fol. 53, quoted in Harbison, *Rival Ambassadors*, p. 54.
11. MacCulloch, ed., "The *Vitae Mariae*," p. 269.
12. Ibid.
13. *Wriothesley's Chronicle*, II, pp. 91–92.
14. Ibid., p. 92.
15. Ibid., p. 93.
16. MacCulloch, ed., "The *Vitae Mariae*," p. 271.

CHAPTER 38. THE JOY OF THE PEOPLE

1. *Wriothesley's Chronicle*, II, p. 93.
2. *CSPS* XI, p. 151.
3. *Wriothesley's Chronicle*, II, pp. 92–95; MacCulloch, ed., "The *Vitae Mariae*," pp. 275–76.
4. *Wriothesley's Chronicle*, II, p. 94.
5. *CSPS* XI, p. 151; *Wriothesley's Chronicle*, II, p. 94.
6. *CSPS* XI, pp. 134, 209.
7. *Wriothesley's Chronicle*, II, p. 95.
8. *CSPS* XI, p. 151.
9. *Wriothesley's Chronicle*, II, p. 95.
10. *CSPS* XI, p. 215.
11. Ibid., p. 172.
12. Ibid., p. 180.
13. Ibid., p. 252.
14. Ibid., p. 130.

15. Ibid., pp. 130–31.
16. Ibid., p. 293.
17. Ibid., p. 132.
18. Ibid., p. 153.

CHAPTER 39. CLEMENCY AND MODERATION

1. Nichols, ed., "The Diary of Henry Machyn," p. 38.
2. R. Garnett, ed. and trans., *The Accession of Queen Mary: Being the Contemporary Narrative of Antonio de Guaras a Spanish Merchant Resident in London* (London, 1892), p. 99.
3. *Wriothesley's Chronicle*, II, pp. 90–91; Garnett, ed., *The Accession of Queen Mary . . . de Guaras*, p. 99.
4. *CQJQM*, pp. 18–19; Tytler, *England under the Reigns of Edward VI and Mary*, II, pp. 230–33; BL, Harley 284, fol. 127.
5. *CSPS* X, i, 184, p. 210.
6. *CSPS* XI, p. 168.
7. Ibid., p. 113.
8. Ibid., p. 168.
9. Ibid., p. 215.
10. Ibid., p. 131.
11. Ibid., p. 134.
12. Ibid., pp. 156–57, 210; Nichols, ed., "The Diary of Henry Machyn," pp. 39–40.
13. *Wriothesley's Chronicle*, II, p. 102.
14. *CSPS* XI, pp. 169–70; Nichols, ed., "Chronicle of the Grey Friars," p. 83.
15. *CSPS* XI, pp. 173–74.
16. Hughes and Larkin, eds., *Tudor Royal Proclamations*, II, p. 5.
17. *CSPV* V, 813, pp. 429–30.
18. *CSPV* V, 836, p. 447.
19. *CSPS* XI, pp. 169–70.
20. Ibid., p. 169.
21. Ibid., pp. 195–96.
22. Ibid., pp. 220–21.
23. Ibid., p. 221.
24. Ibid., p. 240.
25. Ibid., pp. 252–53.
26. Ibid., pp. 393–95.
27. Ibid., p. 395.
28. See ibid., p. 440.

CHAPTER 40. OLD CUSTOMS

1. *CSPS* XI, p. 214.
2. Hughes and Larkin, eds., *Tudor Royal Proclamations*, II, 393, p. 11.
3. Strype, *Ecclesiastical Memorials*, III, p. 34; Nichols, ed., "The Diary of Henry Machyn," p. 43.
4. *CQJQM*, p. 31.
5. Strype, *Ecclesiastical Memorials*, III, p. 34.
6. *CSPS* XI, p. 238.
7. Ibid.
8. Ibid., pp. 238–39.
9. *CSPV* V (15), p. 430. Mary stopped using the title "Supreme Head" at the end of 1553,

but the break with Rome was not officially reversed and England absolved until the third Parliament in November 1554.

10. *CSPS* XI, p. 220.
11. J. R. Planché, *Regal Records; or, A Chronicle of the Coronations of the Queens Regnant of England* (London, 1838), p. 3.
12. College of Arms, MS I 18, fol. 117.
13. *CSPS* XI, p. 262; TNA SP 11/1/16.
14. Planché, *Regal Records*, pp. 4–12; Garnett, ed., *The Accession of Queen Mary . . . de Guaras*, pp. 117–19.
15. Planché, *Regal Records*, p. 6.
16. *CQ JQM*, p. 28.
17. Garnett, ed., *The Accession of Queen Mary . . . de Guaras*, pp. 118–19.
18. J. Mychel, *A Breviat Chronicle* (London, 1554) (STC ggjo.j), sig. Oii.
19. *CSPS* XI, p. 259.
20. *CQ JQM*, p. 29.
21. Stow, *Annales*, p. 1044.
22. *CQ JQM*, p. 30.
23. Ibid.

CHAPTER 41. GOD SAVE QUEEN MARY

1. Planché, *Regal Records*, pp. 12–13; Society of Antiquaries, MS 123, fol. 4v; Malfatti, ed., *Mary Tudor*, p. 32.
2. *CSPS* XI, pp. 239–40.
3. Malfatti, ed., *Mary Tudor*, p. 33.
4. Planché, *Regal Records*, pp. 16–23; Society of Antiquaries, MS 123, fols. 6r–8v.
5. Garnett, ed., *The Accession of Queen Mary . . . de Guaras*, p. 121.
6. Malfatti, ed., *Mary Tudor*, p. 34.
7. *CQ JQM*, p. 31.
8. *CSPS* XI, p. 262.
9. Garnett, ed., *The Accession of Queen Mary . . . de Guaras*, pp. 122–23.

CHAPTER 42. INIQUITOUS LAWS

1. *CSPV* V, 813, p. 431.
2. BL, Cotton Titus B II, fol. 148.
3. *CSPS* XI, p. 305.
4. Ibid.
5. *Cal. Pole*, II, 760, pp. 231–32.
6. *Cal. Pole*, II, 765, pp. 235–37.
7. *CSPV* V, 807, p. 425.
8. *CSPS* XI, p. 418.
9. Ibid.
10. Hughes and Larkin, eds., *Tudor Royal Proclamations*, II, pp. 35–38.
11. Bonner's articles, printed in W. H. Frere and W. M. Kennedy, eds., *Visitation Articles and Injunctions of the Period of Reformation*, 3 vols. (London, 1910), II, pp. 344–45.
12. Frere and Kennedy, eds., *Visitation Articles and Injunctions*, II, pp. 347–55.
13. Strype, *Ecclesiastical Memorials*, III, ii, pp. 37–42.
14. Charles Lethbridge Kingsford, ed., *Two London Chronicles from the Collections of John Stow* (London, 1910), p. 31; Nichols, ed., "Chronicle of the Grey Friars," p. 85.
15. Nichols, ed., "The Diary of Henry Machyn," p. 49.

16. A. G. Dickens, ed., "Robert Parkyn Narrative of the Reformation," *English Historical Review* 62 (1947), p. 82.

CHAPTER 43. A MARRYING HUMOR

1. *CSPS* XI, p. 266.
2. Ibid., p. 282.
3. Foxe, *Actes and Monuments*, book 10, p. 1418.
4. *CSPS* XI, pp. 386–87.
5. Vertot, *Ambassades*, II, pp. 144, 174–82.
6. *CSPS* XI, p. 131.
7. BL, Arundel 151, fol. 195; *LP* VI, 1126, p. 472.
8. *CSPS* XI, p. 165.
9. Ibid., pp. 126–27.
10. Ibid., pp. 177–78.
11. Ibid., p. 213.
12. Ibid., pp. 289–90.
13. Ibid., p. 288.
14. Ibid., p. 310.
15. Tytler, *England under the Reigns of Edward VI and Mary*, II, pp. 260, 263.
16. *CSPS* XI, p. 328.
17. Ibid., p. 331.

CHAPTER 44. A SUITABLE PARTNER IN LOVE

1. *CQJQM*, p. 32.
2. *CSPS* XI, pp. 363–65.
3. MacCulloch, ed., "The *Vitae Mariae*," p. 278; *CSPS* XI, pp. 312–13.
4. *CSPS* XI, p. 364.
5. Ibid., p. 372.
6. Ibid.
7. Grafton, *A Chronicle at Large*, (London, 1569), p. 1327.
8. *CSPS* XI, p. 467.
9. Ibid., pp. 409–10.
10. *CQJQM*, p. 34.
11. Aff. Etr. IX, fol. 99, cited in Harbison, *Rival Ambassadors*, pp. 115–16.
12. *CSPS* XI, p. 407.
13. *CQJQM*, p. 34.
14. Ibid., p. 35.
15. Ibid.

CHAPTER 45. A TRAITOROUS CONSPIRACY

1. *CSPS* XI, p. 426.
2. Aff. Etr. IX, fol. 99, cited in Harbison, *Rival Ambassadors*, pp. 115–16.
3. Harbison, *Rival Ambassadors*, p. 108.
4. *APC* IV, p. 382.
5. *CSPS* XII, pp. 30–35.
6. Ibid., p. 31.
7. TNA SP 11/2/8, fols. 12–13v (*CSPD*, Mary, 30).
8. *CSPS* XII, pp. 40–41.

9.   J. Procter, "The Historie of Wyate's Rebellion," in *Tudor Tracts*, ed. A. F. Pollard (London, 1903), pp. 212–13.
10. Procter, "Wyate's Rebellion," p. 213.
11. *CQJQM*, p. 37.
12. Procter, "Wyate's Rebellion," p. 230; John Elder, *The Copie of a Letter Sent into Scotlande* (London, 1333), reprinted in *CQJQM*, appendix X, pp. 38–39.
13. *CQJQM*, p. 39.
14. TNA SP 11/2/9, fols. 14–15v.
15. Proctor, "Wyate's Rebellion," p. 237.
16. Malfatti, ed., *Mary Tudor*, p. 43.
17. *CQJQM*, p. 40.
18. Cited in S. Brigden, *London and the Reformation* (Oxford, 1989), pp. 539–40.
19. MacCulloch, ed., "The *Vitae Mariae*," p. 281.
20. *CSPV* VI, i, p. 1054.
21. Foxe, *Actes and Monuments*, book 10, pp. 1418–19.
22. Procter, "Wyate's Rebellion," p. 240.
23. Kingsford, ed., *Two London Chronicles*, p. 32.
24. *CQJQM*, p. 43.
25. *CSPS* XII, p. 86.
26. *CQJQM*, p. 48.
27. Ibid., p. 51.
28. *CSPS* XII, pp. 86–88; Nichols, ed., "The Diary of Henry Machyn," p. 55.
29. *CQJQM*, p. 54.

CHAPTER 46. GIBBETS AND HANGED MEN

1.   *CSPS* XII, p. 120.
2.   *CQJQM*, p. 59.
3.   *CSPS* XII, p. 106.
4.   Nichols, ed., "The Diary of Henry Machyn," p. 56.
5.   *CSPS* XI, p. 168.
6.   *CQJQM*, p. 55.
7.   Ibid., pp. 56–59.
8.   Strype, *Ecclesiastical Memorials*, III, pp. 82–83.
9.   Tytler, *England under the Reigns of Edward VI and Mary*, II, pp. 426–27.
10. Strype, *Ecclesiastical Memorials*, III, p. 95; Tytler, *England under the Reigns of Edward VI and Mary*, II, pp. 310–11; Nichols, ed., "The Diary of Henry Machyn," p. 57.
11. *CSPS* XII, p. 125.
12. Ibid.
13. Foxe, *Actes and Monuments*, book 12, p. 2092.
14. L. S. Marcus et al., eds., *Elizabeth I: Collected Works* (Chicago and London, 2000), pp. 41–42.
15. *CSPS* XII, p. 167.
16. *CQJQM*, pp. 70–71.
17. Foxe, *Actes and Monuments*, book 12, p. 2092.
18. Ibid., p. 2093.
19. *CSPS* XII, p. 201.
20. *CQJQM*, pp. 73–74.
21. Nichols, ed., "The Diary of Henry Machyn," pp. 59–60; *CQJQM*, p. 74.
22. *CQJQM*, p. 5.
23. BL, Add 34563, fol. 6r; Revd. C. R. Manning, ed., "State Papers Relating to the

Custody of the Princess Elizabeth at Woodstock in 1554," *Norfolk Archaeology*, 4 (1855), pp. 133–226.

24. Manning, ed., "State Papers," p. 158.
25. *CSPS* XII, p. 162.

CHAPTER 47. SOLE QUEEN

1. Foxe, *Actes and Monuments*, book 10, p. 1419.
2. Hughes and Larkin, eds., *Tudor Royal Proclamations*, II, no. 40.
3. *CSPS* XII, p. 201.
4. Ibid., pp. 216–17.
5. TNA SP 11/1/2, fols. 50–53v.
6. *CSPS* XII, pp. 15–16.
7. Ibid., p. 142.
8. J. D. Alsop, "The Act for the Queen's Regal Power," *Parliamentary History* 13, no. 3 (1994), p. 275. Original is at BL, Harley 6234, fols. 10–25v, which is transcribed in Alsop's appendix.
9. Alsop, "The Act for the Queen's Regal Power," pp. 275–76.
10. *Statutes*, IV, I, p. 222; 1 Mariae, St. 3. c. 1.2.
11. *CSPS* XII, p. 242.
12. BL, Cotton Vespasian F III, Art. 24, no. 19, in French, printed and transcript in Wood, *Letters of Royal and Illustrious Ladies*, III, pp. 290–91.
13. *CSPS* XII, p. 5.
14. Ibid., p. 185.

CHAPTER 48. GOOD NIGHT, MY LORDS ALL

1. Strype, *Ecclesiastical Memorials*, III, p. 127.
2. *CSPS* XII, p. 279; *APC* V, p. 131.
3. *CSPS* XII, p. 309.
4. Ibid.
5. Strype, *Ecclesiastical Memorials*, III, p. 127.
6. *CSPS* XII, p. 295.
7. Malfatti, ed., *Mary Tudor*, p. 49.
8. Nichols, ed., "The Diary of Henry Machyn," p. 66.
9. *CSPS* XIII, p. 1.
10. Hughes and Larkin, eds., *Tudor Royal Proclamations*, II, 413, p. 45.
11. Vertot, *Ambassades*, III, p. 287.
12. John Elder's letter in *CQJQM*, p. 139.
13. Ibid., p. 136.
14. Ibid., pp. 165–66.

CHAPTER 49. WITH THIS RING I THEE WED

1. College of Arms, MS WB, fols. 157r–158r; Malfatti, ed., *Mary Tudor*, p. 51.
2. BL, Add 4712, fol. 79–80.
3. John Elder's letter *CQJQM*, p. 141.
4. Marriage of Queen Mary and King Philip: English heralds' account printed *CQJQM*, pp. 167–72.
5. Bodleian, Wood MS F 30, fol. 49, cited and transcript in A. Samson, "Changing

Places: The Marriage and Royal Entry of Philip, Prince of Austria and Mary Tudor, July–August 1554," *The Sixteenth Century Journal* 36, no. 3 (2005), p. 763.

6. Bodleian, Wood MS F 30, fol. 49r, transcript and cited in Samson, "Changing Places," p. 763.
7. Ibid.
8. John Elder's letter in *CQJQM*, p. 6; *Wriothesley's Chronicle*, II, p. 120.
9. *Wriothesley's Chronicle*, II, p. 121; Hughes and Larkin, eds., *Tudor Royal Proclamations*, II, pp. 45–46.
10. *CSPS* XII, p. 269.
11. Ibid., 11, p. 10.
12. John Elder's letter in *CQJQM*, p. 143.
13. *CSPS* XIII, 11, p. 11.

CHAPTER 50. MUTUAL SATISFACTION

1. C. Weiss, *Papiers d'état du Cardinal Granvelle*, 9 vols. (Paris, 1844–52), IV, p. 285.
2. John Elder's letter in *CQJQM*, *CSPS* XIII, p. 443.
3. John Elder's letter in *CQJQM*, p. 146.
4. *CQJQM*, p. 79.
5. John Elder's letter in *CQJQM*, p. 147.
6. Ibid.
7. John Elder, in *CQJQM's letter* p. 150.
8. Ibid., p. 151.
9. *CSPS* XIII, 53, p. 43.
10. Withington, *English Pageantry*, p. 190.
11. *CQJQM*, p. 81.
12. *CSPS* XIII, 60, p. 49.
13. *CSPS* XIII, 5, pp. 3–4.

CHAPTER 51. THE HAPPIEST COUPLE IN THE WORLD

1. *CSPS* XIII, 30, p. 26.
2. *CSPS* XIII, 7, pp. 3–6.
3. *CSPV* V, 925, p. 527; *CSPS* XII, pp. 291–93.
4. *CSPS* XIII, 12, p. 13.
5. *CSPS* XIII, 33, p. 28.
6. *CSPS* XIII, 37, pp. 30–34.
7. Ibid.
8. *CSPS* XIII, 102, p. 95.
9. *CSPS* XIII, 56, p. 45.
10. C. H. Williams, ed., *English Historical Documents 1485–1550* (London, 1967), V, p. 210; *CSPS* XIII, 37, p. 31.
11. Nichols, ed., "The Diary of Henry Machyn," p. 76.
12. *CSPS* XIII, 111, p. 105.
13. Nichols, ed., "The Diary of Henry Machyn," p. 108; *CSPF*, Mary, 514, p. 231.
14. Harbison, *Rival Ambassadors*, p. 198.
15. TNA SP E 351/3030.
16. *CQJQM*, p. 82.
17. A supplication to the Queen's majeste (1555) (STC 17567), fols. 23v–24.
18. *CQJQM*, p. 35.
19. BL, Cotton Vespasian F III, no. 23.

20. Archivo General de Simancas, Estado 1498, fols. 6–7; quoted by G. Redworth in "Matters Impertinent to Women: Male and Female Monarchy under Philip and Mary," *English Historical Review* 112, no. 447 (June 1999), p. 598.
21. *CSPS* XIII, 75, pp. 63–64.
22. *CSPS* XIII, 94, pp. 79–80.
23. *CSPV* V, 955, pp. 582–83; 957, pp. 584–86.
24. *CSPS* XIII, 115, p. 108.
25. *CSPS* XIII, 97, p. 81.
26. *CSPS* XIII, 97, p. 82.

CHAPTER 52. TO RECONCILE, NOT TO CONDEMN

1. *CSPS* XIII, 63, p. 53.
2. *CSPV* V, 776, p. 398.
3. *CSPV* V, 856, p. 464; *CSPS* XI, p. 263.
4. *CSPS* XI, pp. 420–21.
5. *CSPS* XIII, 111, p. 105.
6. *CQJQM*, p. 159.
7. John Elder's letter in *CQJQM*, p. 160; Foxe, *Actes and Monuments*, book 10, pp. 1476–77.
8. Foxe, *Actes and Monuments*, book 10, p. 1478.
9. *CSPS* XIII, 115, p. 109.
10. Grafton, *A Chronicle at Large*, pp. 550–51.
11. *CSPS* XIII, 118, p. 112.
12. Foxe, *Actes and Monuments*, book 10, p. 1479. See John Elder's letter in *CQJQM*, pp. 162–63.
13. *CSPS* XIII, 127, p. 122.

CHAPTER 53. THE QUEEN IS WITH CHILD

1. *Cal. Pole*, II, 998, p. 380.
2. Tytler, *England under the Reigns of Edward VI and Mary*, II, p. 455.
3. Strype, *Ecclesiastical Memorials*, III, pp. 204–205; Nichols, ed., "The Diary of Henry Machyn," pp. 76–77.
4. *CSPS* XIII, 71, p. 60.
5. *CSPS* XIII, 92, p. 78.
6. *CSPS* XIII, 116, p. 110.
7. *CSPS* XIII, 130, p. 124.
8. Tytler, *England under the Reigns of Edward VI and Mary*, II, p. 455.
9. Foxe, *Actes and Monuments*, book 11, p. 1597.
10. *CSPF*, Mary, 367, p. 172; Tytler, *England under the Reigns of Edward VI and Mary*, II, p. 469.
11. *Statutes*, IV, I, pp. 255–57; 1 and 2 Phil. & Mar. c.10.
12. *Statutes*, IV, I, p. 256; 1 and 2 Phil. & Mar. c.10.
13. Nichols, ed., "The Diary of Henry Machyn," p. 85.
14. *CSPV* VI, i, 67, pp. 57–58.
15. Foxe, *Actes and Monuments* (1563), 5, iii, p. 1731.
16. Nichols, ed., "The Diary of Henry Machyn," p. 86.
17. *CSPV* VI, i, 72, p. 61; *CSPS* XIII, 184, p. 169.
18. Foxe, *Actes and Monuments*, book 11, p. 1596.
19. *CSPF*, Mary, 354, pp. 165–66.

CHAPTER 54. HER MAJESTY'S BELLY

1. *CSPV* VI, i, 89, p. 77.
2. *CSPS* XIII, 193, pp. 175–76.
3. *CSPS* XIII, 216, p. 224.
4. Cited in H. Kamen, *Philip of Spain* (New Haven, 1997), p. 62.
5. *CSPV* VI, i, 174, p. 148.
6. *CSPV* VI, i, 174, p. 417.
7. BL, Sloane I, 583, fol. 15.
8. *CPR*, Mary, III, pp. 184–85.
9. Foxe, *Actes and Monuments*, book 11, p. 1597.
10. Vertot, *Ambassades*, IV, pp. 341–44.
11. *CSPS* XIII, 212, p. 222.
12. *CSPV* VI, i, 116, p. 93.
13. *CSPV* VI, ii, 174, pp. 147–48.
14. *CSPV* VI, i, 142, p. 120.
15. Ibid.
16. *CSPV* VI, i, 174, p. 147; 184, p. 162.
17. *CSPV* VI, ii, p. 1080.
18. *CSPS* XIII, 229, p. 240.
19. *CSPV* VI, i, 190, p. 167.

CHAPTER 55. BLOOD AND FIRE

1. Foxe, *Actes and Monuments*, book 11, p. 1493.
2. *CSPS* XIII, 148, pp. 138–39.
3. Foxe, *Actes and Monuments*, book 11, pp. 1520–21.
4. Ibid., p. 1510.
5. Ibid., p. 1511.
6. Ibid., p. 1592.
7. Ibid., pp. 1592–93.
8. Ibid., p. 1567.
9. *APC* V, p. 118.
10. Foxe, *Actes and Monuments*, book 11, p. 1981.
11. Ibid.
12. Ibid., p. 1945.
13. *CSPV* VI, iii, appendix, 136, p. 1647.
14. *CSPS* XIII, 148, pp. 138–39.
15. *CSPV* VI, 116, p. 94.
16. Cited in Kamen, *Philip of Spain*, p. 62.
17. *CSPS* XIII, p. 151.
18. *CSPV* 934, p. 533.

CHAPTER 56. EXTRAORDINARILY IN LOVE

1. *CSPS* XIII, 228, pp. 238–39.
2. *CSPV* VI, i, 200, p. 173.
3. *CSPV* VI, i, 204, p. 178.
4. Ibid.
5. *CSPV* VI, i, 209, p. 183.
6. *CSPV* VI, i, 213, p. 186.

7. *CSPV* VI, i, 200, p. 174.
8. *CSPV* VI, i, 217, p. 190.
9. *CSPS* XIII, 52, p. 42.
10. *CSPS* XIII, 239, p. 247.
11. BL, Cotton Titus B II, fol. 62.
12. Vertot, *Ambassades*, V, pp. 126–27.
13. *CSPV* VI, i, 246, p. 213.
14. *CSPV* VI, 318, p. 285.
15. BL, Cotton Titus B II, fol. 62.
16. TNA SP 11/6/17, fol. 27v; SP 11/8/71 (i), fols. 121–122v.
17. *CSPV* VI, i, 353, p. 319.
18. *CSPV* VI, i, 245, p. 212; 257, p. 227; 315, p. 281.
19. *CSPV* VI, i, 245, p. 212.
20. *CSPV* VI, i, 332, p. 300.
21. *CSPV* VI, i, 332, pp. 299–300.
22. *CSPV* VI, 309, p. 278.
23. Vertot, *Ambassades*, V, pp. 169–73.

CHAPTER 57. COMMITTED TO THE FLAMES

1. Lord Houghton, ed., *Bishop Cranmer's Recantacyons*, with introduction by J. Gairdner, *Miscellanies of the Philobiblon Society*, 15 (1877–84), pp. 108–10.
2. Letter of Warrant from Mary to mayor and bailiffs of Oxford quoted in G. Townshend and S.R. Cattley, eds., *Actes and Monuments of John Foxe* (8 vols., 1837–41), 6, pp. 531–32.
3. Foxe, *Actes and Monuments*, book 11, p. 1770.
4. Ibid.
5. Ibid.
6. *CSPV* VI, 365, p. 329.
7. Cox, ed., *Miscellaneous Writings and Letters of Thomas Cranmer*, II, p. 563.
8. Ibid.
9. P. N. Brooks, *Cranmer in Context* (Cambridge, 1989), p. 112.
10. Cox, ed., *Miscellaneous Writings and Letters of Thomas Cranmer*, II, pp. 564–65.
11. Foxe, *Actes and Monuments*, book 11, p. 1887.
12. Ibid., p. 1888.
13. *CSPV* VI, 434, p. 386.

CHAPTER 58. A GREAT AND RARE EXAMPLE OF GOODNESS

1. *CSPV* VI, i, 473, pp. 434–47.

CHAPTER 59. STOUT AND DEVILISH HEARTS

1. *CSPV* VI, i, 429, p. 378.
2. Strype, *Ecclesiastical Memorials*, III, p. 286; Nichols, ed., "The Diary of Henry Machyn," p. 101.
3. John Bradford's letter in Strype, *Ecclesiastical Memorials*, III, ii, p. 129.
4. Nichols, ed., "The Diary of Henry Machyn," pp. 94–95.
5. *CSPS* XIII, 161, pp. 147–48.
6. *CSPV* VI, i, 215, p. 188.
7. *CSPV* VI, i, 274, p. 243.
8. *CSPV* VI, i, 258, p. 231.

9. *CSPV* VI, I, 297, pp. 269–270.

10. *CSPV* VI, i, 289, p. 259.

11. *APC* V, p. 224.

12. *CSPV* VI, i, 427, p. 376.

13. *CSPV* VI, i, 434, p. 384.

14. Ibid.

15. *CSPV* VI, i, 434, pp. 384–85.

16. *CSPV* VI, i, 434, pp. 383–84; *CSPF*, Mary, 496, pp. 222–23.

17. Vertot, *Ambassades*, V, pp. 361–63.

18. *Wriothesley's Chronicle*, II, p. 134.

19. *CSPV* VI, i, 440, p. 392.

20. *CSPV* VI, i, 458, p. 411.

21. *CSPV* VI, i, 525, p. 495.

22. *CSPV* VI, i, 570, p. 558.

23. *CSPV* VI, i, 427, p. 376.

24. *CSPV* VI, i, 460, p. 415.

25. *CSPS* XIII, 273, p. 271.

26. Vertot, *Ambassades*, V, pp. 361–63.

27. Aff.Etr. XIII, fol. 24, as cited in Harbison, *Rival Ambassadors*, p. 301.

28. *CSPS* XIII, 279, p. 276.

CHAPTER 60. OBEDIENT SUBJECT AND HUMBLE SISTER

1. *CSPV* VI, i, 505, p. 475.

2. *CSPV* VI, i, 510, p. 479.

3. L. Wiesener, *La Jeunesse d'Elisabeth d'Angleterre* (Paris, 1878), p. 343.

4. *CSPV*, VI, i, 514, p. 484.

5. Strype, *Ecclesiastical Memorials*, III, p. 336.

6. Ibid.

7. BL, Lansdowne 1236, fol. 37, printed in Marcus et al., eds., *Elizabeth*, pp. 43–44.

8. Nichols, ed., "The Diary of Henry Machyn," p. 120.

9. Wiesener, *La Jeunesse d'Elisabeth*, p. 304.

10. BL, Cotton Titus B II, fol. 109.

CHAPTER 61. A WARMED OVER HONEYMOON

1. Nichols, ed., "The Diary of Henry Machyn," p. 129.

2. C. Erikson, *Bloody Mary* (London, 1978), p. 463.

3. *CSPV* VI, ii, 743, p. 835.

4. *CSPV* VI, ii, 723, pp. 808–809.

5. *CSPV* VI, ii, 787, p. 902; 790, p. 907; 795, pp. 916–17.

6. "Instructions," Jan. 22, 1557, Aff.Etr. XIII, fols. 137, 139, cited in Harbison, *Rival Ambassadors*, p. 315.

7. BL, Cotton Otho IX, E321–342, fol. 88; T. Glasgow Jr., "The Navy in Philip and Mary's War, 1557–1558," *Mariner's Mirror* 53, no. 4 (1967), pp. 321–42.

8. Nichols, ed., "The Diary of Henry Machyn," p. 124.

9. Ibid.

10. Aff.Etr. XIII, fol. 157, quoted in Harbison, *Rival Ambassadors*, p. 317.

11. *CSPS* XIII, 289, pp. 285–87.

12. Aff.Etr. XIII, fols. 160, 180, quoted in Harbison, *Rival Ambassadors*, p. 321; *CSPV* VI, ii, p. 956.

13. Aff.Etr. XIII, fol. 182, quoted in Harbison, *Rival Ambassasdors*, pp. 323–24.

14. Aff.Etr. XIII, fols. 182–183, cited in Harbison, *Rival Ambassadors*, p. 324.
15. *CSPV* VI, ii, 864, p. 1019.
16. Aff.Etr. XIII, fols. 182v–183, cited in Harbison, *Rival Ambassadors*, p. 324.
17. François de Noailles to Montmorency, April 5, 1557, cited in Harbison, *Rival Ambassadors*, p. 324.
18. *CSPV*, VI, ii, 743, p. 835.
19. Aff.Etr. XIII, fols. 166–168, cited in Harbison, *Rival Ambassadors*, p. 319.
20. Aff.Etr. XIII, fol. 191, cited in Harbison, *Rival Ambassadors*, p. 326.

CHAPTER 62. A PUBLIC ENEMY TO OURSELVES

1. *CSPV* VI, 870, p. 1026.
2. Strype, *Ecclesiastical Memorials*, III, ii, p. 261.
3. Ibid., pp. 261–63.
4. *CSPS* XIII, 299, pp. 290–91; *CSPV* VI, ii, 873, pp. 1028–29.
5. *CSPS* XIII, 306, p. 294.
6. *CSPV* VI, ii, p. 927.
7. *CSPS* XIII, 339, p. 317.
8. Nichols, ed., "The Diary of Henry Machyn," p. 147; Strype, *Ecclesiastical Memorials*, III (1721), p. 382.
9. *CSPS* XIII, 349, p. 321.
10. Nichols, ed., "The Diary of Henry Machyn," p. 162.
11. George Ferrers, "The Winning of Calais by the French" (1569), reprinted in Pollard, ed., *Tudor Tracts 1532–1588*, pp. 290–98.
12. *CSPS* XIII, 395, p. 348.
13. *CSPS* XIII, 382, pp. 340–41.

CHAPTER 63. THE GRIEF OF THE MOST SERENE QUEEN

1. Reginald Pole, *Epistolae Reginaldi Poli*, ed. A. M. Quirini, 5 vols. (Brescia, 1744–1757), V, p. 24.
2. *CSPV* VI, ii, 849, p. 994.
3. *CSPV* VI, ii, 772, p. 880.
4. Pole, *Epistolae Reginaldi Poli*, V, p. 144.
5. *CSPV* VI, 899, p. 1112.
6. Strype, *Ecclesiastical Memorials*, III, ii, pp. 231–37.
7. *CSPV* VI, 898, pp. 1109–11; 913, pp. 1131–33.
8. *CSPV* VI, 937, pp. 1166–70.
9. *CSPV* VI, ii, 937, pp. 1166–67.
10. *Cal. Pole*, III, p. 464.
11. *CSPF*, Mary, 641, p. 320.
12. *CSPV* VI, ii, 981, p. 1240.
13. *CSPV* VI, 991, p. 1248.
14. Nichols, ed., "The Diary of Henry Machyn," pp. 150–51.
15. Pole, *Epistolae Reginaldi Poli*, V, p. 34.
16. *CSPV* VI, iii, 1209, p. 1482.
17. *CSPV* V, 813, p. 429.
18. C. G. Bayne, *Anglo-Roman Relations, 1558–1565* (Oxford, 1913), p. 24.

CHAPTER 64. READINESS FOR CHANGE

1. *CSPV* VI, ii, 884, pp. 1043–85.

CHAPTER 65. THINKING MYSELF TO BE WITH CHILD

1. *CSPV* VI, iii, 1142, p. 1427.
2. *CSPS* XIII, 382, pp. 340–41.
3. *CSPS* XIII, 413, p. 367.
4. *CSPS* XIII, 425, pp. 378–79.
5. BL, Harley 6949, is the transcript of the will and is printed in D. M. Loades, *Mary Tudor: A Life* (Oxford, 1989), pp. 370–83.
6. *CSPV* VI, iii, 1274, p. 1538.
7. M. J. Rodriguez-Salgado and S. Adams, eds., "The Count of Feria's Despatch to Philip II of 14 November 1558," *Camden Miscellany* 28 (1984), pp. 330, 334.
8. *CSPV* VI, III, 1274, p. 1538.
9. *CSPS* XIII, 498, p. 438.
10. *CSPV* VI, iii, 1285, p. 1549.

CHAPTER 66. REASONABLE REGRET FOR HER DEATH

1. Clifford, *Life of Jane Dormer*, p. 71.
2. Holinshed, *Chronicles of England*, II, p. 1784.
3. Nichols, ed., "The Diary of Henry Machyn," p. 178.
4. *CSPV* VI, iii, 1286, p. 1550.
5. *CSPS* XIII, 502, p. 440.
6. "Ceremonial of the Burial of King Edward IV, from a Ms of the Late Mr Artis, Now in the Possession of Thomas Astle, Esq," *Archaeologia* II (1779), pp. 350–51.
7. *CSPS* I, 1, p. 3.
8. TNA SP 12/1, fols. 32–33.
9. Nichols, ed., "The Diary of Henry Machyn," p. 182.
10. Strype, *Ecclesiastical Memorials*, III, i, pp. 466–67; Nichols, ed., "The Diary of Henry Machyn," p. 182; A. P. Harvey and R. Mortimer, eds., *The Funeral Effigies of Westminster Abbey* (Woodbridge, 1994), pp. 55–57.
11. Nichols, ed., "The Diary of Henry Machyn," pp. 182–83; TNA SP 12/1, fols. 69–80.
12. Strype, *Ecclesiastical Memorials*, III, ii, pp. 277–87.
13. Ibid.
14. "A Sermon Made at the Burial of Queen Mary," BL, Cotton Vespasian D XVIII X, fol. 104; for published version, cited in Strype, *Ecclesiastical Memorials*, III, ii, pp. 277–87.
15. *APC* VII, p. 45.
16. Nichols, ed., "The Diary of Henry Machyn," pp. 183–84.

EPILOGUE. VERITAS TEMPORIS FILIA

1. BL, Harley, 1813, pp. 259–60. *The Epitaphe vpon the Death of the Most Excellent and oure late vertuous Quene, Marie, deceased, augmented by the first Author* (London, 1558?), in *Old English Ballads 1553–1625, Chiefly from Manuscripts*, ed. Hyder E. Rollins (Cambridge, 1920), pp. 23–26, at p. 26. See Marcia Lee Metzger, "Controversy and 'Correctness': English Chronicles and Chroniclers, 1553–68," *The Sixteenth-Century Journal* 27 (1996), pp. 437–51, at p. 450.
2. E. Arber, ed., *A Transcript of the Register of the Company of Stationers of London, 1554–1640*, 5 vols. (London, 1875–77), I, fol. 35.
3. "A fourme of prayer with thankes giuing, to be used every yeere, the 17. of November, beyng the day of the Queenes Maiesties entrie to her raigne, London

1576," reprinted in W. Keatinge, *Liturgical Services, Elizabeth* (London, 1847), pp. 548–58.

4. J. Knox, *The First Blast of the Trumpet against the Monstrous Regiment of Women* (Geneva, 1558), p. 32.

5. Ibid., p. 10.

6. Ibid., p. 9.

7. Foxe, *Actes and Monuments* (London, 1583), p. 2098.

8. R. Garcia, "'Most Wicked Superstition and Idolatry': John Foxe, His Predecessors and the Development of an Anti-Catholic Polemic in the Sixteenth Century Accounts of the Reign of Mary I," in *John Foxe at Home and Abroad*, ed. D. Loades, pp. 79–87.

9. W. C. Sellar and R. J. Yeatman, *1066 and All That: A Memorable History of England Comprising all the Parts You Can Remember . . .* (London, 1930), pp. 64–65.

10. M. Twiss, *The Most Evil Men and Women in History* (London, 2002), pp. 85–97.

11. *CSPV* V, pp. 532–33.

12. J. Aylmer, *An Harborowe for Faithfull and Trewe Subiectes* ("Strasborowe" [i.e., London], 1559) (STC 1005) sig. H3v.

13. Janet Arnold, *Queen Elizabeth's Wardrobe Unlock'd* (Leeds, 1988), pp. 52, 55.

SELECT BIBLIOGRAPHY

UNPUBLISHED SOURCES

MANUSCRIPTS

Bodleian Library

Rawlinson MS B 146; Tanner MS 90; Wood MS F 30

British Library

Add 4712; Add 5841; Add 5935; Add 6113; Add 21481; Add 24124; Add 27402; Add 33230; Add 34563; Add 48126; Add 71009; Arundel 97; Arundel 151; Cotton Caligula D VII; Cotton Caligula D IX; Cotton Caligula E V; Cotton Cleop E VI; Cotton Faustina C II; Cotton Nero B VI; Cotton Otho C X; Cotton Titus B I; Cotton Titus B II; Cotton Titus C VII; Cotton Vitellius C I; Cotton Vitellius V I; Cotton Vespasian C III; Cotton Vespasian C XIV; Cotton Vespasian F III; Cotton Vespasian F XIII; Egerton 616; Harley 284; Harley 416; Harley 589; Harley 3504; Harley 5087; Harley 6068; Harley 6234; Harley 6807; Lansdowne 3; Lansdowne 103; Lansdowne 1236; Royal 14 B XIX; Royal 17 B XXVIII; Royal 17 C XVI; Royal 18 C XXIV; Royal App. 89; Sloane I; Sloane 1786; Stowe 142; Stowe 571

The National Archives

E36; E101; E179; E351; LC 2; LC 5; LS 13; PROB 11; SP 1; SP 10; SP 11; SP 12; SP 46

College of Arms

MS I 7
MS I 18
MS WB

Oxburgh Hall

Bedingfield Papers: Papers relating to Henry Bedingfield

Suffolk Record Office

EE2/E/3: Eye Borough Records
HA 411: Cornwallis family papers

Society of Antiquaries

MS 123

Inner Temple Library

Petyt MS 538

PHD THESES

Braddock, R. C. "The Royal Household, 1540–1560: A Study in Office-holding in Tudor England" (PhD thesis, Northwestern University, Illinois, 1971).
Bryson, A. "The Special Men in Every Sphere; The Edwardian Regime, 1547–1553" (PhD thesis, St. Andrews, 2001).
Carter, Alison J. "Mary Tudor's Wardrobe of Robes" (MA thesis, Courtauld Institute, 1982).
Drey, Elizabeth Ann. "The Portraits of Mary I, Queen of England" (MA thesis, Courtauld Institute, 1990).
Hamilton, D. L. "The Household of Queen Katherine Parr" (DPhil thesis, University of Oxford, 1992).
Lemasters, G. A. "The Privy Council in the Reign of Mary I" (PhD thesis, University of Cambridge, 1971).
Merton, C. "The Women Who Served Queen Mary and Queen Elizabeth: Ladies, Gentlewomen and Maids of the Privy Chamber, 1553–1603" (PhD thesis, University of Cambridge, 1992).
Starkey, D. "The King's Privy Chamber, 1485–1547" (PhD thesis, University of Cambridge, 1973).
Whitelock, A. "In Opposition and in Government: The Households and Affinities of Mary Tudor, 1516–1558" (PhD thesis, University of Cambridge, 2004).

PUBLISHED SOURCES

PRIMARY

Aylmer, John. *An Harborowe for Faithfull and Trewe Subiectes, against the Late Blowne Blaste, Concerning the Government of Women* (London, 1559).
Bonner, Edmund. *Homilies Sett Forth by the Righte Reverence Father in God* (London, 1555).
———. *A Profitable and Necessarye Doctryne* (London, 1555).
Brewer, J. S., et al., eds. *Letters and Papers, Foreign and Domestic, of the Reign of Henry VIII, 1509–47,* 21 vols. and addenda (London, 1862–1932).
Brown, R., et al., eds. *Calendar of State Papers and Manuscripts, Relating to English Affairs, Existing in the Archives and Collections of Venice, and in Other Libraries of Northern Italy,* 9 vols. (London, 1864–98).
Burnet, Gilbert. *History of the Reformation in England,* ed. N. Pocock, 7 vols. (Oxford, 1865).
Byrne, M. St. C., ed. *The Lisle Letters,* 6 vols. (Chicago, 1980).
Calendar of the Patent Rolls Preserved in the Public Record Office: Philip and Mary (London, 1937).
Cavendish, G. *The Life and Death of Cardinal Wolsey by George Cavendish,* ed. R. S. Sylvester (London, 1959).
Clifford, Henry. *The Life of Jane Dormer, Duchess of Feria,* ed. J. Stevenson (London, 1887).
Collins, A., ed. *Letters and Memorials of State in the Reigns of Queen Mary, Queen Elizabeth,*

King James, King Charles the First, Part of the Reign of King Charles the Second and Oliver's Usurption, written and collected by Sir Henry Sydney, 2 vols. (London, 1746).

Cox, J. E. *Works of Archbishop Cranmer*, 2 vols. (Parker Society, 1846).

Crawford, A., ed. *Letters of the Queens of England 1100–1547* (Stroud, 1994).

Dasent, J. R., et al., eds. *Acts of the Privy Council*, 46 vols. (London, 1890–1914).

Du Bellay, Jean. *Ambassades en Angleterre de Jean Du Bellay . . . Correspondance Diplomatique* (Paris, 1905).

Duwes, G. *An Introductory for to Learn to Read, to Pronounce, and to Speak French [1532?]*, ed. R. C. Alston, facsimile (Menston, 1972).

Elder, John. *The Copie of a Letter Sent into Scotland* (London, 1555).

Ellis, H., ed. *Original Letters, Illustrative of English History . . . from Autographs in the British Museum and . . . Other Collections*, 1st ser., 3 vols. (London, 1824).

An Epitaphe upon the Death of the Most Excellent and Late Vertuous Queen Marie (London, 1558).

Foxe, J. *Actes and Monuments of These Latter and Perillous Dayes . . .* (London, 1583).

Frere, W. H., and W. M. Kennedy, eds. *Visitation Articles and Injunctions of the Period of Reformation*, 3 vols. (London, 1910).

Gairdner, J., ed. "Journals of Roger Machado, Embassy to Spain and Portugal, AD 1488," in *Historia Regis Henrici Septimi* (London, 1858; 1966 reprint).

Giustiniani, Sebastian. *Four Years at the Court of Henry VIII: Selection of Despatches Addressed to the Signory of Venice*, ed. and trans. R. Brown, 2 vols. (London, 1854).

Grafton, R. *A Chronicle at Large and Meere History of the Affayres of Englande and Kinges of the Same* (London, 1569).

Grose, Francis, ed. *The Antiquarian Repertory*, 2nd ed., rev. E. Jeffery, 4 vols. (London, 1807–09; first published 1775).

Guaras, Antonio de. *The Accession of Queen Mary: Being the Contemporary Narrative of a Spanish Merchant Resident in London*, ed. and trans. R. Garnett (London, 1892).

Hall, E. *Hall's Chronicle Containing the History of England, during the Reign of Henry the Fourth, and the Succeeding Monarchs, to the End of the Reign of Henry the Eighth, in Which Are Particularly Described the Manners and Customs of Those Periods*, ed. Henry Ellis, 2 vols. (London, 1809).

Halliwell-Phillipps, J. O., ed. *Letters of the Kings of England, Now First Collected from the Originals*, 2 vols. (London, 1846).

Harpsfield, Nicholas. *Archdeacon Harpsfield's Visitation of 1557*, ed. L. E. Whatmore (London, 1950–51).

Haynes, S. *A Collection of State Papers Relating to the Affairs in the Reigns of King Henry VIII, King Edward VI, Queen Mary and Queen Elizabeth from the Year 1542 to 1570 . . .* (London, 1740).

Hearne, Thomas. *Sylloge Epistolarum* (London, 1716).

Herbert of Cherbury, Lord. *The Life and Raigne of King Henry the Eighth* (London, 1649).

Holinshed, R. *Chronicles, &c.*, ed. H. Ellis, 6 vols. (London, 1807–08).

Hughes, P. L., and J. F. Larkin, eds. *Tudor Royal Proclamations*, 3 vols. (New Haven and London, 1964–69).

Jordan, W. K., ed. *The Chronicle and Political Papers of King Edward VI* (London, 1966).

Kaulek, J., ed. *Correspondance Politique de MM. de Castillon et de Marillac* (Paris, 1885).

Kipling, G., ed. *The Receyt of the Ladie Kateryne* (Oxford, 1990).

Knighton, C. S., ed., *Calendar of State Papers, Domestic Series, of the Reign of Edward VI, 1547–1554*, rev. ed. (London, 1992).

———. *Calendar of State Papers, Domestic Series, of the Reign of Mary I, 1553–1558, Preserved in the Public Record Office*, rev. ed. (London, 1998).

Knox, John. *The First Blast of the Trumpet against the Monstrous Regiment of Women* (Geneva, 1558).

Lodge, Edmund, ed. *Illustrations of British History, Biography, and Manners, in the Reigns of Henry VIII, Edward VI, Mary, Elizabeth and James I, Exhibited in a Series of Original Papers* . . . , 3 vols. (London, 1838 ed.).

Luders, A., T. E. Tomlins, J. France, W. E. Taunton, and J. Raithby, eds. *Statutes of the Realm*, 11 vols. (London, 1810–28).

MacCulloch D., ed. "The *Vita Mariae Angliae Reginae* of Robert Wingfield of Brantham," *Camden Miscellany*, 28 Camden Society, 4th series, 29 (London, 1984), pp. 181–301.

Madden, F. "Narrative of the Visit of the Duke of Najera to England in the Year 1543–44; Written by his Secretary, Pedro de Gente," *Archaeologia* 23 (1831), pp. 344–57.

Madden, F., ed. "The Petition of Richard Troughton . . . to the Privy Council," *Archaeologia* 23 (1831), pp. 18–49.

————, ed. *The Privy Purse Expenses of the Princess Mary* (London, 1831).

Malfatti, C. V., ed. and trans. *The Accession, Coronation and Marriage of Mary Tudor as Related in Four Manuscripts of the Escorial* (Barcelona, 1956).

Marcus, L. S., J. Mueller, and M. B. Rose, eds. *Elizabeth I: Collected Works* (Chicago and London, 2000).

Marillac, Charles de. *Correspondance politique de MM. de Castillion et de Marillac*, ed. J. Kaulek (Paris, 1885).

Mayer, T. F., ed. *The Correspondence of Reginald Pole*, 4 vols. (Aldershot, 2002).

Morice, R. "Anecdotes and Character of Archbishop Cranmer," in *Narratives of the Days of the Reformation, Chiefly from the Manuscripts of John Foxe the Martyrologist*, ed. J. G. Nichols, Camden Society 77 (London, 1859), pp. 234–72.

Mueller, J. A., ed. *The Letters of Stephen Gardiner* (Cambridge, 1933).

Mychel, J. *A Breuiat Cronicle* . . . (London, 1554).

Nichols, J. G. *The Legend of Nicholas Throgmorton* (London, 1874).

————. *The Literary Remains of King Edward VI*, Roxburghe Club, 2 vols. (London, 1857).

Nichols, J. G., ed., "Chronicle of the Grey Friars of London," *Camden Miscellany*, Camden Society, 1st ser., 53 (London, 1851).

————. "The Chronicle of Queen Jane and Two Years of Queen Mary, and Especially of the Rebellion of Sir Thomas Wyat," *Camden Miscellany*, Camden Society, 1st ser., 48 (London, 1850).

————. "The Diary of Henry Machyn, Citizen and Merchant Taylor of London, from 1550–1563," *Camden Miscellany*, Camden Society, 1st ser., 42 (London, 1849).

————. *Narratives of the Reformation*, Camden Society, 1st ser., 77 (London, 1859).

Parkyn, Robert. "Robert Parkyn's Narrative of the Reformation," ed. A. G. Dickens, *English Historical Review* 62 (1947), pp. 58–83.

Planché, J. R. *Regal Records: or, A Chronicle of the Coronations of the Queens Regnant of England* (London, 1838).

Pocock, N., ed. *A Treatise of the Pretended Divorce between Henry VIII and Catherine of Aragon by Nicholas Harpsfield*, Camden Society, new ser. 21 (London, 1878).

Pole, Reginald. *Epistolae Reginaldi Poli*, ed. A. M. Quirini (Brescia, 1744–57).

Proctor, John. "The Historie of Wyate's Rebellion," in *Tudor Tracts, 1532–1588*, ed. A. F. Pollard (London, 1903), pp. 201–57.

Robinson, H., ed. *Original Letters Relative to the English Reformation* . . . *Chiefly from the Archives of Zurich*, Parker Society, 2 vols. (Cambridge, 1846–47).

Rodriguez-Salgado, M. J., and S. Adams, eds. "The Count of Feria's Despatch to Philip II of 14 November 1558," *Camden Miscellany*, 28 (1984).

Rymer, T., and R. Sanderson, eds. *Foedera, Conventions, Litterae* . . . , 20 vols. (London, 1704–35).

State Papers Published under the Authority of His Majesty's Commission, King Henry the Eighth, 11 vols. (London, 1830–52).

Stow, J. *The Annales of England* (London, 1605).

Strype, J. *Eccesiastical Memorials, Relating Chiefly to Religion, and the Reformation of It, and the Emergenices of the Church of England under King Henry VIII, King Edward VI and Queen Mary I,* 3 vols. (London, 1721).

Turnbull, W. B., ed. *Calendar of State Papers, Foreign Series, of the Reign of Mary I, 1553–1558* (London, 1861).

Tyler, R., et al., eds. *Calendar of Letters, Despatches and State Papers Relating to the Negotiations between England and Spain; Preserved in the Archives at Vienna, Simancas, and Elsewhere* (London, 1862–1954).

Tytler, P. E., ed, *England under the Reigns of Edward VI and Mary* , 2 vols. (London, 1839).

Underhill, Edward. "The Narrative of Edward Underhill," in *Tudor Tracts,* ed. A. F. Pollard (London, 1903).

Vertot, R. A. de, ed. *Ambassades de Messieurs de Noailles en Angleterre* (London, 1681–1714).

Vives, J. L. *De Institutione Feminae Christianae,* ed. and trans. C. Fantazzi and C. Matheeussen (New York, 1998).

Weiss, C. *Papiers d'État du Cardinal Granvelle* (Paris, 1844–52).

Wood, M. A. E., ed. *Letters of Royal and Illustrious Ladies of Great Britain,* 3 vols. (London, 1846).

Wriothesley, C. *A Chronicle during the Reigns of the Tudors from 1485 to 1559, by Charles Wriothesley, Windsor Herald,* ed. W. D. Hamilton, 2 vols., Camden Society, new ser., 11 (London, 1875–77).

SECONDARY

Alexander, G. "Bonner and the Marian Persecutions," *History* 60 (1975), pp. 374–92.

Alford, Stephen. *Kingship and Politics in the Reign of Edward VI* (Cambridge, 2002).

Alsop, J. D. "The Act for the Queen's Regal Power," *Parliamentary History* 13, no. 3 (1994), pp. 261–78.

———. "A Regime at Sea: The Navy and the 1553 Succession Crisis," *Albion* 24, no. 4 (1992), pp. 577–90.

Anglo, Sydney. *Spectacle, Pageantry and Early Tudor Policy* (Oxford, 1965).

Bayne, C. G. *Anglo–Roman Relations, 1558–1565* (Oxford, 1913).

Beer, B. L. *Northumberland: The Political Career of John Dudley, Earl of Warwick and Duke of Northumberland* (Kent, Ohio, 1973).

Bindoff, S. T. *Kett's Rebellion* (London, 1949).

———. "A Kingdom at Stake, 1553," *History Today* 3 (1953), pp. 642–48.

———. *Tudor England* (London, 1950).

Bourgeois, G. "Mary Tudor's Accession and Cambridgeshire: Political Allegiance and Religion," *Lamar Journal of Humanities* 21 (1995), pp. 37–49.

Brigden, Susan. *New Worlds, Lost Worlds: The Rule of the Tudors* (London, 2000).

Bush, M. L. *The Government Policy of Protector Somerset* (London, 1976).

Carter, Alison J. "Mary Tudor's Wardrobe," *Costume, The Journal of the Costume Society* 18 (1984), pp. 9–28.

Chibnall, Marjorie. *The Empress Matilda: Queen Consort, Queen Mother and Lady of the English* (Oxford, 1991).

Davies, C. S. L. "England and the French War, 1557–9," in *The Mid-Tudor Polity, c. 1540–1560,* ed. J. Loach and R. Tittler (Basingstoke, 1983), pp. 159–96.

Dodds, M. H., and R. Dodds. *The Pilgrimage of Grace: 1536–1537 and the Exeter Conspiracy,* 1538 (Cambridge, 1915).

Doran, S. *England and Europe 1485–1603* (London, 1996).

Doran, S., and T. S. Freeman, eds. *The Myth of Elizabeth* (Basingstoke, 2003).

Dowling, M. *Humanism in the Age of Henry VIII* (Beckenham, 1986).
———. "Humanist Support for Katherine of Aragon," *Historical Research* 57, no. 135 (May 1984), pp. 46–55.
Duffy, E. "Mary," in *The Impact of the English Reformations, 1500–1640*, ed. P. Marshall (London, 1997), pp. 192–229.
———. *The Stripping of the Altars: Traditional Religion in England c. 1400–1580* (London, 1992).
Duffy, E., and D. M. Loades, eds. *The Church of Mary Tudor* (Ashgate, 2006).
Edwards, J. *The Spain of the Catholic Monarchs, 1474–1516* (Oxford, 2000).
———. "Spanish Religious Influence in Marian England," in *The Church of Mary Tudor*, ed. E. Duffy and D. M. Loades (Ashgate, 2006), pp. 201–27.
Edwards, J., and R. Truman, eds. *Reforming Catholicism in the England of Mary Tudor: The Achievement of Friar Bartolomé Carranza* (Aldershot, 2005).
Ellis, T. P. *The First Extent of Bromfield and Yale, Lordships A.D. 1315* (London, 1924).
Elston, T. G. "Transformation or Continuity? Sixteenth-Century Education and the Legacy of Catherine of Aragon, Mary I, and Juan Luis Vives," in *"High and Mighty Queens" of Early Modern England: Realities and Representations*, ed. C. Levin et al. (New York, 2003), pp. 11–26.
Emmison, F. G. *Tudor Secretary* (London, 1961).
Erickson, C. *Bloody Mary* (London, 1978).
Fenlon, D. B. *Heresy and Obedience in Tridentine Italy* (Cambridge, 1972).
Fletcher, A. J., and D. MacCulloch, eds. *Tudor Rebellions* (Harlow, 2004).
Freeman, T. S. "'As True a Subject Being Prysoner': John Foxe's Notes on the Imprisonment of Princess Elizabeth, 1554–5," *English Historical Review* 117, no. 470 (2002), pp. 104–16.
Freeman, Thomas S. "Providence and Prescription: The Account of Elizabeth in Foxe's 'Book of Martyrs,'" in *The Myth of Elizabeth*, ed. S. Doran and T. S. Freeman (Basingstoke, 2003), pp. 27–55.
Friedmann, P. *Anne Boleyn: A Chapter of English History, 1527–1536*, 2 vols. (London, 1884).
Froude, J. A. *The Reign of Mary Tudor*, ed. W. Llewelyn Williams (London, 1910).
Gammon, S. R. *Statesman and Schemer: William, First Lord Paget, Tudor Minister* (Newton Abbot, 1973).
Glasgow, Tom, Jr. "The Navy in Philip and Mary's War, 1557–1558," *Mariner's Mirror* 53, no. 4 (1967), pp. 321–42.
Harbison, E. H. "French Intrigue at the Court of Queen Mary," *American Historical Review* 45, no. 3 (April 1940), pp. 533–51.
———. *Rival Ambassadors at the Court of Queen Mary* (Princeton, 1940).
Harvey, A. P., and R. Mortimer, eds. *The Funeral Effigies of Westminster Abbey* (Woodbridge, 1994).
Hoak, D. E. "The Coronations of Edward VI, Mary I, and Elizabeth I, and the Transformation of the Tudor Monarchy," in *Westminster Abbey Reformed 1540–1640*, ed. C. S. Knighton and R. Mortimer (Aldershot, 2003), pp. 114–51.
———. "Rehabilitating the Duke of Northumberland: Politics and Political Control, 1549–1553," in *The Mid-Tudor Polity*, ed. J. Loach and R. Tittler (Basingstoke, 1983), pp. 29–51.
———. "Two Revolutions in Tudor Government: The Formation and Organisation of Mary I's Privy Council," in *Revolution Reassessed: Revisions in the History of Tudor Government and Administration*, ed. D. Starkey and C. Coleman (Oxford, 1986), pp. 87–115.
Houlbrooke, R. "Henry VIII's Wills: A Comment," *The Historical Journal* 37, no. 4 (1994), pp. 891–99.

Huggard, W. J. "Katherine Parr: Religious Convictions of a Renaissance Queen," *Renaissance Quarterly* 22 (1969), pp. 346–59.

Hughes, Philip. *The Reformation in England*, 3 vols. (London, 1950–54).

Hume, M. A. S. *Two English Queens, and Philip* (London, 1908).

Hunt, A. *The Drama of Coronation: Medieval Ceremony in Early Modern England* (Cambridge, 2008).

Ives, E. W. *Anne Boleyn* (Oxford, 1989).

———. "Henry VIII's Will: A Forensic Conundrum," *The Historical Journal* 35, no. 4 (December 1992), pp. 779–804.

———. "Henry VIII's Will: The Protectorate Provisions of 1546–7," *The Historical Journal* 37, no. 4 (1994), pp. 901–14.

James, M. E. "Obedience and Dissent in Henrican England: The Lincolnshire Rebellion of 1536," *Past and Present* 48 (1970), pp. 3–78.

James, S. E. *Kathryn Parr, the Making of a Queen* (Aldershot, 1999)

Jansen, S. L. *The Monstrous Regiment of Women: Female Rulers in Early Modern Europe* (Basingstoke, 2002).

Jones, M. K., and M. G. Underwood. *The King's Mother: Lady Margaret Beaufort Countess of Richmond and Derby* (Cambridge, 1992).

Jordan, W. K. *Edward VI: The Threshold of Power* (London, 1970).

———. *Edward VI: The Young King. The Protectorship of the Duke of Somerset* (London, 1968).

Kamen, Henry. *Philip of Spain* (New Haven, 1997).

Kelly, H. A. *The Matrimonial Trials of Henry VIII* (Stanford, Calif., 1976).

Levin, C., et al., eds. *"High and Mighty Queens" of Early Modern England: Realities and Representations* (New York, 2003).

Levine, M. *Tudor Dynastic Problems, 1460–1571* (London, 1973).

Loach, J. *Edward VI* (London, 1999).

———. "The Function of Ceremonial in the Reign of Henry VIII," *Past and Present* 142 (1994), pp. 43–68.

———. "The Marian Establishment and the Printing Press," *English Historical Review* 100 (1986), pp. 135–48.

———. "Mary Tudor and the Re-Catholicisation of England," *History Today* 44, no. 1 (1994), pp. 16–22.

———. "Pamphlets and Politics, 1553–8," *Bulletin of the Institute of Historical Research* 48 (1975), pp. 31–45.

———. *Parliament and the Crown in the Reign of Mary Tudor* (Oxford, 1986).

Loach, J., and Tittler, R., eds. *The Mid-Tudor Polity, c. 1540–60* (Basingstoke, 1983).

Loades, D. M. "The Enforcement of Reaction, 1553–8," *Journal of Ecclesiastical History* 16 (1965), pp. 54–66.

———. *John Dudley, Duke of Northumberland* (Oxford, 1996).

———. *Mary Tudor: A Life* (Oxford, 1989).

———. *Mary Tudor: The Tragical History of the First Queen of England* (Kew, 2006).

———. *The Oxford Martyrs* (London, 1970).

———. "Philip II and the Government of England," in *Law and Government under the Tudors: Essays Presented to Sir Geoffrey Elton*, ed. C. Cross, D. M. Loades, and J. J. Scarisbrick (Cambridge, 1988), pp. 177–94.

———. "The Reign of Mary Tudor: Historiography and Research," *Albion* 21, no. 4 (1989), pp. 547–58.

———. *The Reign of Mary Tudor: Politics, Government and Religion in England 1553–59*, 2nd ed. (London, 1991).

———. *Two Tudor Conspiracies* (Cambridge, 1965).

Loades, D. M., ed. *John Foxe: An Historical Perspective* (Aldershot, 1990).

MacCulloch, D. "Kett's Rebellion in Context," *Past and Present* 84 (1979), pp. 36–59.

———. "Kett's Rebellion in Context: A Rejoinder," *Past and Present* 93 (1981), pp. 165–73.

———. *Thomas Cranmer, A Life* (London, 1996).

———. *Tudor Church Militant, Edward VI and the Protestant Reformation* (London, 1999).

Maltby, William S. *The Black Legend in England: The Development of Anti-Spanish Sentiment*, 1558–1660 (Durham, N.C., 1971).

———. *The Reign of Charles V* (Basingstoke, 2002).

Manning, Revd. C. R. "State Papers Relating to the Custody of the Princess Elizabeth at Woodstock in 1554," *Norfolk Archaeology* 4 (1855), pp. 133–226.

Mattingly, Garrett. *Catherine of Aragon* (London, 1942).

Mayer, Thomas F. *Reginald Pole, Prince and Prophet* (Cambridge, 2000).

Mcintosh, J. L. *From Heads of Household to Heads of State: The Preaccession Households of Mary and Elizabeth Tudor, 1516–1558* (Columbia University Press, 2008).

Medvei, V. C. "The Illness and Death of Mary Tudor," *Journal of the Royal Society of Medicine* 80 (1987), pp. 766–70.

Miller, H. "Henry VIII's Unwritten Will: Grants of Lands and Honours in 1547," in *Wealth and Power in Tudor England: Essays Presented to S. T. Bindoff*, ed. E. W. Ives, R. J. Knecht, and J. J. Scarisbrick (London, 1978), pp. 87–105.

Moore, D. "Recorder Fleetwood and the Tudor Queenship Controversy," in *Ambiguous Realities: Women in the Middle Ages and Renaissance*, ed. Carole Levin and Jeanie Watson (Detroit, 1987), pp. 235–51.

Muller, J. A. *Stephen Gardiner and the Tudor Reaction* (London, 1926).

Parker, Geoffrey. *Philip II* (Chicago, 1995).

Paul, J. E. *Catherine of Aragon and Her Friends* (London, 1966).

Pierce, Hazel. *Margaret Pole, 1473–1541* (Cardiff, 2003).

Pogson, Rex H. "Reginald Pole and the Priorities of Government in Mary Tudor's Church," *Historical Journal* 18 (1975), pp. 3–21.

———. "Revival and Reform in Mary Tudor's Church," *Journal of Ecclesiastical History* 25 (1974), pp. 249–65.

Pollard, A. F. *The History of England from the Accession of Edward VI to the Death of Elizabeth* (London, 1913).

Prescott, H. F. M. *Mary Tudor* (London, 1940).

Redworth, G. *In Defence of the Church Catholic: The Life of Stephen Gardiner* (Oxford, 1990).

———. "Matters Impertinent to Women: Male and Female Monarchy under Philip and Mary," *English Historical Review* 112, no. 447 (June 1999), pp. 597–613.

Richards, J. M. *Mary Tudor* (Basingstoke, 2008).

———. "Mary Tudor as 'Sole Quene'? Gendering Tudor Monarchy," *Historical Journal* 40 (1997), pp. 895–99.

———. "To Promote a Woman to Beare Rule," *The Sixteenth Century Journal* 28, no. 1 (1997), pp. 101–21.

Robinson, W. R. B. "Princess Mary's Itinerary in the Marches of Wales, 1525–1527: A Provisional Record," *Historical Research* 71 (1998), pp. 233–52.

Rodriguez-Salgado, M. J. *The Changing Face of Empire: Charles V, Philip II and Habsburg Authority, 1551–1559* (Cambridge, 1988).

Russell, E. "Mary Tudor and Mr Jorkins," *Historical Research* 63, no. 152 (1990), pp. 263–76.

Russell, J. G. *The Field of the Cloth of Gold* (London, 1969).

Samman, N. "The Progresses of Henry VIII, 1509–1529," in *The Reign of Henry VIII: Politics, Policy and Piety*, ed. D. MacCulloch (Basingstoke, 1995), pp. 59–74.

Samson, Alexander. "Changing Places: The Marriage and Royal Entry of Philip, Prince of Austria and Mary Tudor, July–August 1554," *The Sixteenth Century Journal* 36, no. 3 (2005), pp. 761–84.

Scarisbrick, J. J. *Henry VIII* (London, 1968).

Schenk, W. *Reginald Pole, Cardinal of England* (London, 1950).

Sherlock, Peter. "The Monuments of Elizabeth Tudor and Mary Stuart: King James and the Manipulation of Memory," *Journal of British Studies* 46 (April 2007), pp. 263–89.

Skidmore, Chris. *Edward VI: The Lost King of England* (London, 2007).

Starkey, David. *Elizabeth: Apprenticeship* (London, 2001).

———. *Henry VIII: A European Court in England* (London, 1991).

———. *Six Wives: The Queens of Henry VIII* (London, 2004).

Stone, J. M. *The History of Mary I, Queen of England* (London, 1901).

Strickland, A. *Lives of the Queens of England,* 6 vols. (London, 1854).

Thorp, M. R. "Religion and the Wyatt Rebellion of 1554," *Church History* 47 (1978), pp. 363–80.

Thurley, S. *The Royal Palaces of Tudor England: Architecture and Court Life, 1460–1547* (London, 1993).

Tittler, R., and S. Battley. "The Local Community and the Crown in 1553: The Accession of Mary Tudor Revisited," *Bulletin of the Institute of Historical Research* 57 (1984), pp. 131–39.

Waldman, M. *The Lady Mary* (London, 1972).

Walker, Julia. "Reading the Tombs of Elizabeth I," *English Literary Renaissance* 26, no. 3 (1996), pp. 510–30.

Watson, F., ed. *Vives and the Renascence Education of Women* (London, 1912).

Weikel, A. "The Marian Council Re-visited," in *The Mid-Tudor Polity, 1540–1560,* ed. J. Loach and R. Tittler (London, 1980).

———. "The Rise and Fall of a Marian Privy Councillor: Sir Henry Bedingfield 1509/11–1585," in *Norfolk Archaeology* 40 (1987), pp. 73–83.

Whitelock, A. "A Woman in a Man's World: Mary I and Political Intimacy, 1553–1558," *Women's History Review* 16, no. 3 (2007), pp. 323–34.

Whitelock, A., and D. MacCulloch. "Princess Mary's Household and the Succession Crisis, July 1553," *The Historical Journal* 50, no. 2 (2007), pp. 265–87.

Wiesener, Louis. *La Jeunesse d'Elisabeth d'Angleterre, 1533–1558* (Paris, 1878).

Williams, P. *The Council in the Marches of Wales under Elizabeth I* (Cardiff, 1958).

Withington, Robert. *English Pageantry: An Historical Outline,* 2 vols. (Cambridge, 1918).

Wizeman, William. *The Theology and Spirituality of Mary Tudor's Church* (Aldershot, 2006).

Wooding, Lucy E. C. *Rethinking Catholicism in Marian England* (Oxford, 2000).

INDEX

d in the United States
ker & Taylor Publisher Services